American University Studies

Series VII
Theology and Religion

Vol. 2

PETER LANG
New York · Frankfort on the Main · Berne

Herbert W. Basser

Midrashic Interpretations of the Song of Moses

PETER LANG
New York · Frankfort on the Main · Berne

CIP-Kurztitelaufnahme der Deutschen Bibliothek

Basser, Herbert W.:
Midrashic interpretations of the Song of Moses/
Herbert W. Basser. – New York; Frankfort on the
Main; Berne: Lang, 1984.
  (American University Studies: Ser. 7,
  Theology and religion; Vol. 2)
  ISBN 0-8204-0065-3

NE: American University Studies / 07

Library of Congress Catalog Card Number:
83-49003
ISBN 0-8204-0065-3

© Peter Lang Publishing Inc., New York 1984

Printed by Lang Druck Inc., Liebefeld/Berne (Switzerland)

in loving memory of my father

לזכר נשמת אבי ז"ל

III

TABLE OF CONTENTS

PISKA INDEX

DEUTERONOMY 32

METHOD OF TRANSLITERATION

Transliteration is used sparingly in preference of keeping Hebrew characters. Where transliteration is used, efforts have been made to approximate modern Israeli pronunciation except for certain classical works, such as tractates in the Talmud, whose titles are rendered by the "Ashkenazi" convention (and standard abbreviations) of the older lexicons and translations.

FREQUENTLY USED ABBREVIATIONS

ARN = Avoth de Rabbi Nathan

B = Bibliography (at end of this work)

BDB = Brown, Driver Briggs. See Bibliography

B.T. = Babylonian Talmud

CBQ = Catholic Biblical Quarterly

EJ = Encyclopedia Judaica

F = Finkelstein's edition of Sifre on Deuteronomy (New York, 1969)

Friedmann = Friedmann's edition of Sifre de-be Rab (Vienna, 1864)

Hoffman = Hoffman's edition of Midrash Tannaim

HTR = Harvard Theological Review

HUCA = Hebrew Union College Annual

ICC = International Critical Commentary

IDB = Interpreter's Dictionary of the Bible

JBL = Journal of Biblical Literature

JE = Jewish Encyclopedia

JJS = Journal of Jewish Studies

JQR = Jewish Quarterly Review

JSJ = Journal for the Study of Judaism

JSS = Journal of Semitic Studies

KS = Kiryath Sepher

L.F. = Louis Finkelstein

Lichtenstein = Lichtenstein's commentary of Zera Avraham to Sifre

Ln = London (British Museum) manuscript of Sifre

M.T. = Massoretic Text

PAAJR = Proceedings of the American Academy of Jewish Research

P.T. = Palestinian Talmud

Pardo = Pardo's commentary to Sifre

R.Q. = Revue de Qumran

Schorr = J.H. Schorr, "The Method of the Sages etc.", HeHalutz, vol. 12, 5647, Heb.

Targum Yerushalmi = Fragment Targum

VT = Vetus Testamentum

OTHER ABBREVIATIONS

Abbreviations of the works of Philo follow those of the Colson edition.
Biblical abbreviations are standard. An important notational usage in
the following work is to be noted:

"Ex"(likewise "Sx", "Lx", "Tx") refers to a section of text-
translation in Sifre Ha'azinu designated by a letter (E,S,L,T)
and a number (x). Thus "E1", Piska 306, refers to that section
of the text marked by E1. The " " notations are found frequently
in notes and conveniently allow the reader to locate a specific
text in the translation. On the other hand, plain notations such
as: E1., Piska 306, refer to those notes found in the sections
following the translation and labelled by notational symbol (e.g.
E1.) in the appropriate Piska-division (e.g. Piska 306).

Biblical verses in Deut. 32 are noted appropriately in the left margin
of the translation.

PREFACE

Translators are fond of quoting Bialik's dictum to the effect
that reading poetry in translation is like kissing a woman through a
veil. Since midrash in its original Hebrew is itself cloaked by a
veil, it must follow that midrash in translation is cloaked by two
veils. In the present work I have tried to let the **pulse** of midrash
Sifre Ha'azinu permeate the outer veil of translation by resorting to
paraphrase at times and by including the original Hebrew at other times.
The inner veil, those difficulties posed by the midrash exclusive of
translation problems, has, now and then, been gently moved and perhaps,
infrequently, forced aside out of the need to find coherence in
ambiguous texts. The copious notes which are designed to deal with
this inner veil may occasionally reflect more an imagined kiss rather
than the vital force of the midrash but such is **the** romantic nature
of this enterprise. To use the homilists' frame of reference we
may say that midrash "drops like rain (Deut. 32:2)" and thereby
describe our "Rabbinic Shakespeares" in the words of De Quincey:

> "O mighty poet! Thy works are not as those of other men, simply
> and merely great works of art; but are also like the
> phenomena of nature, like the sun and the sea, the stars and
> the flowers; like frost and snow, rain and dew, hailstorm
> and thunder, which are to be studied with entire submission
> of our own faculties, and in the perfect faith that in them
> there can be no too much or too little, nothing useless or
> inert -- but that the further we press in our discoveries,
> the more we shall see proofs of design and self supporting
> arrangement where the careless eye had seen nothing but accident."

IX

As for my own encounter with midrashic scholarship, I am grateful for the guidance I have received from a number of individuals. This book originated as a Ph.D. dissertation (Sifre Deut. to Ha'azinu: Rabbinic Interpretations of Deut. 32, especially the Song of Moses, University of Toronto, 1983) under the able guidance of Prof. Lou Silberman. His perceptive comments appear in almost every section of my work. Prof. Harry Fox provided me with Geniza fragments, manuscripts, books and scholarly insights. My colleagues at Queen's University kept me employed while I researched the necessary materials to produce this work. The encouragement of my wife, Elaine, and seven children, Yocheved, D'vora, Ya'acov, Fagie, Tova, Nechama and Yehuda, lies behind the completion of this book.Finally, I must acknowledge the extensive editorial help I received from Profs. R. Sweet and R. Sarason; as well as the useful advice I received from Profs. E. Clarke, E. Birnbaum and W. Oxtoby. I am indebted to my typist, Janet Cooperberg, who arranged the text and notes in the present format. Without the dedication,of the above named individuals,to serious scholarship I should not have succeeded in my task of elucidating a section of Rabbinic literature.

Herbert W. Basser
Sept. 18, 1983
Department of Religion
Queen's University.

INTRODUCTION

1. <u>Purpose</u>. The purpose of the present study is to portray

the process whereby a Tannaitic midrash* which comments upon a

poetic part of the Pentateuch assumed its present form. I have

selected that unit of midrash Sifre (the <u>Books</u>: referring to the

books of Numbers and Deuteronomy) which examines the liturgical

portion of the Pentateuch known as <u>Ha'azinu</u> (<u>Give</u> ear, the introductory

word), i.e. Deuteronomy 32. The first forty-three verses of this

chapter, which stand out from their prose environment by virtue of

their poetic structure, are presented in Scripture as a song (<u>shirah</u>)

spoken by Moses shortly before his death (Deut. 31:30, 32:44);

hence their common designation as the <u>Song of Moses</u>.

The midrash of Sifre Deuteronomy has been divided into sections

or <u>Piska'ot</u> and Sifre <u>Ha'azinu</u> is contained between Piska 306 and

Piska 341 inclusive (the <u>Song</u> midrash ends already at Piska 333).

The following translation and commentary of Sifre to Deut. 32 may

serve to introduce the major methods and themes of a Tannaitic

midrash on a poetic section of Scripture (stressing Israel's historic

election, present suffering and future redemption) to those who are

not familiar with the Rabbinic method of making acoustic shifts in

words of Scripture to reveal unsuspected references to Covenant,

Torah, and the Messianic Era.

The reader who is interested in the history of traditions concerning

---

*Major midrashim generally considered to be of the Tannaitic period
(2-3c. redaction) are (see EJ s.v. <u>Midreshei</u> Halakha): <u>Mechilta</u>
(Ishmael and bar Yochai) on Exodus, <u>Sifra</u> on Lev., <u>Sifre Numbers</u> and
<u>Sifre Deut.</u>

Sifre Deuteronomy is referred to the fine study of the extant manuscripts and commentaries of Sifre Deut. by L. Finkelstein: "Prolegomena to an Edition of the Sifre on Deuteronomy", PAAJR, vol. 3 (1932).

2. Assumptions about Sifre. The following presuppositions have guided this investigation of Sifre Deuteronomy to Ha'azinu. Rabbinic literature functions as an organic whole. Despite its wide extent and diversity, Rabbinic literature shows a surprising unity in its ideas. Its various parts seem to have exerted a mutual influence on one another, and a clear line of historical development is not evident. Allusions to current events and conditions in the society in which the homilists lived are not used to explain Israel's existence in terms of single historical events, but serve either as examples of Scripture's word or as eternal possibilities, ready to occur again and again at all points of Israel's existence[1]. The midrashim upon the poetic sections of Scripture portray events in Scripture and the lives of the Rabbis as models for the living of a proper Rabbinic Jewish life in all times and circumstances.

The underlying assumption of my work in Sifre Ha'azinu is that the text is Palestinian[2]. I believe that some traditions can be traced as far back as First Temple times (i.e. to the time of Hosea, see Conclusion, no. 7) while the bulk of material dates from Hasmonean times[3] to the third century[4] when they were collected and redacted in much the same form as they are today. This third century date is given by J.N. Epstein who, in my opinion, has dealt with these questions in a more satisfying way than have Albeck[5] and others[6].

3. How to read this study. The following work contains notes

which are designed to bring the reader to a better comprehension of
the symbols and images found in the midrashim on the Song of Moses in
Sifre. For the sake of completeness, I have included a translation and
notes to that section of the Sifre midrash on Deut. 32 which is not
part of the Song midrash. The notes are sectioned according to the
following headings:

"S" Scriptural

"T" Textual

"L" Linguistic

"E" Exegetical (while the translation of the text is based on the
most literal understanding of the words, "E" is designed to
offer other possible interpretations, including some which may
be preferable to what is offered in the translation).

"B" refers to important books listed in the Bibliography.

The reader will note that the present translation is of the version
of Ha'azinu in Sifre Deuteronomy published by L. Finkelstein[7].
Finkelstein's text is eclectic and at times conjectural. I have
therefore also included interesting readings of the text of the London
Manuscript[8]. The reader will note also that Finkelstein's edition is
the more complete one as London omits sections, probably due to
homoioteleuton. Nevertheless, London does preserve exceptionally fine
readings which were not incorporated into the body of the text of
Finkelstein. I have chosen London because it represents the manuscript
closest in readings to the first edition of Sifre (Venice, 1545-6). It
is a relatively early manuscript (13c) which S. Lieberman characterized
as "very accurate" in Kiryat Sepher (vol. 14, 1937-3, p. 329).

I have also included an Introduction and a Conclusion so that my
work as a whole may be seen to be a concentrated effort to explain

midrash Sifre Deut. to Ha'azinu in such a way that the midrash emerges
not only as an important document of Jewish theology but also as a
significant literary record for the academic study of religion[9]. The
reader may himself investigate the insights of Friedmann[10], Hoffman[11],
and Finkelstein[12] by consulting their editions of Sifre or Midrash
Tannaim. For traditional commentaries on Sifre Ha'azinu, he may consult
Pardo[13], A.Y. Lichtenstein[14], Ashkenazi[15], and Malbim[16]. For
traditional commentaries on Deut. 32 (incorporating much material from
Sifre Ha'azinu) he may turn to Rashi[17], Leqah Tob[18], and Ramban[19].
I have mentioned such works only where I have regarded the author's
comment as particularly noteworthy.

My major focus in this work is solely on the thought processes of
those who helped shape the Sifre Deut. to Ha'azinu. I have selected
this section for investigation because it has been traditionally
assumed that Deut. 32, the Song of Moses, is a summary of Israel's
total history, from inception until the end of days. To see how the
Rabbis understood this scripture in the light of their world-view
requires patience and thought. The reader may rest assured that the
midrash upon this scripture is an important piece of homiletic
literature. No commentator on Deut. 32 among the Jews has ever
strayed from its guidance. Sifre Deut. to Ha'azinu remains the basis
of traditional commentary upon Deut. 32 up to the present day. The
reader must therefore take the trouble to consider very carefully the
materials incorporated into this midrash.

As for the sense of the Biblical verses of Deut. 32 according to
modern scholarship, I refer the reader to P. Craigie, The Book of
Deuteronomy (Eerdman's, 1976), 373-390 (with full references to
earlier scholarship). One suspects that the Rabbis assumed the audience

knew the text and its "literal" meaning but wished to expand the
poetry of the text to make it a perfect mirror of the Rabbinic world-
view.

   4. Sifre Deuteronomy 32:1-43 as a literary unit. The midrash on
the Song of Moses should probably be considered an independent unit
that may be treated in isolation from the rest of Sifre Deuteronomy to
Ha'azinu. It is noted in the London Manuscript that Piska 333 is the
"end of the Song". A recurrent feature of the midrash on the Song (Piska'ot
306 - 333) is that a second or subsequent tradition is introduced by
the formula "another interpretation," which is something not found in
Piska'ot 334-341. It is also noteworthy that the midrashim on the
Song depend for much of their material upon an acoustical shift of
words (paranomasia) whereas the other midrashim in Sifre Ha'azinu depend
more upon meanings suggested by the context in which a given word
occurs. The context allows the midrashist to weave a story around the
verse in question. Since the language and the material of Scripture
are of a different order in the Song from that in the rest of
Deuteronomy 32, we should not be surprised if the midrash of the Song
circulated as an independent unit.

   The redactor has furnished us with an introduction to the Song
midrash as a whole in his comments on the first three verses of the
Song in Piska 306. His first proof text on the first verse speaks of
Israel witnessing against themselves, while his last proof text upon
this verse speaks of God as witnessing against Israel. The exposition
of the second verse begins with a discussion of Torah-study and ends
with the notion of the Resurrection of the dead. The third verse is
discussed in terms of Moses' inferiority to the angels, then in terms

of the purpose of martyrdom for glorification of the Name, and
finally in terms of Israel's superiority over the angels. Taken as
a whole, "the Piska 306-introduction" anticipates the midrash of the
entire Song. Thus, while the first pericope downgrades Israel, the
introduction as a whole presents the glory of Israel as a constant
progression. The forms of the introduction are also different from
those of the rest of the Song in that they are sometimes dramatic (as
at the beginning of Piska 306), sometimes proverbial (לעולם הוי), and
usually quite verbose. In these ways the first Piska (i.e. 306) of our
midrash introduces the remainder of the Song of Moses midrash. Indeed,
the size of the Piska'ot generally decreases as they progress from
beginning to end. In this way they resemble the format of Talmud which
has lengthy opening chapters (and sugyot within chapters) compared with
the remainder of the texts. I believe that this feature of the midrash
on the Song of Moses, namely, that it begins with a lengthy introduction,
is indicative of its being an independent unit of midrash[20].

5. Song midrash. A basic point of view which has informed the
present study is that, in order to understand the Tannaitic midrashic
enterprise of commenting on the poetic sections of Scripture in general
and of the Song of Moses in particular, we should bear three factors
in mind: a) the midrashic understanding of reality, b) Scripture,
c) the literary process.

The midrashic understanding of reality evaluates every event in
Israel's "experienced" history (including "past" national myths and
"future" national myths) by reference to three certainties of faith;
namely, Israel's election[21], Israel's suffering[22], and Israel's final
redemption[23]. God's existence and revelation are accepted as givens

in the Rabbinic evaluation of reality and are not open to speculation.
The above stated certainties of faith provide the foci of what I will
call "the midrashic understanding of reality".

Scripture was expected to abound in allusions to these certainties
of faith. But in fact they are often not apparent in a superficial reading.
The Rabbis therefore devised a method which worked the scriptural word
into such a frame (henceforth called "exposure") that the word revealed
these certainties of faith to the satisfaction of the Rabbis.

The literary process to be observed in the study of midrashim upon
a poetic section of Scripture consists of the "exposure" within
Scripture, whether explicit or not, of one or more of these certainties
of faith. The editors juxtaposed interpretations of a phrase of
Scripture in such a way that, wherever possible, a reference to election
is followed by a reference to suffering and this in turn is followed
by a reference to future redemption, even though the primary reference
may be to the second or third of these three[24].

6. Implications of observing these three factors for the study
of the Midrash. The above point of view has many implications for the
researcher of midrash. The researcher must be sensitive to the
particular genre of Scripture which is being subjected to the literary
process. For example, when a midrash on a poetic section of Scripture
is being examined, the researcher must always be aware of which factor
he wishes to analyze. Is he concerned at that moment with describing
the midrashic understanding of reality? Or is it the wording of the
Scriptures that is his concern? Perhaps it is the literary process
which is under scrutiny. Once the researcher is aware of the object
of his study he may then choose an appropriate method to initiate the

study. "The midrashic understanding of reality" and "the literary
process" must never be confused. It is easy to confuse the two since
the literary process has been guided by the authors' understanding of
reality which is the Rabbinic world-view. The researcher must also
realize that the origins of the "midrashic understanding of reality"
are beyond the reach of the scholar who has only the midrash before
him. Here the historian, the psychologist, the sociologist, and the
anthropologist are needed[25]. The midrashic scholar's task is to
describe the "midrashic understanding of reality" succinctly and show
how it controls the religious mind of the midrashist. By doing this,
he clarifies the distinctive world-view of the early Rabbis.

Because scholars of midrash have been reluctant to view midrash
in terms of the Scriptural genre with which a given midrash deals,
gross simplifications of midrash, its world-view, and process have
resulted[26]. Thus at the outset of my investigation I must distinguish
between understanding the ad hoc function of Tannaitic midrash on
poetic scripture (i.e. the community's perception of the conscious
function and role of such midrash) and understanding the integral
sense of such midrash (its literary meaning explicable as the development
of traditions influenced by internal and external conditions, i.e. the
particular setting which determined the modes of language and emphasis
of theme inherent in any midrash[27]. These are two separate enterprises,
the sum total of which will provide the researcher with an interpretation
of midrash as a phenomenon in the academic study of religion.

How should the researcher study midrash? First, the researcher of
midrash must realize his limitations. Midrash both instills and feeds
off a culturally determined vision of the world. This vision is an

experienced one. If it is to be reduced to scholarly description it
must be understood fully. The twentieth century researcher can only
approximate the contours of the experience of the ancient Rabbinic
Jew. He must use the literature judiciously and realize that what he
has in his eye is the testimony of the documents which shaped Jewish
culture, in its ideal state, not in its real state. Then he must
realize the nature of the documents he is studying. They represent a
search for "prophetic" revelation. By searching their religious
traditions, the authors of midrash reveal their own understanding of
reality. The system is entirely closed. It does not attempt to
interpret history, history "interprets" it. "History", for the Rabbinic
Jew, is what the midrashic world forecast. Nothing happens except
that which was expected; and once experienced, it proves the "correctness"
of the "midrashic understanding of reality." The researcher, at the
outset, must not naively attempt to unravel such views by asking if
the community had indeed understood its "present" condition as the
outgrowth of a set plan, or whether preachers only convinced them of
this after the fact. Midrash does not deal with specifics but with
eternals. It is only when we know how earlier midrashim were recast
into new pronouncements that we can entertain such notions. Each
tradition must be considered on its own terms as no one has yet
satisfactorily established a general, reliable method for determining
the literary history of traditions. Most important, the researcher of
midrash must always remember that the "Israel" of the midrashim is not
so much a nation as a "literary notion". By this I mean to say that
the nation is not separable, for the Rabbis, from the literary image
of the people. It is this insight which yields the truly religious

character of the work and the people. The self-image is that of Israel--
Knesset Yisrael--suffering for its sins to bring to fulfilment the
ultimate will of God--Knesset Yisrael, heir to God's past, witness of
the present and heirs to His future. The point is that if God is
accessible to Israel, it is because He is known through the midrashim
that picture Him as king[28] or father[29]. The midrashist, like his
audience, is the product of the Rabbinic enterprise, he is not its
creator.

To study midrash, then, one must study all of Rabbinic literature.
One must always realize that the forms of Rabbinic literature are the
forms of the Rabbinic Jewish self-image: the struggle of the Biblical
word to express its true meaning in the midrashic framework is the
very struggle of Israel to realize its potential meaning in the world.
This world is static, hovering between the poles of promise given and
promise realized, and the word is static as it hovers between the same
two poles--sometimes bending as promise given[30], sometimes as promise
realized[31], sometimes seeing the present and the future in terms of the
past[32] and vice versa[33]. This is the basic "cognition" of midrash
which the researcher must acknowledge.

7. Characterization of midrash. Midrash communicates a frame of
mind, a perspective through which every object in existence can be
appraised and placed into the proper setting within the midrashic context.
Thus it provided the Jew with a grammar by which he might speak of his
world and his existence[34]. So it is that midrash exists as a cultural
organism in its own right, allowing for historical and sociological
studies to emerge if they are done cautiously and judiciously[35]. Most
importantly, midrash exists as documents which vibrate with the religious

vitality of the Rabbinic world-view which is confirmed by the fact of
its own existence. We must remember that for the Rabbis, message alone
deadens the fact of midrash; for midrash provides instantaneous impact--
it is a human creation filled with the light of all that is divine.
The historical setting of the midrash was important for the homilist
only to the extent that it provided a stage to present the "experience"
of the certainties of faith. To read midrash merely as a historical or
sociological document is to destroy midrash[36]. That is not to deny
that an important part of reading midrash is the detailed understanding
of "the presentation of the style of language, the importance of words,
the beliefs of the period, its morality, morals, and actually, if the
text so requires, even the social and political situation"[37]. These
are the background components involved in the understanding of any given
midrash, but they are not the specific point of midrash and they do not
provide us with an appreciation of midrash. These are the paints,
canvas, and brushes of the midrashist. His creation can only be
understood, in the final analysis, if we can see his blend of colors.
And, unless we know the functional context of all midrash, we shall
never appreciate any single midrash.

8. Style and form of midrash on poetic Scripture. Since I have
postulated that midrash is an integrated system of expression and thought,
dependent for the most part upon the formation of past traditions for
its development, I raise the question here whether the development of
midrash is characterized by recurrent standard features. My answer is
that, in so far as midrash must remain midrash, its development does
indeed show such features. These appear in respect to both form and
content. The features of form are simple. There exist traditional

forms of argument, paraphrase, allegorical identification and narrative.

The employment of these conventional forms informs the audience that

these traditions are part of the "Rabbinic canon" and that the entire

corpus of Rabbinic tradition, its views and its methods, is somehow

being expressed in the midrash under discussion. The features of

content (I exclude paraphrastic, exegetical asides for they are not

prominent in the "Song of Moses midrash"[38]) are also simple. Israel's

covenant demands that Israel serve God through obedience to halacha[39].

Israel suffers because the nation has not followed halacha[40]

sufficiently (and has not studied Torah sufficiently) or because God

needs to show the nations His power through mighty acts which can only

be proportionate to the depths of Israel's suffering[41]. In the Future

Era God will provide a perfect existence for every faithful Jew who

will be resurrected at that time, for Israel is unique and is God's

beloved child[42].

The general impression one has after reading the repetitious,

although never monotonous, volumes of midrash is that midrash appears

to foster and preserve a marked rhythm of life. How does it do this?

To answer this question we must look at the anatomy of a midrashic

specimen. We will find that at its center lies a word which is subjected

to acoustic or semantic shifts (if our specimen is typical[43]). These

shifts are accomplished by bringing given words into contact with other

words which have a specific emotional charge in the Rabbinic corpus and

which can expose a similar charge in the given words[44]. In this way

the given word or phrase attains a "fuller shape[45]". By exploiting

all the possibilities of exposing the charges of the given words, the

midrashist discovers hidden layers of emotional impact beneath the surface

of the words he is examining. Thus, some slight acoustical shift in
a word or phrase permits the discovery of charges inherent in the word
of Scripture under analysis. More than midrash is a product of Jewish
history, Jewish history is a product of the harmony of expectation
inherent in the "midrashic charge". Midrash, as a phenomenon, is not
essentially intended to communicate an idea, although ideas are its
major components, but rather to instill a belief-system which is claimed
by the framers of midrash to be no less than the rhythm to which the
world and Israel march[46].

A few words must be said about midrashic art, for midrash is a
controlled, literary art-form. Midrashic method realizes the power of
dialectic and polarity as a reality in the world and as a literary device
in art. In many midrashim, particularly in the genre of which Sifre
Deut. to the Song of Moses is very typical, we find that the midrashist
begins by challenging the Rabbinic world-view in such a way that the
concept of God's love for Israel appears under threat[47]. Tension is
a major key in the initial movement of midrash. The tension usually
results from the experience of Israel's subjugation which strains the
word of divine promise[48]. The final movement in a typical midrashic
panel ingeniously manipulates words and images to show that all is
going according to the plan originated by God in eternity. Israel must
have faith and remain loyal to her traditions[49]. This tension and its
resolution are portrayed in the classic forms of midrash: how can word
"X" which clearly means "X" now be taken as "A"! The midrash, when
successfully understood, shows that the "A" sense is precisely the "true"
sense[50]. The pattern of midrash is holistic. It plays upon familiar
images, familiar forms. The past is not merely translated into the

present; the present is also translated together with the past into the
eternal. Past, present and future are seen to be projected into a single
cone of Scriptural expression[51]. Midrash is not concerned with
questions of "historicism" but with the question of time. Time, as we
experience it, does progress, but experiences in time are held by the
midrashist to be static--eternal. The crisp, short "punch" of a midrashic
statement is suited for this message. These statements constantly
present the old, the known, in new ways--the impression is sure.
Whatever appears to be new is only illusion, the base of the world is
Parmenidean--changeless. Only the Biblical word and the Rabbinic
traditions are open to new insights; however, when all is said and done,
these insights are nothing more than the old insights developed from a
Biblical passage in a novel way. Sometimes the midrashist uses a
Rabbinic tradition which was primarily used to show one "truth" to show
now another "truth"[52]. Hidush-innovation, midrashic genius, is in
exegetical manipulation, sleight of word, not in innovation of form or
content. The midrashic artist ties together acoustic impressions,
Biblical images and community experience through the forms, teachings,
and affirmations of Rabbinic Judaism.

   9. Importance. What can we learn from Sifre to the Song of Moses?
Since midrash is a search for the meaning of Jewish existence in the
world through the medium of the written Scriptural word, by careful
analysis of the midrash's reflection upon the nature of reality we can
discover how Jews were taught to view the world. As this teaching has
not undergone radical change[53] since the midrashim were developed,
we can probe midrash to understand the Jewish psyche and imagination.
We can learn how Jews saw systems of thought other than the midrashic

system as evil and perverse[54]. We can see that Jews conceived of
Scripture as a "speaking document" whose words are able to be articulated
in many fashions. If we are astute, we can read behind the midrashim to
sense the threat of Gnostics, Jewish sectarians, Christians and pagans
who appear to have attacked the Rabbinic way of life[55]. It does not
take more than a glance at the literature to see how Jews reacted to the
might and power of Rome and to see the pride of the Jew as he thought
of his culture as superior and more eternal than that of pagan Rome[56].
We should not draw hasty conclusions from the paucity of references to
the figure of the Messiah in our midrashim of the Song of Moses. There are
definite tones of subdued messianism, referring more to the end of days
than to the person of the Messiah[57]. Klausner explains this phenomenon
by positing that the Rabbis had thus defused heightened messianism after
the fall of the Temple and after the Bar Kochba rebellion [58]. We
could imagine another conclusion--perhaps the community was upon the
verge of expecting the Messiah imminently, an expectation which did not
require reinforcement. What the preachers did have to talk about were
those things which people habitually need to be reminded of: sins[59],
the justice of suffering[60], divine mission[61], and ultimate glory[62].
The scenes and background of midrash assume the poverty of Israel[63],
the wealth of Rome[64], the plundering of the Palestinian community[65],
and the need of the people to stay in their land[66].

10. Midrash and the Academic Study of Religion. J.Z. Smith[67]
says the historian should study the "radical and arbitrary reduction
represented by the notion of canon and the ingenuity represented by the
rule-governed exegetical enterprise to apply the canon to every dimension
of human life," which he calls "that most characteristic, persistent and

religious activity." His words, particularly in view of his term "reduction," may be applied to the self-definition of midrash since we must follow the assumption of Rabbinic Judaism that the religious dimension of life, having been "reduced" into the canon, is precisely that which results with full clarity from the "exegetical enterprise". If I understand Smith correctly here, we are not being asked to examine canon itself, but the midrashic process (as far as Judaism is concerned) as a way of understanding the world-view of the midrashists and their audiences. For the Rabbis, canon is the "map" of the "midrashic understanding of reality" while midrash itself is the "legend" (pun intended). Since the interpreter of the cryptic word was held in wide esteem long before Rabbinic Judaism declared itself, we must bear in mind that while midrash is totally Rabbinic in method and outlook, the enterprise of interpretation, and perhaps of forming many traditions now embedded in midrash, is not exclusively Rabbinic. Ecclesiastes 8:1 defines the sage (חכם) as one who understands the interpretation (פשר) of a word (דבר). Both Joseph (Gen. 41:15, פתר) and Daniel (5:26, פשר) are pictured as sages (Gen. 41:39, חכם ; Dan. 1:20, חכמת בינה) who are able to interpret the words and images of dreams. In all these cases, a cryptic passage is shown to have some bearing upon a sequence of events which have ultimate significance for the progress of Israel's sacred history. The author of Isaiah 24:16,17,18[68] was understood by the targum to have unravelled a cryptic phrase "fear and pit and trap" in such a way as to disclose an insight into Israel's subjugation or redemption (as in other circumstances did the authors of Daniel and Genesis). The targum may be quite right. The author of Isaiah appears to be uncovering a phrase, a _raz_ (cf. Is. 24:16,17,18 and Dan. 2:28), just as the Rabbis uncovered razei Torah[69]. The Rabbis referred to

themselves as "sages (חכמים)". Thus the Rabbi is heir to an enterprise

that is as old as Scripture itself. Yet, for the Rabbi, it is of major

importance to show that no "song midrash" introduces new beliefs or

changes any previous views of the world. The midrashists, the commentators,

the redactors, and students of such midrash enhance traditions by

adducing proof texts and similar traditions to those under discussion.

Thus midrash is the finding of new sources for that which was already

known--and every new source in some way makes the tradition more sure,

more real.

The study of midrash has been greatly aided in recent years by

the appearance of English and German translations based on editions of

midrashim[70], complete with sound notes and scholarly introductions.

There also exist many fine articles on midrashic forms and ideas, and

substantial studies of the theology of the midrashim[71]. My work is a

continuation of this process and an addition to the previous commentaries

of the Rabbinic analysts of the traditional school of enquiry, as well as

an addition to the scholarly commentaries of the scientific school of

research, particularly of the academic study of religion.

-----------------　　　-----------------　　　-----------------

Deut. 31:30: THEN MOSES SPOKE THE WORDS OF THIS SONG TO THEIR

COMPLETION IN THE HEARING OF THE WHOLE ASSEMBLY OF

ISRAEL.

Midrash Leqah Tob: Words of reproof--he spoke to them twice, once

when he wrote and once when he read: there does not remain a single

word which he did not say to them in order to strengthen them in the

Torah of the eternally living God.

1.   See Piska 321, "E9", Piska 322, "E9", Piska 316, "E3" and "E4".

2.   See J.N. Epstein, Introduction to Tannaitic Literature, Magnes Press, Jerusalem, 1957, p. 710f.

3.   See Piska 329 "E4".

4.   If our reading is trustworthy in Piska 306, "E34", we have mention of Rabbi Yehuda HaNasi (early third century). The very latest tradition recorded in our text may be that of Piska 311, "E4" (see "E4" where a similar statement is adduced in the name of Rab who also lived in the third century). Epstein finds that our section of text has a complicated history. Redacted by the school of Yishmael, containing much Akiban material, our midrash appears to have origins in the school of Shimon bar Yochai (cf. Epstein, p. 629 who discusses anonymous traditions in Piska'ot 306, 313, and 336 brought elsewhere in the name of Yochai or his school). Says Epstein (p. 630): "It appears that it was composed in the days of the students of Rabbi." There is a general consensus that in Sifre Deut. Piska 55 to Piska 304 emanates from Akiba's school while Piska 1 to Piska 54 and Piska 304 to Piska 357 (in which our text occurs) comes from Yishmael's school (see Epstein, p. 625ff. and p. 703ff.).

5.   Ch. Albeck, Untersuchungen über die halachischen Midraschim, 1927, p. 119.

6.   See "Sifre" in Jewish Encyclopedia and Encyclopedia Judaica.

7.   Finkelstein set forth his goals and methods in "The Mekilta and its Text", PAAJR, vol. 5(1934), p. 5ff., and in "Prolegomena to an Edition of the Sifre on Deuteronomy", PAAJR, vol. 3(1932), p. 3ff. In this work Finkelstein presents an excellent description of: the editions of Sifre Deut. (p. 3, n. 1), the manuscripts (pp.4-7), and the manuscript families (p.38). The major problems in Finkelstein's edition of Sifre Deuteronomy has been discussed by J.N. Epstein (Tarbiz, vol. 8, 5697, p. 375ff.) and S. Lieberman (Kiryat Sepher, vol. 14, 5698, pp. 323-336). Unfortunately, Finkelstein was not able to use the Cairo geniza fragments to good advantage because they remain uncollated. Finkelstein realized that more work had to be done to produce an excellent edition (cf. HUCA, vols. 12-13, 1937-38, p. 253). The edition of Finkelstein, which appeared in the ominous years in Berlin of 1934-39, had been started by H.S. Horovitz. The edition survived Nazi atrocities through its republications (photo-print) by the Jewish Theological Seminary of America in 1969. The section of Ha'azinu has escaped major criticism as it (unlike other sections in F) generally provides trustworthy variants in the apparatus. The text of Ha'azinu in F is eclectic and even conjectured in one or two places but is very readable. Friedmann's edition of 1864 is eclectic as well but not always readable. If there is any merit in eclectic texts, then Finkelstein's edition is superior. In order to aid the reader I have included in my translation of Sifre Ha'azinu interesting readings from the London manuscript of Sifre. This manuscript was dated by Margoliouth (British Museum, 341 Add 16406) to the twelfth century and thought to be possibly of Greek origin. Prof. E. Birnbaum of the University of Toronto has told me that he considers the manuscript to be late thirteenth century Italkian (a similar date is given by M. Kahana,

<u>Prolegomena</u> <u>to</u> <u>a</u> <u>New</u> Edition <u>of</u> <u>the</u> <u>Sifre</u> <u>on</u> <u>Numbers</u>, unpublished
diss. Hebrew University, Jerusalem, April, 1982, p. 23). Since the
manuscript contains a notation to the effect that it had once been
part of the Rezzi collection and was sold to one Isaac Finzi, and
since Finkelstein has noted the affinity of Ln with the first printed
edition, 1545-6 (see his "Prolegomena etc" in <u>PAAJR</u>, vol. 3, 1932,
p. 10, n. 2, and p. 38) it is certainly plausible that the manuscript
is of Italian origin. If we select a date close to 1250 we shall not
be too far wrong.

8.   See "Prolegomena etc.", p. 10.

9.   The two texts present a good range of the possibilities of
readings. A comparison of the text (see "T") shows us how homoioteleuton is widespread in Ln. To be sure, Ln's readings, at some points,
are exceptionally fine and allow us to glimpse multi-level meanings in
traditions. Sometimes, different textual readings highlight different
meanings of a midrashic tradition which is common to both texts.

10.   <u>Sifre</u> <u>de</u> <u>be</u> <u>Rab</u>, <u>Meir</u> <u>Ayin</u>, Vienna, 1864.

11.   <u>Midrasch</u> <u>Tannaim</u> <u>zum</u> <u>Deuteronomium</u>, Berlin, 1909.

12.   See the commentary on the "inside" of the page in F.

13.   P. Pardo, (Commentary to) <u>Sifre</u> <u>devei</u> <u>Rav</u>, Salonika, 1799.

14.   A.Y. Lichtenstein, <u>Zera</u> <u>Avraham</u> (on Sifre), vol. 2, Radwil, 1820.

15.   M.D. Askenazi, <u>Toledot</u> <u>Adam</u> (on Sifre), Jerusalem, 1974.

16.   M.L. Malbim, <u>HaTorah</u> <u>veHaMitzvah</u> 'im <u>Mechilta</u>, <u>Sifra</u> <u>veSifre</u>,
<u>Otzar</u> <u>HaPerushim</u>, vol. 2), Jerusalem, 1956.

17.   Rashi, <u>Commentary</u> <u>to</u> <u>the</u> <u>Pentateuch</u>, ed. Berliner.

18.   <u>Midrash</u> <u>Leqah</u> <u>Tob</u>, ed. Katznellbogen.

19.   Ramban, <u>Commentary</u> <u>to</u> <u>the</u> <u>Pentateuch</u>, ed. Chavel.

20.   Precisely how the various materials in Sifre Deut. were assembled
and how the divisions were determined are open questions. Finkelstein
("Studies in Tannaitic Midrashim", <u>PAAJR</u>, vol. 5, 1934, p. 228)
conjectured that the original divisions of Sifre Deut. were in the form
of <u>parashot</u> like those we find in Sifra. Then the divisions were made in
terms of "verses". Copyists wrote פליק at the end of the comment to
each verse and פסוק after this, to introduce the next verse. He imagines
that the use of פליק led to aramaicizing פסוק which then became
understood as פיסקא . The net result was that the two word פליק and
פיסקא were read as סליק פיסקא which led to the idea that the
text was to be divided into <u>Piska'ot</u>. It is my belief that the <u>Piska</u>
division tells us something about the redaction of the text. Surely
Finkelstein realizes that there is not a one to one correspondence between
a verse and a Piska. Piska 306 comments upon three verses.

21.   E.g. see Piska 306, "E8".

22.   E.g. see Piska 307, "E22".

23.   E.g. see Piska 317, "E23". Also cf. Piska 311.

24.   E.g. see Piska 313, "S1", "S8", "S9", "S10", "S11".

25. Fine studies have been done by S. Baron, G. Alon, M. Stern,
S. Safrai, A. Büchler, S. Freyne, J. Gager, S. Klein and others (see
Bibliography).

26. See Piska 329, "El" where I discuss A. Segal's inattentiveness to
the sensitivity of midrash in dealing with Biblical verses as a series.
He was not attentive to the genre of the midrash he was discussing. See
Piska 330, "El" for a similar error on the part of Hayward. For examples
of the Song and Blessing genre of midrash see Gen. R. to Gen. 27:8, Gen.
R. to Gen. 49:1-33, Mechilta to Ex. 15:1-18, Sifre to Deut. 32:1-43,
Sifre to Deut. 33:1-29.

27. One must distinguish between a tradition which was generated for
purposes other than anti-Christian polemic (as its internal dynamic) and
the function such a tradition may serve as anti-Christian polemic
within the community's perception. Thus, if we find two points of view
expressed in one source, we may be certain that the editor did not have a
polemic in mind (he weakens any polemic by bringing a view that casts
doubt upon it). However, if in another source we find only one of the
views given and the context supports polemical function (e.g. we are told
to answer minim with the exegesis), then we are safe in seeing a polemic.
E.g. see Piska 308. If Friedmann is correct and Rabbi Yehuda's view is a
gloss external to the text, then we have a polemic here as both Meir's
view and Yehuda's view occur elsewhere. My opinion is put forward in
El , Piska 308.

28. Eg. Piska 306, "E10".

29. Ibid. In most "King" parables, Israel is cast in the role of
"prince".

30. See Piska 317, "E23".

31. See Piska 317, "El".

32. See Piska 318, "E6".

33. See Piska 313, "El". The Rabbis considered the sum total of
Rabbinic learning which was to develop in the academies to have been
shown to the Israelites at Sinai. For them, Scripture had to be reduced
(expanded?)to the sum total of Rabbinic dicta. These dicta formed the
Rabbinic reality, which Scripture was "shown" to mirror. Since future
was seen as past, and all of Scripture considered as a closed unit, such
that every word of Scripture was of necessity informed by every other
word of Scripture regardless of when the words were authored, a very
complex construct of understanding texts evolved. The complexity of
these texts is the object of study in this work and it must be noted that
the ideas we are discussing in this introductory remark were fused into
the consciousness of those who read or heard midrash.

34. I.e. Rabbinic Jews did not live so much in history as a "history"
rich in symbol lived in them, which they used to interpret their experiences
in terms of "midrashic reality".

35. See "Methodological note for the Study of Rabbinic Literature",
(B107) in W.S. Green ed., Approaches to Ancient Judaism: Theory and
Practice, Missoula, 1978, p. 29ff.

36. See the Introd. of J. Goldin to Song at the Sea, (B175) p. 19, also

ibid, p. 66.

37.   This quotation from Emil Staiger is cited by Gy. M. Vajda in Literature and Its Interpretations, (B280) (L. Nyiro, ed.) Mouton, The Hague 1979, p. 220.

38.   See Piska 320, "And I will know what they are at their end".

39.   E.g. see Piska 306, "E26", Piska 306, "E25" (And the Sages say), Piska 323 "E1".

40.   See beginning of Piska 323.

41.   See Piska 306, "E66".

42.   See Piska 317 "E21", Piska 306 "E53", Piska 308 "E1", Piska 309 "E1".

43.   E.g. Piska 320 "E7" (acoustic shift), Piska 322, "E3" (semantic shift).

44.   E.g. see Piska 309 "E6", where the word "possess" is brought into the context of Torah-Israel-Temple.

45.   The sense of the word possess now indicates the manner of Israel's relationship with God -- through Torah and Temple. It is evident that this midrash exists as a unit and is independent of the verse exegesis of Sifre Ha'azinu. Nevertheless, we find that the midrash works well because it illumines our verse (which is referred to in the course of this midrash) and charges the words "that possess thee" along the lines indicated by Scripture (a unique relationship between God and Israel) but with greater intensity and fuller shape in the context of "loaded" words -- Torah and Temple. The triad form of the midrash shows the author has charged "Israel" with the sacred valences of the Temple and the Torah.

46.   See Piska 333 "E10". It is not the invention of midrash on the songs of Scripture, nor an invention of the early Jews on the basis of unwritten tradition. That the Song of Moses is seen to be the score which history follows is due to the presentation of these Scriptures themselves. The entire Song, when carefully examined, can be seen at its most basic level to be a poetic epic of Israel's journey in history. The introduction to the Targum (B 54) of the Song of Songs sees the Songs of Scripture as acknowledgements of the fulfillment of progressive portions of Israel's history, as promised, at those points, where the unfolding of this history has been made manifest (cf. Mechilta.Y.,Ex.15:1):

Promise of Sifre Deuteronomy   Song acknowledgement in Targum:
   to Ha'azinu:

Piska 307-308, Piska 328	Remission of Adam's sin
Piska 306	Splitting of Sea
Piska 313	Well supplied in desert
Piska 318	Moses' rebuke before death
Piska 306	The stopping of the sun
Piska 324	The victory over Sisera
1 Sam. 2:1-11 parallels our Song	Hannah's praise for Samuel
See "S" references to Psalms	David's miracles
Piska 314	Solomon's song
Piska 333	Song of final redemption

I am not arguing that we have a conscious parallel structure but that the

genre of Rabbinic interpretation of poems of Scripture is a unified
conceptual construct, just as the Songs themselves are a genre sui
generis in Scripture. See above n. 6. The midrash Canticles R. is
a fine example of a midrash on poetic Scripture;it has much early
material if the ascriptions are taken as indications.

47. See beginning Piska 306.

48. E.g. see Piska 320.

49. E.g. see end of all Piska'ot and end of Song, Piska 333.

50. E.g. see Piska 306, "E33".

51. See Jonah Fraenkel, "Time and its Shaping in Aggadic Literature",
(B 164)Studies in Aggadah, Targum etc., p. 133ff. (Heb.), cf. Piska
313 further.

52. See Piska 306: "And the Sages say...", also see how the expression
"Torah min hashamayim" is used in Piska 306 "E27".

53. See Jacob Katz, Exclusiveness and Tolerance,(B 218)Schocken,
New York, 1962, Introd.: XIII.

54. See Piska 322 "E8".

55. See Marmorstein, Studies in Jewish Theology, p. 11.(B 259)

56. See Piska 318 "E4". See also Piska 323 "E16".

57. The person of the Messiah is not mentioned at all in our text.
Nevertheless, the "generations of the Messiah" is mentioned in Piska
310 "E4", and the "Days of the Messiah" is mentioned, Piska 318 "E15"
and elsewhere.

58. See J.Klausner, The Messianic Idea in Israel,(B 231)Macmillan,
New York, 1955.

59. E.g. Piska 319 "L2", cf. Piska 306 "E51".

60. See Piska 307.

61. See end of Piska 306.

62. E.g. see end of Piska 324.

63. See Piska 326 "E2".

64. See Piska 317 "L2".

65. Ibid.

66. See Piska 333 "E9".

67. See J.Z. Smith, "Sacred persistence: Towards a Redescription of
Canon",(B 303)in Approaches to Ancient Judaism, (W.S. Green, ed.),
Scholars Press, Missoula 1978, p. 18.

68. See J. Niehaus,"raz-pešar in Isaiah XXIV", (B 277)VT vol. 3,
(1981), no. 3, p. 376f. Also see L. Silberman, "Unriddling the riddle,
a Study in the Structure and Language of the Habakuk pesher",(B 318)
R.Q. 3 (1961) no. 11, p. 330-333.

69. See P.T. Avodah Zarah 2:7.

70. E.g. W.G. Braude, The Midrash on Psalms, New Haven, Yale University,
1959. W.G. Braude and J.J. Kopstein, Tanna debe Eliyahu, Philadelphia,
JPS, 1981, and Pesikta deRab Kahana, Phila., JPS, 1975. W.G. Braude,
Pesikta Rabbati, New Haven, Yale University, 1968. M. Kadushin,
A Conceptual Approach to the Mekilta, New York, JTS, 1969. In German we
have A. Wuensche (ed.), Bibliothica Rabbinica, George Olms, Hildesheim,
1967, on Gen. R., Ex. R., Lev. R., Deut. R., Ruth R., Kohelet R.,
Esther R., Canticles R., Lamentations R., Pesikta de Rab Kahana. Also
G. Kittel, Rabbinische Texte, Tannaitische Midraschim on Sifra and Sifre
(not complete), W. Kohlammer, Stuttgart, 1933. And of course no example
of such works would be worthy without mention of Judah Goldin's Song
at the Sea, New Haven, Yale University Press, 1971.

71. For some examples see R.S. Sarason "A Select Bibiliography of (B303)
Scholarship on Midrashic Literature", Studies in Aggadah, Targum, etc.
p. 71ff and Lee Haas, "Bibliography on Midrash" in The Study of Ancient
Judaism (B184).

An English Translation of

Sifre Deuteronomy to Ha'azinu:

being the section of Rabbinic Midrash in Sifre (i.e. the Books of
Numbers and Deuteronomy as opposed to the Book of Leviticus) to Deut. 32
as found in the edition by L. Finkelstein, Sifre On Deuteronomy (New York,
1969). Brackets or asterisks have been used to signify interesting
readings in the London Manuscript which are not found in Finkelstein.
The translation is accompanied by notes to aid in the understanding of
the work.

"Give ear, ye heavens, and I will speak..."

Rabbi Meir[T1] says: When Israel was pure they would give witness to themselves, as it is said, "And Joshua said unto the people, 'Ye are witnesses to yourselves'."[S1] But then they subverted themselves, as it is said, "Ephraim compasseth Me about with lies and the House of Israel with deceit."[S2] So, He brought the Tribe of Judah and of Benjamin to give witness to them, as it is said, "And now, O inhabitants of Jerusalem and men of Judah, judge[E1] I pray you, betwixt Me and My vineyard.[S3] What could have been done more to My vineyard...."[S3a] Then the tribe of Judah and Benjamin became corrupt, as it is said, "Judah hath dealt treacherously...."[S4] So, He brought the Prophets to give witness to them, as it is said, "Yet the Lord witnessed to Israel, and Judah by the hand of every prophet (and every seer)...."[S5] Then they subverted the Prophets, as it is said, "But they mocked the messengers of God...."[S6]

S1. Joshua 24:22.   S2. Hosea 12:1.   S3. Isaiah 5:3.
S3a. Isaiah 5:3.   S4. Malachi 2:11.   S5. 2 Kings 17:13.
S6. Chronicles 36:16.

T1. While both Ln and F read "Meir" here, the variant "Bena'ah" is the preferred reading of Epstein (p. 628, B112).

E1. Throughout my translation of Biblical verses I have kept an eye on JPS (1917) and RSV (1952) but I have not hesitated to present the scriptural text as it was viewed by the Rabbinic preacher. In the case of very complex word plays, I have sometimes included the Hebrew word. Joshua's alleged statement ("S1") should chronologically have followed that of Moses ("S7"). However, our teacher does not intend to give us a history lesson but rather a lesson of history: Israel has continued to ignore and subvert God's witnesses who are His messengers to guarantee the covenantal relationship between God and Israel. The Rabbis understood the word "judge" as used in these proof texts to be of a "lawsuit" nature referring to the witnessing of the covenantal

So, He brought the Heavens to give witness to them as it is said,

"I call heaven and earth to witness to you this day...."[S7] Then they

subverted the Heavens, as it is said,[T2] "Seest thou not what they

do...."[S8] And then it states,"the children gather wood, and the fathers

kindle the fire, and women knead the dough, to make cakes for the

queen[T3] of heaven."[S9] So, He brought the Earth to give witness to

them, as it is said, "Hear, O earth; behold, I will bring evil...."[S10]

Then they subverted the Earth, as it is said, "Also their altars are

as heaps upon the furrows of the field...."[S11] So,[T4] He brought the

paths to give witness to them, as it is said, "Thus saith the Lord;

stand ye in the ways and see...."[S12] Then they subverted the paths,

as it is said, "Thou hast built thy lofty place at every head of

the path...."[S13] So, He brought the Gentile Nations[E2] to give witness

to them, as it is said, "Therefore hear, ye nations, and, know

O congregation, what is against them...."[S14]

---

terms. For the construction of the "Song of Moses" as a "lawsuit" (B 351)
see G.E. Wright, "The Lawsuit of God", Israel's Prophetic Heritage
Essays in Honor of James Muilenberg ed: B.W. Anderson et al, 1962.

S7. Deuteronomy (4:26) 30:19.   S8. Jeremiah 7:17.   S9. Jeremiah 7:18.
S10. Jeremiah 6:19.   S11. Hosea 12:12.   S12. Jeremiah 6:16.
S13. Ezekiel 16:25.   S14. Jeremiah 6:18.

T2. Ln likely influenced by the preceeding האזינו ,reads האזינו
in lieu of האזין . The error is simply to be ignored.

T3. Ln reads מלאכת "work of heaven" in lieu of מלכת "queen of
heaven". If it is not simply an error it is a scribal euphemism for
the idolatrous term --"queen of heaven".

T4. The "path" passage "S12" is missing entirely in Ln. This lack may
be indicative of the late addition of the passage to the midrash rather
than of a homoioteleuton. This suggestion is based upon structural
considerations within the passage.

Then they subverted the Gentile Nations, as it is said, "And

they mingled themselves with the nations, who learned their

works..."[S15] [E3] So, He brought the Mountains to give witness to

them, as it is said, "Hear, O ye mountains the Lord's controversy..."[S16]

Then they subverted the Mountains, as it is said, "They sacrifice

upon the tops of the mountains...."[S17] So, He brought the cattle to

give witness[E4] to them, as it is said, "The ox knoweth his owner

(and the ass, his master's crib)...."[S18] Then they corrupted the cattle,

as it is said, "And they exchanged their glory for the likeness of an

ox that eateth grass...."[S19] So, He brought the birds[*] [T5] to give

witness to them, as it is said, "Also the stork in the heavens knows

her appointed times...."[S20] Then they subverted the cattle, beasts and

birds, as it is said, "And I went in and saw; and behold every form

of creeping thing and detestable beast...."[S21] So, He brought the fish

to give witness to them, as it is said, "Or speak to the Earth and

---

* f: birds -- Ln: beasts

E2. The Rabbinic usage of the word אומות is like that of the Latin
gentiles. Since the English "gentile" commonly refers to non-Jewish
individuals, I have adopted the title "Gentile Nations" as the proper
translation of אומות .

S15. Psalms 106:35.   S16. Micah 6:2.   S17. Hosea 4:13.
S18. Isaiah 1:3.   S19. Psalms 106:20.   S20. Jeremiah 8:7.
S21. Ezekiel 8:10.
T5. Ln reads "beasts" while F reads "birds". The proof text in both
mentions the "stork" who is called to witness while both share a
further proof text which refers to "beasts" who are subverted.
Neither reading is clearly superior.

E3. The verse is literally rendered as "and they learned their works".
The subject of "learned" could be either the Jews or the nations. Here,

it shall teach thee; and the fishes of the sea shall declare unto

thee...."[S22] Then they subverted the fish, as it is said, "And thou

---

the midrashist understands the subject to be the <u>nations</u>, the closest
possible antecedent in the verse. I have therefore rendered "...nations
<u>who</u> learned" which is the interpretation the midrashist preferred.

E4. The so-called "witnesses" are claimed here to "testify" in one
of two ways: either as an appointed official to report actions to
a court, or by giving warning (and later testifying) by providing a
good example. In either case breach of responsiblity is punishable
when the witness establishes that:
   1) the accused was aware of his responsibility;
   2) clear infraction occurred (cf. B.T. Makkoth 6b and ibid 9b).
The following proof text comes from Isaiah 5:3-4: "And now, O inhabitants
of Jerusalem and men of Judah, judge I pray you...." This pericope in F
is not parallel to the format of the other pericopes. The other
pericopes read " קלקלו ב "(subverted) while the Judah pericope
reads " קלקלו "(became corrupt), (Ln: קלקלו ב). This
pericope also omits the particle " את " which occurs in all the other
pericopes. A speculative explanation of the divergence of the
pericope mentioning the Tribes of Judah and Benjamin (inhabitants of
Jerusalem) is that this pericope formed the earliest layer of the
midrash. In this earliest layer the preacher has taken Deut. 30:19
to mean that Moses has called Israel (בכם) to testify with (את)
the heavens and the earth.
      The earliest form of the midrash may have read:
            He brought the Tribes of Judah and Benjamin to
            give witness to them, as it is said...
            The Tribes of Judah and Benjamin became corrupt, as it is
            said...
            He brought the heavens and the earth to give witness to
            them, as it is said...
L. Silberman has suggested to me that some redactor or preacher
of the midrash, not only brought the verses, but brought, at times,
glossed comments also (eg. the ant pericope, ."S24").
      Perhaps our midrash has been structured according to witnessing
language (eg. Lev. 5:1), the "witnesses" arranged in order of
importance, developed in three separate stages. I draw attention
to the following:
      1) The "Judah" passage may be of the earliest layer of the
midrash as its usages of העיד (and not העיד את) and of קלקלו vary from
the rest (Ln: קלקלו ב appears to be a scribal harmonization and can so
be explained while F is difficult to explain unless it is "original").
      2) The "earth" passage is apparently a later transitional passage
designed to eliminate the witnesses of the earlier section of the
midrash. Its use is awkward.

makest men as the fishes of the sea..."[S23] So, He brought the ant to

give witness for them, as it is said, "Go to the ant, thou sluggard...

she provideth her bread in the summer..."[S24]

Rabbi Shimon the son of Elazar said: How humble[L1] would that

man have been who was supposed to take instruction from the ant!
--Had he actually taken instruction and acted accordingly he

---

3) If the passages containing a witnessing term (e.g. Lev.
5:1) be gathered and compared they will show perfect consistency
in style and usage. These passages may represent the second stage
of the development of this midrash.

4) The "path" pericope has no fixed place in this midrash.
Its proof texts vary from recorded source to recorded source and it
presents a forced usage of בהם להעיד which does not accord
with its proof texts. These may be signs of the late addition of
this passage into the midrash. Yet, the internal order is so well
edited that the above discussion must be taken as mere speculation.

S22. Job 12:8.   S23. Habakuk 1:14.   S24. Proverbs 6:6.

L1. For the sense of עלוב as "humble" see Avoth de Rabbi
Nathan "A" ch. 23:   זה שהוא עלוב כמשה רבנו שנאמר
                          והאיש משה עניו מאד
This shows that עלוב may have a meaning of "humble" in its
most positive sense. Jastrow, s.v. עלוב recognizes that
עלוב does mean "humble" in Piska 306 but understands it in its most
negative sense (i.e. "humiliated"). However, as Harry Fox indicated
to me in private discussion, עלוב here should be rendered in
its most positive sense: "Had he actually learned from the ant,
how humble a man he would have been indeed!"

As usual, the use of איל here signifies a conditional
statement. However, when accompanied with a negative particle
(לא, איל), I believe it often has the force of
exclamatory rhetoric. Thus, (e.g. "E 14") it is followed by
statements denying the exclamatory rhetoric. I shall refer to this
use of איל as "exclamatory" throughout this work.

would have been humble. But he "was supposed to take instruction"
from her ways and, in fact, did not take instruction.

At the time of the Future Judgement, the community of Israel will
address the Holy One, blessed be He:

> Master of the Universe, I fear for my witnesses exist, as
> it is said, "I call heaven and earth to witness against you
> this day."[S25]

He will say to her:

> Fear not for I will remove them, as it is said, "For behold
> I will create a new heaven and a new earth." [S26]

She will address Him:

> Master of the Universe, I fear for I see places that I have
> shamed... and I am ashamed, as it is said, "See thy way[E5]
> in the valley."[S27]

He will say to her:

> Fear not, for I will remove them, as it is said, "Every valley
> shall be lifted up."[S28]

She will address Him:

> Master of the Universe, I fear for my name exists.

He will say to her:

> Fear not, for I will remove it, as it is said, "And thou
> shalt be called by a new name." [S29]

S25. Proverbs 6:8.   S26. Isaiah 65:17.   S27. Jeremiah 2:23.
S28. Isaiah 40:4.   S29. Isaiah 62:2.

E5. The reference in Jeremiah 2:23 is to the worship of the
baals which the Israelites practised in the valleys.

She will address Him:

Master of the Universe, I fear for[T6] [*] my name has been

associated with the name of the Baals.

He will say to her:

Fear not, for I will remove it, as it is said, "And I shall

remove the name of the Baals..."[S30]

She will address Him:

Master of the Universe, nevertheless the household[E6] will

mention it.

He will say to her:

"And they shall no more be mentioned by their name."[S31]

---

* F: my -- Ln: Your

S30. Hosea 2:19.   S31. Hosea 2:19.

T6. There are two possibilities of understanding F here. In Ln
it is clear that Israel feels the guilt of having associated God's
name with the Baals--they have syncretized their worship of
the Deity with polytheistic practices. If we take F literally
the passage claims that Israel worshipped Baal. No mention is made
of "associating God's name with the Baals. "My name" (Israel's)
has been associated. However, according to Palestinian traditions
recorded in B.T. Sanhedrin 63a "association of God's name with
idols" is a more severe crime than is idol worship. It is therefore
possible that F has used a euphemism "my name" but really means
"Your name" (God's). Thus   the intent of Ln and F may agree
--both refer to God's name being associated with the Baals.

E6. The term "household" is not likely to refer to the Jews or
non-Jews of the Land of Israel who syncretized Jewish practice
with non-Jewish practices. {The structure of the pericope may have
been determined by the preceding pericope. The preacher wishes to
refute the notion that Israel is eternally condemned. Although the
preceding pericope does not assume that any one witness is eternal,
it does assume that there is an eternal sequence of witnesses. L.
Silberman takes "At the time of the Future Judgement the Knesset Yisrael...
furthermore..." as one piece. The previous section concluded with
"witnessing" ants - the new section stresses that God will cancel out

---

the witnesses. He suspects we have here an anti-Christian polemic.
It is true that the homilist places in the mouth of Knesset
Yisrael the words of a polemic that was used against Jews.
Talmudic passages as well as Christian sources indicate that
Israel had been accused of severing herself eternally from God by
her rejection of Him in favor of idols. (See B.T. Yevamot 102b;
B.T. Avodah Zarah 4a; B.T. Hagigah 5b (top)). Some sources indicate
that Christians said the name "Israel" was meant to testify the
evil of the Jews and that the prophecy of "new heavens and a new
earth" was a reference to the Kingdom of Christ. (See A.P. Hayman's
edition of the "Disputation against Sergius" in Corpus Scriptorum
Christianorum Orientalium tome 153, Scriptores Syri vol. 339, p. 52.
Also see ibid. p. 64, p. 66, p. 76).
The accusations are dismissed in these pericopes which claim
that God himself sanctions their dismissal. Since divine authority
is invoked to refute the charges we may surmise that Jews were
bothered by the onslaught of the Christian or Min polemic.
See ibid, tome 152, vol. 338, p. 26 regarding prophecies. E.g. when
Isaiah spoke to the כנושתא (Knesset) telling them that they would
be called by a new name, he was replacing the כנושתא by TSTMH
A'DTA, the Body of Confessors. Also see Ephraem's Sermon against
the Jews (220B)(B 141) and Aphraate's Demonstrations 1,090.(B91)
Also Verecundi Iuncensis, "Commentarii Super Contra Ecclesiastica",
Corpus Christianorum Series Latina, XCIII, p. 16. (B 341) In this
6th century work we find a commentary upon the Song of Moses (Deut.
32) along the same theme as Origen presented in his commentary to
Canticles. Accordingly, the first verse of Deut. 32, in this
allegorical commentary, alludes to the spiritual Church by the term
"heaven" and to the materialistic Synagogue by the term "earth".
Just as Christians interpreted the songs of Scripture in ways to
refer to the body of the Church so did Jews interpret the songs in
ways to refer to the Synagogue of Israel (Knesset Yisrael).
Urbach's ("Homiletical Interpretations etc") contention of direct
influence of the commentaries of the Christian and Jewish scholars
upon each other appears to be somewhat overstated. However, it appears
to be the case that the terms used to refer to the body of the
Christian community in these works and to the Jewish establishment
in the texts have been chosen with an apologetic motif in mind.
Knesset Yisrael is deemed to be the saved community in the World to
Come in Jewish texts while the Body of the Confessors is deemed to
be that in Christian commentaries. To posit a direct dialogue within
these texts places a strain upon the interpretation of the texts.
Suffice it to say that both textual traditions wish to accomplish
the same ends for their respective communities and use similar terms
to refer to their establishments. Undoubtedly, some interpretations
do reflect an actual interchange between the communities but it
would be difficult to establish exactly which verses are based upon

Furthermore, on the Future Morrow, at the time of the Future

Judgement, she will address Him:

> You have yet written,"...saying: If a man put away his wife,
>
> and she go from him, and become another man's, may he return
>
> unto her again?"[S32]

He will say to her:

> I wrote[E7] nothing other than "a man". Yet has it not been stated,
>
> "For I am God and not a man."[S33]

---

an actual interchange. Urbach's argument shows mutual concerns,
polemic and apologetic. He has not established actual proof of
dialogue. See also Marmorstein, The Old Rabbinic Doctrine II:
Essays in Anthropomorphism, p.9.} Here "household" may refer to the
angels of the heavenly court (=familia), who would remember Israel's
perfidy. Cf. Philo, (ed. Colson), Virtues, ch. 11-12: "He
convoked a divine assemblage of the elements of all existence and
the chiefest parts of the universe, heaven and earth, one the house
of the mortals, the other, the house of the immortals." Or perhaps,
the term בני ביח is to be taken as בני ביתי see Yalk.
Shim. Isaiah 506. בני ביתי means "household servants" cf. Gen.
15:2f. and Midrash Ruth R6:2, also see Goldin, AJS Review 5(1980) [B172]
p. 53 n. 42. Servants were semi-proselytes and their behavior
"could affect" God's benevolence towards Israel. (cf. Hebrew-English [B69]
Dictionary, Lexicon of the Bible s.v. בוה .)

S32. Jeremiah 3:1.   S33. Hosea 11:9.

E7. The tone of this passage may have been influenced by Christian
claims that the Gentile has supplanted Israel, e.g. see Irenaeus' [B207]
Proof of the Apostolic Teaching, p. 104 ch. 95 and Justin [B261]
Martyr's Dialogue with Trypho, p. 325, ch. 115. Ln reads
here "dictated" rather than F's "wrote".

Another interpretation:[T7]

--O House of Israel, are you my divorcees? But has it not

yet been stated, "Thus saith the Lord: Where is the bill of your

mother's divorcement, wherewith I have put her away? Or which

of my creditors is it to whom I have sold you?"[S34]

Another interpretation:

"Let the heavens give ear":

This may be explained by a parable of a king who entrusted

his son to a tutor[L2] to take conscientious care of him. The son

declared, "Father, do you think it will do any good to deliver me over

to a tutor? I will make sure that he eats and drinks and goes to

sleep and then I will go about my own interests." His father said,

"I have delivered you over to a tutor from whom you cannot

escape."

So did Moses say to Israel, "Perhaps you think that you can

escape from beneath[*] [T8] the wings of the Shekina[L3] or that you

can move away from the presence of the earth!"

---

* F: beneath   -- Ln: the presence of

S34. Isaiah 50:1.

T7. Missing in Ln. for sense of " דבר אחר " see Piska 307, "E6".

T8. See "L3", Piska 306. Ln's reading here is as meaningful as
F's. Neither reading is clearly superior.

L2. Although Joseph Smith (see St. Irenaeus etc., p. 215, n. 377)
takes "paedagogue" in Galatians 3:24("The Law was our paedagogue
in Christ...") as the slave who accompanied the Roman child to
school, Fürst, s.v. פדגוג finds the paedagogue to be a "tutor
and governor" of the child. I believe we should understand the
word in this way in our midrash and perhaps in Galatians as well.

In our midrash the role of the tutor is explained in one reading
to refer to the protective custody of God: beneath the wings of
the Shekina (allusion to שמים Deut. 32:1),or to the custody
of the presence of the earth (allusion to ארץ   Deut. 32:1),
cf. Bauer s.v. παιδαγωγός   . For the sense of
another reading see next note.
L3. The words "wings of the Shekina" must be looked at carefully
in this pericope. E.E. Urbach maintains that this phrase always
refers to divine protection. This is certainly its meaning here.
However, Urbach (Sages, p. 47) thinks that the variant כנפי
שמים (which is sometimes found in parallel sources to midrashim
which refer to   כנפי השכינה) is not significantly different
from   כנפי השכינה so that the two expressions are nearly
synonymous. Yet, his very example throws his contention into
doubt (see Sages, p. 704 n. 36 and n. 39). We see that "wings
of the Shekina" and "wings of heaven" may have somewhat different
meanings. Urbach examined a passage in Mechilta de Rabbi Shimon
bar Yochai (to Ex. 17:15-20). This midrash expresses concern that
'Amalek will destroy "Your children from under the wings of heaven".
He believed that this statement was practically synonymous with
the passage in Mechilta de Rabbi Yishmael, to the same verses,which
reads "When Amalek came to destroy Thy children from beneath the
wings of...their Father in Heaven..." However, inspection of the
passages leads me to conclude that Mechilta de Rabbi Shimon bar
Yochai is referring to "Your children whom You will scatter to the
four corners of the heavens." "Wings of heaven" here means "corners
of heaven". See also Mechilta of Rabbi Yishmael which also has
such a tradition and alludes to Zech. 2:10. In the passage of
Mechilta de Rabbi Yishmael the reference is to the covenantal
protective role of God as is the image of wings in Targ. to Ez. 16:8
(ואגינית במימרי   ). Perhaps   כנפים here refers to
hems (=grace), see E. Greenstein "To grasp etc." p. 218 (B 178)
Heb.   וראפרש כנפי. In like fashion we may explain the reading
of F and Ln, "wings of the Shekina", to refer to convenantal watching
(allusion to השמים in Deut. 32:1). Another reading, mentioned
in F's critical apparatus (Sifre Deut. p. 330) is: "So Moses
said to Israel: Are you able to cross over from under the corners
of heaven (כנפי שמים) or to move from off of the earth?".
According to his version (cited in the name of R. Yehuda), one cannot
escape the physical limits of the universe. L. Silberman understands
the passage to mean that Moses said - Perhaps you think you can
escape heaven and earth but heaven and earth will inform even
when you thought you had escaped.

And furthermore[E8] the Heavens publish, as it is said, "The

heavens shall reveal his iniquity."[S35] And from whence do

we know that even the earth informs? As it is said, "And the

earth shall rise up against him."[S36]

At the time of the Future Judgement: the community of Israel[E8a]--

she will stand in judgement before God and address Him:

Master of the Universe, I do not know who has subverted

whom and who has changed His relationship to whom?

S35. Job 20:27.   S36. Job 20:27.

E8. L. Silberman says that the idea here is that even if one has
escaped heaven and earth, one will ultimately find that these
"guardians" will have the last word. An important point here is that
"writing" (publish = כותבים) is considered equivalent to "revelation"
(= יגלו). This is the axiom of aggadic thinking. What Scripture
imparts in the way of written shapes is transformed by the aggadic
mind into the revelation of Israel's past, present and future
history. To the midrashist it is the written word which reveals.
He "learns" of truth by examining the written word of Scripture.
The preacher then gives us an example of this axiom. Since
witnesses rise to give testimony (see B.T. Shevuoth 30b) and since
the Scripture states that the earth is to "rise up", the midrashist
finds that a personified earth will testify on Judgement Day.
For the style of the Rabbinic mashal see D. Stern, "The Case of
the Mashal", (B 325) Prooftexts, Sept. 1981, vol. 1, no. 3,
p. 262ff., and R.M. Johnston,"The Study of Rabbinic Parable: Some
Preliminary Observation", (B209) SBL Seminar Papers, 1976
(112th annual meeting), Scholars Press, p. 377ff. (esp. see p. 342ff.)

E8a. Do we have here a discussion of problems encountered in
"Knesset Yisrael" passages rather than an actual "Knesset Yisrael"
passage itself? Perhaps some redactor or gloss tells us that whenever we find "In the Future, Knesset Yisrael..." in a midrash, the
reference is to the time when she will stand in judgement before God.
And when we find: "And she will say to Him: Master of the Universe..."
then I (the redactor) do not know how to interpret these midrashim.
Whose faults are being addressed? Is Israel complaining against God's
"desertion" of Israel? But to the contrary Israel had "deserted" God.
(cf. Targumim to Deut. 31:20 where:= וישנון ית קיימי
                                      הפר את בריתי   )

Did Israel subvert God and did God (not) change[T9] His relationship
to Israel?--Since Scripture says, "And the heavens tell of His
righteousness",[S37] it is certainly the case that Israel subverted
God but God did not "change His relationship with Israel." And
so Scripture says, "For I the Lord change not."[S38]

Another interpretation:

"Give ear, ye heavens..."

Rabbi Yehuda says:[E9] This may be explained by a parable[E10] of a king

---

S37. Psalms 50:6.   S38. Malachi 3:6.

T9. We should suspect a euphemism in Ln here. F reads "...did
God change His relationship..." while Ln reads "...did God not
change his relationship...". Since there is a principle that
what is uttered by the lips may come to pass (see B.T. Moed Katan
18a), the custom at times prevails to avoid saying things like
"God change his relationship", even in hypothesis, lest it come
to pass by the mechanism of "opening the mouth to Satan"
(see B.T. Ber. 19a). Indeed "change relationship" itself
means to "break the covenant" - see E8q Piska 306.

E9. The midrash, like many others in our text, is attributed to
Rabbi Yehuda the son of Ilai. He flourished in the Land of Israel
circa 150 C.E. and was said to be the "greatest of the preachers"
(see B.T. Menachoth 103b and Strack's Introduction etc. p. 115).
It is said that the redaction of Sifra to Leviticus followed the
teachings of Yehuda (see B.T. Shabbath 137a, B.T. Yoma 41a,B.T.
Erubin 96b). Yehuda was a student of Akiba and over six hundred (B 326)
traditions are recorded in his name (see Strack p. 115)
and Amoraic sources tend to favor his decisions (see Seder HaDoroth,
"Tannaim veAmoraim", p. 169 (B 186)).
E10. Our parable is designed around the verses which the fable
itself cites in explanation. Deut. 28:12 mentions that the heavens
are God's storehouse. The midrashist has translated the image of the
storehouse-heaven into an image of his own time. The heavens are
seen as the "apitropos" (see L4., Piska 306) who collects taxes
and nourishes the family of the king. The apitropos is no mere
messenger. Sifre to Numbers 12:8 claims that the apitropos
represents the king's authority. There need not be any discrepancy
between those sources which do not allow for intermediaries to
control rain flow (e.g. B.T. Ta'anith 2a) and our pericope. God,
here, is seen to have ordered the heavens to observe Israel's

who had two administrators[L4] in the country and he entrusted[L5]

them with everything he had. Then he put his son into their charge

---

behavior and to send them rain when they are worthy of God's blessing.
The heavens cannot act contrary to God's wishes. In this way the
parable of the apitropos is quite appropriate (see Judah Goldin's "Not
by means of an Angel and not by means of a Messenger", (B 173)
Studies in the History of Religions, 1968. p. 412ff.). The midrashist
connects Deut. 32:1 and Deut. 12:8 to suggest the image of the
apitropos in order to indicate that Israel's physical welfare is
dependent upon its spiritual welfare. L. Silberman notes that F:
"two administrators" is derived from the form of the dual " שמים "
in Scripture. See my interpretation further E12.

L4. The term "apitropos bamdina (במדינה   אפיטרנפוס   )"
requires examination. In Sifre to Numbers 12:8 (B 49   ) we find the
following parable:

> To what can this be compared? To a king who had
> his apitropos in the country and the inhabitants of
> the country insulted him. The king said, "Not my
> servant have you insulted but it is I whom you have
> insulted...

According to the usage of אפיסרופוס במדינה   here we may assume
that the apitropos (Gk. epitropos: trustee, guardian, governor)
was a royal spokesman who spoke with the authority of the king who
sent him to administer. Midrash Haggadol to Ex. 4:13 compares the
"tishlaḥ", the divine representative, to the apitropos. In this
comparison in Midrash Hagadol we find an apparent gloss comment
which claims that the word אפיסרופוס   refers to "one who nourishes
the king's household (understanding "epitropos" as if from Gk.
"tropos" (a feeder), equivalent to   המפרנס). Rashi believed the
term "   אפיסרופוס של מלך " (see Rashi to B.T. Shabbath
121a) refers to the man appointed over the king's monies and the man
who supervised the fiscus. Targum Pseudo-Jonathan to Gen. 41:34 sees
the "apitropos" as the king's financial deputy who administered the
land taxes. Lam. R.(to Lam. 5:12), the Gospel of Luke (3:11), the
Gospel of Matthew (20:8), the Syriac "Testament of the Apostle Addai"
(beginning)uses "apitropos" to refer to the proconsul. Other midrashim
use the term (see Jastrow, s.v.   אפיסרופוס   ) to refer
to a guardian and Matthew 21:37 uses it to refer to the steward of
a vineyard (see also Gal. 4:2). Thus, there are many usages of the
word. However, אפיסרופוס , when qualified by   במדינה , alludes
to an official representative of the king and not merely a child's
guardian. He administered the monies of the king and was responsible
for providing the needs of the king's household. See further, Liddell
& Scott, s.v. ἐπίτροπος) . Sifre to Num. 12:8 and Krauss,Persia
and Rome etc., (B 235) p. 140f. L. Silberman likes the reading
in F because שמים is dual and so R. Yehuda indicates two administra-

and said to them, "Whenever my son fulfills my wishes, thou shalt
delight him and indulge him by giving him to eat and by giving
him to drink. Whenever my son does not fulfill my wishes he may
not taste [E11] anything of mine."

So what does Scripture have to say about Israel whenever[E12]
they (Israel) fulfill the wishes of God? --The Lord will open unto
thee His good treasure the heavens..."[S39] And what does Scripture
have to say about them whenever they do not fulfill the wishes
of God? --"And the anger of the Lord will be kindled against you,
and He shut up the heavens, so that there shall be no rain, and
the ground shall not yield her fruit."[S40]

---

tors.
L5. For the usage of שלם in the sense of "entrusted" see Targum
Onkelos to Exodus 31:3, also see B.T. Baba Mezia 85a and B.T. Yoma
83b. See also Jastrow, s.v. שלם . The attestations are in
Aramaic and we possibly have an Aramaicism here.

S39. Deuteronomy 28:12.   S40. Deuteronomy 11:17.

E11. Dining at table with guests in Rabbinic lore is indicative
of friendship and mutual trust (e.g. see B.T. Sanhedrin 23a which
tells how the   נקיי הדעת   of Jerusalem would dine only
with those they knew).
E12. God feeds Israel by providing rain. This rain represents
the bond between God and Israel. The "two administrators"
of version F are meant to signify the "heavens" and the "earth"
from whose sustenance Israel eats.

Another interpretation:

"Give ear, ye heavens":

Rabbi Nehemiah says: This may be explained by a parable of a king whose son fell upon evil ways. He began to complain about him to his brothers, then he began to complain about him to his friends , then he began to complain about him to his neighbours, then he began to complain about him to his relatives. That father did not leave his constant complaining until he said, "Heavens[E13] and Earth! To whom may I complain about you except for these."

Therefore it is said, "Give ear, ye heavens, and I will speak." Another interpretation:

"Give ear, ye heavens":

Rabbi Yehuda says: Is the measure given the righteous at all insufficient! But the world where they live is given a measure of largesse.[E14] For when Israel fulfills the will of God, what is said about them? "The Lord will open unto thee His good treasure the heaven..."[S41] And "opening" is distinctly an expression of "enlarging"[L6] as it is said, "And He opened her womb."[S42]

S41. Deuteronomy 28:12.   S42. Genesis 29:31.

E13. "Heavens and Earth!" may possibly be explained here as an expression of desperation and last resort. (However, the king may, perhaps, be seen to be exorcizing his son. For the expression "By heaven be exorcized, by earth be exorcized!" see Studies in Biblical and Semitic Symbolism, p. 139.(B149)) That קבל certainly implies a request for rebuke see Sifra Kedoshim to Lev. 19:17, Sifre Deut. Piska 1, and B.T. Arachin 16b. In Yalkut Shimoni Ha'azinu 942 this tradition is recorded in the name of Rabbi Nachman. As Nachman is not a known name amongst Tannaitic teachers we are faced with three or four possibilities: The name is a

corruption(probably for Nehemiah (as in Finkelstein) whose name
is paired frequently with that of Yehuda}; we have here an Amoraic
tradition; there was a Rabbi Nachman who was a Tanna; or the name
is pure invention. I prefer the first possibility because Yehuda
was the recorded tradent of the passages surrounding this one.
The point of these midrashim is to stress the material benefits which
befall the righteous. It is possible to see here traditions which
would have had profound significance for a community whose legal
system had been threatened such as occurred during the Hadrianic
persecutions. Heaven and Earth are capable of punishing infractions,
human courts are not necessary. Thus the preacher may have been
telling his audience that Jewish laws remain in force at all times
and should not be abandoned under threat of persecution.
E14. The point here is that not only the reward given to the
righteous is extremely ample but also the part of the world where
they live --including the heavens above them (for according to the
bounty of the rain is the bounty of the crop) --is blessed on their
account. The usage of דיין follows that of B.T. Shabbath 31b
(דיין לרשעים), B.T. Sotah 12b (דיין לצדיקים), and
Gen. R. 84:1 (דיין לבעלי תשובה). For the use of
רוח and דוחק see Avoth de Rabbi Nathan "B" edition
Schechter ch. 35, p. 82. Our midrashist understands " פתח לך " =
"will be given largesse where you are". The use of אילו here
is in the sense of "as if it were not sufficient" and is best
translated into English idiom as a rhetorical statement which it
intends to be. Heaven and earth not only punish but also reward.

L6. This passage seems to be an expansion of "E12",(Piska 306).
Both passages are cited in the name of Yehuda and both relate
Deut. 28:12 and Deut. 11:17 to Deut. 32:1. While the proof texts
which speak of "the heavens" are made to apply to the "world" we
should note that here the state of the heavens controls the bounty
of the earth. Also the stretching of the Land to contain the blessings
of heaven is alluded to in Rabbinic literature. In B.T. Gittin
57a we find that a heretic accused Rabbi Hanina and his colleagues of
transmitting the false report that Israel had once been inhabited
by large populations. The retort came: Scripture refers to the
Land of Israel as the "Land of the Deer" --just as the shrunken skin
of the skinned deer cannot contain its flesh once its flesh is removed,
so the Land of Israel, stretched to contain its inhabitants, contracts
when it is not inhabited. (Cf. Josephus, Wars (Whiston) 6:9:3 records
large populations). So too,in our midrash does the space of the
righteous grow to accommodate bounties and comforts. See ARN "B"
ch. 25 (ed. Schechter, p. 82) where דוחק has the sense of
"discomfort" and רייח has the sense of "ease".

Is the measure given the wicked at all insufficient! But

even the world where they live is given a measure of depression.

For when they do not fulfill the will of God, what is said about

them? "And the anger of the Lord be kindled against you and He

shut up the heaven..."[S43] And "shutting up" is distinctly an

expression of "depressing" as it is said, "For the Lord had

fast constricted..."[S44]

Another interpretation:

"Give ear, ye heavens, and I will speak":

The Holy One, blessed be He, said to Moses: Tell Israel,

"Consider the heavens[E15] which I have created to serve you.

Perhaps it has changed its custom? Or perhaps the orb of the sun

has said, "I will not ascend from the East and light up the entire

world."? But this matter is according to that of which it is said,

"The sun also ariseth and the sun goeth down."[S45] And moreover

it is happy[T10] * to do my will, as it is said, "And it is like a

---

* F: it is happy   --   Ln: the sun

S43. Deuteronomy 11:17.   S44. Genesis 20:18.
S45. Ecclesiastes 1:5.

T10. Has שמח such as in F become corrupted to שמש   in
Ln?

E15. The heavens and the earth are here, in a sense, considered to
be models for Israel to consider and in this way will show Israel's
treachery if Israel does not perform well.

bridegroom coming out of his chamber."[S46]

"And let the earth hear the words of my mouth":

Consider the earth which I have created to serve you. Perhaps it has changed its custom? Perhaps you have sown in it and it has not grown? Or perhaps you have sown wheat in it and it brought forth barley? Or perhaps a cow has said, "I will not thresh and I will not plough today."? Or perhaps a donkey has said, "I will not carry the load and I will not go."?[E16] And likewise concerning the sea[T11] it says, "Fear ye not Me? saith the Lord; will ye not tremble at My presence? Who have placed the sand for the bound of the sea..."[S47] For from the time that I set my decree upon it, has it changed its custom and said, "I will arise and drown the world."?[E17] But this matter is according to that of which it is said, "And I have prescribed for it My decree

---

S46. Psalms 19:6.   S47. Jeremiah 5:22.

T11. Since the proof texts clearly indicate that the <u>sea</u> ים is meant here I suspect that Ln's "Day" יום is a scribal corruption and should be ignored as such. The corruption of ים to יום is not difficult to envision.

E16. The mention of the <u>cow</u> and <u>donkey</u> here may have been influenced by Isaiah 1:3: "The ox knoweth his owner and the ass his master's crib."

E17. In Babylonian mythology, the Sea, Tiamat, rose to destroy creation. Biblical references here seem to refer to that story in some form and show that now Yam, the Sea, is obedient. See <u>E.J.</u> (B 140) s.v. Creation and Cosmogony, vol. 5, p. 1063.

and set bars and doors, and said: Thus far thou shalt come, but
no further; and here shalt thy proud waves be stayed."[S48] But
it[E18] is troubled and does not know what to do. The matter is
according to that of which it is said, "They toss themselves but
they cannot prevail..."[S49] And can it not be argued a fortiori:

> Since these[E19] which are not destined for reward
>
> or for deprivation, i.e. if they behave well they
>
> receive no reward and if they do ill they receive
>
> no punishment, and they care not for the welfare
>
> of their sons and their daughters--these have not
>
> changed their customs; and you do care for the
>
> welfare of your sons and daughters, a fortiori
>
> you must not change your customs![E20]

S48. Job 38:10.   S49. Jeremiah 5:22.

E18. The Sea is troubled.
E19. I.e. the components of Nature.
E20. Perhaps this argument is not meant to be taken as a strictly
logical formulation. It is midrashic art. The artist takes a
traditional form of argument and contrives to fashion his point
using this form in a convincing manner. It is only after close
inspection of the argument that we realize his picture is not real
but painted. Here the midrashist ties together the Torah and Nature
into a unified harmony. His concluding message is that natural
law dictates that Israel should be true to the Torah. The author
knows that the components of nature really do not have free will as
does man. He carefully chooses scriptures which seek to indicate that
these items do have choices. He thereby utilizes the mythic
expressions of the Bible as if to say that the Bible intended the
artful argument presented by the midrashist. By using a Rabbinic
legal form to mold his image, he gives it the aura of an authentic
teaching. A fuller discussion of these types of "artifical" arguments
can be found in Chaim Hirschensohn's Berure haMiddoth (B 199)
(Jerusalem 5689), ch. 1-10. A similar argument is found in Marqah
4:8,"The heavens say...earth and what it contains also say: We have not

Another interpretation:

"Give ear, ye heavens (and I will speak)":

Rabbi Benaya used to say:[E21] When a person is found guilty in judgement, only his witnesses may stretch out their hands against him at first, as it is said, "The hand of the witnesses shall be first upon him..."[S50] And gradually, afterwards, that of the people, as it is said, "And afterward the hand of all the people."[S51] So it is that when Israel does not do the will of God, what is said about them? "And the anger of the Lord be kindled against you and he shut up the heaven..."[S52] Gradually afterwards come more ills, as it is said, "And ye perish quickly..."[S53] And when Israel does the will of God what is said about them? "And it shall come to pass in that day, saith the Lord, I will respond with the heavens (and the earth shall respond)..."[S54] and then it says, "I will sow her unto Me

_____

accepted foreign gods — with what recompense shall I be recompensed for this?"

S50. Deuteronomy 17:7.   S51. Deuteronomy 17:7.
S52. Deuteronomy 11:17.   S53. Deuteronomy 11:17.
S54. Hosea 2:23.

E21. Punishments here are not limited to the agency of the heavens and the earth -- although these punishments do come first. The same holds true of the rewards -- they are also not limited to the agency of the heavens and the earth. Cf. Koran sura 5:66.

by the earth."[S55]

Another interpretation:

"Give ear, ye heavens, and I will speak":

Rabbi Yehuda the son of Hananiah used to say: When Moses said, "Give ear, ye heavens. And I will speak" the Heavens and the utmost Heavens[E22] were silent. And when he said, "And let the earth hear the words of my mouth," the Earth and everything upon it were silent.[E23] And if you are bewildered by the matter

---

S55. Hosea 2:25.

E22. The usage of "the Heavens and the Utmost Heavens" is Biblical (see Deut. 10:14, I Kings 8:27, 2 Chronicles 2:5, and ibid. 6:18). According to the midrashist's view the proof texts cited in this passage confirm that the righteous have supernatural power over nature. He, Moses, silenced the earth and all which it contains as well as שמים and שמי שמים . The reference to שמי שמים requires clarification so as to understand how the Rabbi understood this Biblical term. According to B.T. Hagiga 12b, Rabbi Yehuda said that Deut. 10:14 ("Behold unto the Lord thy God belongeth שמים and שמי שמים.") referred to two heavens: שמים and שמי שמים . The double heavens were also discussed in Deut. R. 2:23, Midrash Tehillim 114:2 (ed. Buber p.471)(B 27) and in Mechilta de R. Yishmael Jethro to Ex. 18:20 (ed. Horowitz-Rabin, p. 216) שמים is qualified by the term "lower" while שמי שמים is qualified by "upper". The same description appears in Gen. R. 4:1. I. Gruenwald (Apocalyptic and Merkabah Mysticism, (B 180) , unpublished Ph.D. thesis, Hebrew University, p. 129) notes that the traditions which count שמים and שמי שמים as separate heavens are almost certainly traditions of the Land of Israel. Interestingly, this Sifre passage does not concern itself with exhorting or consoling Israel as do the other passages of Sifre Ha'azinu. Its purpose is solely to demonstrate the complete power of the righteous man. Sifre Deut. Piska 47 cites Daniel 12:3 ("And thee who make the multitudes righteous are as the stars forever...") and remarks, "Just as the stars govern and have power from one end of the universe to the other, so do the righteous." For the Rabbis it was not the magician who had power over the world, -- it was the zaddik, the righteous man.

go out and see that which is said about Joshua: "And he said in
the sight of Israel: 'Sun be thou still upon Gibeon; and thou moon,
in the valley of Aijalon'.[S56] And the sun was still and the moon
stayed...[S56a] And there was no day like that before it...."[S56b]
We find that we have been taught that the righteous have power over
the entire universe.

Another interpretation:

"Give ear, ye heavens...":

Since Moses was close to heaven, therefore he said, "Give ear,
ye Heavens." And since he was far from the earth he said, "And let
the Earth hear the words of my mouth." Isaiah came and stated in
conjunction with this usage --"Hear, ye Heavens."[S57] This was because
he was far from heaven. --"And give ear, ye Earth."[S58] This was because
he was close to the earth.[E24]

E23. The imperative "Listen!" implies "Be quiet!" The righteous man
can control nature. A.Y. Lichtenstein (B 247) sees Joshua as
commanding the sun's silence (וידום) see Rashi to B.T. Avodah
Zarah 25a - " וידום " and Introduction to Tanhuma Buber para. 14,
p. 128.

S56. Joshua 10:12.   S56a. Joshua 10:12.
S56b. Joshua 10:14.   S57. Isaiah 1:2.   S58. Exodus 20:19.

E24. It is implied that שמע   is addressed to someone distant
and האזין   to someone close because one can be told to put one's
ear to a speaker (literally) if the speaker is close by. The point
here appears to be related to Sifre Deut. Piska 340 where we see that
Moses has discharged his authority to Joshua. The question now is:
Does Moses still retain his gift of "highest prophecy" or not? (In
his commentary to this verse, Rabbenu Bahya claims that the sense of
the passage is that as Moses neared death he became aware that he was
approaching the heavens. If this is the case it is difficult to
understand why some (see E25 next) would argue so vehemently against
that passage.) The view that Moses was closer than Isaiah to the

heavens, which I take to mean that his prophecy was superior, is
attributed to Akiba (cf. Machiri to Isaiah 1:2, Devarim Rabba
(ed. Lieberman) beginning of Ha'azinu, and the printed Tanhuma to
Deut. 32:1. See further Saadiah's Book of Doctrines and Beliefs
(B 38)Landauer, 213.21ff tr. S. Rosenblatt, 1948).
According to the sages here Isaiah merely followed the halachic form
of Moses, according to his precedent, and the question of prophetic
supremacy (if that is what the question was) was not germane. It
may have been the wish of the "sage" pericope to argue that the
narrative portions of the Bible should be separated from the legal ones,
such that all poetic prophecy could be considered on the same
"inspirational" level while halachic imperatives were of a more distinct
communication. (L. Silberman thinks the problem may concern an
"imputed" angelic nature to Moses.) Likewise in B.T. Makkoth 24a-b
one may find a passage claiming that the words of Moses had been
refuted by later prophecy (Ezekiel). For Frag. Targ, and Targ. Ps.-
Jon. to Deut. 32:1, "Give ear!" may suggest a close audience (i.e.
put your ear close to my mouth) while "Hear!" may suggest a more
distant one. Others argued, halacha dictated the sense of Scripture
and not vice-versa. The homilist will next present an interpretation
of Deut. 32:1 in defense of the rule that witnesses must clearly witness
the same event in the same way, cf. B.T. Sanhed. 29a and P.T. Sanhed.
3:9. The rules of testimony are applied to the way in which Moses
charged his witnesses. Our initial tradition intimated (contrary to the
halacha) that Moses charged the heavens by asking them to "give ear"
(as if he were interested in having Israel's verbal utterances recalled
whether they were intelligible or not) while Moses charged the earth
to "hear" matters (that were clearly intelligible). Since "give ear"
and "hear" may have different meanings it is not clear that the
witnesses had understood their duties to be of the same nature and
the result would be that their testimonies could not be used to
substantiate each other as the halacha requires. The preacher espouses
a method of reading the verse which B.T. Pes. 21b refers to as the
method of Meir (cf. Marmorstein, Old Rabbinic Doctrine II, Essays in
Anthropomorphism.p. 108) who did not read verses according to the
structure in which they are written. The homilist structures the verse
to mean that the heavens and the earth were both instructed to "give
ear and to hear". He finds confirmation in the words of Isaiah who
used "give ear" to charge the earth and "hear" to charge the heavens,
which is the reverse order of Deut. 32:1. This "proves" that Isaiah
understood Moses to have applied equivalent instructions to both
heaven and earth since he undoubtedly based his words upon those of
Moses. Thus both the statement of Moses and that of Isaiah are to
be read as halachic and not according to their written structure.
To both verses we may apply the principle (Mechilta (p.2 line 11)
to Ex. 12:1) --i.e. where Scripture contains a word order and its
reverse, we consider the terms of equal weight and sharing common
circumstance.

Another interpretation:

Since the <u>heavens</u> are pluralities--he specified them[L7] by the

plural form; and since the <u>earth</u> is singular--He specified it by

the singular form, "And let the Earth hear the words of my mouth."

Isaiah came and stated in conjunction with[L8] this usage --"Hear, ye

---

L7. In our pericope we find the expression:פתח להם בלשון מרובה.
I have translated this as: "Since the heavens are pluralities, he
specified them by the plural form." That is to say, Moses used the
plural form " האזינו " and hence defined the object of his address.
In <u>Hebrew</u> <u>Studies</u> (1979-80), p.60, I have argued that פתח can have
the meaning of "define", "specify", "clarify" in Rabbinic usage.
Previously, J. Heinemann had argued {<u>Scripta</u>, (1971) p. 109} that
פתח means "to deliver a sermon" because the sermon was delivered
in the opening section (begin = פתח) of the Scriptural lectionary
service in the synagogues of old. Yet, even prior to him, Bacher
(<u>Erche</u> <u>Midrash</u>,[B 61] p. 111 and p. 272) traced the sense of פתח as
"to explain" to Tannaitic times. He cites Gruenhut and Loew who also
came to this conclusion. Ugolino[B335] (<u>Thes</u>. vol. 16) agreeably
renders פתח in this Sifre passage by "exposuit". Cf. "he opened
(διανοίγω) to us the scriptures," Lk. 24:32, i.e. explained.

L8. I take סמך as a term indicating the bolstering of a new concept
by fitting it into the contextual framework of an existing Biblical
idea, cf. P.T. Berachoth 2:3 and P.T. Eruvin 10:1: Rabbi Yochanan
said: For every tradition which is not explicitly stated we bolster
it (מסמכין לה) from many places -- in Scripture. In P.T.
Shevi'ith 10:2 we find: מכאן סמכו לפרוזבול שהוא מן התורה
which is explained to mean: כשהתקין הלל סמכוהו לדבר תורה
i.e. the Rabbis bolstered the enactment of the <u>Prosbul</u> by fitting it
into the context of a Biblical statement. סמך means here "to fit
into for the purpose of strengthening." Both Torah legislation and
Rabbinic enactment are mutually strengthened by bolstering Rabbinic
enactments through Scriptural exegesis. The enactment will be readily
accepted while the authority of Torah tradition will be upheld.For the
use of סמך meaning "to fit into for the purpose of strengthening,"
see Kohut,[B 170] <u>Aruch</u> <u>Completum</u> s.v. סמך , and L. Ginzberg <u>On Jewish Law</u>
<u>and Lore</u>, p. 258, n. 14. See also Bacher <u>Erche</u> <u>Midrash</u>, s.v.
סמך . The use of בא in passages which refer to the strengthening
or weakening of Scriptural passages is well known: "Isaiah <u>came</u> and
established them (613 commandments) on six principles (B.T. Makkoth
24a)". Or again, "Moses said "...". Amos <u>came</u> and annulled it(Ibid.).
Perhaps the statement in Matthew 5:17 (cf. B.T. Shab. 116b) --"I have
not come to annul them but to give them their completion" --is of this

Heavens, and give ear, ye Earth." --in order to apply the plural to pluralities and the singular to individuals.[E25]

---

form. Thus I have rendered בא ישעיה וסמך לדבר as: "Isaiah came and stated in conjunction with this usage..." i.e. he bolstered his words by fitting them into the context of Deut. 32:1 and this context likewise became strengthened. Isaiah found precedent in the usage of Moses and thereby made this usage a preferred usage of Biblical terminology. The point is that by looking carefully at the ways Moses and then Isaiah used their terms we can determine their precise usages.

E25. This paragraph, although placed before the statement of the sages is actually a refutation of their position. They claim that both Moses and Isaiah addressed the heavens and the earth in precisely the same words. This paragraph attempts to refute this notion by showing that the statements of Moses and Isaiah were by no means equivalent. Moses addressed the heavens by the term האזינו and he used the proper grammatical construction of a plural verb to refer to the plural "heavens". On the other hand he addressed the earth by the term תשמע and he used the proper grammatical construction of a singular verb to refer to the singular "earth". Isaiah also used proper grammar and we find that he did not use the same terms Moses had used to refer to the same entities. He addressed the plural "heavens" by the plural שמעו and the singular earth by the singular האזיני (Isaiah 1:2). Thus they did not use the same terms to address the witnesses whom it appears they summoned separately. The editor appears to have introduced this grammatical argument here to create "another interpretation". The internal evidence of the passage shows that the "sage" pericope was first intended to refute the claim that Moses was closer to the heavens when he recited the Song than was Isaiah when he began his book. The sages' words, retaining "is not so", refer to the statement making the claim of Moses' greater proximity to the heavens, a claim they wish to refute. Their reading of the text misses the grammatical nexus of singulars and plurals and logically this counter argument should have followed the " sage " pericope. The editor has arranged his placement of the traditions in such a way as to allow for the viability of the two positions as if they were not in conflict: 1) Moses was the superior prophet; 2) Moses uses proper halachic form (albeit poor grammar) to summon his witnesses. Midrash leqah Tob [B 21] explains the grammatical argument here: "The heavens are plural because they are a tiered plurality."

And the Sages say: The interpretation is not so! Rather, when witnesses come and testify their testimony stands if their words are mutually oriented, and if they are not, then their testimony does not stand. So it was that if Moses had said, "Give ear, ye Heavens" and stopped there, the Heavens would have said, "We only listened by giving ear." And had he said, "And let the Earth hear the words of my mouth," the Earth would have said, "I only listened by listening." Isaiah came and stated in conjunction with this usage --"Hear, ye Heavens and give ear, ye Earth" in order to apply "giving ear" and "listening" to the Heavens and "giving ear" and "listening" to the Earth.

Another interpretation:

"Give ear, ye heavens, and I will speak":

This was said with reference to the fact that the Torah was given from the Heavens,[E26] as it is said, "Ye, yourselves, have seen that I talked with you from the Heavens."[S58]

"And let the earth hear the words of my mouth":

For Israel stood upon it -- And they said: "Of all which the Lord has spoken we will do and we will hearken."[S59]

Another interpretation:

"Give ear, ye heavens...":

This was said on account of the fact that Israel did not

S58. Exodus 20:19.   S59. Exodus 24:7.

E26. It is because the heavens and the earth were present at the formal covenantal gathering that they are able to act as witnesses.

do the commandments, which were given to them, "of the Heavens."[E27]

And these are the commandments which were given to them, "of the Heavens": The intercalation of the years and the fixing of the months, as it is said, "...and let them be for signs, and for seasons, and for days and years."[S60]

"And let the earth hear":[T11a]

This was said on account of the fact that Israel did not do the commandments which were given to them --"Upon the Earth" and these are the commandments which were given to them "Upon the Earth": the gleanings, the forgotten sheaves, and the corners of the fields; heave offerings and tithes; sabbatical years and jubilee years.

Another interpretation:

"Give ear, ye heavens":[T11a]

This was said[E28] on account of the fact that they did not do

---

S60. Genesis 1:14.

T11a. A scribe in the Ln tradition appears to have omitted here by homoioteleuton --"This was said on account".

E27. The midrashist explains the term תורה מן השמים which properly refers to the divinely revealed Torah מן (literally: "from the heavens") as "The teaching which concerns (= מן =of) the heavens". The midrashist has played with the sense of מן here to yield this sense. Enforcing observance of calendrical and agricultural regulations were important facets of Rabbinic power. Friedmann suggests that in the preceding paragraph, the terms "teachings from the heavens" and "teachings upon the earth" refer to divinely and Rabbinically ordained rules respectively. This "another interpretation" paragraph may well be a creative expansion of the phrases "Torah given from (= מן) the heavens" and Torah given upon it (the earth)" which appear in the preceding paragraph of the Sifre text. (see next note).

E28. This appears to be the earlier form of the midrash before some learned master actually spelled out in "E27" what specific commandments

all the commandments, which were given to them, "of the Heavens".

"And let the earth hear the words of my mouth":

This was said on account of the fact that they did not do the commandments, which were given to them, "of the Earth".

Moses brought to witness against Israel two witnesses which exist eternally and for ever and ever,[T12] as it is said, "I call to witness against you this day Heaven and Earth."[S60a] And the Holy One, Blessed Be He, brought the Song to witness against them, as it is said, "Now therefore write ye this Song for you...."[S60b] We do not know whose testimony "prevails" --is it the Holy One's,

---

were at issue. The order of the passages deserves comment.
  Tradition 1) Israel did not perform the commandments מן שמים specifically listed here. Israel did not perform the commandments בארץ specifically listed here.
  Tradition 2) Israel did not perform any of the commandments מן השמים (no listing). Israel did not perform any of the commandments בארץ (no listing).
It appears that Tradition 1) is meant to explain that Tradition 2) should not be taken to mean that Israel broke all the commandments. Therefore Tradition 2) must have come first. Exactly what that tradition meant in the first place cannot be deciphered. Friedmann suggested that it referred to Torah injunctions (i.e. from the Heavens=divine) and Rabbinic injunctions (i.e. from the Earth=human). I suspect that 1) is a "commentary" passage that reworks 2) by taking מ as if it meant "concerning". Whatever the actual intent of 2) it is clear that 1) has been introduced to defend Israel's behavior, the viability of the covenant {both issues jeopardized by a literal reading of 2)}; yet, the homilist still castigates the neglect of certain key injunctions which were unique to the inhabitants of the Land.

S60a. Deuteronomy 30:19.   S60b. Deuteronomy 31:19.

T12. Ln has omitted some passages here, apparently due to homoioteleuton ("For ever and ever").

Blessed Be He, or is it Moses'? Since Scripture says, "and this
Song shall testify before Him as a witness..."[S61] --thus the Holy
One's, Blessed Be He, "overcomes"[L9] Moses' and Moses' does not
"overcome" the Holy One's. And for what reason did Moses bring against
them two witnesses that live and exist eternally and for ever and
ever?[T12] He said: "I am flesh and blood and tomorrow I die. If
Israel wanted to say, 'We did not receive the Torah', who could
contradict them?" Therefore he brought against them two witnesses
that live and exist eternally and for ever and ever.[E29]

S61. Deuteronomy 31:21.

T12. Ln has omitted some passages here, apparently due to homoioteleuton ("For ever and ever").

L9. For this usage of מקיימת (1.v. מכחשת) = תיובתא (counterargument)
see Aruch Compl. s.v. קם (cf. Job 16:8). The other point seems to
be that Moses appointed two witnesses and God appointed one witness.
According to Jewish Law, at least two witnesses are required for
juridical action to proceed. In this tradition we hear that Moses
appointed two witnesses against Israel, Heaven and Earth, and also
there are two other witnesses, God and the Song, which observe
and guarantee Israel's future. For our understanding of this pericope
which claims God and the Torah can deny the validity of Moses'
witnesses see Hoffman p. 183 and E29 , Piska 306.

E29. In "S26" we saw that the heavens and the earth were not eternal
witnesses! Targum Yerushalmi to Deut. 32:1 reads:
(1   כיון דמטא קיציה דמשה למסתלקא מן גו עלמא אמר מאי אנא
מסהיד בעלמא האילין מילין דלא טעמא (ין) מיתו..מסהיד אנא
בהון שמיא וארעא
(2   דלא בלין בעלמא (הדין) ברם סופיהון דבליין לעלמא דאתי
דכן הוא כתבא מפרש ואמר...ברם אנא עתיד ברי שמיא חדתין
וארעא חדתא.
A close inspection of the text reveals a harmonizing (accomplished
by ברם) of a controversy between two opposing Traditions, 1 and
2. These two traditions are found in Sifre Ha'azinu Piska 306.
לפיכך העיד בהם שני עדים שהם חיים וקיימים לעולם ועולמי
עולמים
is a tradition found in "E29" which states that Moses found immortal
witnesses in the heavens and the earth. Another tradition (see above

"S26" , הריני מעבירם שנאמר כי הנני בורא שמים

חדשים וארץ חדשה

states that the heavens and the earth that Moses commissioned
would not survive to the Era of Judgement. Even in "E29" it may well
be that there are two combined traditions – one that God will
obliterate the testimony of the witnesses and another that they are
eternal. There is a relationship between Targ. Yerushalmi's assertion
that Israel will not be destroyed since her witnesses will be
obliterated (בלייו=), and Targum to Mal. 3:6 which reads "And ye sons
of Jacob, are not obliterated(כלייתם)". Targ. to Mal. 3:6 refutes
the notion of Targ. Yer. to Deut. 32:1.

Targ. to Mal. 3:6 states: ארי אנא ה' לא אשניתי דמן עלמא

ואתון בני ישראל אתון סדמן דמן דמאת בעלמא הדין

דיניה פסיק.

so that the contention of Targ. Yer. to Deut. 32:1, "Yet in finality
(the witnesses) will be destroyed" is met in Targ. Mal. 3:6 with "And
you, Children of Israel, imagine that whoever dies in This World has
his judgement terminated!" The Targum here understood Mal. 3:6 to
mean --"And ye, O sons of Jacob, shall ye not be consumed!" Such an
interpretation can only be a retort to those who found in Mal. 3:6
complete exoneration for sins committed in This World, so that every
Jew would have a guaranteed place in the World to Come: ואין המקום

שנה בהם בישראל רכן הוא אומר כי אני ה' לא שניתי.

The tradition that suggested that the "heavens and the earth" were to
be destroyed at the close of the world before the advent of the Messianic
Era provided a belief in redemption without recourse to Temple or
heretical methods of achieving salvation. However, such a tradition
could have easily given rise to "new heaven and new earth" theories which
proclaimed that in the Messianic Era, the Torah – covenant, witnessed
by heaven and earth, would no longer be in force. The tradition that
said the "heavens"and "earth" were immortal witnesses preserve the
notion that the Torah is to exist for eternity and that there will be
eternal responsibility for its observance. See further G. Scholem,
The Messianic Idea in Judaism and other Essays on Jewish Spirituality,
Schocken, New York, 1972, p. 3ff.(B 311) We may develop the following
theory of the pericope's history. The pericope at first contained only
one statement. The witnesses Moses had commissioned would not have the
final word. The Promise of Deut. 32:43(to the effect that Israel's
enemies would be punished and Israel would find atonement)would prevail
if Moses' witnesses attempted to condemn Israel. We then have a
secondary tradition that is meant to explain this early tradition. If
the Promise of the Song would prevail why then did Moses appoint
witnesses? How could the testimony of the Song overcome the testimony
of two witnesses --Heaven and Earth? Jewish Law requires two witnesses.
Thus the secondary tradition explains that the Heaven and the Earth were
useful witnesses to establish that Israel had received the Torah but
Israel's history and final glory were not in the hands of Heaven and
Earth but in the hands of the Song and of God. The pericope is in the
tradition of "S26", Piska 306.

And the Holy One, Blessed Be He, brought the Song to witness against them. He said: "The Song will witness against them from below and I from above." And from where do we know that God is called "a witness"? As it is said, "And I will come near to you in judgement; and I will be a swift witness...."[S62] And Scripture also says: "For I am He who knows and a witness," saith the Lord,[S62a] and Scripture states "And let the Lord be witness against you, the Lord from His Holy Temple."[S63]

2)

" לקחי shall drop ⟨יערף⟩ as the rain":

לקחי can only mean "the words of the Torah";[E30] as it is said, "For I give good לקח to you, forsake not My Torah."[S64]

S62. Malachi 3:5.   S62a. Jeremiah 29:23.
S63. Micah 3:5.   S64. Proverbs 4:2.

E30. Our midrash now begins an entire section of interpretation which will portray the centrality of תורה דברי in Rabbinic Judaism. " דברי תורה " refers to the entire corpus of Rabbinic studies. For the sense of איר...אלא לשון see S. Lieberman, Hellenism etc.,(B 250) p. 49ff. The point of this passage is to show the equation of the word לקח (literally: taking) with "the study of the Torah". By showing this equation he will be able to proceed to construe Deut. 32:2 as a lesson in the proper methodology of Torah study. The passages he selects to show this equation:
   1) equate "good לקח" with "Torah".
   2) equate קוח with "instruction" and "instruction" with "Torah" and "hearing wisdom".
   3) equate קוח with "words" and "words" with "the Decalogue".
   4) equate לקח with "grasping instruction".
Now Deut. 32:2 refers only to לק and not to "good לקח" so that it is not clear from proof #1 that Deut. 32:2 refers to Torah. Statement #3 is not general enough to accomplish the exact equation. Statement #2 accomplishes the task well and introduces three verses which speak of "not letting go of the Torah". This is the midrashist's point: לקח refers to Torah methods of study because one must take hold of the Torah, one must retain it. The more references he finds to this effect, the more forceful is his argument that Torah is that which must be retained.

Likewise Scripture says: "   My instruction, and not silver."[S65]
Now "instruction" distinctly[L10] means "the words of the Torah", as
it is said, "Hear my son, the instruction of thy father, and forsake
not the Torah of thy mother."[S66] And Scripture also says, "Hear
instruction and be wise and refuse it not."[S67] And likewise Scripture
says, "Take fast hold of instruction, let her not go."[S68] Likewise
Scripture says, "וקח with you words and return...."[S69] Now "words"
distinctly means "the words of the Torah, as it is said, "These words
the Lord spoke unto all your assembly...."[S70]
"As rain":

Just as rain is life to the world so are the words of the Torah
life to the world. But if it is as you say, then should it not
follow: Just as some of the world is gladdened by rain

and some of the world is distressed by it --he

whose pit is full of wine and whose threshing

floor is readied before him is distressed by

it --I might think that such should be the

reaction to the words of the Torah!
Therefore Scripture states, "My speech shall distill as the dew,":
Just as the whole world is gladdened by dew so is the whole world
gladdened by the words of the Torah.[E31]

S65. Proverbs 8:10.   S66. Proverbs 1:8.   S67. Proverbs 8:33.
S68. Proverbs 4:13.   S69. Hosea 4:3.   S70. Deuteronomy 5:19.

L10(לשון) אלא....אין is here rendered "distinctly" to show that a
word in Scripture may have a secondary sense which is the specific
sense required in the context of the verse. A proof text is usually
adduced to illustrate the secondary sense. L. Silberman clarifies

"As the rain winds upon the grass":

Just as rain winds[L11] fall upon the grass and raise them and promote their growth, so do the words of the Torah raise you and promote your growth. And so does Scripture say, "Exalt her and she will raise you up."[S71]

"And as רביבים winds upon the herb":

Just as rain-drop winds fall upon the grass and make them delightful and fine, so do the words of the Torah make you delightful and fine. And so does Scripture say, "For they shall be a chaplet of grace upon thy head."[S72] And Scripture also says, "She will give to thy head a chaplet of grace."[S73] [E32]

---

the point by showing how the homilist noted קח was used with תורה=מוסר so that תורה=לקח.

E31. The preacher explains the need of the double simile "as the rain"..."as the dew" in Scripture--Torah study is "as rain" in that it nourishes but it is unlike rain in that it does no harm; it is as harmless "as the dew". That the whole world is gladdened by Torah is essentially a Biblical doctrine according to Bright,[B 114] p.440.

S71. Proverbs 4:8.   S72. Proverbs 1:9.   S73. Proverbs 4:9.

L11. The midrashist in "E47", Piska 306 considers these words to describe winds as do the Targumim. However, "E31" and "E33", Piska 306, take them as referring to the rain itself. The words are obscure. See Craigie,[B 122] p.376 n.10.

E32. Torah study not only promotes intellectual growth but also refines one's character. רביב is taken by the aggadist as "coronating" as in Targum to Psalm 2:6.

Another interpretation:

" לקחי shall drop ⟨יערף⟩ as rain":

Rabbi Nehemiah[*T13] used to say: Indeed you should accumulate

the words of the Torah as general rules. I might think that just

as you are to gather them as general rules you should set them forth

as general rules! Yet, Scripture states, " לקחי shall drop

⟨יערף⟩ as rain." And יערף is distinctly a mercantile[L12]

term. For example, one does not say to another, "Break this sela

into small units for me," but rather " יערף this sela for me."

So you should accumulate the words of the Torah as general rules

and you should break them into smaller units and set them forth as

"drops of dew" and not as "drops of rain" which are big units.

Rather, you should set them forth as "drops of dew" which are small

units.[E33]

---

* F: Nehemiah   -- Ln: Yehuda

T13. Ln reads Yehuda while F reads Nehemiah here. There is no
reason to select one reading as preferable but it is of interest to
recall the passage of the Passover Haggadah (= Sifre Deut., F,p 319):
רבי יהודה היה נותן בהם סמנים דצ"ך עד"ש באח"ב

L12. The term כנעני here is used in its Scriptural sense as
referring to "trade" (cf. Prov. 31:24 and see Tanhuma Ma'asei 9 and
B.T. Baba Bathra 75a   אין כנען אלא תגרים .
ערף in Syriac means to "exchange currency" (possibly related to
Heb.   ערב :to barter, see Ez. 27:9, 2K. 12:5) and thus here means
"to change money". See also Targ. Onk. to Gen. 33:19 (חורפן).

E33. This is another explanation of the double simile "as rain...as
dew". Torah teachings should be memorized in their most comprehensive,
compact form ("rain drops") but then studied and applied with attention
to fine detail ("dew droplets"). See further "T16" for Meir's version
of this pericope. We should also note that שעירים is taken as משחרת
(ם=ע) and   hence as   שפפש ספפש (משחרת=שפפש ספפש =search out). However in

"As the rain winds upon the grass":

Just as rain winds fall upon the grass and penetrate[L13]them so they will not become wormy, so you should penetrate the words of the Torah in order that you should not forget them. And so Rabbi Yaacov the son of Hanilai* said to Rabbi,[E34]"Come and let us penetrate (the words of the Torah) the Halachot, in order that they will not become mouldy."

---

passage "L17" we find that שעירים is exegeted as מעלים ומגדלים but it seems that this exegesis is not based on שעיר but is actually based upon the word רביב. This exegesis likely understands רביב = תרבות {i.e. "raising up" (= מגדל) B.T. Avodah Zarah 22a}. B.T. Baba Bathra 25a does have the form of the exegesis I propose: ברביבים -- מעלה ומגדלת. A common way of codifying related traditions is to compare various parts of these traditions to each other and extract a common principle. Some Mishnayot, identified by De Vries ("Concerning the Form of the Halachot in the Tannaitic Era", Studies [B 132] in Talmudic Literature, Mossad HaRav Kook, Jerusalem 1968, pp.81 -95) as belonging to the earliest strata of the tradition, are phrased in terms of general principles but in general the earliest traditions in the Mishna were taught in short apodictic (even enigmatic) phrases which enumerated specific laws and their circumstances. When we find statements of general principle which follow a group of apodictic phrases --usually introduced by the term זה הכלל , we find that these generalizations belong to a later layer of teaching whose purpose is to summarize. Condensing is necessary, says Sifre here, as a method of retaining and organizing materials, but not for teaching or practical use.

* F: Hanilai   --Ln: Hanina

L13.   פשפש means "to investigate by examining closely". I have understood the term here to refer to thorough and repetitive action and so I have freely rendered פשפש as "penetrate" which could apply to a liquid (such as rain is) and may imply an action of cleansing.

E34. Rabbi Yehuda HaNasi, the compiler of the Mishna, is generally referred to as "Rabbi".

"And as רביבים drops upon the herb":

Just as rain drops fall upon the herbs and cleanse them and enrich them, so you should enrich the words of the Torah by scrutinizing them two, three, four times.[E35]

" לקחי shall יערף as rain":[T14]

Rabbi Eliezer the son of Rabbi Yosi Hageliti says: " יערף " is distinctly an expression of "killing",[E36] as it is said, "And they shall break the neck ⟨ערפו⟩ of the heifer there in the valley."[S74] For which sin does the heifer atone? For bloodshed. And so do the words of the Torah atone for all sins.

"As שעירים upon the grass":

And for which sin do goats⟨שעירים⟩ atone? For unintentional sins.[E37] So do the words of the Torah atone for unintentional sins.

S74. Deuteronomy 21:4.

T14. Ln has omitted passages here, possibly due to homoioteleuton (" לקחי shall drop as rain").

E35. L. Silberman takes מפסטים as a hithpa'el written defectively and translates "and encircled them, so you should be encircled by words of Torah". At any rate, the point is that every time Torah is studied, a new insight is gained. B.T. Erubin 54b mentions that subjects are to be studied four times. I suspect that מרבב (רביבים) is exegeted as if it came from רב (much) and hence is rendered by מפסטים while סנקים likely is based on the exegesis of תזל as if it meant "shiny" or "clean", see "E48", Piska 306.

E36. The midrashist wants to explain why the rare and difficult word יערף is used here. He says that this word is used to subtly allude to the atoning heifer (ערפו). He does not wish to argue against the other interpretations of this verse but only to point out that יערף was used specifically for purposes of allusion and we derive an extra insight from this usage.

E37. See Lev. 4:28 (goats atone for unintentional sins).

"And as רביבים upon the herb":

Just as unblemished lambs ⟨רביבים⟩[L14] atone so do the words

of the Torah atone for every sin and transgression.

Another interpretation:

" לקחי shall drop as rain":[T14]

The Sages say: Moses said to Israel, "Perhaps you do not know

how much I suffered over the Torah and how much I labored in it and

how much I travailed in it."

--This is according to the matter of which Scripture states:"And

he was there with the Lord forty days and forty nights...."[S75]--

And Scripture states, "Then I abode in the mount forty days and forty

nights."[S75a]

"I entered amongst the angels and I entered amongst the Hayyot

and I entered amongst the Seraphim, any one of whom is capable of

burning the entire world and its inhabitants." This is according to the

matter of which Scripture states, "And above Him stood the Seraphim."[S76]

S75. Ex. 34:28.　　　　　S75a. Deuteronomy 9:9.
S76. Isaiah 6:2.

T14. See previous page.

L14. Ben Yehuda (p. 6368 n.2) notes that רביבים refers both to clouds
and to sheep. The relationship between clouds and sheep appears to be
the puffy white appearance of both objects. Ben Yehuda also notes that
in the French language both clouds and sheep are referred to by the term
"moutons". Furthermore (p. 6371), he claims that רביב refers to
sheep because sheep flock together in myriads (רבבה). He cites
by way of illustration Ez. 36:37 --"I will increase them with **men**
like a flock (ארבה אתם כצאן)", Ps. 107:41 --"He maketh his
families like a flock." Ps. 144:13 --"Whose sheep increase by thousands
and ten thousands (רבבות) in our fields." Ben Yehuda equates
רביב with כבש (p. 6378).

"I have expended my life upon it; I have expended my blood
upon it. Just as I studied it in suffering, so you should study it
in suffering."

But if you say thus, should it not follow that just as you learn
it in suffering so you should teach it in suffering? Therefore
Scripture states, " תזל My word as tet lamed.[E38]--You should
look upon it as if it is inexpensive, between 1/3 and 1/4 bushels*
a sela.

---

* Ln omits "bushels".

E38. I.e. "סל (dew)" --Here   this apparently redundant word is
explained: When one teaches others about Torah it should be considered
as if it were a cheap commodity (we have seen that "dew" was taken to
refer to the detailed teaching of the Torah in "E33", Piska 306). סל
{(30) = ל and (9) = ס } is understood perhaps as 9/30 (18/60) which
is between 1/3 (20/60) and 1/4 (15/60). The midrashist stresses the
importance of one's willingness to suffer to acquire the knowledge
of the Torah and finds support for this stress in Scripture's repitition
of Moses' abstinence. It must be noteworthy and therefore is to apply
not only to Moses but to everyone. Moses endangered himself by entering
the realm of burning Seraphim (Seraph=burn) so that he could study the
Torah.
It would appear that this midrash is meant to follow the pericope
which states that the Torah is to be laboriously studied, two, three
and four times. This is the position of our midrash in Ln and it
would appear that such was its original place. The pericope which
compares the atonement by the heifer to that by the words of the Torah
may well be a very early interpolation. Thus the editor wanted to build
upon the notion of extended study by showing that Moses himself labored
and suffered to learn the Torah.
The midrashist has carefully instructed his audience not to make
others suffer in their acquisition of the Torah. One should share his
knowledge freely and consider the Torah as of little monetary value.
One should not charge money for teaching Torah but consider its monetary
value as inexpensive. The word "תזל " is interpreted in this play on
words, not as "pouring forth" but as "זיל " (inexpensive). How
inexpensive? As inexpensive as "tet" (9) out of "lamed" (30) which is
3/10. The word " סל " (dew) has been broken into its numerical value
of 9 and 30. According to a possible understanding of the text in Ln one
(omits "bushels") would be able to purchase between three and four bushels

"As the שעירים upon the herb":

When a person first goes[E39] to study Torah it falls upon him like a שעיר . And שעיר specifically means "demon", as it is said, "And the wild-cats shall meet with the jackals, and the שעיר shall call to his fellow."[S77] And Scripture also states, "And שעירים flutter there."[S78]

---

per sela. The "bushel" need not be mentioned in Sifre but can be taken for granted as it was the standard measure, cf. Rashi to B.T. Hulin 92a (" חומר "). Mishna Erubin 8:2 places wheat at four bushels per sela. Now P.T. Peah 8:6 relates that teachers are to be supported from the charity stores of those who have lived in their city for at least twelve months. The Mishna behind this comment stipulates that the quality of wheat those supported by charity may buy is the quality of that cheap wheat which sells for four bushels a sela. The reading of F appearing to say --"between 1/3 and 1/4 bushels per sela" should perhaps be construed as --"between 1/3 and 1/4 sela per bushel.

S77. Isaiah 34:14.   S78. Isaiah 13:21.

E39. The beginning Torah student is often bedeviled by the massive problem of fitting traditions together in a consistent fashion until he masters the methods of the Rabbis. See comment of Schorr in E43 further. The form of this tradition suggests that it be viewed together with a further tradition in this section of Piska 306, ("E43"). The further text begins with the catch word שעירים but ends with a proof text mentioning רביבים . I suspect that we have a single tradition which I reconstruct as:
    "As שעירים upon the herb":
        When a man first goes to learn Torah it falls upon him
        like a שעיר and שעיר can only mean demon....("E39")
/"As רביבים upon the herb":/
        He does not know what to do until he learns two sections
        of Mishna or two books of Scripture and afterwards it will
        follow after him like lambs (רביבים)....("E43")
    I have added the part contained between /.../ which I suggest became displaced by analogy with the first tradition (i.e."E39") which lead verse was taken to refer to "E43" as well. The traditions are now found separately suggesting a later interpolation of materials and the wordings, themes and continuity of the midrashic exegesis show that these midrashim were once a unified tradition.

Another interpretation:

" לקחי shall יערף as rain":

Rabbi Benaya used to say: If you study[L15] the words of the
Torah without ulterior motive, the words of the Torah will give
you life, as it is said, "For they are life to them that find them."[S79]
But if you do not study the Torah without ulterior motive, they (the
words of the Torah) will bring you death,[E40] as it is said," לקחי
shall יערף as rain." And " עריפה " specifically means "killing"
as it is said, "And they shall break ⟨וערפו⟩ the neck of the heifer
there in the valley."[S80] And Scripture also says, "For she hath cast
down many wounded; yea, a mighty host are all her slain."[S81]

S79. Proverbs 4:22.   S80. Deuteronomy 21:4.
S81. Proverbs 7:26.

L15. The parallel in B.T. Ta'anith 7a shows that עשה here refers
to the study of the Torah. Cf. Mishna 5:14 and the commentary attributed
to Rashi ad loc., also see N. Broznik, (B 115) " עשות ספרים הרבה
אין קץ " (קהלת יב-יב),
Beth Mikra 25(1980) p.213ff. For the meaning of לשמה see Sanders,
Paul, etc. p.121. B.T. Gittin 20a, B.T. Sukka 9a (correct intention
validates), B.T. Gittin 45b, B.T. Shab. 116a (improper intention makes
void).

E40. We now find another version of "E36" tradition but now ערף does
not refer to the atonement qualities of the heifer but to its death.
The message is that the Torah, if studied improperly, can be an
instrument of death. Since the Torah, according to the Rabbis, teaches
the way to achieve life immortal its misuse could deprive one of such
immortality. Also judges may literally cause an innocent man to die
if they neglect the study of the finer points of Torah teaching (see
also Pirke Avoth 5:11) (B 271) For "study" as "life giving elixir" see
Moore, Age etc., vol. 2, p. 242, p. 306, pp. 96-97.

Another interpretation:

" לקחי shall drop as rain":

Rabbi Dostai son of Yehuda says: If you accumulate the words of the Torah in the way that water accumulates in a cistern, in the end[T15] you will merit to behold your Mishna learning, as it is said, "Drink waters out of thine own cistern."[S82] But if you accumulate the words of the Torah in the way that rain accumulates in a narrow pit, a lengthy ditch, and a spacious cavity,[E41] in the end[T15] you will water and irrigate others, as it is said, "And running waters out of thine own well."[S83] And Scripture also states, "Let thy springs be dispersed abroad."[S84]

Another interpretation:

" לקחי shall יערף as rain":

Rabbi Meir[*] used to say: Indeed, you should accumulate the words of the Torah as general prinicples. For if you accumulate them as specific cases they will exhaust you and you will not know what to do.[T16] This is like the parable of the man who went to Caesarea and needed 100 or 200 zuz for expenses. If he took them in small change it would have exhausted him and he would not have known what to do.[T16]

---

* F: Meir   --Ln: Yehuda

S82. Proverbs 5:15.   S83. Proverbs 5:15.   S84. Proverbs 5:16.

T15. Apparent omission due to homoioteleuton in Ln ("in the end").

T16. Apparent omission due to homoioteleuton in Ln ("what to do").

E41. Perhaps the lesson of the text is that if you practise and apply what you have learned then you do not merely store water as in a cistern, but irrigate others with your learning (cf. Avoth de Rabbi Nathan "B" ed.

Rather, he should combine them and change them into <u>selaim</u> and

then break these into smaller change which he will spend at every

place when he so desires. Likewise, whoever goes to Bet Ilnis,[E42]

to the market, and will need a hundred <u>manot</u>[L16] or two <u>ribua</u> for

expenses, if he combines them and changes them into <u>selaim</u> they will

exhaust him and he will not know what to do. Rather, he should

combine them and change them into golden <u>dinari</u> and break these

into small change which he will spend at every place when he so

desires.

"As שעירים upon the herb":

When a man first goes to learn Torah he does not know what to

do until he learns two books of Scripture or two sections of Mishna

and afterwards it will follow after him like lambs (רביבים)[E43]

For such reason was it said, 'כרביבים upon the herb."

Schechter,[(B 1)] p. 83: "Whoever learns Torah for his own needs...
Drink water out of thine own cistern"). L. Silberman writes here that
he thinks the contrast is between one who considers his own learning
exclusively as compared to one who considers the learning of others as
well.

L16. <u>Mina</u>, (100 zuz) see Jastrow, s.v. מנה and Devarim Rabba (ed.
Lieberman) p. 126, n.2.

E42. See Hoffman, <u>Midrash Tannaim</u>, [(B 26)] Vol. 2, p. 252, בית
אלנים is equated with בוסנה as in P.T. Avodah Zarah 1:4
(ירידי של בוסנה) and as in Gen. R. 47:12 : ירד
בסנו . Hoffman mentions that in Hieronymus' commentary to
Jeremiah 11, our בית אלנים is referred to as Botane (Gk.
plant = Aram: אילן) in reference to the "trees" Abraham planted.

E43. The text here appears to have been corrupted and continues the
tradition of "E39", (שעירם). It appears most likely that the
<u>midrash</u> here should have begun with the words כרביבים (not כשעירם).
The point of the wording (like the tradition of "E39"),is to encourage

Another interpretation:

"   לקחי   shall drop as rain":

Just as the rain falls upon the trees and gives the specific

flavor to each one according to its specie: to the vine according

to its specie, to the olive according to its specie, to the date

according to its specie, so are the words of the Torah all-inclusive.

In it are Scripture, <u>Mishna</u>, <u>Talmud</u>,[*][T17] <u>Halachot</u> and <u>Haggadot</u>.[E44]

"As שעירם upon the herb":

Just as the rain drop winds fall upon the grass and raise

them up, such that there are some grasses which are red,[L17] some

which are green, some which are black, and some which are white, so

do the words of the Torah, such that are some (masters of the Torah)

wise people, some honest people, some righteous people, some pious

people.

---

the student to pursue his studies and not to give up. The plural
רביבים   accounts for two (books or sections).   Schorr suggests
we have a play on the words for "herb" such that

  דשא   =   διαζω   (irresolute)
  עשב   =   εὐσάφα   (clear); also   שונה
(learned) here means "to study the oral traditons of".

* F: Talmud   --Ln: Midrash

T17. For the variants "Talmud" (F) = "Midrash" (Ln) and "Midrash"
(F: "L18") = "Mishna" (Ln: "L18"), see L. Finkelstein, "Midrash,
Halachot, and Aggadot", <u>Yitzhak F. Baer Jubilee Vol.</u>, p. 28ff.

L17. אדום can refer to various shades and colors and need not match
our precise understanding of "red", likewise   ירוק   need not precisely
match our ideas of "green".

E44. Here again the simile "as rain"..." is explained in reference to
the various methods of the Rabbis who studied Jewish traditions.

Another interpretation:

Just as you cannot see the rain until it comes --and so it says,
"And it came to pass in a little while that the heaven grew black with
clouds (and wind)"[S85] ---so you cannot recognize a student of the Sages
until he teaches Midrash,[*][L18] Halachot and Haggadot or until he is
appointed as a public officer[E45] over the community.

Another interpretation:

"...shall drop as the rain":

Not like the rain which comes from the south which causes only ruin,
causes only disease, and causes only curse, but like the rain which
comes from the west[E46] which causes only blessing.

Rabbi Simaye used to say: From whence is it that just as Moses
brought the Heavens and the Earth to witness against Israel so he
brought the Four Winds of the heavens to witness against them? We
know it from that which is said: " לקח יחם shall drop (יערף) as

---

* F: Midrash   --Ln: Mishna

S85. 1 Kings 18:45.

L18. F reads   סדרש   and Ln   משנה . They may be referring to
the same body of study. Cf. B.T. Kiddushin 49a where the question is
asked, "What is Mishna?" and Rabbi Meir responded, "Halacha!" while
Rabbi Yehuda said, "Midrash!". Generally speaking, "Mishna" refers to
Oral Law usually taught without reference to Biblical verses while
"Midrash" refers to Oral Law taught with reference to specific verses
of Scripture.

E45. For the parnes as a spiritual leader see G. Alon[(B 90)] p. 413,
n. 113.

E46. The aggadist takes   יערף as equivalent to ערב by applying a
ב=פ   interchange. Such interchanges occur frequently in the
midrashic techniques used in Sifre Ha'azinu and reflect known linguistic
principles which are now creatively applied by the homilist.

rain." This describes the west wind which is the underpinning

(ערפו) of the world --which causes only blessing.[E47]

E47. The "Simaye" tradition keeps יערף as it is and renders it according to its substantive meaning, "underpinning" or "back". He thus finds in יערף a reference to the West because west winds were considered "beneficial" and so must have come from the underpinning of the world (see Rashi to B.T. Baba Bathra 25a). Perhaps Simaye also wished to explain why "West" is called מערב . By appealing to an idea as found in tradition "E46" previous , he may have determined that the West is called מערב because that is the underpinning of the world (יערף) from which beneficial winds come. What is very clear to him is that יערף refers to the west wind. (I like L. Silberman's suggestion here to refer to Levy III p. 705 which tells us that the orientation of the world is considered to face East so that the back part of the world (ערפו של עולם) is in the West.) The various traditions in Ln are difficult to reconcile with each other in regards to which winds are beneficial. The variants provided by the Talmud (see references in F to this pericope) show us the difficulty in attempting to establish a sound reading here. See Daniel 7 for the concept of the "Four Winds of Heaven". The form of the pericope follows an ideal format, more obvious in those traditions which are based upon oral transmissions (as I assume Talmud and later midrashim were) than upon literary ones(like Sifre - see Conclusion of my work, n. 6):

    a) teasing a suitable catchword in Deut. 32:2 to yield a meaning which describes a wind.

    b) relating this catchword by a philological artifice to the name of the wind.

    c) explaining the significance of the wind by means of an etymological play based upon the Scriptural catchword.

We can illustrate this format as follows:

    a)   יערף

    b)   מערב

    c)   ערפו (של עולם)

See the following note for a more detailed example.

This represents a very late, composite
form. However, structural uniformity
here permits us to glimpse the intent of
earlier forms of the tradition.

"It distills as the dew my word": This describes the north wind which makes the sky lambent[E48] as gold.

"As שעירים upon the grass": This describes the east wind which renders the sky dark as goats.[E49]

E48. There is a complicated word play here that relates "distilled dew", "north", and "lambent as gold". תזל = מזלת =(shining)= הצפין = צפון = זהב . It is useful here to compare the format of our midrash as presented in B.T. Baba Bathra 25a-b.

    a) The homilist teases the catchword תזל in Deut. 32:2 which is understood as a term referring to the sluicing of gold to make it shine (להצפין). In Canticles Rabba 4:30 מזיל refers to sluicing for the purpose of making objects shine: Rabbi Azariah says, "This one sluices part of the matter and that one sluices part of the matter until the halacha emerges as a shiny thing"(cf. Canticles Rabba 5:10 --"This refers to the halacha; for they wash it in pairs until they make it pure (בקי) as milk.").

    b) Thus תזל has been related to sluicing --making something shine - מזלת . It is therefore the equivalent of להצפין --"to make shine". And להצפין has the same root letters as צפון --the North Wind.

    c) This wind (תזל = מזלת = צפון) is significant because it causes things to shine like gold.

While the Babylonian tradition is blatant in its presentation:
a)   תזל   b)   רוח צפונית   c)   מזלת את הזהב
Sifre is more subtle: a)   תזל   b)   רוח צפונית
c)   נקיה כזהב   (cf. Cant. R. 5:10).

The gists of the other passages are:
--the West Wind, " יערף " --it supports (ערף) the world by its blessing.
--the East Wind, " שעירים " --it disfigures the sky (שעירים -- demon-like).
--the South Wind, " רביבים " --makes the sky like a fleecy lining (רביב).

For the relationship between these descriptions and the names of the winds see next note. L. Silberman notes that these word plays are most abtruse--"This is a game for scholars not for ordinary people".

E49. Since שעירים can refer both to rain winds and to goats the midrash wants to explain the etymology of the word by showing the relationship between darkened rain clouds and goats. שחיר = שעיר (morning sun; thus East. Also to darken --from root שחר). ח and ע are interchanging letters to the midrashist. The catchword כשעירים is used according to the above formula, of which our text, against readings in Talmud and later sources, presents the most obvious form

"And as רביבים upon the herb": This describes the south
wind which lines the sky as fleece.[E50]

---

of the tradition. This I take to be a sign that the wording here
is based upon oral sources which have not been cast into a literary
mould, unlike other Sifre Ha'azinu wordings.
   a) We are presented with a catchword " כשעירים ".
   b) The homilist "philologically" relates השעיר = השחיר =the
      rising of the sun = זרח = the East.
   c) Thus the East wind is connected to " שעיר " = the demon-like,
      ill East wind which is said to blow "no-good". Leqah Tob reads
      מטהרת (cleanses) instead of משחרת and thereby
      attempts to remove the contradiction of understanding משחרת
      as "morning rising" in reference to the East (מזרח) wind
      but as "darkness" in reference to the function of the wind
      (השחיר =darkened). B.T. Baba Bathra 147a reads מסערת
      ("storm") but does not show us how the word "East" is to be
      derived from it. However if we think that משחרת = מזרח
      (taking ש as if ז) is the basis of the exegesis then
      Babli's מסערת = מזרח (taking ס as if ז) is
      less forced.
The form here is proper: a) כשעירים b) זו רוח מזרחית
c) משחרת...כשעירים

E50. Since רביב can refer both to rain clouds and to fleece linings,
the midrash wants to explain the relationship between the billowy clouds
and fleece. רבב =(to line) דרב =(south) דרום . ב and ס
are interchanging letters. The reading which corresponds to our
formulated expression here (and hence I suppose of unworked oral
materials) can be found in Leqah Tob where we have:
   a) The catchword " כרביבים ".
   b) The homilist philologically relates רבב (to line) = דרב
      = דרום (=South).
   c) The South wind (דרום) is said "to line" (דרב , ב and ס
      interchange) the "world" as a fleece.
Here again we find the proper form of the tradition:
a) וכרביבים b) זה רוח דרומית
c) שהיא מרבבת...כרביב
The reading of the Sifre --"Which weaves the sky as with a fleece" is
meant to explain רבב as "to line" but replaces the "catchword"
(מרבבת) with מארגת to make the play more subtle, a feature
I identify as literary editing of oral traditions.
   In regards to the word דרב we should look at the comment of
Samson of Sanz to Kilaim 9:7, "And a shoe of זרב " --which means
"to warm" as in (Job 6:17) "at the time יזורבו " and refers in the
Mishna to a shoe constructed to warm the foot. The shoes are made
with double walls and between these walls are inserted silk or flax
and one should not be anxious that perhaps they are lined with wool.

Another interpretation:

" לקחי shall drop as rain":

And also did Rabbi Simaye used to say: These four winds were

mentioned by Scripture specifically in relationship to the Four

Winds of Heaven which blow;

> Northern -- in the sunny season it is beneficial[*] and in the rainy
>
> season it is harmful,[*]
>
> Southern -- in the sunny season it is harmful and in the rainy
>
> season it is beneficial,
>
> Eastern -- always harmful,[*]
>
> Western -- always beneficial.[*T18 E50a]

The reading of the Aruch here is זרר . The Yerushalmi explains "shoe
of זרב " by saying that there are places where they line on the
inside with wool....
    In considering the texts we find that the variants mentioned by
Samson, זרב and   זרד , mean "to line with fat or something soft".
זרב   and   זרד seem to be equivalent terms and both readings may be
correct. Now the homilist equates רבב (line) =   זרב (זרב =
זרם) = דרום (ד = ז), cf. Eben Shoshan vol. 2, p. 696, זרב
close to זרם . Thus the South wind דרום = זרב = רבב
lines as with a fleece. (רביב). Cf. W.D. McHardy "The Horses in
Zechariah", In Memoriam, Paul Kahle p. 178. Are the colors mentioned in
our midrash related in any way to the colors of the horses in Zech. 6:6-7
which go towards the various directions of the compass?
    It is important here to note that Sifre reads רקיע while Leqah
Tob reads   עולם . This corresponds to the sense of Exodus R. 15:28
which also equates רקיע = עולם . Thus I suspect that phrases
such as   מסוף העולם עד סופו mean "from one end of the
heavens to the other," the reference being to that space which is above.
Thus, perhaps, Moses was able to see high above himself with his miraculous eyesight according to Piska 338, (alternatively עולם in Piska
338 may refer to the Land of Israel as in Piska 315).

* Ln: Northern in sunny season is harmful and in rainy beneficial.
  Eastern is always beneficial. Western is harmful.

T18. F's mention here of the west wind as beneficial is consistent with
"E46" and "E47". Is Ln a variant tradition, a harmonization with B.T.

The north wind is beneficial to wheat when it is one-third

ripe and harmful to olives[*] when they are ripe. The south wind

is harmful to olives when they are one-third ripe and beneficial

to wheat when it is ripe.

And Rabbi Simaye also used to say: All creatures who are

created to be heavenly, their soul and their body is of the

---

or equivalent to F but using a different terminolgy here (i.e. one
names a wind according to the direction it blows <u>from</u> while the
other names it according to the direction it blows <u>towards</u>) ?

E50a. This tradition was known to the Babylonian Amoraim and is
quoted in B.T. Yoma 21b. However there appears to be an interesting
variant there.
> "The East wind is always beneficial,
> the West wind is always harmful
> the South wind is harmful to wheat when it is one third ripe and
> beneficial to olives when they are ripe."

In conflict with this B.T. tradition our Sifre passage in F
declares that the East wind is harmful and the West is beneficial, (Ln
seems , presumably, to have been harmonized with B.T.),the South
wind is harmful to olives when they are one-third ripe and beneficial
to wheat when it is fully ripe. Sifre also contains traditions
concerning the North wind --beneficial to wheat when it is one-third
ripe and harmful to olives when they are ripe. Now B.T. Yoma 21b supplies us with the following mnemonic: "The Temple Table (on which
sat loaves of wheat) is in the North part of the Temple --the Lamp
(which held olive oil) in the South part". <u>North</u> corresponds with
<u>wheat</u>, <u>South</u> with <u>oil</u>. The reading in B.T. is not a scribal corruption
but represents a Babylonian (cf. Baba Bathra 147a and 25b) version of
our pericope. Will the mnemonic work for the version in the Sifre
text? The Sifre text does not fit the mnemonic (the South wind is said
to be harmful to olives which are one-third grown in Sifre) whereas
B.T. mnemonic says the South wind is beneficial to olives.

[*] F: olives   --Ln: wheat

heavenly realm. All creatures which are to be earthly, their

soul and their body are of the earth; except for Man. For his

soul is of the heavenly realm and his body is of the earthly realm.

Therefore, if a man learns Torah and does the will of His Father who

is in heaven, then he is as[E51] the creatures of the upper realm, as

it is said, "I said, ye are godlike beings, and all of you sons of

---

E51. The point here is that the soul is always "heavenly" --it is
the man which is neutral and can either become "earthly" (materialistic) or "heavenly" (spiritual). For gnostics, the body could never
become "heavenly" although the soul could become "earthly"
(cf. Introduction to Tanhuma Buber p. 154 in reference to Ps. 8:7.). The
series of statements here, related in the name of Simaye, place the
heavens as the spiritual part of man and the earth as the physical part
of man, (cf. Urbach, Sages, p. 221, Mechilta de R. Shimon Bar Yochai
(B 114) 15:1, also B.T. Sanhedrin 91a, Lev. R. 4:5). L. Silberman
points to the possibility of a collection of "heaven and earth"
traditions which has been incorporated here. Silberman points to a
more intricate text of this type in the Introd. to Buber's Tanhuma.
Simaye's equation: "heaven" = "soul", "earth" = "body" reads Ps. 50:4
to show that the soul is judged with (reads עמו as opposed to
Massoretic   עמ) the body. Now the judgement will be, he claims,
at the time of the resurrection based upon Ezekiel's discussion of Four
Winds. Elsewhere we have seen in Piska 306 that Deut. 32:2 refers to
the rain-wind witnesses against Israel and here also the "winds of
heaven" are taken to refer to those four winds which the homilist
discovered in Deut. 32:2 were the North, South, East and West winds.
An exegesis of Ezekiel demonstrates how the heavenly spirit will be
carried by the four winds into the earthly corpse and judged ("that
these may live.").This midrash favors the view that Israel's witnesses
will indeed confront her at the time of the Resurrection. Simaye
supports his contention by claiming there are allegorical ways to
interpret every section of Scripture (if only we knew how) to find
teachings concerning the Resurrection. In these passages one may find
polemics aimed at those who denied that Resurrection was mentioned in
Scripture, against gnostics --who believed that the soul, the spirit,
would be saved but that the body was intrinsically evil and doomed. See
further Marmorstein's "The Doctrine of the Resurrection of the Dead",
Studies in Jewish Theology, p. 149f. and p. 156f.

the Most High."[S86] If he does not learn Torah and does not do the will of his Father who is in heaven then he is like the creatures of the lower realm, as it is said, "Nevertheless ye shall die like men."[S87] [E52]

And Rabbi Simaye also used to say: There is no section of Scripture which does not refer to the resurrection of the dead; however, we do not have the required capability of interpretation, as it is said, "He will call to the Heavens above and to the Earth, that He may judge His people."[S88] "He will call to the Heavens above," -- this refers to the soul; "and to the Earth to judge His people," -- this refers to the body which is judged with it. And from whence do we know that this specifically alludes to the resurrection of the dead? As it is said, "Come from the four winds, O wind, and breathe upon these slain...."[S89] [E53]

S86. Psalms 82:6.   S87. Psalms 82:7.   S88. Psalms 50:4.
S89. Ezekiel 37:9.

E52. Here as elsewhere in Rabbinic literature the point is made that there is no need of magical praxis or theurgic "raz" to make one a member of the heavenly realm. The study and practice of Rabbinic Judaism is all that is necessary. See my article, "The Rabbinic Attempt to Democratize Salvation and Revelation", Studies in Religion (B 102).

E53. Here as elsewhere (see the references in F to this pericope) body and soul are judged together. Rabbinic dualism is certainly not the same as gnostic dualism. See also I. Abrahams, Studies in Pharisaism, (B 84), Series I, ch. 12, pp. 93-106, for Indian and Christian parallels also see Neave's Greek Anthology (B 273) p. 197f. : "The blind man lifts the lame man on his back etc." and other Greek parallels. The utilization of the image to portray the interdependence of body and soul seems to be originally Jewish.

"For I will proclaim the name of the Lord":

We find that Moses mentioned the name of the Holy One, Blessed Be

He, specifically after twenty-one words.[E54] From whom did he learn this?

From the Ministering Angels; for the Ministering Angels do not mention

---

E54. The tetragrammaton occurs in the Song only after 21 words, i.e.
as the 22nd word. The preacher noted that God's name is not mentioned
in Deut. 32 until the twenty-second word. He explained as follows:
    Moses knew that the angels would only mention God's name
    after three words of praise. Being seven times inferior
    to the angels he would only mention the Name after (3 x 7)
    words. That is why God's name appears as the twenty-
    second word in the Song of Moses. (Cf. Hoffman's Midr.
    Tann., p. 186, Leq. Tob. and Hizk. to Deut. 32:3).
We might also note here that if some considered Moses as angelic in any
sense, cf. Marqah 5:3 - He ascended from human status to that of the
angels, (see David Lenz Tiede, The Charismatic Figure as Miracle Worker,
(B 333) Missoula, SBL, 1972, p. 154, p. 104f. and p. 112-131) our
homilist shows otherwise. In regards to the responses uttered by the
congregation when they hear the divine name Sifre embodies an interesting tradition attributed to Rabbi Nehoraye. Although it may mean
that the uncommissioned soldiers attack while the commissioned ones
get the glory, I take it to mean that the Galearius "whets" (incites
the commissioned officers to battle by his praises of them) but they
do not win the war. This is consistent with the sense of the passage
in B.T. Berachoth 53b (cf. end B.T. Nazir): "the one who answers is
superior to the one who began the praise; for he who began it only
whetted the appetite while he who finished it accomplished the feat."It
is not clear exactly how the statement is meant to function in the
Talmud where it is brought in reference to the "amen" response in
prayer. Perhaps the original setting of the statement should be this
Sifre passage. See "L19", Piska 306. L. Silberman refers here to the
entry in Krauss (Lehnwörter: Galearius) and writes me " The young knight
invites to battle -- the heroes win the battle" i.e. ברכו is the
invitation to which we have response but the order is reversed. In our
case the "hero" invites while the "young knight" responds.

the Name except after saying "Holy!" three times, as it is said,

"And they called one to the other and said: קדוש, קדוש, קדוש

the Lord of Hosts."[S90] Moses said, "It is sufficient for me to be .

reduced one-seventh of the Ministering Angels."[E55] And behold the

matters should be argued a fortiori:[T19]

> And just as Moses, who was the wisest of the wise, and
>
> the greatest of the great and the father of the prophets
>
> did not err by mentioning the name of God but did it
>
> after twenty-one words --so it is that he who mentions
>
> the name of God in vain does err a fortiori.[E56]

Rabbi Shimon the son of Yochai says: from whence do we know

that one should not say, "To God is this burnt-offering,";[E57] "to

---

S90. Isaiah 6:3.

T19. Apparent omission due to homoioteleuton in Ln ("a fortiori").

E55. In Hebrew idiom, "sevens" are considered full units (see
Studies in Biblical and Semitic Symbolism,(B 149) p. 139). By
mentioning the Name after a full multiple of seven words after that
of the angels, it is claimed that Moses clearly showed his station to
be a full rank less than that of the angels.

E56. For attitudes towards the use of the divine name during Second
Temple times see G. Alon(B 90) p. 235ff. The midrashic argument
here states that had Moses, who had good reason to mention the Name,
not treated the Name with utmost diffidence he would have erred and
so does he err who has no reason to mention the Name and mentions it
without diffidence. See Sifra to Lev. 22:32 and Sifre Deut. to Deut.
33:3.

E57. See B.T. Nedarim 10b and Sifra to Vayikra (i.e. Lev.) 1:2.

God is this meal-offering"; "to God is this peace-offering"; --but

rather, "this burnt-offering is to God"; "this meal-offering is to

God"; "this peace-offering is to God"? We know it from the Scripture

which states, "An offering to God."[S91] Is this not an argument a

fortiori:[T19]

> And just as concerning these offerings, which are hallowed
>
> for divine purposes, the Holy One, Blessed Be He,[*] said,
>
> "My name shall not be conferred upon them until after they
>
> have been hallowed --lest one does wrongly, so does he who
>
> mentions the name of the Holy One, Blessed Be He, vainly
>
> or in a place of shame all the more so do wrongly.

"For I will proclaim the name of the Lord":

Rabbi Yosi says: From whence do we know that we respond,

"Blessed is the Lord who is to be blessed for ever and ever" after

they who stand in the synagogue recite, "Bless the Lord who is to

be blessed"? We know it from that which is said, "For I will

proclaim the name of the Lord[L19] --Give praise unto our God".

---

* Ln: HaMakom

S91. Leviticus 1:2.

T19. See previous page.

L19. Targum Yerushalmi (Gins. vs. 3, pg. 66) translates ואדברה (Deut.
32:1) by מדבר שמא which it takes to refer to a call to praise
(Rabbinic Bible ורבו): הבו יקר ותושבחתא ורומסו .
This refers to גודל (cf. Deut. 32:3). In a similar way we find
Targum Ps. -Jon. renders גודל by (Gins. p. 357).
                                          הבו איקר ורבותא
It is possible that the tradition tied together אקרא and גודל
in reflection of Deut. 5:21 which Ps. -Jon. (Gins. p.312) renders:
       (Heb.   את כבודו ואת גודלו)
            .ית שכינת יקריה וית רבות תושבחתיה

This reference is to the experience of God's actual presence, the experience of the Name and of the praise being contained in the term גודל (cf. P.T. Megilla 3:7, B.T. Yoma 69b, P.T. Peah 7:3 in ref. to Neh. 8). Perhaps Deut. 32:3, " אקרא " has been taken in the sense of Aram. " יקרא " (=Heb. כבוד)while " גודל " has been taken to refer to God's presence. It is also possible that the midrashist understood אקרא as אקריא , see B.T. Sotah 10a where וקרא of Gen. 21:33 is so interpreted. It is noteworthy here that, interestingly, both in the midrash and in the Targumim of Ps. - Jon. and Yerushalmi reference is made to the kedusha prayer of the angels mentioned in Isaiah 6:3. The word קדוש I take to mean "blessed", as explained by Philo (Glatzer p. 46) who equates "holy" and "blessed". We can now see why Lev. 22:32 was understood by the Rabbis to refer to a quorum for publicly blessing the presence of God. The term of Lev. 22 ונקדשתי itself was understood to refer to "blessing the divine presence". Cf. B.T. Megilla 23b, B.T. Berachoth 21b, Mishna Meg. 4:3, P.T. Ber. 7:3, P.T. Meg. 4:4, Soferim ch. 10. The statement of Nehoraye here is somewhat perplexing. It is worthwhile here to note the commentary of M.L. Malbim to Isaiah 42:13: the verse states,"The Lord goeth forth like a warrior, as a man of wars hath stirred the anger---over his enemies he shall be victorious." Malbim comments:(B 254) "The warrior has strength in his "loins" and goes to battle alone which is the sense of "goeth forth like a warrior". But the man of wars is no warrior. He is knowledge-able in the battle arrangements. And so the man of wars who has studied many battles and is expert in the ways of war, does not himself parti-cipate himself but stirs up the anger. That is, he knows the strategies to quicken the warriors and to stir anger in their hearts...and through such strategy he overpowers his enemies."

It is not beyond question that our midrash is based upon the verse in Isaiah. The commentary of Malbim appears quite correct and corres-ponds to the understanding of battle techniques discussed in our pericope. And so it is that the warrior can only win if he be stirred into battle against the enemy. Nehoraye uses this imagery to explain (see Silber-man's view Piska 306, E58) the order of praising God according to the liturgy. First one is stirred up and then one responds. It is of interest to note that the angels who praise God are sometimes pictured as armies. Canticles R. 2:18 reads:

> Rabbi Eleazar says he gave them an oath according to
> the heavens and the earth --"according to the armies"
> --the heavenly army and the earthly army.....they
> would deliver their souls for the sanctification of the
> name of the Holy One Blessed Be He. Rabbi Hoshaye said:
> God told Israel: Wait for me and I will make you as the
> heavenly army (צבא).

Also see גדיד מלאכים end of Pesikta Rabbathi 20.

Rabbi Nehoraye said to him: By Heaven! It is the usual procedure

for the soldiers' aides to stimulate others in regard to war and for

the warriors to win."[E58]

In summary it appears that Targum Yerushalmi understood Deut.
32:1 הַאֲזִינוּ הַשָּׁמַיִם to mean that the angels, the heavenly host,
allowed Moses to hear their prayer so that וְתִשְׁמַע הָאָרֶץ -people,
the earthly host, could learn the proper call to prayer אִמְרֵי פִי.
This call was a studied program of 21 words which gave one proper access
to the divinity. To do less would be to insult God. Thus a proper
<u>kedusha</u> prayer has an introduction of no less than 21 words before God's
name is referred to. According to Targum Yerushalmi, Moses had to train
his mouth to recite the Blessed Name, and according to B.T. Yoma 3b-4a
proper training to serve God requires a seven day induction period. Thus
the explanation of Sifre that the three-fold <u>kedusha</u> was practised for
a space of 21 words (3 x 7) is intelligible. On the wider scale of the
<u>Song</u> it is to be noted that the reason for Israel's covenantal history
is to bring Israel and the nations eventually to praise the name of the
Lord. It is against the hostile lawlessness of the nations that the
covenant is formed and its progress towards fruition is measured.

E58. According to the way Scripture is interpreted here, Moses
("the synagogue cantor") appears to have an inferior position in regards
to blessing the Lord. He merely instigates the blessings but does not
bless by himself --"When I proclaim God's name --you are to give praise."
Thus our pericope suggests that this is a surprising situation since it
is only the job of the underling to stimulate battle but the hero's
task is to win it (so Moses here is the underling). According to this
view the cantor did not repeat the blessing as is the usual custom today.
Cf. B.T. Nazir 66b and B.T. Berachoth 53b. For my translation "to
stimulate" see how root גרז works in Targ. Onkelos (B 8) to Num. (B 25)
21:6. Also see Num. R. (B 23) 18:3 and printed Tanhuma Korach
3 " להתגרות ": "to stir up against" and see P.T. Peah 1:1 "Temptation
will stir up someone against you (Joseph)". For a causative understanding of אקרא see "E66" to Piska 306. L. Silberman suggests, that for
R. Nehoraye, Moses is indeed the hero and is not the young knight so that
in the synagogue the usual battle practice is reversed.

Piska 306

And from whence do we know that we do not participate in זימון [L20] unless there are three? We know it from that which is said, "For I will proclaim the name of the Lord--give praise to our God."[E59]

And from whence do we know that we recite "Blessed is His glorious sovereign name for ever and ever"? We know it from that which is said, "For I will proclaim the name of the Lord."

And from whence do we know that we say "Amen" after the blesser?[E60] We know it from that which is said, "Give praise to our God."[T20] [E61]

T20. This "Amen unit" may be a gloss in the text--it is located after "E59" in Ln.

L20. For the sense of זימון as "invite" see Targ. to 1 Sam. 9:22, where זמינא = הקרואים and cf. Mishna Berachoth 7:1.

E59. זימון is the introductory blessing for the saying of grace when three males have shared bread together. See Aruch Completum[B71] s.v. זמן "I will proclaim" refers to one person while "Give Praise" (הבו) is in the plural form which is used to address a minimum of two people. Thus there is a minimum of three people involved in the process of זימון. See Mishna Berachoth 7:1-3 and Gen. R. 43:8. For the Tannaitic sources related to our pericope see E.Z. Melamed, The Relationship between the Halachic Midrashim and the Mishna and Tosefta,[B265] Jerusalem 5727, p. 142ff.

E60. I.e. "Amen" is an expression of praise (גדולה). The refrain "amen" came into vogue as a replacement of "blessed be His glorious sovereign name for ever and ever" in past Temple times (see B.T. Ta'an. 17b). I suspect that "amen"-liturgical traditions were adapted from(see 'E62') earlier "blessed be..." traditions which were readapted for synagogue rather than Temple usage. Our midrashist refers here to synagogue practice. He mentions the "beth knesseth" and refers to the morning and evening barchu calls to prayer for the recital of the shma. He also knows the kaddish doxology and we may infer that the leader says:
יתגדל ויהקדש...ובזמן קריב ואמרו אמן
which is answered by the congregation:
אמן...יהא שמיה רבא...לעולם ולעולמי עולמים
the leader repeats: יהא שמיה רבא מבורך
the congregation repeats: לעולם ולעולמי עולמים
(See D. de Sola Pool , p. 45ff.).

E61. A literal understanding of the phrase, "When I proclaim the name of the Lord--you are to give praise". In conclusion we note:

For the meaning of נרוך שם כבוד מלכותו לעולם ועד
see Kaddish by D. de Sola Pool, p. 45. According to Mishna Yoma
ch. 3, mishna 8, the High Priest would recite a formula which
mentioned the divine name:
> And they answer after him, "Blessed is His glorious sovereign name
> for ever and ever." (See David de Sola Pool , The Kaddish, p. 45
> and Ephraim Urbach, the Sages, p. 127, p. 130).

B.T. Yoma 37a comments here:
> We have learned that Rabbi says, "For I will proclaim the name
> of the Lord, give praise to our God"--Moses said to Israel: "When
> I mention the name of the Holy One, Blessed Be He, you should give
> praise."
> Rabbi Hananiah, the brother of Rabbi Yehoshua, says: "The mention
> of the righteous one is for blessing --the prophet said to Israel,
> "When I mention the Righteous One of Eternities you should give
> blessing." (Cf. Mechilta $^{(B \; 15 \;)}$ p. 61 to Ex. 13:2).

The practice of responding with a doxology after the mention of the
divine name appears to have been an ancient practice which the above
sources seek to justify through the discovery of proof texts which
purport to relate the source to the custom of Moses. While the form in
Babli Yoma 37a --scriptural text followed by midrashic paraphrase --
is a common halachic and aggadic form, the form in Sifre --"From whence
do we know..." --appears to be set in an halachic form, only rarely used
in aggadic materials. Thus, the statement may have originally been part
of an halachic midrash which has now been taken into an aggadic passage.

According to B.T. Yev. 79a, the act of "sanctifying God's name, i.e.
in bringing others to recognition of His supreme authority, is considered
the greatest act a Jew can perform (see Urbach, Sages, pp. 355-360, p.
147)." קדוש ה' " is a term which has commonly been applied to the act of
public martyrdom. On the other hand, "desecrating the Name" (חילול ה')
is considered to be the gravest sin that one may commit (see B.T.
Sanhedrin 107a) as it casts aspersions upon the sovereignty of God.
Thus according to B.T. Krithoth 7b, blasphemy may actually be a worse
offense than idol worship --blasphemy attempts to uproot divine authority while idol worship does not directly attempt to uproot divine
authority (since it does not recognize it to begin with).

Having said this we can analyze the logic of this Sifre pericope.
a) Moses takes great care to mention the divine name in a more humble
   manner than the angels. The Name must be treated with care and
   respect.
b) With the exception of those passages which deal with the "amen"
   response (are these passages interpolated by the redactor so as
   to relate "amen" traditions with "blessed is His glorious..."
   traditions?), the homilist mentions the doxologies which are
   known in Jewish legal literature as דבר שבקדושה , "the
word that ascribes holiness and blessing".
c) The homilist then tells us that the greatest sanctification of
   God's name is not verbal --it is historical. The trials,
   tribulations and redemptions of Israel are one great historical

doxology to demonstate God's sumpreme authority to non-
believers. Their ultimate verbal praise of God mirrors the
divine praise inherent in all of the events that beset Israel's
relationships with the nations.

d) The homilist now ends his discussion of Deut. 32:3 by showing
that Israel's ultimate confession of faith lies in their recital
of the shma formula (The Lord our God, the Lord is One). But
Israel's profession is not verbal (shma) in toto for in this
profession they acknowledge that they are the tools of the
historical process to sanctify God's name --with all their lives.
And so the homilist comes full circle --Israel is the one who will
bring the praise of God into the world. Spiritually inferior
to the angels, they glorify; and their praise is of greater
purpose and value than that of the angels. Thus the angels are
not able to sanctify and bless God's name until Israel has done
so. Israel is the actual tool, the angels merely the observers
of the establishment of God's glory upon earth.

The homilist-redactor has thus anticipated the entire Song of Moses
and at the close of the opening section has introduced the theme of Deut.
32 as the "blessing of God" as a function of Israel-Nation history which
history of necessity must conclude with הרנינו גוים --the blessing of the nations and the blessing of the angels (cf. LXX to Deut 32:43).
The Song itself is the source of all doxology. This presentation is more
than a literary device --it is fundamental to the midrashic understanding
of Scripture. The whole is contained in the part --at the outset all has
been ordained. History is an unfolding of a divine plan, as S. Alkabez
poetically summarized (" לכה דודי "):

. "סוף מעשה במחשבה תחילה"

We are now in a position to evaluate the unity of structure imposed by
the homilist. The homilist began the pericope by reference to Israel's
inferiority to the angels and concluded with their superiority. In
between these statements he discussed the purpose of Israel's history as
that which is to lead the nations to the recognition of God. He has
presented a micro-version of the whole structure of Ha'azinu. It is
interesting to see, for the homilist of Sifre Deut. 32:43 (Piska 333),
the last verse of the Song, also refers back to the opening verses of
Deut. 32. Those who were to witness against Israel will end by praising
them --the heavens and the earth, the mountains and the nations. Now
it is (cf. Bloch, Midrash etc. p. 47) impossible to tell, on any given
passage where a Hebrew text is lacking in evidence, whether Septuagint
readings reflect variant Hebrew texts whose traditions were relegated
to midrashic lore by the Rabbis to preserve them or whether the
Septuagint translator has used a midrashic interpretation to present
his version. Yet, it seems to me that the Septuagint tradition of
Deut. 32:43,("Rejoice ye heavens with Him and let all the angels of
God worship Him." (cf. S. Hidal "Reflections on Deut.32" p.17), whether
as a midrash or as a text,)was known to the homilist of Piska 306. He
incorporates this tradition by identifying Israel with the "morning
stars" and the angels with the "b'nai elohim" mentioned in Scriptures.

And from whence do we know that we respond, "To eternity
and for ever and ever" after they who recite "May His Great Name
be blessed." We know it from that which is said, "Give praise to our
God."[E62]

And from whence do you say that our ancestors specifically
descended to Egypt so that the Holy One, Blessed Be He, could perform
miracles and wonders for them and this, so that His Great Name should
be sanctified in the world? We know it from that which is said, "And
it came to pass in the course of those many days that the king of
Egypt died...."[S92] [E63] And it further states, "And God heard their
groaning and God remembered His covenant."[S93] And it further states,
" When I cry upon the name of the Lord--Give praise to our God."[*]

And from whence do we know that God specifically brought
retribution and specifically brought the Ten Plagues upon Pharoah and
upon Egypt to have His Great Name sanctified in the world? We know it
because at the beginning of the episode he[E64] stated, "Who is the Lord

---

Philo too seems to have both Deut. 32:1 and Deut. 32:43 in mind when he
speaks of the divine and earthly assemblage and the "choir of the stars"
which heard the Song of Moses (On Virtues 73-75).(Cf. Marqah 4:7 "Moses
praised, the angels rejoiced and said "Praise the Lord" --The glory and
all the angels then praised....") In this way we can see that the
midrash holds together as a well ordered whole based closely upon
scriptural tradition and is not merely a string of midrashim loosely
strung together without a strong principle of organization. In this
manner, the midrash is a well constructed literary unit and uses a
format which exemplifies its message --the unity of Israelite history as
a vehicle to bring about the universal praise of God.

[*] "Give praise..." not in Ln. L. Silberman prefers Ln here noting the
verse is out of place in F.

S92. Exodus 2:23.   S93. Exodus 2:24.

that I should hearken unto His voice..."[S94] while at the end of

the episode he said, "The Lord is righteous and I and my people are

wicked."[S95]

And from whence do we know that God specifically performed

miracles and wonders at the Sea and at the Jordan and at the Valley of

Arnon to have His name sanctified in the world? We know it from that

which is said, "And it came to pass, when all the kings of the Amorites,

that were beyond the Jordan westward and all her kings...."[S96] And

likewise did Rahab say to the agents of Joshua, "For we have heard how

---

E62. See D. de Sola Pool., Kaddish [(B 286)], p. 50. According to D.
de Sola Pool., the congregation would recite לעולם ולעולמי before
the leader but then would recite the entire doxology of יהי שמיה
after hearing ואמרו אמן .

E63. I.e. the events of those times, the groaning and the slavery, were
the effects of God's invoking the Patriarchal covenant: --"ויזכר ה".
The midrashist understands ותעל שועתם as --"their salvation
(ישועתם) which would be accounted (תעל) to God on account
(סם)[(B 271)] of their labor". For the concept of קדוש ה' see Moore Ages
etc., vol. 2, p. 102ff. Also see Sifre to[(B 15)] Lev. 23:33 and
Sifre Deut. to Deut. 23:5 also Mechilta R. Yishmael to
Exodus 15:2 and see P.T. Baba Mezia 2:5 (others should bless his name).

E64. Or perhaps: "It (Scripture) says...." For similar ideas see Sifra
to Lev. 23:33, Sifre to Deut. 23:5.

S94. Exodus 5:2.   S95. Exodus 9:27.
S96. Joshua 5:1.

the Lord dried up the water of the Red Sea before you."[S97] Thus

does Scripture state, "For I will proclaim the name of the Lord."[E65]

And from whence do we know that Daniel specifically descended
into the lions' den for the purpose that the Holy One, Blessed Be
He, would perform miracles and wonders for him and so that His
Great Name would be sanctified in the world? We know it from that
which is said, "For I will proclaim the name of the Lord."[E66] And
Scripture also states, "I make a decree, that in all the dominion of
my kingdom men tremble and fear before the God of Daniel."[S98]

And from whence do you say that Hananiah, Mishael, and Azariah
specifically descended into the fiery furnace so that the Holy One,
Blessed Be He, would perform miracles and wonders for them in order that
His Great Name would be sanctified in the world? We know it from that

---

S97. Joshua 2:10.   S98. Daniel 6:27.

E65. As for verses "S96" and "S97", L. Silberman points out the
unstated ends of the verses and the following verses contain the
essential proof texts. Also "...give praise to our Lord" is understood
here. For the concept of חלול ה see Sifra to Lev. 22:32 and
Sifre Deut. to Deut. 33:5
                    (...כשאני קורא בשמו הוא גדול ואם לאו).

E66. Since this pericope places the text "For I will proclaim the
name of the Lord" prior to the proof text showing that the gentile king
praised God, we may well assume that the midrashist here is reading
אקרא as hiph'il אקריא . Perhaps this understanding of
קראapplies throughout the passage so that "E58", Piska 306, takes
אקרא as if it were indeed an expression of instigation rather than
of blessing. See B.T. Sotah 10a and D. de Sola Pool , Kaddish, (B 286)
p. 43, for the understanding of קרא as hiph'il.

which is said, "It hath seemed good unto me to declare the signs and wonders that God the Most High hath wrought toward me."[S99] And Scripture also says, "How great are His signs and how mighty are His wonders."[S100]

And from whence do we know that the Ministering Angels[E67] do not mention the name of the Holy One, Blessed Be He, in the heavenly realm, until Israel mentions it in the earthly realm? We know it from that which is said, "Hear, O Israel, the Lord our God, the Lord is One."[S101] And Scripture also states, "When the morning stars sang together"[S102] --and afterwards --"And all the godly ones shouted."[S103] "The morning stars" --These refer to Israel who is compared to stars, as it is said, "And in multiplying I will multiply thy seed as the stars of the heavens,"[S104] "And all the godly ones shouted," --These refer to the Ministering Angels; and so does Scripture state, "And the godly ones came to present themselves before the Lord."[S105]

END OF PISKA

S99. Daniel 3:32.   S100. Daniel 3:33.   S101. Deuteronomy 6:4.
S102. Job 38:7.   S103. Job 38:7.   S104. Genesis 22:17.
S105. Job 1:6.

E67. Does the sun symbolize the heavenly host? See Josephus Wars (Whiston),[B 13] 2:8:5 where the Essens pray at sunrise as if to cause the sun to rise. See also B.T. Hulin 91b. Also see Devarim Rabba[B 19], ed. Lieberman, p.68.

4

"The Rock (צור)":

I.e. the craftsman (צייר). --For He first fashioned the world and then He formed man within it, as it is said, "And the Lord God crafted (וייצר)[E1] the man."[S1]

"His work is perfect":

His work is perfect in respect to all who have come into the world and none may criticize His works, not even in the least. And none may consider and say,[E2] "Would that I had three eyes...," or "Would that I had three hands...," or "Would that I had three feet...," or "Would that I walked upon my head...," or "Would that I had my face turned backwards...":..."how suitable it would be for me." For Scripture states, "For all His ways are justice." --He sits in

---

S1. Genesis 2:7.

E1. The midrashist here plays upon the similarity of sound between צור (rock), צור (to form), יצר (to fashion), צייר (craftsman). The point is that man is considered God's handiwork. Cf. ICC Driver, (B 137) p. 351 for Greek versions taking צור as if from יצר or נצר. We noted that God is referred to as צור because He created (יצר) man and the world. Marmorstein (see "Background," p. 5ff.) adduces similar "creation" midrashim aimed at refuting the claims of dualists. Perhaps the midrashist polemicizes here to show that the creator of the world is certainly the creator of "man" and that the world is not hostile to man. Scripture describes God by אמונה because "He declared the world worthy (האמין)". Marmorstein, "Background", Studies in Jewish Theology, (B 259) p. 10, rendered this as "God trusted the world" (see his discussion ibid., pp. 7-11). The point is that man is designed perfectly for his environment by the same craftsman who designed it.

E2. See A.F. Segal, Two Powers in Heaven,(B 315) p. 141ff. Also see E.E. Urbach, Sages (B 339) p. 58; p. 788, n.82 and also S. Lieberman, Tosefta Kifshuta, (B 249) Moed, p. 583.

judgement in respect of each and every one and provides him with
what he deserves.[E3]

E3. God knows the root of each person's character and gives each one
what is fitting for him. Cf. Ben Sira (B 44) 16:15, 32:24, also
IQS 10:17-21, also 2 Cor. 5:10, see further Marmorstein, Studies in
Jewish Theology, (B 259) p. 11. The pericope is indicative of theodic
speculation, cf. Mishna Sanhedrin 10:3 (in reference to the Generation
of the Flood, the Generation of the Tower or Dispersion and the people
of Sodom). Korach (B 16) is mentioned in the following mishna (10:4).
See Marqah (B 16) 4:5, "He recompenses every doer according to his
deed and He reveals the truth in that event." See Marmorstein, "The
Background of the Haggadah", Studies in Jewish Theology, (B 259)
Oxford University Press, London, 1950, p. 7ff., who says that the
author of the midrash is Shimon bar Yochai (2nd c.) who wanted to
ridicule Marcionite ideas about the pusilliates of the demiurge-creator.
Urbach, Sages, p. 202, denies that this pericope is anti-marcionite but
upholds the notion that it is certainly anti-gnostic. Marmorstein goes
so far to say that our pericope's exposition of God's bestowal of
punishments and favors, as just, is also anti-marcionite (see
"Background etc.", (B259) p. 20f. and p. 17). There are close parallels
to our pericope in Marqah 4:3,4,5. Are they then also anti-marcionite!
Cf. also Marqah 4:7 - "The works of the Lord are blemishless."
Marqah interprets Deut 32:4:

"For all his ways" is a pointed allusion to the Day of Vengeance
...The Lord will be too righteous for us (4:3).
When he scattered the people of Babel, there was no iniquity;
When he burned Sodom and Gommorah and overthrew them there was
no iniquity...
Abraham when he was summoned and he came with a pure heart was
recompensed justly...Likewise all of them when they submitted
themselves to their Lord with purity were justly recompensed
(4:4). "God of faithfulness"...and completed the two worlds
...by saying the words "without iniquity" and then further
"just" --which is a perfect world devoid of all imperfection (4:4).
These statements are parallel in sentiment and close in form to those of
our pericope.

"A God of אמונה":

For he declared the world worthy (האמין)[L1] and created it.[E4]

"And without iniquity":

For He did not create people to be wicked but to be righteous.[E5]

And likewise does Scripture state, "Behold, only this I have found

that God made man upright, but they have sought out many inventions."[S2]

"Just and right is He":

He deals rightly in respect to all who have come into the world.

Another tradition:

"The Rock":

I.e. The Mighty One.[E6]

S2. Ecclesiastes 7:29.

L1. See Mandelkern s.v. אמן II who understands that the root sense
of the word refers to that which endures. In Rabbinic literature it
often means to "confirm" or to "declare worthy". For the expression
מחת פורענות see Y. Ben-David "מחת פורענותן של רשעים" in Lĕšonenu,
vol. 41 (1977), no. 4, p. 294ff.

E4. Another possible rendering is: "For He declared the world worthy
and created him." More likely is this: "For He declared the world worthy
which He created." (B 307) Also see S. Schechter, Some Aspects of Rabbinic
Theology, p. 62: "...when He created it." and cf. "Some Aspects (B34)
of Rabbinic Theology", JQR 6, (1894) p. 638. Cf. Philo, Mut. 34, 182f.
God's faith is His knowledge and it is perfect. Hence it cannot be
criticized. (B 33) See also Philo, On the Migration of Abraham, ch. 25 (ed.
Glatzer).

E5. I.e. evil is not God's creation; it is man's.

E6. Rock = Strength = Royal authority = Omnipotence. See S. Schechter,
Some Aspects of Rabbinic Theology, (B 307) p. 305 and see A. Marmorstein,
Old Rabbinic Doctrine, etc., p. 95. (B 260) For usage of בעל הפקדון see
Marmorstein op. cit., (B 260) p. 146. Cf. M. Lehrer, "In the Heavens etc.",
(B 243) De Vries Memorial Volume, p. 106. Now the tradition marked
here as "another interpretation" is act   variant of the tradition
which preceded it. In that tradition   God's physical endowment
of people which was at issue while here   His merit system that is at

"His work is perfect":

His work is perfect in respect to all those who have come into the world and none may criticize His works, not a whit of criticism. And none may consider and say: "How did the people of the Flood Generation deserve to be drowned in water?"[E7] Or, "How did the people at the tower deserve that they should be dispersed from one end of the world to the other?"[E8] Or, "How did the people of Sodom deserve to be deluged by fire and brimstone?"[E9] Or, "How did Aaron deserve to receive the Priesthood?"[E10] Or, "How did David deserve to receive the King-ship?"[E11] Or, "How did Korach and his assembly deserve that the earth

---

issue. At times the phrase דבר אחר "another interpretation" may signal a completely new facet while at other times it introduces a variant tradition, different in detail but similar in intent to the tradition which it follows (B 95) See W. Bacher, Tannaim, p. 32ff. Also see Yehuda L. Bohrer (B 108): "The material which is introduced by the term "another interpretation" or in the form of "petiḥot" gives the impressions of random collections. This is not the case. It actually belongs to the essential text and offers enlightenment from a different perspective." (Y.L. Bohrer, "A Historical and Methodological Exposition of Aggadic Sources", Samuel K. Mirsky Memorial Volume: Studies in Law, Philosophy and Literature,editor: G. Appel,Yeshiva University, N.Y., Sura Institute for Research, 1970, p. 155ff.

E7. See Gen. 6:4.

E8. See Gen. 11:9.

E9. See Gen. 19:24. "Deluged" (שטף) means here "destroyed".

E10. See Numbers 17:17, also see S. Schechter, Some Aspects of Rabbinic Theology, (B 307) p. 306.

E11. See 2 Sam. 7:16,cf. S. Schechter, Some Aspects of Rabbinic Theology, (B 307) p. 306.

should swallow them?"[E12] For Scripture states, "For all his ways

are justice." --He sits in judgement of each and every one and gives

him what he deserves.

"A God of faithfulness":

    I.e. The trustee .[E13]

E12. See Num. 16:32.

E13. Cf. Koran, sura 53:41. God has given Man a world of assets and
He will demand repayment. God will not subtract due punishments from
due rewards or due rewards from due punishments. The accounting will be
exact --punishments will be meted out as owed and rewards will be meted
out as owed. See E. Sanders, Paul, etc., (B 302) p. 126f. and S. Schechter,
Some Aspects of Rabbinic Theology, (B 307) p. 306. Perhaps the point of
saying, God is "the trustee" and can be relied upon to collect His
personal debts after He has distributed what He owes, is also a way of
indicating that no one will escape death and judgement for God claims
the soul when it is due to return to Him. For halacha of deducting from
debts due when paying off loans see Rabbenu Tam in Sefer Hayashar, (B 328)
Berlin,1898, 34a, p. 55,n.4. Our pericope can best be understood by
understanding the frame of reference of Devarim Rabba (ed. Lieberman)
ekeb 3. We learn there that the words "faithful God (אל נאמן)"
(Cf. Deut. 32:4 אל אמונה ואין עול) are to be related to the words of
Jeremiah 2:5 --Did your fathers find in Me iniquity (עול). The expositor
maintains that both verses are intended to show that God pays off His
debts fully. In Sifre Deut. Piska 307 we find the same word complex
as in Dev. R.--"נאמן" and "עול". The terms "אמונה" and "עול" in both
sources are interpreted to show that "While He is owed outstanding debts,
He also fully pays off his debts". The conclusion is that God is in a
position to pay in full and "collect in full". Dev. R. continues the
discussion by giving examples of debts that God had paid off long ago:
the promise to Abraham that He would give his children wealth and
redemption and other examples of debts that man owes God. (See Alon,
p. 458ff. for a discussion of the term "strategoi" used in this Dev.
R. pericope.) Our Sifre pericope also notes God's justice in this
regard. Rewards and punishments are kept separate. God exacted
punishment from the wicked generations of the Flood and the Tower,
while David and Aaron were given Kingship and Priesthood duties.
God bestows, upon each one, that which keeps the balance of payments
due and owing in precise tally.

"And without iniquity":[T1]

He collects His debts after meeting His obligations. The customs of the Holy One, Blessed Be He, are not like those of flesh and blood. The custom of flesh and blood is that when one, who owes one hundred, gave his creditor a purse of two hundred in trust and now comes to retrieve his purse --he can be told, "subtracting the hundred that you owe me --here is the rest!". And likewise when a workman, working for his boss to whom he owes a <u>dinar</u>, comes to collect his wages --he can be told, "subtracting the <u>dinar</u> that you owe me --here is the rest!"

But "He who spoke and the world was" is not like this, but "He is a faithful God" --i.e. the trustee. "And without iniquity."[T1] --i.e. He collects his debts after meeting his obligations.

"Just and right is He":

This is according to the Scripture which states,[E14] "For the Lord is righteous, He loveth righteousness."[S3]

Another interpretation:

"The Rock":

I.e. The Mighty One.

S3. Psalms 11:7.

T1. Omitted in Ln apparently due to a homoioteleuton ("and without iniquity").

E14. For the concept of God's righteousness see A. Marmorstein, <u>Doctrine</u> <u>of</u> <u>Merits</u> etc.,[B 260] p. 7ff. and E. Urbach, <u>Sages</u>,[B 339] p. 652f, p. 264ff. Also see Moore, <u>Ages</u> etc.,[B 271] vol. 2, p.249, n. 10. Also see Marqah 4:5,[B 16] "The Rock...perfect" --He designated their sins for them for the great day of judgement.

"His work is perfect":

The dues of those who have come into the world are perfectly administered by Him, the bestowing of reward due the righteous and the placing of punishment due the wicked.[E15] The former receive nothing due them in This World[T2] and the latter receive nothing due them in This World. And from whence do we know that the righteous receive nothing due them in This World? We know it from that which is said, "O how abundant is thy goodness which thou hast laid up for them that fear thee."[S4] And from whence do we know that the wicked receive nothing due them in This World?[T2] We know it from that which is said, "Is this not laid up with Me, sealed up in my treasuries..."[S5] When shall both these and those receive it?

S4. Psalms 31:20.   S5. Deuteronomy 32:34.

T2. Omitted in Ln apparently due to a homoioteleuton ("receive nothing due them in this world").

E15. As in "E7", Piska 307, the use of "another interpretation" here is to present a variant tradition rather than a new interpretation of the verse. The point here is that faithful God collects his debts from the wicked in the Next World and will not reduce the punishment by exacting a loan against the wicked in This World through doling out premature punishment in This World. Likewise He pays the righteous in the Next World their full due and will not reduce their credit by exacting a loan against this reward through doling out credit prematurely in This World. L. Silberman notes that the problem addressed here is the problem of why the righteous suffer while the wicked prosper. See further Bacher, Tannaim, (B 95) p. 77, n.2. Also see S. Schechter, Studies in Judaism (1st series), (B 308) JPS, Phila., 1919, p. 215ff. See above "E13" and Moore, Age, (B 271) Vol. 2, p. 255.

"For all His ways are justice":

--On the Future Morrow[E16] when He sits upon the Throne of
Justice in respect to the judgement of each and every one and gives
him what he deserves.[E17]

"A God of faithfulness":

Just as He pays the completely righteous man in the Next World
the reward for the precept fulfilled in This World, so does He pay
the completely wicked man in This World the recompense for the
light precept[T3] done in This World.[T4] And[E18] just as He exacts
punishment from the completely wicked man in the Next World for the
sin committed in This World, so does He exact punishment from the
completely righteous man in This World for the sin committed in This
World.[T4]

T3. F has mention of "light precept". These are acts that cost little
and are easily done (e.g. See Mishna Hulin 12:5).

T4. Omitted in Ln apparently due to homoioteleuton ("in this world").

E16. Each part of Scripture here is analyzed in the form of a continuous
commentary. The "Future World" in these passages seems to refer to
the world of resurrection when God will judge each one. See Piska 318,
"L2".

E17. This interpretation of Deut. 32:4 includes Man's present existence,
Israel's past history and the Future Judgement.

E18. God keeps the record book straight by not allowing credits and
debits to offset the tally. The wicked man receives his reward in This
World for the little good he may have done while the righteous man
receives the punishment here for any evil he may have done. In this way
the future punishment or reward will be paid with fulness in the Next
World and cannot be offset or reduced by rewards or punishments which
would still be forthcoming had God not disposed of these already in
This World. See E. Sanders, Paul, [B302] p. 142, p. 203.

"And without iniquity":

When a man departs from the world all his deeds come before him

to be enumerated and he is told: "Such and such you did on this

certain day and such and such you did on that certain day. Do you

declare these words to be worthy?" And he says, "Yea!"

He is told: "Sign!" This is as it is said, "By hand, every man shall

sign that all men may make known their deed."[S6] [E19]

"Just and right is He":

And he declares the judgement to be righteous by saying: "I

have been judged properly."[E20] And so does Scripture state, "That thou

mayest be justified by thy words."[S7]

Another tradition:

"The Rock His work is perfect":

When Rabbi Hanina the son of T'radyon was apprehended, it was

decreed that he[T5] should be burned with[*] his scroll. They said to him:

---

* F: He should be burned with his scroll --Ln: It was decreed that his
  scroll should be burned.

S6. Job 37:7.   S7. Psalms 51:6.

T5. Perhaps Ln's omission of mention of Hanina 's death is out of
respect for the scholar and instead the euphemism "Torah" is used. The
mention of the verses of צדוק הדין as related in the name of Rabbi
illustrate that the tradition was known that Hanina was killed. The
words attributed to Philosophus indicate that the word "Torah" refers
to the scholar: "You have burned the Torah...may my portion be with them".
F's tradition may be a later expansion which combined the story of the
death of Hanina as told outright and the tradition as in Ln which spoke
of "the burning of the Torah". F's reading may have combined both
stories as has, perhaps, B.T. Avodah Zarah 18a.

E19. The accounting is so perfect that one will sign confessions when
confronted with the hard evidence of his behavior. See Sanders, Paul,
p. 126ff. and A. Marmorstein, The Doctrine of Merits etc. p. 7ff. and

"It has been decreed that you are to be burned with your scroll."

He recited this Scripture, "The Rock, His work is perfect."

They said to his wife: "It has been decreed that your husband

is to be burned[*] and that you are to be decapitated."[L2] She recited

this Scripture, "A God of faithfulness and without iniquity."

They said to his daughter: "It has been decreed that your father

is to be burned and your mother is to be decapitated and that you are

to perform duty."[E21] She recited this Scripture, "Great in counsel,

and mighty in work; whose eyes are open...."[S8]

The Old Rabbinic Doctrine etc., p. 192ff.[(B 260)]

E20. Even sinners will justify God's retribution system in the Future
World.

* F: That your husband   --Ln: Decreed upon your husband to burn the
  scroll. (To daughter...upon your father to burn the scroll).

S8. Jeremiah 32:19.

L2. See Jastrow, s.v. הריגה. Each of the martyrs are dealt specific
ordeals of a tortuous nature. Thus it is reasonable to assume that הריגה
(which can mean "an unspecified execution") is being used here to refer
to a specific method of execution, i.e. to decapitation, which הריגה at
times signifies. It is my contention that the redactor (the Tannaim
called such euphemisms תקון סופרים --see Jastrow s.v. תיקון) of our
materials was fond of using euphemistic expressions and that Ln's
reading of "Torah Scroll" in fact refers to the burning of Hanina himself. For the Rabbinic espousal of circumlocutions see Sifre Bamidbar
Piska 105 to Num. 12:12 where the Rabbis claim that "his mother" is a
euphemism for "our mother" and "his flesh" is a euphemism for "our flesh".
Also see Sifre Zuta (ed. Horowitz, p. 277) where we are told that one
should speak of unagreeable occurences which one experiences as if
another had experienced them. (Discussed by S. Lieberman, Hellenism etc.,
p. 32.)

E21. I.e. she was forced to work in a brothel, see B.T. Avodah Zarah
18a and G. Alon,[(B 90)] p. 254, n. 6. Bacher, Tannaim,[(B 95)] p. 116ff.
sees קובה של זנות as the language of the original tradition, as found
in B.T. Avodah Zarah 18a but he fails to say why he holds that view.
Does he think euphemistic expressions represent later alterations to
existing texts?

Said Rabbi: "How great were these righteous people who in their hour of suffering readily specified the three verses which remain unparalleled in all of Scripture for their acknowledgement of God's righteous[L3] judgement!"[E22]

The three of them directed their hearts and justified the judgement that came upon them.

Philosophus opposed his commander. He said to him: "My lord, boast not that you have burned the Torah,[E23] for to the place from

---

L3. צדוק הדין is a term which has come to designate acceptance of God's righteousness in matters of death. A blessing of ואסף אתכם בדין is mentioned in B.T. Berachoth 58b. Custom has it that the verses noted in our midrash are to be recited after burials. These rites are mentioned in Amram Gaon's siddur (p. 55a) and in Shevilei Haleqet ("Semachot" 13) we hear that the recital of the Kaddish at the grave site is on account of the verses of צדוק הדין which are mentioned in our midrash (cf. B.T. Avodah Zarah 18a; see also Sifre Deut. 304). It seems that Marqah 4:4 also knew this verse referred to צדוק הדין: "Adam said it when Abel was killed."

E22. See E. Sanders, Paul etc.,(B 302) p. 198, n. 85.

E23. It seems to me that the word Torah in Ln actually is a euphemism to refer to the "master of the Torah", i.e. to Hanina himself. The claim of B.T. Avodah Zarah 18a to the effect that Hanina was burned with his scroll appears to be a different version than that found (with interpolative discussion) in B.T. Avodah Zarah 17b--18a which does not mention the Torah scroll and which wording closely agrees with our Sifre text. It may well be that the second tradition in the Talmud is related to the reading in F. Whether F is merely an elaboration of the "Torah" of an earlier tradition (Ln) which is also recorded as a separate tradition (first) in the B.T. or whether F is a harmonizing of the reading in Ln and the second tradition in the B.T. (dying with the scroll) cannot be determined for certain. The evidence that "scroll" was merely a euphemism for the "Torah scholar" can be found in Philosophus' pericope which refers only to the burning of the "Torah" (and not to Hanina, but means "Hanina") throughout all mss. (and which is absent in B.T.) in his allusion to the Future Morrow (resurrection of the dead) thus showing that the term "Torah" is meant to refer to people. The second tradition in B.T. Avodah Zarah 18a does allude to an executioner who is granted a share in the World to Come but the relationship of that story with our pericope is not clear.

which it came has it returned --to its Father's house." He replied:"To-

morrow shall your judgement be as　　　theirs." He said to him:

"You have announced glad tidings to me that on the Future Morrow my

portion may be with them in the Next World."

Ln's reading appears to be consistent　with　the "Philosophus
pericope"　where we read　:　"Tomorrow shall your judgement be
as theirs --On the Future Morrow may my portion be with them in the
Next World." This is a response to his commander's threat that Philosophus
would join them ("the Torah") on the Morrow. The words "boast not
that you have burned the Torah" make sense in Ln where the preceding
pericope referred only to burning a scroll(Hanina) while in F the reference
to the "Torah" does not relate as well to the story preceding the pericope.
See A. Marmorstein, Studies in Jewish Theology,(B 259) p. 142, p. 167,
p. 174,where the second tradition in B.T. Avodah Zarah 18a concerning the
death of Hanina and the burning of the Torah is shown to share literary
motifs with other stories in Rabbinic literature,and this suggests to me
that the Tannaitic tradition recording the burning of Hanina and the
scroll is a later telling of the story than the one where just Hanina
dies and no mention is made of a scroll (in B.T. Avodah Zarah 17b, first
story). The second tradition, (in B.T. Av. Zar. 18a) bearing the marks
of an editorial stylist, may be a dramatic expansion of the first story
or may be completely independent of it. The former suggestion appears
more tantalizing because the passage is highly stylized. Discussions of
the story of the martyrdom of Rabbi Hanina and his family can be found
in Urbach, Sages, p. 442, p. 515, p. 918,n. 31, A. Büchler The Galilean
Am-Haretz, Jerusalem, Mossad HaRav Kook, 1964, p. 199, Marmorstein,
"The Holy Spirit in Rabbinic Legend",(B 259)(Studies in Jewish Theology),
p. 142f. In the Sifre version we find the name Philosophus (var.
P'lsolos, Pilospus, Plispus) and it may be that this name refers to the
father of Proklus who is mentioned in Mishna Avodah Zarah 3:4: "Proklos,
the son of Philosophus, asked Rabbi Gamliel". L. Silberman wonders if
the name Philosophus means he was a philosopher.

T6. The word "tomorrow" is important here indeed . "Tomorrow"
acts as a trigger for his response concerning the Next World or as it
is more commonly called, "the World to Come". In Rabbinic parlance
מחר = עולם הבא.

Another interpretation:

"The Rock His work is perfect":

When Moses descended from Mount Sinai, Israel gathered about

him. They said to him, "Our master Moses, tell us what heavenly

justice is like."[E24]

E24. The issue of מדת הדין here addresses the problem of how God
insures maintenance of justice in the world. The answer is that Man's
courts are supposed to vindicate the innocent and fault the guilty as
Moses is believed to have directed in Deut. 25:1. Nevertheless, even
where human justice fails by faulting the innocent or exonerating the
guilty, God brings ultimate justice to prevail although man remains
ignorant of the process by which this is accomplished. Cf. B.T. Makkoth
10b where the criminals are justly punished through "accidents" in such
a way as to receive the fitting punishments for their crimes. A.
Marmorstein, (Studies in Jewish Theology, p. 9, n. 2)(B 259) believed
our Sifre passage was only partially preserved. He assumed its purpose
was to combat heretical opinions (Studies in Jewish Theology, (B 259)
p. 11). See also E. Sanders, Paul etc.,(B 302) p. 169ff. Pardo sees
here a justification for the age old problem of "the righteous who
suffer and the wicked who prosper" --only God knows exactly how justice is
to work and man cannot question this. Cf. 2 Cor. 5:10 and 1 QS 10:17-21.
Also see Bonsirven, Palestinian Judaism, (B 110) p. 20 ff. For the
setting of this passage at the time of Moses' descent from Sinai cf.
Tanhuma Buber Jethro 5 (vol. 2) p. 72. The image conjured by the term:
the "measuring" of deeds, recalls the image of Nemesis: "Nemesis checks
with cubit and bridle, Immoderate deeds, and boastings rash and idle."
(as cited in The Greek Anthology,(B 273) p. 152). Various suggestions
have been offered to unravel the obscure text. Pardo discusses a view
that paraphrases:
     Certainly God does not do anything else than vindicate the
     innocent and fault the guilty but he also will not cancel
     out a due punishment because of some due reward, or vice
     versa.
Pardo points out that חלף never has the meaning "to cancel" or "to
reduce" that it is given in this interpretation.
     Another view, that of Moshe David Ashkenazi(B 92) (Toldoth Adam)
states:
     There is no problem when we see that God vindicates the
     innocent and faults the guilty; yet, when it appears, that
     the reverse is the case, you may rest assured that there is
     just reason for it.
Although Pardo likes this latter interpretation, I should object
that the understanding of the wording here does not indicate a sense
of "when it appears that the reverse" but rather indicates "when the

reverse...". LE, apparently following the comment of Elijah of Wilna,
claims that the text's "vindicate the innocent" is in fact a euphemism
to state --indict the innocent. Accordingly the passage means:
> I have not said to you that God indicts the innocent and
> frees the guilty, but even to think that God perverts justice
> is wrong (cf. Sifre Deut.307, "E13") because God is just.

This interpretation is possible but, if the passage intended such, it
could have read in clearer style: "You should not say" (rather than
"I have not said..."). My own solution is to dismiss the notion that
we are concerned here with the problem of why the righteous suffer and
the wicked prosper. Rather, I think, we are here concerned with the
question of ultimate justice: Is perfect justice to be found in This
World? The answer is --"Always!"

> Have I not told you (in Deut. 25:1) to justify the righteous and
> to condemn the wicked? Even if the judges do not proceed
> to do this, God's ultimate justice prevails in spite of human
> shortcomings.

In this way the midrashist understood the two sections of the verse
--   1) God is faithful, 2) He has no iniquity --i.e. 1) God has faith
in human courts ("el emuna" --elohim can refer to human courts, cf. Targ.
Onk. to Ex. 21:6); 2) He allows no iniquitous miscarriage of justice
(cf. Urbach, Sages, p. 448ff. and p. 461). We need not be concerned
that the midrashist understands citations of Deuteronomy to have
been propounded before Moses descended from Mount Sinai (as told in
Exodus). The Rabbis (see B.T. Pesachim 6b and P.T. Rosh Hashannah
1:1) did not think that the Hebrew Bible was written in chronological
order.

Memar Marqah 4:12 (4th c. according to IDB,(B 70) s.v. Samaritans)
contains a tradition affixed to Deut. 32:39:

> "And there is none that can deliver out of My hand":
> --"Is the Lord's hand waxed short? (Num. 11:23)", the
> Lord's hand first created and by its magnitude is all
> restituted to its principal state. Therefore he said,
> "hand (Deut. 32:39, יד)"--"He will judge (Deut. 32:36,
> ידין, i.e. hand = the hand (יד) of justice (ידין)". If
> he was innocent, woe to the witness; but if he was a liar,
> then the witness will be honored.

> "And there is none that can deliver out of My hand":
> --He said: This matter concerns witnesses. Before the
> false witness was ever recognized, when the hand of the
> witness was stretched forth to slay the innocent "then
> there is none that can deliver him out of My hand" and
> he will not be saved from Me. But when he slays the
> guilty --Moses, his predecessor, killed an Egyptian.

Now this passage is intended to show that God's justice is absolute and
will not allow the frailty of human court process to interfere with this
justice. Although Marqah attaches his statement to Deut. 32:39 and our
midrash to the same effect is placed in Deut. 32:4, we should recognize

He replied to them, "Have I not told you to acquit the innocent and declare the guilty liable?[E25] But even were the matters to be reversed -- He is a God of faithfulness and without iniquity."

END OF PISKA

---

the relationship between the two statements. If my analysis of Piska 307 is correct then the homilist had referred to Deut. 25:1. The Rabbis interpreted Deut. 25:1 (see B.T. Makkoth 2b.) to refer to the case of false witnesses. Thus our Piska is concerned with the same problem facing Marqah (or his source) --what safeguards are to enforce justice? The response is that God guarantees ultimate justice. We may not know that the Egyptian deserved to die or that some apparently honest witness deserved to meet with a fatal accident but God guides justice perfectly.

E25. The reference is most likely to Deut. 25:1: "...and judges judge them by justifying the righteous and condemning the wicked." The problem to be rectified by God is the one caused by erroneous judgements in the courts. For the midrashist, justice is always absolute in God's worlds. See also Canticles R. 1:6.

5

"Is corruption His? No; His children's is the blemish":

Even though they are full of blemishes they are called "His

children". These are the words of Rabbi Meir. --As it is said,

"His children's is the blemish"...

Rabbi Yehuda says:[*] They have no blemishes, as it is said, "Not

His children's is the blemish."[E1]

---

* Ln: And so does Rabbi Yehuda say...

E1. Cf. Luke 6:35, Matthew 5:45 and Philo, On Rewards and Punishments,
115:5, 163:72, also see Philo, Sob.ch. 10f.(B34) which equates the
term "children" with "lack of reasoning" which argument does not accord
with our midrash. While Philo is a masterful apologist for the man of
reason, the Rabbis were apologists for the people of Israel, saints and
sinners alike.
   Our present text supposes that Rabbi Meir pauses after לא, while
Yehuda pauses before לא. The parallel texts to this section are found in
Sifre Deut. Piska 96 (to Deut. 14:1):
   ("You are children to the Lord your God":)
   Rabbi Yehuda says: If you behave like children, then
   you are children. But if you do not, then you are not
   children.
   Rabbi Meir says: Whether you do or you do not --"you
   are children to the Lord your God". And likewise it
   says, "Yet the number of the children of Israel (shall
   be as the sand of the sea...ye are the children of the
   living God)."
And also B.T. Kiddushin 36a:
   As we learned: "You are children to the Lord your God":
   When you behave like children you are called children,
   When you do not behave like children you are not called
   children. These are the words of Rabbi Yehuda.
   Rabbi Meir says: Whether you do or do not, you are still
   called children, as it is said, "They are sottish children",
   and also it says, "Children in whom there is no faithfulness ",
   and also it says, "A seed of evil doers, children that deal
   corruptly ", and also it says, "Instead of that which was
   said unto them: 'Ye are not My people', it shall be said
   unto them, 'Ye are the children of the living God'."
The following observations are to be made:
   The form of Sifre Deut. Piska 308 has --
   a) statement of Meir (+supporting proof text)
   b) statement of Yehuda
   c) proof text as if to support Yehuda

d) proof texts supporting Meir.
Sifre Deut. Piska 96 and B.T. Kiddushin 36a have --
a) statement of Yehuda
b) statement of Meir
c) proof texts supporting Meir.
In B.T. Kiddushin and Sifre Deut. Piska 96 (Is this an example of a
transformed Midrash as discussed by Ch. Albeck, "The Method of the Sages'
Exegesis", p. 23ff.?) we have no proof texts to support Yehuda. Sifre
Deut. Piska 308 joins the Yehuda proof text --מומם בניו לא-- to a proof text
which obviously supports Meir's contention.   Friedmann (followed by
L. Finkelstein "Studies in the Tannaitic Midrashim," PAAJR, vol 5,
1933-1934, p. 211f.) would omit the statement of Yehuda from the text
(i.e. sees it as a gloss). However we may find here a dialogue:
(R.T. = received tradition).
        R.T.a: Meir --Even if full of blemishes they are called "children"
                (editor adds --as it is said "His children's is the blemish"
                editor adds-- Yehuda "says" they are called children only
                when they have no blemishes as it is said, "Not His
                children's is the blemish.")
        R.T.b: And so does Scripture state....
R.T.a ends with the words "the words of Rabbi Meir". R.T.b belongs to
a "separate" tradition which brought proof texts for Meir as we find
in the other traditions of this type. It may be that R.T.a and R.T.b
were once connected but that R.T.a was brought into Sifre Ha'azinu alone
and after the tradition had been cast into the edited form, another
redactor added R.T.b to restore the earlier tradition. R.T.b is
secondary to the purposes of Sifre Ha'azinu and is out of sequence in
the framework of the midrash as it belongs after the statement of Meir,
not at the end of the passage as it now stands. Only in a passage that
gives a single view (e.g. Meir alone) may we see an intent to show that
people of Israel have not been disowned by God and they are still His
children (see Marmorstein, "Judaism and Christianity in the Middle of
the Third Century", p. 219-224). The point of such a midrash may be to
take a Biblical verse which appears to be offensive towards Israel and
to take that very verse to show that the covenant is still in force even
when Israel sins. Urbach, Sages, p. 528 finds the spirit of Akiba in
Meir's words. I suspect that the word "son" or "child" here actually
is to be understood as a "covenantal partner" --the Almighty (Father)
has bound himself to protect his "children" (see Piska 314, "El").
The dispute between Meir and Yehuda may be more than just a debate over
terms --not: are Israelites who sin able to be called children? but:
is God still bound to protect Israel when they sin? Yehuda's position
here is consistent with his position in Piska 322 where he interprets
Deut. 32:28 to mean that Israel has lost divine favor because they have
abandoned his Torah. In Piska 323, further, Yehuda announces that
Israel, because of the treachery of their leaders and righteous ones, are
still in the category of having the curse of Adam upon them. According
to Marmorstein's interpretation of the passage, even the revelation of
Sinai --now rejected, is not able to help them, (see Marmorstein,

...And likewise does Scripture state, "A seed of evil-doers, children that deal corruptly."[S1] If they are called "children" even when they deal corruptly; if they would not deal corruptly how much more so should they be called "children"![E2]

A similar argument to this is:

"They are wise to do evil":[S2] And are not these words subject to an a fortiori interpretation?

--Since they are called "wise" even when they do evil; if they would do good, how much more so should they be called "wise"!

A similar argument to this is:

"They are sottish children":[S3] Since they are called "children", even when they are sottish; if they would be judicious, how much more so should they be called "children"!

A similar argument to this is:

"And they will come unto thee as the people cometh and sitteth before thee as My people and hear thy words":[S4] I might think that they will hear and do them. But Scripture states, "But do them not...."[S5] And are not these words subject to an a fortiori interpretation:

Since they are called "My people", even when they hear but

האמונה בנצח ישראל בדרשות התנאים והאמוראים, Studies in Jewish Theology, p. 10f.).

S1. Isaiah 1:4.   S2. Jeremiah 4:22.   S3. Jeremiah 4:22.
S4. Ezekiel 33:31.   S5. Ezekiel 33:31.

E2. See E. Sanders, Paul etc., (B 302) p. 96ff. (B 124) Also see D. Daube, New Testament and Rabbinic Judaism, p. 276ff.

do them not; if they would hear and do them, how much

more so should they be called "My people"!

They said in the name of Abba Hadores:[*] [L1] Israel extirpated

every "thou shalt not" in the Torah! --And why use such an

exclamatory expression? --In order to silence potential arguments

of the wicked to the effect that whenever we sin before Him, "we"

are pained before Him.[E3]

To what may the matter be compared? --to one who went to be

executed and his father cried for him and his mother threw herself

before him. The one said, "Woe is me!" and the other said, "Woe

is me!" But this woe is produced only for he who goes out to be

executed.[E4] And likewise does Scripture state, "Woe unto their soul

when they have recompensed them with calamity."[S6]

---

* Ln: of a preacher

S6. Isaiah 3:9.

L1. F reads: אבה הדורס, Friedmann reads: אבא דורש, Ln reads: דורש.
It is probably a name. Pardo says he was so called because he was a
darshan (a homilist). Silberman believes we somehow have here a
reference to Herod, the wicked, whose behavior is being criticized.

E3. "We are pained before Him" should be read as a euphemism for "We
cause Him pain". R.M. Johnston, op. cit., (B 209) p.350 attempts to
show how editors placed euphemisms in texts. The point of the Sifre
passage before us appears to be that the verse could be read (and
perhaps some read it this way) as: "They have done harm (שחת) against
Him (לו), His children, the "do-not" (לא), by their blemish." The
position of the negative particle "לא" (here taken as single "do-not"
prohibition) allows for such a reading. Perhaps some minim really did
argue from here that they could hurt God by doing a sin. "They have
harmed --against Him (לו) -- His children, the 'do-not (לא)',
by their blemish."

E4. The preacher explains that this "heretical" interpretation is
unreasonable because it is a matter of everyday experience that parents

"A generation crooked and twisted":

Moses said to Israel, "You are crooked and twisted people and you will go nowhere except into the fire". --To what may the matter be compared?[L2] To one who had in his hand a twisted staff and he gave it to the craftsman to repair. He repairs it by fire, and if this does not work, then he straightens it by the press, and if this does not work then he chisels it with an adze and casts it into the fire.[E5] And likewise does Scripture say, "And I will hand thee into the hand of men of burning, skilful to destroy."[S7]

---

are not pained by the blemishes of their children as they are when their children are executed. According to the preacher, God was pained (לו) by the deaths (שחת) of the "do-nots" (i.e. all of them were transgressed). The midrashist notes that the word "children" is used in the verse to refer to the commandments and therefore assumes that the imagery of the verse would have to be consistent with parent-child relationships as known from common experience. For the idea of commandments as children cf. Gen. R. 30:6[B 17] Alternatively L. Silberman interprets "No one is sorry until he is caught"; the verse here is taken as "They have acted corruptly against Him in regard to לאוין=לא." --Why does Scripture say this? In order to prevent the wicked from saying "Whenever we sinned against Him, we were sorry!"

S7. Ezekiel 21:36.

L2. See the notice in S. Lieberman, Greek in Jewish Palestine, p. 155. He compares ps. Diogenian 6:92 ("There is no straightening of a crooked stick, for it is difficult to produce good from bad") with our Sifre passage. Schorr, p. 13, suggests דור = δόρυ (wood) and פתלתל : פתל = ψόλός (fire), תל = αιθαλόω (burning).

E5. The midrash plays upon the Hebrew word for generation, "דור" by taking it as "מדורה", a pile of fire (see above "L2"). Pardo interprets the verse in accordance with this midrash as "To the fire-pile you [B 248] crooked and twisted people." Cf. S. Lieberman, Greek etc., p. 155, who finds the imagery here parallel to Greek adages of Politis and Pseudo-Diogenian. L. Silberman says that he thinks our text once may have read "...adze. And if this does not work, he casts it into the fire." Aaron Moses Padwa of Karlin in his commentary to Midrash Leqah Tob [B 21] takes the word בוערים of Ez. 21:36 to mean burning and thus explains the text of the midrash, in its Midrash Leqah Tob version.

Another interpretation:

Moses said to Israel: "In the way in which you have behaved, I have behaved towards you."[E6] --for so does Scripture state, "With the pure thou dost show thyself pure; and with the <u>crooked</u> thou dost show thyself <u>subtle</u>[S8] (עקש תתפל) --"A generation crooked and פתלתל."

END OF PISKA

The order of repair is --straightener and adze, then peeling and firing in a kiln. Leqah Tob adds a proof text not found in Sifre versions, "And I will bring the third part through the fire". The Sifre midrash continues here the theme of punishing the wicked by adducing the principle of מדה כנגד מדה, measure for measure. מדה (lit. measure) is often used in the sense of "customary behavior" (see Piska 306) because the measure of one's character determines one's usual behavior. The idea of "measure for measure" is ancient. (See Urbach, <u>Sages</u>, p. 371ff, p. 438ff. and p. 458ff. Also B.T. Yev. 197b, B.T. Shab. 105b, B.T. Ned. 32a, B.T. Sotah 8a, B.T. Sanhed. 90a, Matthew 7:2, Luke 6:38, Mark 4:24.) The homilist may see the words, Deut. 32:5 דור עקש - ופתלתל here as "the crooked generation --He deceives".

S8. 2 Samuel 22:27.

E6. The "measure for measure" concept here is derived from word usages in this verse and in other places in Scripture, which are attached to words which show similar phonology while expressing "tit for tat". For example 2 Sam. 22:27 תתפל (to subtly punish an עקש) sounds like Deut. 32:5 פתלתל (an עקש subtly does evil). Similarly 2 Sam. 22:27 תתבר (doing acts of kindness) sounds, (indeed תתבר comes from the same root) as נבר (to reward kindly). Since the sounds of "deed" words match "reward" words, the midrashist believes that Scripture utilized these expressions to indicate that to the exact degree that one has behaved well or ill so are his desserts justly given. See E. Urbach, <u>Sages</u>, (B 339) p. 371ff, p. 438ff, p. 458.

6

"Do ye thus requite the Lord":

They told a parable: To what may the matter be compared?--
To one who stood in the market place and hurled insult against a councilman. Those who heard him said, To whom, you common fool, do you
stand and hurl insult: against a councilman! What if he wanted to beat
you or to tear your garment or to incarcerate you in prison, could you
possibly check him? Were he a <u>centurion</u>,[L1] who is of higher rank than
he, how much more so would you be a fool, and were he a councillor, which
is of superior rank to both of these, how more so would you be a fool!"

"Do ye thus requite the Lord":

A parable: To what may the matter be compared?--To one who stood
in the marketplace and hurled insult against his father. Those who
heard him said to him: "You common fool, against whom do you stand and
hurl insult! Against your father!! Listen--how much he toiled for you,
how much did he labor for you! If in the past you have not[*T1] honored
him you must now honor him lest he inscribe[E1] all his property to others."

---

* F: You have not honored   --Ln: I have honored

T1. Ln ("I have honored") may be a euphemism for F's reading ("You
have not honored Him").

L1. See Fürst, p. 198 s.v. קטרון who discusses the textual readings.

E1. See Justin Martyr's <u>Dialogue with Trypho</u>[(B 261)] (p. 350, ch. 30),
"For just as you angered Him...so has He deemed them, idolaters,
worthy to know His will and to share His inheritance." Also see <u>ibid</u>.
p. 352, ch. 132.

So Moses spoke to Israel: If you do not remember the miracles
and wonders that the Holy One, Blessed Be He, did for you in Egypt,
acknowledge how many kindnesses He will ultimately provide for you in
the World to Come.

"O foolish people and unwise":

"Foolish -- about that which is past.[E2]

"And unwise" -- about the Future to Come.

A similar exegesis is:

"But Israel doth not know"[S1] -- about the past.

"My people doth not consider"[S2]-- about the Future.

And what was the cause that made Israel to be foolish and unwise?
--They did not gain enlightenment through the words of the Torah. And
so does Scripture state, "Is not their tent-cord plucked within them?
They die, and that without wisdom."[S3] [E3]

S1. Isaiah 1:3.   S2. Isaiah 1:3.   S3. Job 4:21.

E2. The phrases are read together as a single thought: "If you are
foolish about that which is past, then you learn nothing from past
mistakes and you will be doomed to repeat them unwisely and thus cause
yourselves ill fortune in the Future to Come." Thus, this pericope is a
continuation of the section which immediately preceded it and which
pointed out that the Jew has no cause to hurl insult at God and may
suffer serious consequences if he continues to do so. If Israel were not
ignorant of the past favors and the future bliss that God provides the
Jews she would not revile the Lord. In this pericope the verse is
explained to mean that Israel is indeed ignorant of the past help God has
given and of the future happiness that God has promised. The midrashist,
aware that every word of Scripture is to be interpreted, finds the
apparently redundant phrases "foolish" and "without wisdom" to mean that
Israel lacks two kinds of knowledge -- that of the past and that of the
future. He supports this interpretation by showing that Scriptural
proof texts warrant this conclusion.

E3. The "tent-cord" is the peg of learning; it is the Torah word. The
proof text is read in such a way as to show that the failure to use

"Is He not thy Father קנך"[L2]

Shimon the son of Halafta says:[*T2] If you were a weak person on
top and there was a strong warrior beneath, who would prevail? Could
you perhaps subdue him! And all the more so will the upper party
prevail when the strong warrior is above and the weak person beneath.
And so does Scripture state: "Be not rash with thy mouth and let not
thy heart be hasty to utter a word before God; for God is in heaven
and thou upon earth."[S4 E4]

---

the "inner tent-cord (enlightenment from the Torah)" has resulted in "un-
wisdom". Thus the proof text is seen to explain the verse, "O
foolish people and unwise". The causes and effects of history can
only be appreciated through the "words of the Torah". Cf. Tanna Deve
Eliahu ch. 30 concerning Jeremiah 10:20 - just as it is impossible for
a tent to exist without pegs and tent cords so is it impossible for
Israel to exist without scholars. --Tent-cords (מיתרי) refers to the
scholars of Israel who permit the permitted and forbid the forbidden
and are for Israel as eternal tent-cords. (Seder Eliahu Rabba,[(B 42)]
p. 148).

* Ln: Rabbi Shimon the son of Halafta says in his(?) name.

S4. Ecclesiastes 5:1.

T2. Not clear whose name is meant in Ln -- Halafta's? Perhaps the
passage was taken from elsewhere and tradent's name has now been lost.

L2. See further E4 for a speculative interpretation based on Greek
homophony. It is possible that קנך here has been understood as "he has
dominion over you," "who subdues you"{cf. BDB s.v. קנה, also see Is. 1:3
(קונהו) and Num. R. 4:4 (He girds his loins with a belt like a slave
before his master i.e. קונו)}

E4. The sense of Deut. 32:6 is that one is foolish to think he can
spite God with impunity. Perhaps, the verse has been understood as if
part of it were in Greek (by homophony): "Could you act so to God?
-You are foolish and senseless people (=common fool).-- cf. Haupert[(B188)]
Heb: halo / hu / avi   ka / ka   neka /   ,
Gk: ἀλλὰ / ὁπὸ / (τοῦ)   κακοῦ /   νικῶ /   ,--
But rather let yourself be vanquished beneath the hand of an evil man!"
So it is that our various Sifre midrashim speak here of a conquering
hero (νικησας   ), insulting (νεικος) an officer (i.e. an evil

"Is He not thy Father that hath gotten thee":

Moses said to Israel: You are his beloveds, you are his

acquisition, but you are not His inheritance.[E5]

This is comparable to the matter of one whose father bequeathed

ten fields to him. He arose and acquired a field of his own and he

loved it better than all the fields his father bequeathed him. And

likewise it is comparable to the matter of one whose father bequeathed

him ten residences and he arose and acquired one residence of his own

and he loved that one more than all the residences his father had left

him.

So Moses said to Israel, "You are His beloveds; you are His

acquisition; you are not his inheritance."

Roman, Κακos), and insulting one's father (אביך). Does the Greek lie
behind our Hebrew Sifre versions so that ὑπὸ τοῦ κα(κοῦ)
= הפתקם (councillor)? If so our Hebrew Sifre reflects homophonous
explanations of a Greek "midrash" which itself is a homophonous explanation of a Hebrew verse! (cf. Romans 12:21 : μὴ νικῶ ὑπὸ τοῦ κακοῦ ,
Romans 12:19 refers to Deut 32:35 while Romans 13:1-7 speaks of being
subject to God and authority --Would you have no fear of him who is in
authority?-- Does Paul know of a sermon similar to our midrash?)

E5. Justin Martyr, Dialogue with Trypho,(B 261) p. 338f, ch. 123, shows
that the Gentiles are the "inheritance". Our midrash is concerned with
showing that what Christians called "the election of the Jews" is not
shared with others. The midrashist wishes to show that the Jews are more
than God's "inheritance". Israel did not automatically "fall" to God
because they were descended from Abraham. God possessed them by saving
them from the Egyptian bondage. It may well be that such a notion was
known to Josephus who never uses the Septuagint term for covenant,
"diatheke", because the word implies "testament" and "inheritance".

"That possesses thee" (קנך):

This is one of the three which are called "possessions of God" (קנין). The Torah is called "God's possession", as it is said, "The Lord possessed me as the beginning of his way."[S5] [E6] "Israel is called God's possession", as it is said, "Is He not thy Father that possesses thee." The Temple is called "God's possession",[T3] and so does Scripture state, "This mountain, which His right hand had possessed."[S6]

"Hath He not made thee and thy כונן":

Rabbi Meir used to say: The walled[L3] city[E7] that contains all:

S5. Proverbs 8:22.   S6. Psalms 78:54.

T3. Ln appears to be corrupt, the scribe having omitted words later filled them in awkwardly. The text is surely meant to be like that of F.

L3. Perhaps כרכא here refers to a bundle as in Syriac, cf. Aruch Compl., s.v. כרך and as such it midrashically renders כונן which can have the sense of that which is "tied" or "twisted". See M. Moreshet and Y. Klein "בשורש כנן בלשון חז'ל באנאלוגיה לאכדית" Lĕšōnenū , vol. 40 (1976), no. 2, p. 95ff. Also see, Ch. Rabin, "הערות לשרש קנן/כנן" Lĕšōnenū ,vol. 40 (1976), no. 3-4, p. 291f.

E6. The speaker of the verse is supposed to be Wisdom, identified by the Rabbis as "Torah". See "E6", Piska 317.

E7. כרכא refers to something twisted. I have followed Rashi to B. T. Hulin 56b in translating "walled city". Josephus, Antiquities (ed. Thackery), 14: 115-116 refers to Abraham using such a picture: "From a single sire, ye have grown so great".

Priests from its midst, prophets from its midst, sages from its
midst, scribes from its midst. And likewise does Scripture state,
"Out of them shall come forth the corner-stone, out of them the
stake...."[S7]

Rabbi Yehuda says: He made you full of cavities.[E8]

Rabbi Shimon the son of Yehuda says: He placed you upon your
foundation;[E9] He stuffed you with the plunder of the Seven Nations.[L4]
He gave you what He promised you and He bequeathed to you what He
promised you. Rabbi Dostaye the son of Yehuda says: He arranged
your inner structure to be full of chambers such if one of them would
infringe upon another, you could not exist.[E10]

END OF PISKA

S7. Zechariah 10:4.

L4. The foundation (כונן) here refers to the Land. Thus the seven
nations refer to those nations which inhabited Canaan before Joshua
destroyed them. Cf. Deut. 20:14 and Joshua 11:14.

E8. The midrash takes ויכוננך as if it were כינין (chambers).

E9. The midrashist understands ויכוננך as כונן "to make a base". For
the use of the past tense in this homily see E. Sanders, Paul etc.; (B 302)
p. 104.

E10. The midrash here ingeniously captures the intent of the scriptural
verse: You are so frail; how can you challenge God? Think of all
you owe God who arranged your inner structure in order.

7

"Remember the days of old":

He said to them: Remember what I did to the first Generations,[T1]

that which I did to the people of the Generation of the Flood, and

that which I did to the people of the Generation[T1] of the Dispersion

and that which I did to the People of Sodom.

"Consider the years of generations and generations":

You do not find a generation in which there is not the likes

of the people of the Generation of the Flood and you do not find

a   generation in which there is not the likes of the People of

Sodom; however, each one[E1] is judged according to his deeds.

T1. Possibly omitted in Ln due to homoioteleuton ("What I did
to the people of").

E1. The preacher begins by rephrasing the verse so that "days of old"
is understood as "first Generations". He then looks at the next verse
(Deut. 32:8, see Piska 311) and interprets בהנחל (see "L4" Piska 311)
as if it referred to a current downflow (נחל). The "current downflow"
is seen as an allusion to the Flood and the Inundation of Sodom by fire
and brimstone. Schorr, p. 13 says הנחל = ἀνοχλέω   (remove them
harshly). Likewise the verse "When He separated the children of men"
becomes an allusion to the Dispersion of the people of the Tower of
Babel. Now the midrashist also notes that the term "days of old" refers
to group happenings (as opposed to an event that happens to an individual) which recur because the group as a whole is told to remember them
as evidenced by the use of the singular verb --   , זכור .   On
the other hand, the parallel   phrase, "generation and generation" must
then refer to individual happenings which are to be constantly considered
since the verb בניו is in the plural form which suggests that
individuals are being addressed separately. Thus the apparent redun-
dancy of the terms "days of old" and "generation and generation" is
explained as referring to different time periods, the one to events
(group punishments) prior to the fall of Sodom, the other (individual
punishments) after the fall. The preacher seems to indicate (cf. Piska
311) why the story of Abraham's tribulation is told in Gen. 20 following
the story of the fall of Sodom when it appears to properly belong in the
cycle of Gen. 12 ff. The point is that we have a contrast between group
punishments and individual punishments. Deut. 32:7 refers to two
generations according to the midrashist -- "generation and generation".
He takes the dual reference to be to both the Generation of the Flood

"Ask thy father and he will declare unto thee":

This refers to the <u>Prophets</u>.[L1] It is according to the Scripture

which states, "And Elisha saw it and he cried, "My father, my

father....".[S1 E2]

"Thine elders and they will tell you":

This refers to the <u>Elders</u>.[L2] It is according to the Scripture

which states, "Gather unto Me seventy men of the Elders of Israel...."[S2]

Another interpretation:

"Remember the days of עולם":

He said to them: Whenever the Holy One, Blessed Be He, brings

---

and the Generation of Sodom. In constructing the verse to refer to
individuals (בינו -- plural) he finds that we are no better than these
"years"(Schorr, p. 13, says שנות = συνήθης   i.e. of like habits)
of the two evil generations but our punishments are meted out individual-
ly rather than groupwise. This allows the world to continue. He concludes that we should not assume that because God has not brought upon us
a communal disaster that we are better than earlier generations or
that God does not punish anymore. Cf. Ben Sira 1:10. Also see
Gen. 18:23:Sodomites as individuals.

S1. 2 Kings 2:12.   S2. Numbers 11:16.

L1. The Rabbis considered the Prophets and Elders to have been the
custodians of the Oral Tradition handed to Moses at Sinai. (Cf.
Jer. 7:25; Amos 2:7; Joshua 24:31; Judges 2:7) see Mishna Avoth 1:1,
ARN ("A" and "B") 1:1.

L2. See "L1" above.

E2. Cf.F.'s <u>New Light From the Prophets</u>,[(B 156)] p. 33ff. and p. 121. L.
F. thinks much of the Sifre material dates from the time of the Exile
(p. 23) but that references in Sifre Deut. to demons and to the Four
Kingdoms were added at a later date (see Piska 313, "E14" and "E17").

suffering upon you, remember how many good things and consolations[L3]
He will ultimately bestow upon you in the World to Come.[E3]

"Consider the years of generation and generation":

This refers to the Generation of the Messiah which will have in

it three generations,[E4] as it is said, "They shall fear you as long as

the sun endureth and so long as the moon, throughout generation --

generations."[S3] [E5]

S3. Psalms 72:5.

L3. In this pericope עולם is taken as עולם הבא .
The midrashist introduces the notion of consolation here because he
understands from the verse that Israel must consider the goodness to
come in the future. But how can Israel know the future? The midrashist
assumes that one need do no more than examine the Song of Moses, Deut.
32:36 -- ועל עבדיו יתנחם which he acknowledges as alluding to the
bestowing of comforts in the Next World.

E3. See E. Sanders, Paul etc.,[(B 302)] p. 169ff. The sense of "עולם "
here is taken as "עולם הבא " i.e. Remember "The World to Come
(=ימות עולם)".

E4. See J. Klausner, Messianic Idea in Israel,[(B231)] p. 408ff. Also see
ibid. p. 420-426. Cf. Y. Zakovitch, The Pattern of the Numerical
Sequence 3-4 in the Bible,[(B 354)] Hebrew University (Ph.D. diss.), p.177,
where it is claimed that punishment lasts three generations while redemption comes in the fourth according to the model of the promise given to
Abraham (Gen. 15:16) where redemption of Israel is based on the fulness
of the sins of the Amorites. Also see R. Le Déaut, La Nuit Pascale,[(B 242)]
p. 147ff.

E5. The midrash is based upon the observation that the literal
"generation -- generations" can refer to no less than three generations
since a singular generation refers to one while a plural refers to no
less than two. The sum is no less than three generations.

Piska 310

"Ask thy Father and He will declare unto thee":

In the Future Era Israel is destined to see and hear as they

who hear from the mouth of the Holy One,[E6] Blessed Be He, as it is

said, "And thy ears shall hear a word behind thee, saying...."[S4]

And Scripture also states, "Yet shall not thy Teacher hide

Himself anymore but thine eyes shall see thy Teacher."[S5]

"Thine elders and they will tell you":

Of that which I showed the Elders on the mountain. This is

according to the matter of which Scripture speaks, as it is said,

"And unto Moses He said: Come up unto the Lord...."[S6] [E7]

END OF PISKA

S4. Isaiah 30:21.   S5. Isaiah 30:20.
S6. Exodus 24:1.

E6. Elitism will not be part of the Future existence. All will be
capable of the highest visions. (See "E4" to Piska 336.) יגד is taken
in the sense of "He (Father God) will 'teach' you" -- cf. B.T.
Pes. 52b.

E7. What has been related by tradition will be personally experienced
in the future -- there will be no doubts. The mountain referred to
here is Sinai. According to the end of the verse 70 Elders beheld
a vision on Horeb.

8

"When the Most High gave to the nations their inheritance":

Before Father Abraham came, the Holy One, Blessed Be He -- as if

it were possible -- judged the world ruthlessly. When the people of

the Generation of the Flood sinned, He inundated them as[*] the winds

upon the surface of the waters. When the People of the Tower sinned

He scattered them from one end of the world to the other. When the

People of Sodom sinned He destroyed them with brimstone and fire.

But when Father Abraham came to the world he achieved the merit

of accepting the suffering which gradually[E1] began to be manifested.

This is according to the Scripture which states, "Now there was a

famine in the Land and Abram went down to Egypt."[S1]

---

* Ln: בזיקים   = by means of strong winds (preferred reading by
  L. Silberman).

S1. Genesis 12:10.

E1. General Introduction to Piska 311 and 312
   The verses cited in these piskaot have midrashic fields
(comparisons of Israel and the nations referring to ratio of 1:2,
rejection of Torah by nations, nations in Hell) which are also
witnessed by the later midrashim. These later midrashim may provide
insights to help us understand our Sifre texts:
   Tanhuma Buber Beha'alotecha para. 16, 52:
   Do not mix with those who say there are two gods in the world for
   their destiny is to perish from the world as it is said, "And
   there shall be in all the earth, saith the Lord, a double portion
   that shall be annihilated and the third part shall remain there
   (Zech. 13:8)." Who is meant by the "third part"? It is Israel,
   as it is said, "On that day Israel shall be its third part...
   (Is. 19:24)."

   Tanhuma Buber Shoftim, para. 9f., p. 32:
   It teaches us that God came around to all the Gentile Nations of
   the World and they did not accept it... the Holy One, Blessed Be
   He, shall bring down the Gentile Nations of the World to Gehenna...
   "And there shall be in all the earth, saith the Lord, a double portion that shall be annihilated and the third part shall remain
   there."....This refers to Israel who are of the third part of the

earth, children of three fathers.

Tanhuma Buber Bamidbar, para. 10, p. 9:
So the Holy One, Blessed Be He, created seventy nations and He
did not find pleasure in any of them save in Israel...and He loved
none but Israel...and Scripture states,"There are sixty queens
(and eighty concubines and maidens without number), My dove,
my perfect one, is only one...(Canticles 6:8f)." This refers to
Sinai from whence He taught me Torah...

Tanhuma Buber Shmini, para. 10, p. 28:
"He stood and measured the earth...(Hab. 3:6)."...if it had not
been for Israel who accepted it (Torah)..."He looked and shook the
nations" -- R. Aha said: He shook them into Gehenna. ,

Devarim Rabba, Lieberman, Ve'etchanan, p. 65:
"And there shall be in all the earth, saith the Lord, a double
portion that shall be annihilated and the third part shall remain
there."...This refers to Israel, as it is said,"Israel shall be its
third part."...such did God apportion his world to the Gentile
Nations of the world as it is said, "When the Most High gave the
nations their inheritance (Deut. 32:8)."...You chose Me so I
chose you -- from whom did Israel gain this merit?...Abraham my
grandfather sired two sons (good Isaac and evil Ishmael)...so did
my father sire two sons (good Jacob and evil Esau)...And I (Jacob)
sired twelve sons (all of them good).
Also cf. Deut. R. 2:23, Num. R. 15:14 and Tosefta Sukka 4:12.
The complexities of our Sifre text can now be seen to involve three
major themes.   Like Abraham 1) Israel accepted God's gift (suffering and
Torah) and 2) Israel is separated from the other nations by a ratio
of one to two and 3) Israel is destined for glory while the others are
destined for punishment.   As for this 1:2 ratio we may note that the
"midrashic fields" above centred upon Zech. 13:8 and Is. 19:24.   These
verses may lie behind our Sifre texts as well where:
2 generations are destroyed but Abraham survives in exile;
2 nations of Ishmael and Esau (and others) (total 140) refuse God's
Torah while Children of Israel (=Jacob) (sum of 70) go into exile.
The midrash implies openly that Abraham's legacy (to be numerous as
stars and to be God's people) is only to go to the children of Jacob
while the legacy of the two generations (punishment and torment)
is destined for the other nations.   Just as Abraham accepted suffering for the sake of heaven, so did the Children of Israel accept
the Torah.   A close reading of the proof texts concerning Abraham's
descent to Egypt and Israel's descent there will show this to be
the case.   The point of our midrash is now clarified.   The sequence
of traditions signalled by progressive units of "another interpretation" moves "chronologically" from the remote-past traditions to
the end-of-days traditions.

The final proof text cited in Piska 311 is enlightening:
"With seventy souls your ancestors came down into Egypt (and now
the Lord your God has set you as the stars of the heavens for a
multitude)." This text of Deut. 10:32 parallels Gen. 12:10
mentioning Abraham's descent into Egypt which opened the Piska
and also reminds us of the legacy of God's promise to Abraham
(i.e. his children would be numerous as the stars and so Marqah
4:10 explains the verse למספר בני ישראל:ויהי זרעך ככוכבי שומיה)
Thus, we are brought into our Ha'azinu text once again by associating these progressions throughout Israelite history with our verse--
"according to the number of the Children of Israel."
    The proof text of Deut. 10:22 occurs in a Scriptural section which
concludes "and in order that you will prolong your days upon the earth...
a land flowing with milk and honey." The very Scripture itself mirrors
the progressions of the "other interpretations" offered in Sifre. This
Piska also sets the stage for the following Piska 312 which militates
against the idea that any nation can share Israel's legacy.
    See "El." to Piska 310 for the initial midrashic exegesis of Deut.
32:8. It is probable that Abraham is meant to be the recipient of the
suffering here rather than the world (עולם); for, as we saw in Piska
310, the point here seems to be that punishments became individual after
the Generations of the Dispersion and Sodom. Indeed, we find that
Abraham argues in Gen. 18:23 against the concept of group punishment.
Perhaps the further point of the midrash here is to posit that suffering
allows the punishment to be protracted over a period of time and allows
the individual to continue his life. The group thus survives, albeit in
an unhappy state. Thus suffering was seen as an instrument, of protection and hence of mercy, which protected against the harms which were
due to arrive because of sin. On this point see K. Grayston, "Hilaskesthai and related words in LXX", NTS, vol 27, Oct. 1981, no. 5., p. 640ff,
for the "cruelty of God" towards the Generation of the Flood see
Marmorstein, Old Rabbinic Doctrine,(B 260)p. 207. For the expression
כביכול see S. Schechter, "Some Aspects of Rabbinic Theology I," JQR vol.
6 (1894), p. 419,n. 2.
    Urbach, Sages, p. 526 discusses the implications of suffering in
this passage from 2 Maccabees:
        That our people were being punished by way of chastening and not
        for their destruction. For indeed it is a mark of great kindness
        when the impious are not let alone for a long time, but punished
        at once. In the case of other nations, the Sovereign Lord in His
        forbearance refrains from punishing them until they have filled up
        their sins to the full, but in our case, He has determined otherwise,
        that His vengeance may not fall on us in after-days when our sins
        have reached their height. Wherefore He never withdraweth his
        mercy from us; and though He chasteneth His own people with calam-
        ity, He forsaketh them not.
    We find here a thought that is expressed in our Sifre passage which
claims that in prior times God let sins pile up against peoples until
they were obliterated in a single blow. But in the time of Abraham,

And if you should ask: Why does suffering come? --Because of
the belovedness[**] [T1] of Israel: "He set the גבולות of the peoples
according to the number of the sons of Israel."[L1] [E2]

---

punishments were administered immediately after infractions so
that there would not result an accumulation of punishment which
would obliterate Israel. See further S. Schechter, Studies in
Judaism (1st. series),[B308] Philadelphia, JPS, 1919, p. 225-232.
     Urbach attributes to R. Akiba the notion that suffering is a
privilege and is not related to the idea of suffering for the sake of
atonement. E.P. Sanders,[B301] ("Rabbi Akiba's View of Suffering",
JQR, vol. 53 (1973), 332ff.) thinks Akiba did view suffering as a means
of atonement and not a "privilege". However, a careful analysis of
Sanders' criticisms shows that Urbach's premise, that "beloved is
suffering" midrashim are a result of the reflection of Jews upon the
Hadrianic persecutions and the ensuing revolt, is quite plausible.
That the reason for this "belovedness" is purely privilege or atonement
is not clearly discernible in the sources and both concepts may have
been current. That the Jews suffered persecution for their adherence
to the law was perhaps best understood in terms of one view at one
occasion while the other view was more advantageous at another occasion.
The ultimate theology that derived from this was evident in the
tradition which questioned the martyrdom of Akiba by responding[B95]
"Silence! So I have decided!" (see further W. Bacher, Tannaim,
vol. 1,[B249] pt. 2, pgs. 66ff. and S. Lieberman, Tosefta Kifshuta, Moed,
p. 824). We have already seen at the end of Piska 306 that
the greatest act that a person can perform is to suffer so that through
this suffering God's saving of the remnant will be made manifest to all
others in the world. God would choose for such an important service
only the most beloved of all. This is not to deny that sinners may
suffer as atonement for their sins and this too is an indication of
one's belovedness. The nations will be judged at once and destroyed
on account of the accumulation of their sins (see Piska 321 further),
not so Israel, who is beloved amongst the nations.

** F: חיבתך   -- Ln: חובתן , their sins.

T1. Ln seems corrupt --חובת as compared with F --חיבת .

L1. This verse belongs here since it is a proof text which shows the
belovedness of Israel. To the extent it is seen to declare that
all the world turmoil revolves upon the relationship between Israel
and the Land, the verse serves the homilist's purpose. The homilist
takes יצב of Deut. 32:8 as if it were related to צבא , "to take
delight in". Perhaps גבול is seen as גמול or as חבל so that the
verse is read as: "There is international turmoil for He takes
delight in the numbers of the Children of Israel." According to Targ.

Another tradition:

"When the Most High gave to the nations their inheritance":

When the Most High gave the world to the nations He separated the boundaries of every nation in order that they should not become inter- mixed. He sent the Gomerians to Gomer, the Magogians to Magog, the Medians to Media, the Yavonites to Yavon, the Tubalites to Tubal. He separated the boundaries of the nations in order that they should not enter the Land of Israel: "He set the borders of the peoples."

Another interpretation:

"When the Most High gave to the nations their inheritance":

When the Holy One, Blessed Be He, gave the Torah to Israel, He stood and looked out[E3] and contemplated, as it is said, "He standeth

---

Ps. -Jon. (Deut. 32:8), lots (יצב = פיס') were cast and Israel won God's land. Thus they fell to be His beloved .

E2. The proof text here may intend to teach that the borders of the nations have been designed to incorporate the exiled number of Jews. Thus exile is either a punishment or a protective device which comes as a result of God's great love for Israel. See the meshalim in Yalkut Shimoni Deut. (B 60) 850 which relates the midrash of Gen. R. 40:2 to the concept of "afflictions of love" (cf. Yalkut Shimoni 303). See also E. Sanders, Paul, etc., (B 302) p. 189ff. I am not certain if the midrash- ist of our Sifre passage here intends us to take the verse as literally stated in the Hebrew text or whether he wants us to think of מספר as מסבל and גבול as גמול . While such transformations are midrashically possible they are not necessary here to read the midrash.

E3. צפה (looked out) may be taken as "looked into the future" accord- ing to E. Sanders, Paul etc., (B 302) P. 92 (citing Taylor). See also Marmorstein, Old Rabbinic Doctrine, (B 260) p. 156, n. 22, and also see Moore, Notes, (B 271) Vol. 3, n. 48 to Vol. 1, p. 278. The text of the midrash plays upon the words "יצב the borders of the peoples". The word is often used to mean "to stand" but also "to be in a prophetic state" (e.g. Ex. 33:21, Ex. 34:2). It also refers to one in a state to divulge a prophecy (e.g. Gen. 38:13, Num. 22:23, Ps. 118:89). Thus our midrashist is not engaging in mere word play when he renders (interchang- ing ב with פ) יצב as צפה . The verse is taken to mean that God

and measureth the earth, He looks and makes the nations to tremble."[S2] [L2]

And there was no nation amongst the nations which was worthy to receive

the Torah except Israel: "He set the borders of the peoples."

---

prophetically visited the nations but divulged His Word (ספר) to
Israel alone. Cf. L. Silberman,"A Survival Myth", CCARJ. Sum. '77.
Incidentally it is interesting to note (we may be concerned with
anti-Jewish Polemic) that Justin Martyr, Dialogue with Trypho, [B261]
p. 350, ch. 131 takes this verse in The Song of Moses to mean that the
Gentiles are heirs to God's promises together with Israel. See "E6" to
Piska 311. Urbach, Sages, [B339] p. 291f, makes the point that both
the Rabbis and Philo understood the word גבול to refer to Oral
traditions and he cites evidence; thus גבולות = Torah. Also, Philo may
have Deut. 32:8 in mind when he comments, (Conf. ch. 128, 145, [B34]),
that the one portion granted to Israel is virtue, i.e. "tradition and
law" (does tradition mean Oral Torah here and law mean written Torah?),
because Philo Plant. [B34] does use this verse to show that "virtue is
the hegemony of God". Ben Sira, [B44] like Targ. Neofiti [B53] 1 and
the Targ. Yerushalmi in the Rabbinic Bible (cf. B.29) understands that
the Land of Israel (or Canaan) was divided into twelve sections even
before the Israelites arrived:ויציבהו לשבטים לחלק שנים עשר
(Ben Sira 44:32, Targum Neof. and Yerushalmi to Deut. 32:8). Also cf.
Philo Post. [B34] ch. 26-27, 89-92 and Ben Sira [B44] 50:25. As for
the Septuagint reading, "sons of God (i.e. angels), we may note that our
midrashist may have this tradition in mind thinking that God offered all
the guardian angels of the nations His Law but Israel was victorious in
getting it. Ben Sira [B44] knows a version of the LXX reading as well
(17:17): הקים שר . Milik, Enoch, [B268] p. 254 cites a fragment in
4Q: גבולות עמים למספר בני אלים .
Cf. W.F. Albright,"Some Remarks on the Song of Moses in Deut. 32," VT
9 [B89] p. 343. Targum Ps. Jon. knows of the tradition in the
Septuagint. Cf. Moore, Notes, [B271] vol. 3, p. 62, n. 2 to vol. 1,
p. 244. See also Conclusion n. 7.

S2. Habakuk 3:6.

L2. Since the proof text verse ends הליכות עולם לו and since B.T.
Sotah 22a (see Mishna ad loc. and B.T. Megilla 28b) finds these words
to refer to "הלכה " we may suppose that הליכות here has been understood to refer to the laws of the Torah.

Another interpretation:

"When the Most High gave to the nations their inheritance":

When the Holy One, Blessed Be He, gave the Gentile Nations of the World their inheritance, their portion was in Gehinnom, as it is said: "Assyria is there and all her company...";[S3] "There are the princes of the North and all the Zidonians";[S4] "There is Edom, her kings...."[S5 E4]

And if you should ask: "Who shall take their wealth and their glory?" --I should say, "It is Israel.": "He set גבולות [L3 E5] of the peoples."

S3. Ezekiel 32:22.   S4. Ezekiel 32:30.   S5. Ezekiel 32:29.

L3. Perhaps the midrashist has added an embellishment to his interpretation by taking גבול in its sense of "fattening up" as in B.T. Baba Mezia 69a.

E4. The end of the proof verse reads "with them that go down to the pit" (i.e. to hell).

E5. The preacher understands the verse to mean: "He will give the territories of the peoples to the numbers of the Children of Israel." The proof text here is from Hab. 3:6 and is also used in a similar tradition in Lev. R. 13:2. In Lev. R. [B 28] the tradition is stated in the name of Shimon bar Yochai, (p. 272ff.). The Amoraim (Lev. R. p. 274) state a tradition concerning the verse of Hab. 3:6 and play upon its wording to the effect that the wealth of the nations and their royal belts (i.e. their authority) are to be removed (התיר a play upon ויתר Hab. 3:6). Thus the question arose, "Who gains these things?". The answer is now found in Deut. 32:8 "He will set the properties of the nations to the multitude of Israel." Since our midrash uses the expression "wealth and glory" it may be that our pericope is related to that of Lev. R. 13:2 where we hear that Rav suggested wealth was taken and Rabbi Huna (רבה דציפורי - probably a student of Yochanan) suggested the glory of royal power was taken.

Another interpretation:

"When the Most High gave to the nations their inheritance":

When the Holy One, Blessed Be He, gave His inheritance -- it was through[E6] those nations which were fearful of sin and honest.[E7]

"When He separated the children of men":

This refers to[*] the Generation of the Dispersion, as it is said, "And from thence did the Lord scatter[L4] them abroad upon the face of all the earth."[S6] [E8]

---

[*] Ln: This refers to Lot, as it is said, "And they separated themselves, the one from the other." S6a.

S6. Genesis 11:9.   S6a. (Ln) Genesis 13:11.

L4. The midrashist understands "הפריד" as "scattering" and proves his point by taking "יצב" as its parallel in vs. 8. "יצב" is then equated with "נפץ" (interchanging ב and פ), the word used to describe the scattering of the generation of the Dispersion in Gen. 11:8f. Rashi (to Deut. 32:8) seems to equate יצב with הצף (=שטף, drown) which then suggests the water punishments given to the Generation of the Flood and the torrents of fire which destroyed Sodom. This is the inheritance of the nations {נחל = inheritance = downflow = inundation (cf. עיקר שפתי חכמים to Deut. 32:8)}.

E6. The text reads הנחיל מן which means "inherited from". The sense requires that we understand that God gave the inheritance to them. The word from here is a literary device, a euphemism or wishful thought. Cf. E. Sanders, Paul, etc.(B 302) p. 207 and A. Marmorstein who sees a reference here to the pious gentiles receiving a share in future life, Doctrine of Merits,(B 260) p. 192.

E7. The word "עליון" in the verse is considered here in the sense of "upright". This tradition may be quite old and form the basis of Justin Martyr's comment referred to in "E3" to Piska 311. This passage may refer to the concept of "the righteous of the nations". See also E. Sanders, Paul etc.,(B 302) p. 207.

E8. Perhaps pericope "E7" continues in "E8" and the sense is -- originally God gave land to the righteous nations but then they became corrupt. Cf. Marqah(B 16) 4:10 "...possesses the land and all those boundaries appointed from the days of Peleg for in his days the earth was divided (Gen. 10:25)."

Rabbi Eliezer the son of Rabbi Yosi Haglili says: Behold

Scripture states, "There are three score queens and four score

concubines."[S7] The sum is one hundred and forty. The number of our

ancestors which descended to Egypt was but "seventy souls",[E9] as it is

---

Targum Pseudo-Jonathon to Deut. 32:8 states:
WHEN THE MOST HIGH GAVE TO THE NATIONS THEIR INHERITANCE
--when the Most High gave the inheritance to those peoples who
came from the children of Noah.
WHEN HE SEPARATED THE CHILDREN OF MEN
--when He separated the scripts and languages of the children of
men in the Generation of the Dispersion.
HE SET THE BORDERS OF THE PEOPLES ACCORDING TO THE NUMBER OF THE
CHILDREN OF ISRAEL
--at that time He cast lots with the seventy angels, the princes
of the peoples, with whom He had gone to see the city. And at
that time He established the borders of the peoples according
to the number of the seventy souls of Israel who went down to
Egypt.
FOR THE PORTION OF THE LORD IS HIS PEOPLE
--and when the lot of the Holy One fell upon the Holy Nation, Michael
opened his mouth and said, "For the blessed portion is of the
name of the Memra of the Lord."
    Now the comment of Sifre here זה דור הפלגה; suggests that the
homilist had before him the tradition as in Targ. Ps.-Jon:"דור הפלגה ".
His point is the nation of Israel is the reference point from which
history develops. Nevertheless, one may posit that the homilist knows
of the interpretation of the Septuagint and the Targ. Ps.-Jon.(which
also preserves the Septuagint tradition) and has fought against it
by showing that the verse refers to "female" borders of "queens and
concubines" and in Piska 309 this homilist or another states that
Israel is no mere windfall but an actual entity which God bound to
himself.

S7. Song of Songs 6:8.

E9. Here Israel is seen to be one of the three major peoples of the
world. Perhaps the Rabbis held the notion that Persia, Rome and
Israel dominate the ideologies of the world. Targ. Onk. to Deut. 32:8
understands that Israel dominates one half of the world --70 nations
and 70 descendants of Jacob. See Moore, Notes, (B 271) vol. 3, p. 62,
n. 2 to vol. 1, p. 227. S. Lieberman, Greek etc., (B 248) p. 15, n. 2
connects an Incantation text republished by Deissmann, which mentions
140 languages, with our pericope.
    What number is meant in Deut. 32:8 (=number of Children of Israel)?
Both the traditions of the Septuagint reading and the Massoretic reading

said, "Thy father went down into Egypt with three score and ten

persons."[S8] And likewise does Scripture state, "The borders of the

peoples": -- "גבולי עמים" "[T2] is not written here but "גבולות עמים". *[L5]

_____

were known to Ben Sira:
   Septuagint reads in Deut. 32:8 -angelon theou; cf. S. Hidal,
   "Reflections etc."[B198] p. 16, and "Qumran Fragment" (Milik,
   Enoch,[B268] p. 254):   יצר גבולות עמים
למספר בני אלים   which suggests 70.

On the other hand Yerushalmi and Neofiti Targums read (cf. B.T.
Hag. 12b): קבע תחומים לאומיא למנין שבטיא דבני ישראל   which suggests
12.

Ben Sira 17:17 (p. 103) reads (cf. Greek Version) הקים שר in a paraphrase
of Deut. 32:8 (suggesting 70) while Ben Sira 44:32 (p. 307) reads also in
a paraphrase of this verse: ויציבהו לשבטים לחלק שנס עשר   (suggesting 12)
(Cf. Marqah 4:10 -- למספר בני ישראל ויהי זרעך ככוכבי
שומיה תרין עשר לעל תרין עשר לרע)

L.F, in his notes to Piska 311, mentions a manuscript commentary
which explains our pericope in reference to the descendants of the sons
of Noah, Amon, Moab and Edom and in reference to the descendants of
the concubines of Abraham, Ishmael and Esau. The preacher sees Israel
as one of three dominant influences in the world. The other two world
powers he has in mind may well have been Parthia and Rome. He has thus
interpreted the verse --"number of Israel (מספר is sing.) "=70,
the territories of the nations (גבולות is plural)" =140, --to show that
the non-Jewish empires derive their power from the divine plan which
fixed the political set-up of the world in accordance with Israel's
position. Such sermons undoubtedly gave the Jews a feeling of international importance in a world which was in political and ideological
struggle against them. The plan of history had been laid out in
Scripture and redemption had been promised. If the subjugation had
already come to be, could redemption be far away?

* Ln: "גבול עם " is not written here but, "He set גבולות עמים ".

S8. Deuteronomy 10:22.

T2. Ln reads --גבול as compared with F --גבולות . Ln distinguishes
between singular and plural forms. F distinguishes between male and
female forms. The female form גבולות may have been taken as an
allusion to the queens and concubines in the major proof text.

L5. The crux of this interpretation depends upon L.F.'s observation that
גבולות here is in the feminine form and so must refer to females
--60 queens and 80 concubines.

The Gentile Nations of the world merit to possess a double portion
in relation "to the number of the Children of Israel".

END OF PISKA

9

"For the portion of the Lord is His people":

This is comparable to the matter of the king who had a field[El] and

---

El. This parable uses the "inheritance" image of Deut. 32:8. It is
possible that the LXX reading "sons of God" has influenced this parable
so that "True sons of God" (spiritual heirs) is paralleled with "His
people, Jacob" (vs. 9.) (B 261) Justin Martyr, Dialogue with Trypho,
p. 350, ch. 131, and p. 331, ch. 119, interprets the Song of Moses to
support the Christian view of the legitimate place of the Gentiles in
God's promises. The nations share Israel's legacy because Israel has
shown herself faithless. God promised Abraham a righteous nation of
like faith, and a delight to the Father but it is not the Jews...
"in whom there is no faith (Deut. 32:20)". The term "His people
(Deut. 32:9)" is interpreted by Justin Martyr to mean "the Patriarchs
and the faithful". Also see Sanders, Paul etc., (B 302) p. 92, n. 27;
that the core of the tradition here may be pre-Christian; see Conclusion
no. 7.
     The image of "the field" was popular in Hellenistic times to symbo-
lize the idea of covenant. According to Marqah (4:4), "Abraham planted
a garden and proclaimed there in the name of the Lord (cf. Gen. 21:33)
...Isaac walked in that way...Jacob hastened in that way."
     If the parable has not been formed by reference to the LXX tradition
(so that here King = God; and God's sons = Children of Israel as opposed
to "dreg nations"), then I suggest another good key to the Sifre parable
which is as follows:
          king = God and Patriarchs, (cf. Lichtenstein here) Noah, and Adam
               (refers to covenant).
          the first group of tenant farmers = (Ishmael and the children of
               Ketura --Ln) Flood Generation (F).
          the second group of tenant farmers = (Esau and the chiefs of
               Edom --Ln) Ishmael and the children of Ketura (F)
          the third group = Esau and chiefs of Edom (F)
          son of the king = the sons of Jacob; i.e. the Children of Israel.
     The point is not to find fault with Abraham or Isaac but to show that
their legacy was not worked upon properly by those who should have taken
care of it. That some of their progeny were evil is not the fault of the
Patriarchs. These progeny are neither spiritual descendants nor heirs.
In the parable the tenant farmers (Esau) are made to be ("behavioral")
descendants of earlier farmers. The king's son (12 tribes) is not related
to them ("behaviorally") at all. So it is not so much the question of
blood relationships which is at stake here as it is the question of proper
behavior. The covenant is considered as the Patriarchal (and God's) fields
while the sons of Jacob are considered the Partriarchal son. God and the
Patriarchs(the covenantal partners) can be partial (מכיר) to the property
now that their son is caring for it. The "dregs", though of blood lineage,
are not "true sons" as are the "children of Jacob". These "dregs" have
been set apart from "the number of the Children of Israel" who are the
true heirs.

The midrash is a literary production which sees the Divine and
Patriarchal covenant as land and the unworthies as bad workers of
the land. Ishmael and Esau are seen as a bad line while the 12 tribes
are seen as a good line. As Urbach points out (Sages, p. 530) the closing
midrash here which establishes Jacob as the seal of the Patriarchs is a
later addition to the opening midrash which has a separate theme. The
introductory phrase of this later piece: "From whence does God show
partiality, i.e. associate Himself, to his portion" is artificially
introduced as if to connect the earlier parable with the end section of
the midrash which establishes Jacob as the link between the nation
of Israel and the Patriarchs. This connecting link may erroneously lead
one to interpret the previous midrash as if the "king's son" should
be taken as Jacob himself rather than the tribes, as Eugene Mihaly has
done (HUCA, (B 267) vol. 35 (1964),KTAV, N.Y. 1968., pp. 103-105). In
reality, the midrashim should be taken separately.

Now Mihaly's "A Rabbinic Defense of the Election of Israel"(B 267)
proposes that the parable of this Piska is to be explained as follows:
Israel was elected when God chose Jacob. The "election" of Israel
therefore did not begin with Abraham but with Jacob.

According to Mihaly, the midrash is intended to refute the
Christian position that Abraham was chosen to be the father of the
elect because of his faith prior to circumcision and that "election"
is primarily a matter of grace rather than familial descent. The
Chrisitan position is evidenced by Romans 4 and Barnabas 13. Mihaly
claims Sifre refutes the Christian position by relating this parable
which shows that Abraham and Isaac were unworthy. Only Jacob was
worthy. Mihaly also claims the midrashist of the parable went on
to preach that Israel chooses God now and will do so forever until the
Messianic Era.

According to his interpretation the homilist disengaged Jacob from
the family of Isaac and Abraham. He supposes:

> King = God
> tenant farmer = Abraham
> tenant farmer = Isaac
> King's son = Jacob

Nevertheless in most readings here Abraham and Isaac are termed "our
father" and Jacob is not so termed (although in some he is). Also,
Mihaly assumes the entire Piska is a single unit. However, even his own
thesis suffers because the midrash ends by comparing Abraham, Isaac and
Jacob to a threefold braid. (The status of the Patriarchs is equal;
if Jacob merits to have his name associated with the nation it is because
he was the final strand in the rope.) This is a far cry from the
thief and evil doer appellations that Mihaly would have attributed to
Abraham and Isaac in the parable. Why in an anti-Christian polemic
would one wish to have an individual identified as a "son of God"? That
the "Children of Israel" are to be identified with God's sons is another
matter (see for example, Baba Bathra 10a). The claim is obviously only
metaphorical in such case and can in no way be taken literally. Furthermore, the usual form of this kind of parable has the final line of the

---

parable state the point of the story under investigation in such a
way as to show how the parable has given meaning to the verse (cf. further
Piska 313).There is a reading in Midrash Haggadol which follows such
a form:

> The Almighty said to the nations, "Get off My land, I do not
> want you on my property, give Me my portion that I may have
> it identified as mine."

The parable, then, is about Children of Israel versus the nations; not
Jacob versus Abraham. The text to which the parable is attached has been
understood as "For the portion of God belongs to His people." "People"
means "the Children of Israel" according to the parable.
Let us see Sifre Deut. Piska 343 (to Deut. 33:2):

> Another interpretation:
> This is comparable to one who wanted to give a present to one of
> his sons. He was anxious on account of his brothers, friends
> and relatives. What did that son do? He arose and identified
> himself by declaring his worth. The king said to him, "To you
> I give the present." In a similar way when Abraham came into
> the world there issued from him the dreg of Ishmael and the sons
> of Ketura. When Isaac came there issued from him the dreg of
> Esau and all the chiefs of Edom, but there was no dreg in
> Jacob. This is according to the Scripture which states, "And
> Jacob was a perfect man dwelling in tents." The Almighty said
> to him, "To you I am giving the Torah." Therefore does it
> state. "The Lord came from Sinai and rose from Seir unto them..."

The parable is meant to show that Israel proved her worth (שׂעיר-- play
upon שׂעיר in Deut. 33:2)and therefore received the Torah. The point of
these midrashim which refer to the dreg of Ishmael etc., is to show that
the nation is called Israel because Jacob's children were all whole and
therefore merited to receive the Torah while the other nations descended
from Abraham and Isaac were not so. It is not the Patriarchs who are
disparaged in these midrashim but the unworthy progeny. The worthy
progeny are named after their father. I believe the proof text that forms
part of this formula --"perfect man dwelling in tents" - has been taken
to mean that his "children conceived in tents were derived from perfect
seed".

Now let us look at Sifre Deut. Piska 31:

"Hear O Israel, the Lord our God, the Lord is One":

> Why is Israel stated in this Scripture? Because it is said,
> "Speak to the Children of Israel." It is not said, "Speak to
> the children of Abraham, Isaac and Jacob." For Jacob, our
> father, merited that it should state the "speaking" to his
> children because Jacob was anxious all his life: "Woe to me,
> perhaps dreg will issue from me as it did from my fathers
> --from Abraham issued Ishmael, from Isaac issued Esau, my
> brother."

and let us see further Exodus Rabba 1:1 :

> ...Similarly did Isaac impart wisdom to Jacob...as it is said,
> "And Jacob was a perfect man dwelling in tents"...and also Jacob

imparted wisdom to his sons and chastened them. For so it
is written, "And these are the names of the children of
Israel who came down to Egypt with Jacob..." All of them are
compared to Jacob for all of them were righteous.

And as a final example, let us note Leviticus Rabba 36:5[B 28]
(p. 899):

Why does Scripture state "even" in regards to Abraham and
Isaac but it does not state "even" in regards to Jacob?
--Because his litter was complete. Abraham -- there issued
from him Ishmael and all the sons of Ketura. Isaac -- there
issued from him Esau and all the chiefs of Edom. But Jacob
-- his litter was complete and all his sons were righteous.
This is as Scripture states -- "All of us are the sons of
one man."

These midrashim show that all the sons of Jacob were complete and
therefore the nation is called after him. The nations that descended
from Esau and Ishmael have no inheritance with Israel. That is not to
say that there was any defect in Abraham or Isaac (cf. Sifre Deut. Piska
8) but only that a defect was in their children and so their unworthy
children could not inherit their convenantal dues. Only the sons of
Jacob were worthy as they in every way were followers of Jacob. They
are real sons of Jacob and therefore they merit exclusive rights to the
Torah because their monotheism is beyond question and they will not
misuse the laws in idolatrous practices. For Israel the Torah-covenant
is indeed "the portion of God". As for the end section of the Piska
we may dismiss Mihaly's forced views that in it we are still encountering
an anti-Christian polemic and agree with Urbach who sees here a completely separate tradition (Sages, p. 530, and p. 926, n. 21.) This tradition
states that not only was Israel chosen by God -- they chose God as well.
We need not think that this point is necessarily an anti-Christian
polemic. The Rabbis could have been expressing a theological view of why
Israel was "elected" --through their own merit. Mihaly's view that we have
an anti-Christian polemic in the opening section of the Piska is
acceptable but his understanding of the polemic (i.e. that Abraham is
not the founder of Israel but that Jacob is) is wrong. The parable is
supposed to convince us that only the Children of Israel, i.e. the
descendants of Jacob are God's chosen while the descendants of Esau
and Ishmael are not. The end of the Piska is not necessarily concerned
with polemic at all but with a theological question -- why was
Israel chosen?

gave it to tenant farmers.[L1] The tenant farmers began to plunder it.
He took it from them and gave it to their children who began to be
worse than their predecessors.[T1] He took it from their children
and gave it to their grandchildren.[*] They became much worse than
their predecessors.[*][T1] When a son was born to him, he said to them,
"Get off my property, I do not want you to be on it. Give me my
portion that I may have it identified as mine."

In like fashion, when Father Abraham came into the world[T2]
there issued from him the dreg of Ishmael and all the children of
Ketura. Isaac came into the world[T2] --there issued from him the dreg
of Esau and all the chiefs of Edom. They became much worse than their
predecessors. When Jacob[**] came no dreg issued from him but all his

---

[*] absent in Ln. (Derrett , "Allegory etc.", p.426, discusses the reading).
[**] Ln: Father Jacob

T1. Omitted in Ln apparently due to homoioteleuton ("their predecessors").

T2. Omitted in Ln apparently due to homoioteleuton ("came into the world").

L1. For the etymology of אריס , see Kohut, Aruch Compl. s.v. אריס.

children were born upright people. This is according to the matter

of which Scripture states, "Jacob was a perfect[E2] man dwelling in

tents."[S1]

From whence does God have His portion identified as His? From

Jacob, as it is said,[T3] "For the portion of the Lord is His people, Jacob

the lot of His inheritance." And the Scripture also states,[T3] "For

the Lord Jacob hath chosen."[S2] [E3]But the matter still remains[T4]

ambiguous[L2]and we do not know whether the Holy One, Blessed Be He, chose

Jacob or Jacob chose the Holy One, Blessed Be He. --Scripture states,

---

S1. Genesis 25:27.   S2. Psalms 135:4.

T3. Possibly another homoioteleuton (introductory formula to proof text) in Ln.

T4. Omitted in Ln apparently by homoioteleuton ("but the matter still remains ambiguous".)

L2. Literally reads "depends upon that which is not dependable".

E2. Cf. Exodus R. 1:1 :
   ...Similarly did Isaac impart wisdom to Jacob...as it is said, "And Jacob was a perfect man dwelling in tents."...and also Jacob imparted wisdom to his sons and chastised them and taught them his ways for there was no dreg amongst them. For it is so written, "And these are the names of the Children of Israel who came down to Egypt with Jacob" -- all of them are compared to Jacob for all of them were righteous..." Philo (B 34) notes (Praem. 58f) that Abraham had only one faultless son, Isaac had one kind one,while Jacob had no faulty sons. See B.J. Bamberger, Philo and the Aggadah, (B 99) HUCA 48 (1977), p. 167.

E3. This could mean "For the Lord hath chosen Jacob" or it could mean "For Jacob hath chosen the Lord". See E. Urbach, Sages, (B 339) p. 925, n. 19, n. 2, p. 926, n. 21 for the expression דבר תלי בדלא תלי.

"Israel, to be His treasured one."[S3] [E4] But the matter still remains[T4]

ambiguous and we do not know if the Holy One, Blessed Be He, chose

"Israel to be His treasured one" or if Israel chose the Holy One, Blessed

Be He. --Scripture states, "And the Lord thy God hath chosen thee to

be His own treasured people."[S4] [E5]

And from whence do we know that Jacob also "chose the Lord"?

We know it from that which is stated, "Not like these[E6] is the portion

of Jacob. (For He is the former of all things and Israel is the

חבל of His inheritance, the Lord of Hosts is His name)."[S5]

--"Jacob the חבל of his inheritance": חבל distinctly means

"allotment", as it is said, "The allotments (חבלים)[E7] are fallen

---

S3. Psalms 135:4.   S4. Deuteronomy 14:20.
S5. Jeremiah 10:16.

T4. See previous page.

E4. Does this mean "Israel chose God to be his treasured one" or
does it mean "God chose Israel to be His treasured one"?

E5. For the sense of סגולה as "נחלה " see J. Muilenberg, "The
Form and Structure of the Covenantal Formulations",(B 272) V.T. 9,
(1959) p. 355. For the fluency of identification of סגולה with חבל
we find the expression חבלתו וסגולתו in Tanhuma Buber Balak,
vol. 2, p. 142.(B 24)

E6. Unlike the false gods is the God who is clearly identified here
as Jacob's portion, i.e. the One whom Jacob chose.

E7. "Allotments" here appears to refer to "chosen lots". See also
4QP Isaiah 6-7 (2:4) where חלק = חבל (Qumran Interpretations of
Biblical Books).(B 204)

unto me in pleasant places."[S6] And Scripture also states, "And there
fell ten allotments (חבלים) to Manasseh,";[S7] "Out of the
allotments (חבלים) of the Children of Judah was the inheritance of
the Children of Simeon."[S8]

Another tradition:

Just as a rope (חבל) is triple braided so was Jacob the third
of the Patriarchs and received the advantage[L3] of all the others.
--Concerning Abraham's birth, what does Scripture say? "And a
brother is born for adversity."[S9] [L4] --Concerning Isaac's birth, what
does Scripture say? "Two are better than one."[S10] --And concerning
Jacob's birth, what does it say? "And a three-fold cord is not
quickly broken."[S11] [E8]

END OF PISKA

S6. Psalms 16:5.   S7. Joshua 17:5.   S8. Joshua 19:9.
S9. Proverbs 17:17.   S10. Ecclesiastes 4:9.   S11. Ecclesiastes 4:12.

L3. Literally reads "received the reward" --i.e. the benefit. Jacob
put on the finishing touches and thereby reaped the benefits of his
predecessors.

L4. We may note that צרה in Proverbs 17:17 has been taken to refer to
Abraham because midrashically צור (see Isaiah 51:1-2, אברהם = צור)
refers to Abraham. Thus Abraham (צור) who had no ancestor to draw
strength from was constantly subjected to turmoil (צרה).

E8. J.D.M. Derrett, "Allegory and the wicked vinedressers and Sifre
Deut. Piska 312", Journal of Theological Studies, 25 (1974), p. 426ff.
sees this Piska as showing God's forbearance unto the third generation.
If so, that point is merely incidental.

10

"He found him in a desert land": [E1]

This refers to Father Abraham. It is like the parable of the king

who went out with his soldiers to the desert. His soldiers left him in

a place of distress, in a place of invaders, in a place of robbers, and

they went upon their way. A certain warrior[E2] was appointed[L1] to him.

He said, "My lord King, let not thy heart be faint and have no fears.

By thy life, I shall not leave you until you enter your royal residences

and sleep upon your bed." --This is according to the matter of which

Scripture states, "I, the Lord* [E3] who brought you out of Ur Casdim."[S1]

---

* Ln: "And He said to him, I, the Lord..."

S1. Genesis 15:7.

L1. The sense of התמנה is "appointed himself" or "became counted together with".

E1. This verse forms part of a recitation of beneficent gestures which Deut. 32 says God performed for Israel. Christians like Justin Martyr used these verses to show that the Gentiles were destined to inherit the promises made to Israel since Israel had received so many blessings in the past and still proved faithless (See Dialogue with Trypho, (B 261) ch. 123ff., ch. 20ff., ch. 119ff., ch. 131ff.)

E2. In this parable we assume (with some reservation) that Abraham is the warrior (cf. Gen. R. 42:4 where he is said to have been להזדווג to God and see var. on Sifre here in F.)and that God is the king in this passage. (It would not entirely be in keeping with the mashal form to assume anything else although Lichtenstein reverses the identification.) The passage then appears to say that Abraham rescued God from His plight of being deserted by earlier generations. The point may be that God had no real earthly kingdom until Abraham showed his constant loyalty to Him. See S. Schechter, Some Aspects of Rabbinic Theology, (B 307) p. 33, p. 62, p. 83ff., p. 37, cf. Gen. R. 59:8.

E3. Although A.Y. Lichtenstein's interpretation preserves the literal intent of the verse (knight = God), I suspect the midrashist took this verse as either "AdoNaI (אני) compare Gen. 15:7 with Gen. 15:8 = אדני ה . Cf. A. Hoffer, (B 200) p. 144 who cites in support M. Landau Machzor (5596) and another book Zauberwesen p. 134 . Perhaps אודנה=אונה (lobes),קדמא = קמא (early) suggested the play אנ אדנ), Lord, you whom

I brought out of Ur Casdim", or more likely, "I am the Lord who was
brought out with you (הוצא אתך   ) from Ur Casdim." For the reading
of verses in such a way that they may offend the omnipotence of God
see Marmorstein, The Old Rabbinic Doctrine of God, II: Essays in
Anthropomorphism,(B 260   ) p. 126-129 who treats the term כבכיול) (B 84   )
Also see the discussion in Abrahams, Studies in Pharisaism
pt. 16, p. 180, who mentions Bacher's view that it means
        אלו נאמר במי שאי יכול אתה לומר זה
"sit venio verbo". (For a similar mashal (concerning Moses) see
L. Finkelstein, "The Transmission of Early Rabbinic Tradition",
Exploring The Talmud (editor: H.Z. Dimotrovsky), Ktav, N.Y., 1976, p. 241 ff,
cf. PAAJR, 6(1935), p. 206 ff.(B 161))
        The proof text Gen. 15:7 is used to underlie the words of the knight
in the parable: He said to him, "O lord king...I shall not set you
down until you enter your palaces and sleep upon your couch."
Of course these problems of adjusting the verse to fit Abraham will not
occur if we, like Lichtenstein, take the knight to be God but such an
interpretation would be difficult to maintain as it would seem to cast God
in an inferior role to Abraham. The plausible explanation will be found
by an examination of P.T. Sukka 4:3 (cf. Tanhuma Buber, Acharei Mot 18).
This passage reflects the theme of the protected journey across sea
and desert whereby the hero grows to maturity. The hero in P.T. Sukka
is "God-Israel". It is a joint journey to full maturity. That is to say,
it is the relationship between God and Israel which grows to maturity in
this venture. The hero is truly neither God nor Israel but their
relationship:
        Rabbi Abahu learned the Mishna in the name of Rabbi Yochanan thus:
        "I and He -- please save, I and He please save!"
        "(Ps. 81:3) And come You to save us" -- And You (are to be saved)
        -- is the profession.
        Rabbi Basrongeh also interpreted:
        "(Zechariah 12:7) The Lord shall save the tents of Judah first."
        -- shall be saved is the written sense.
        Rabbi Zekhaya explained:
        "(Micah 4:10) For now shalt thou go forth out of the city and shalt
        dwell (שכנת   ) in the field." --My Shekina (שכנתי) is in the
        field.
        Hananiah, the son of the brother of Rabbi Yehoshua says:
        "(Exodus 20:2) I am the Lord thy God who took thee out of the Land
        of Egypt." --You who took thee out... is the written sense.
        (So Korban haEdah,   Pnei Moshe: הוצא אתך   --who was brought out
        with you.)
What allows this interpretation to succeed is the alleged reading of
הוצאתך which is allowed to drop the yod from הוצאתיך   . The verse has
been read to mean that God was redeemed. The "You" here is the Eternal
Thou -- it is a euphemism perhaps for the divine "I". It is even possible
that the reading mentioned in the apparatus of F here-- "So did the Holy
One, Blessed Be He, say to father Abraham..." understood God to say that
He was brought out of Ur Casdim in accordance with the type of midrash

found in P.T. Sukka 4:3. Cf. A. Marmorstein, The Old Rabbinic Doctrine II, Essays in Anthropomorphism, p. 127, n. 55. Harry Fox has convinced me of this distinct possibility by pointing out the profound sense of P.T. Sukka 4:3. God needs man to recognize Him so that He may have dominion in the lower worlds. Our Piska definitely says as much explicitly in the following sections. It is my contention that these passages speak of the divine relationship with Israel more than they speak of God or Israel per se. It is the relationship which is saved. The imagery, as Harry Fox points out, is in terms of God being saved but the sense is that God and Israel are intertwined into a single history by virtue of their covenantal relationship. See also Tanhuma Buber Acharei Mot p. 71 for other examples of this phenomenon. Thus the problems of "who is the knight and who is the king and how is Gen. 15:7 to be read?" are intentionally created by the homilist who thereby intertwines Abraham and God into a unified whole -- a single relationship -- which was redeemed. The choseness of Israel is not by grace but by mutual need and singleness of purpose. God and Israel are a unit -- as I suggested in my key to the parable in Piska 312.

The major points of interest in the rest of the Piska concern the midrashic understandings of Scriptural vocabulary.

יסובבנהו = He caused him to wander about

יבוננהו = (perhaps understood in the parable as נתמנה . ב and מ interchange) He caused him to have appointment.

יצרנהו כאישון עינו = He distressed him concerning the pupil of his eye.

ימצאהו = He made it ready

יבוננהו = He caused him to be distinguished from the nations.

המוליכך = He caused to rule over you (see Deut. 8:15)

יסובבנהו = elder (זקן = סב)

יבוננהו = prophet (נביא)

We may briefly note that סובב in Deut. 32:10 is taken as שומע in Mechilta[B 15] to Ex. 20:15 and refers to the hearing of the commandments. We might also note here that Marqah 4:10 also interprets Deut. 32:10 "יסובבנהו " as "bringing to meet God (שומע)": "He encircled him...": "Then Moses brought the people out of the tent to meet God (Exodus 19:17)." יסובבנהו ויבננהו - ויוציא משה את העם׳

לקראת האלוהים מן המחנה - בדיל ישמע עמה בממללי עמך

The traditions concerning Israel's behavior during the theophany as they chased the "Word" can be found in Rashi to Shabbath 88b, Frag. Targ. to Ex. 20:2 and Exodus R. 5:9. The point of the redaction of our Piska is to show through a three-fold reading of the verse that the protected journey-relationship between God and Israel began with Abraham, continued through Sinai and the oral-tradition leadership period (Elders and Prophets) and will continue into Messianic times. Israel's redemption is God's redemption. Israel's salvation history is the history of the redemption of God-Israel. In the Abraham years the relationship began, it grew to fruition in the time of the Exodus and progressed during Israel's early history. The relationship will further blossom in the Future Era.

Piska 313

"He compasseth him about":

This is according to the matter of which Scripture states,[E4]

"And the Lord said to Abram, 'Get thee out of thy land'."[S2]

"He instructed him":

Before Father Abraham came into the world, the Holy One, Blessed Be He, -- as if it were possible, was only the king of the heavens, as it is said, "The Lord, the God of heaven, who took me...."[S3] However, when Father Abraham came into the world, he accorded Him dominion over the heavens and over the earth. This is according to the matter of which Scripture states,[E5] "And I will make thee swear by the Lord, the God of heaven and the God of earth".[S4]

S2. Genesis 12:1.   S3. Genesis 24:7.   S4. Genesis 24:2.

E4. This pericope does not appear to be part of the midrashic framework which surrounds it. It appears to be an interpolation of a passage that related the verse of Deut. 32:9 to Abraham; yet, unlike the images which precede and follow this Sifre passage (Abraham saves God). This pericope states that it was God who favored Abraham and caused him to travel about (=יסובבנהו).

E5. Here we have the continuation of "E2" above. The point is that not only does God save Israel, Israel saves God (cf. Sifre Deut. 33:5 and Tanhuma Buber, Acharei Mot, para. 18). Thus God's responsibilities to Abraham's descendants are matched by their responsibilities to God. The effect of the midrash here is to soften the condemnation of Israel which follows. This implies that God is "limited" by Israel's actions. See the polemic against this idea in Koran, sura 5:64.

"He kept him as the apple[L2] of his eye":

Even if God had wanted his eyeball he would have given it to Him. And not only his eyeball would he have given but also his soul which was more dear to him than anything, as it is said, "Take I pray thee, your son, your only one, Isaac."[S5] And is it not obvious that this, his son, was his "only one"? -- But it is the soul which is called "the only one",[E6] as it is said, "Deliver my soul from the sword, mine only one from the power of the dog."[S6]

Another interpretation:

"He found him in a desert land":

This refers to Israel, as it is said, "I found Israel like grapes[L3] in the wilderness."[S7]

S5. Genesis 22:2.   S6. Psalms 22:21.   S7. Hosea 9:10.

L2. The sense of "eye-ball" here for אישון accords with its usage in Ben Sira. אישון is used quite often by Targum Yerushalmi to mean "the fixed time" -- its usage in Syriac. See Kohut, Aruch Compl. s.v. אשן .

L3. Or "vines".

E6. "Soul" and "only one" are taken as in apposition. See Philo, On the Migration of Abraham, (B 33) ch. 24 (ed. Glatzer), where Philo appears to render "your only one" (Gen. 22:2) as "his very being and soul".

"And in the waste, a howling wilderness":

In a place of distress, in a place of invaders, in a place of robbers.

"He compassed him about":

Before Mount Sinai. This is according to the matter of which Scripture states, "And thou shalt set bounds unto the people round about, saying...."[S8]

"He instructed him":

Through the Ten Commandments. It teaches us here that when the utterance went out from the mouth of the Holy One, Israel could see[L4] it and they gained knowledge from it* and they knew how much Midrash there is in it, and how much Halacha there is in it, and how many a fortiori arguments there are in it and how many arguments by analogy[E7] there are in it.

---

* Ln: Israel reflected upon it and they knew....

S8. Exodus 19:12.

L4. L. Silberman points out that ראה (see) here may mean "To have pleasure in".

E7. For a discussion of גזרה שוה see S. Lieberman, Hellenism etc., (B 250) pp. 59-79. Also see E. Slomovic, "Towards an Understanding of Exegesis in the Dead Sea Scrolls", (B 321) Bar Ilan, vol. 7-8, (1970), p. 50, n. 8, p. 51, n. 10.

"He kept him as the apple of His eye":

Going twelve <u>mil</u> and returning twelve <u>mil</u> in conjunction with every utterance, but they were frightened neither by the sounds nor by the torches.[E8]

Another interpretation:

"He found him in a desert land":

Everything was ready-made* and prepared for them in the desert. A well arose for them, manna came down for them, quail was prepared for them, The Clouds of Glory surrounded them.[E9]

---

* Ln: appointed and fixed.

E8. See Mechilta <u>Jethro</u> (Horowitz-Rabin p. 235: <u>Baḥodesh</u> 9) and also see Targ. Ps.-Jon. to Ex. 20:2 for the way in which the Decalogue was spoken. That the Tradition argues against angelic mediation at Sinai as believed by Christians see R. Kimelman, "Rabbi Yochanan and Origen on the Song of Songs: A Third Century Jewish-Christian Disputation",(p. 571,n. 49) <u>HTR</u>, 3 (1980), no. 3-4.[B 219] Also note the protective aspect of "God's eye" in similar circumstances according to Ben Sira,[B 44] p. 103, 17:8, 17:19 and this acts as a "seal" - Ben Sira[B 44] 17:22 אישון = חותם (cf. Scholem, <u>Jewish Gnosticism</u>[B 309] p. 69 and also his Appendix "C" para. 16. Note also Targ. PS.-Jon[B 55] (etc.,) to Ex. 28:30 where knowledge of God's name assures   a) revelation
        b) protection.)
That אישון refers to the ball of the eye is evident from Ben Sira 3:25, p. 19.

E9. The midrashist sees ימצאהו (found him) as מצוי (ready-made). Indeed in Numbers 11:22 מצא actually refers to "supplying". It is remotely possible that the midrashist found in the expression אישין עלינו a reference to the miraculous well עין which watered the Israelites. The feats mentioned here are later ascribed to Moses in Piska 339. Justin Martyr,<u>Dialogue with Trypho</u>,[B 261] p. 178, ch. 20 understands these verses in a similar vein as the midrashist: "...for after you had eaten the manna in the desert and had seen all the miracles God wrought for your sake." Justin Martyr again alludes to this notion: "Yet you were delivered from Egypt...Sea was divided ... pillar of light...manna..." (p. 351, ch. 131). For the way in which יבוננהו was used to note distinction of Israel's election see "Ll" to Piska 313. Since it is unlikely the midrashist copied Christian sources, these interpretations must date back to pre-Christian times and are common to both Jewish and Christian

"And in the waste, a howling wilderness":

In a place of distress, in a place of invaders (in a place

of filth) in a place of robbers.

"He compassed him about":

With banners -- three on the north, three on the south, three on

the east, three on the west.[E10]

"He instructed him":

Through two gifts -- so that when one from the Gentile Nations

would extend his hand to misappropriate some manna -- his hand would not

receive anything; to fill up with water from the well -- his hand would

not receive anything.[E11]

"He kept him as[L5] אישון עינו ":

This is according to the matter of which Scripture states,[T1 E12]

"Rise up, O Lord, and let thine enemies be scattered: and let

them that hate thee flee before thee":[S9]

---

literature.

S9. Numbers 10:35.

T1. Omitted in Ln possibly due to homoioteleuton, ("as it is said").

L5. Perhaps the sense is best rendered as "guard by His watchful eye".

E10. For the shape of this "encompassing formation" and its power to
protect see Numbers 2:1-32, Tosefta Sota 3:4, and Tanhuma Buber,
Bamidbar 14, vol. 2, p. 13.

E11. Through these two gifts the nations learned of Israel's election.
Also Origen misappropriated these symbols of God's love: "...Christ
was in...the rock which...to afford them drink...and the Manna, the
Word of God." (Song of Songs, Comm., [B 282] Book 2, p. 155.)

E12. It seems that אישון here is associated with שונא . God
scatters the שונא thus protecting the אישון .

Another interpretation:

"He found him in a desert land":

This refers to the Future to Come. As it is said,[T1] "Therefore, behold I will allure her, and bring her into the wilderness and speak tenderly unto her."[S10 E13]

"And in the waste, a howling wilderness":

This refers to the Four Kingdoms. This is according to the matter of which Scripture states, "Who led thee through the great and dreadful wilderness."[S11 E14]

S10. Hosea 2:16.   S11. Deuteronomy 8:15.

T1. See previous page.

E13. This desert is not threatening; for here God deals gently with Israel.

E14. In the proof text of Deut. 8:15 המוליכך is understood to mean "cause to rule over you" as if it were a form of מלך . See New Light From the Prophets,[B 156] p. 121, where LE calls into question the term "Four" here and prefers to read only "Kingdoms". He does this because he thinks that the passage is earlier than Greece's domination of Israel and thus the allusion to the Greek domination and the Roman is a later interpolation. L.F. aside, it seems to me that the 4 plagues (נחש שרף ועקרב וצמאון) referred to in Deut. 8:15 are seen as the "Four Kingdoms" so that our midrash is not as early as LE thinks because Deut. 8 serves as a point of reference to our midrashist throughout the midrash even where the homilist does not acknowledge to have done so. For example, the water and manna are explicitly referred to in Deut. 8:15-16. See Piska 313 "E11" above which may well have been associated with this verse. Thus the midrash is a complete unit based upon Deut. 8:15-16 and not a unit into which an interpolation has fallen. Thus, it seems to me, LE's thesis of an interpolation falls apart as does his early dating of this tradition. However, the roots of these traditions may indeed go back to early times. See Conclusion further no. 7.

"He compassed him about (יסובבנהו‎)":

Through the Elders.[E15]

"He instructed him":

Through the Prophets.[E16]

"He kept him as the apple of His eye":

He guarded them from the demons that they should not harm them.[E17]

This is according to the matter of which Scripture states, "Surely

he that toucheth you toucheth the apple of His eye."[S12]

END OF PISKA

S12. Zechariah 2:12.

E15. The midrash plays upon סב‎ = elder (See Targ. to Is. 3:2).

E16. The play here must be יבוננהו‎ = נביא‎ = prophet.

E17. The word נגע‎ refers to "demons" as well as to plagues. See "E8" to Piska 313.

11

"As an eagle that stirreth up his nest":

Just as an eagle before coming to his nest, painstakingly with his
wings between two trees or two thickets, causes a disturbance for his
children, in order that they should be stirred up so as to have the
strength to receive him; so when[E1] the Holy One, Blessed Be He, came[L1]

L1. In this pericope I have translated the word "נגלה " by "come"
although the word literally means "revealed". My purpose in doing such
was to show the shared tradition of Targum and midrash which uses the
conventional נגלה to refer to God approaching man, cf. the Targumim
to Ex. 19:18 (יתגלי = ירד) and Deut. 33:2 (יתגלי = בא). Since the
midrashist compares the approach of the eagle and the approach of God,
he uses the conventional terminology in regards to the deity when he
speaks of the eagle's approach. Cf. Ps.-Jon. to Deut. 32:11. Cf. Ex. R. 5.9

E1. The point may be that God did not reveal His Law at once at the
dawn of history but slowly allowed the notion of covenant to be manifested.
In this way the people were prepared by the covenants with Adam, Noah and
Abraham for the covenant with Moses. Or, perhaps, the comment is meant to
express the gentleness with which the revelation to the whole people took
place. See printed Tanhuma Jethro 9 . For the relation of "קנו "
(nest) with Torah it may be suggested that Prov. 8:22, "קנני " is the
source of the identification. Interestingly, the Palestinian cycle of
Parshiot readings was 154 or 155 (= קנ'ה) see A. Epstein, "Some Sources"
(B 143) p. 54, p. 58. The comparison between the eagle and God is
a striking one. For the midrashist the point of comparison can be found
in the image of the eagle as a creature that warns his young of his
approach so that they will not be startled. He rustles the branches far
in advance of his coming so he might alert his young that he is
approaching. In like fashion, the midrashist says, did God slide through
Israel's history, giving advance notice of their election and responsibilities in all possible ways. Israel could not but notice the various forms
of revelations that preceded the giving of the Torah. The homilist
poetically expresses how Israel must have caught glimpses of God and His
laws prior to the startling theophany at Sinai. In such way, the midrashist tells us, was Israel prepared to receive the ultimate revelation
at Sinai. Having now established God's way of anticipating Israel's
history the redactor provides continuity of theme by adducing another
tradition. The Messianic Era also approaches slowly. The final
revelation for Israel is prefigured by her past. God's rustling in
present history beckons the Jew to hear the approach of a new dawn. The
sound of the approaching eagle is the sound of God approaching directly
into Israel's history. The signs of His love and of the coming redemption are audible. He is not yet in sight. Thus the midrashist cites
Canticles 2:8 which speaks of the sound of the beloved whose approach is

to give the Torah to Israel, He did not come to them from one direction

but from four[*] directions, as it is said, "The Lord came from Sinai

and rose from Seir unto them...." Which is the fourth direction?

--"God cometh from Teman."[S1]

"Spreadeth abroad his wings, taketh them":

This is according to the matter of which Scripture states: "And

in the wilderness, where thou hast seen how that the Lord thy God bore

thee...."[S2]

"Beareth them on his pinions":

This is according to the matter of which Scripture states:

"And how I bore you on eagles' wings...."[S3] [E2]

---

sure. The image of the eagle's wing is one of protection. Thus Targum
to Ezekiel 16:8 renders ואפרס כנפי by ואגינת במימרי עליכון while
ואגינת במימרי is also the phrase used by Targ. Onk. to render Ex. 33:22:
ושכותי כפי. According to Hayward the image is that of the actively (B190)
redeeming God who manifests Himself in history (see <u>Divine Name etc.</u>,
p. 22f.). For the identification of קנו with "the giving of the Torah"
see Piska 317, "E6". Cf. Marqah 4:9, "That flutters over its young":
...my power brought about your deliverance.

* Ln: two directions.

S1. Deuteronomy 33:2.   S2. Habakuk 3:3.   S3. Deuteronomy 1:31.

E2. Cf. Mechilta de R. Yishmael to Ex. 19:4, p. 208, (ed. Hor-Rab.):
How is the eagle different from all other birds? For all other birds
place their young beneath their legs because they fear other birds who
fly above them but the eagle fears only man who shoots an arrow at him.
The eagle prefers the arrow to strike him rather than his young. This is
like the parable of one who was walking on the way with his son in front
of him. When thieves arose to threaten him from the front he took his son
from the front position and placed him in the rear, when a wolf came to
tear him apart from behind he placed the child in front. And so when
thieves came from in front and wolves from behind he took the child and
placed him on his shoulders, as it is said, "And in the desert where thou
hast seen how the Lord thy God carried you (as a man carries his son...).
Also see N. Leibowitz, <u>Studies in Shmot</u>, (B 245) p. 290ff. Both here and
in the following proof text, the conclusion of the verses (omitted in the

Another interpretation:

"As an eagle that stirreth up his nest":

This refers to the Future to Come, as it is said, "The voice of my beloved, behold he comes...."[S4]

"Spreadeth abroad his wings":[E3]

This is according to the verse which states: "I will say to the north: 'Give up', and to the south: 'Keep not back...'."[S5]

"Beareth them on his pinions":

This is according to the matter of which Scripture states: "And they shall bring their sons in their bosom."[S6]

END OF PISKA

---

text) are necessary to appreciate the midrash.

S4. Isaiah 43:6.   S5. Isaiah 43:6.   S6. Isaiah 49:22.

E3. "Wings" here is to be understood as "corners" or "directions". The reference is to the ingathering of the exiles in the Messianic Age when it is believed that Jews from all corners of the earth will return to their "promised land". Cf. N. Leibowitz, Studies in Shmot, (B 245) p. 294 and note connections between Deut. 32:11 and Ex. 19:4.

PISKA 315

12

"The Lord did set them down alone":

The Holy One, Blessed Be He, said to them, "Just as you have dwelt[L1] alone in This World and have no benefit from the Gentile Nations at all, so ultimately will I cause you to dwell alone in the Future and not one of the Gentile Nations shall have benefit from you at all."

"And there was no strange el with him":

--Such that any of the angels[L2] of the Gentile Nations may **not have** authority to come and rule over them.[E1] This is according to the matter of which Scripture states, "And when I go forth, lo, the angel of Greece shall come"[S1] ; "But the angel of the kingdom of Persia withstood me"[S2] "Howbeit, I will declare unto thee that which is inscribed in the writing of the truth...."[S3]

S1. Daniel 10:20.   S2. Daniel 10:13.   S3. Daniel 10:21.

L1. יַנחנו is considered to have been derived from "חנה ", "dwell".

L2. I take the point to be that no guardian angel of the Gentile Nations can have authority over Israel ('s guardian angel = "him"). L. Silberman suggests that it means no guardian angels are on God's level (=with Him) and he points to the end of the proof text "S3":
ואין אחד מתחזק עמי. For my view of this see next note (E1.).

E1. I.e. a foreign "el". Accordingly, this refers to the angels (elim) which are the guardians of the various "foreign nations". Michael is the guardian angel of Israel and according to this interpretation in the Sifre, he continues to rule over Israel even while they are in exile. Israel thus remains a full nation even when she has been swallowed amongst the other peoples of the world. The preacher introduces an apocalyptic motif from the book of Daniel. I believe he renders the verse in Daniel as follows: The guardian angels of the Gentile Nations cannot hold my people (עמי is read as "with me" in M.T. but the preacher likely takes it as "my people"). Perhaps this pericope was brought here to fit the theme introduced by the previous pericope. There, Israel was contrasted to the guardian angels of the nations. It should also be noted that the midrashist uses the expression to rule "over them" when he means "over you" ("you" being his constant reference throughout the passage) because of "euphemis-

Another interpretation:

"The Lord did set them down alone":

Ultimately[L3] I am to cause you to inhabit possessions from one
end of the world to the other. And so does Scripture state:

"...From the east side unto the west side: Asher one portion,";[S4]

"...From the east side even unto the west side: Reuben one portion,";[S5]

"...From the east side even unto the west side: Judah one portion,".[*] [S6] [T1]

What is it that Scripture states: "Asher one portion,"; "Reuben
one portion,"; "Judah one portion,"? --It is that ultimately Israel is
to take; lengthwise; from the east unto the west, by widthwise: twenty-
five thousand rods which measurement is seventy-five mil.[E2]

---

tic convention". One does not utter unhappy words in connection with
Israel.

[*] Ln: N to W: Dan 1, Judah 1, Asher 1, "S6". E to W: Menasseh 1, Naftali 1.

S4. Ezekiel 48:2.   S5. Ezekiel 48:6.   S6. Ezekiel 48:7.

T1. The difference in readings here between Ln and F has almost no
bearing upon distinguishing a different sense between the two passages.

L3. That is, in the World to Come.

E2. The boundaries of the Land of Israel are here given in an interesting interpretation of Ezekiel 48. The recurring phrase, "From the east
side even unto the west side" supposes that each tribe will inherit property equal to the entire width of the land as it existed in the days of
the Judges. However the length of the land will be only seventy-five
mils. Ezekiel 41:8 fixes the length of the "measuring rod" at 6 cubits.
Since Ezekiel 48:8 puts the allotted portions at 25,000 reeds, this
distance can be calculated to be 150,000 cubits (6 x 25,000). Since one
mil contains 2000 cubits, we find that our 150,000 cubits must measure
75 mils. (150,000/2000). See further, the commentaries of Rashi and
Radak to Ez. 48:7.
    My understanding of the pericope follows the reading of Midrash
Haggadol as cited by Hoffman in Midrash Tannaim (B 26) to this verse.
The same theme is developed in Devarim Rabba (ed. Lieberman), p. 52.
The word נוחלים in this pericope will mean "individual allotments of

"And there was no strange <u>el</u> with him":

So that there will not be amongst you men who worship idols.[E3]

And so does Scripture state, "Therefore by this shall the sin of

Jacob be expiated...."[S7] [E4]

---

each tribe", such that each allotment will have a length equal to the
existing length of the entire land as it now stands. Each tribe will
have what is now one length of Asher, one length of Reuben, etc. Thus
it is that each tribe of Israel will take as its length ·an amount·
equal to the east-west measurement of the entire land that now exists while
the width of each tribe has been calculated such that it will be 75 <u>mils</u>.
To understand in this way assumes:

1. נוחלים refers to tribal inheritances. It appears our midrashist
   placed this comment here because he took ינחנו as ינחלנו .
   (See Piska 318 at end where "r" falls out, here "l" is added.)
2. בדד is taken as בָּדַד , "scattered afar" (see <u>Aruch Compl.</u>) s.v.
   בָּדָד .
3. עֹולם is understood to refer to a unit of land, in this case, the
   existing Land of Israel. Cf. "E 14" to Piska 306, and "E5" to
   Piska 338).
4. ישראל   is a "tribe" of Israel.

Jer. 3:19 appears to be the reference behind these traditions:
ואתן לך ארץ חמדה נחלת צבי .
It would appear that the homily upon this verse as expressed in B.T.
Gittin 57a to the effect that the Land of Israel can stretch like a
deer's skin was known to our midrashist who alludes to the verse and
its homily by picking up the word of Deut. 32:12 ינחנו   and equating
it with נחלת   of Jer. 3:19. It is likely that the homilist saw in the
wording of Deut. 32:8 a veiled statement of this teaching which he thinks
vs. 12 is alluding to ישראל . למספר (השבטים) גבולות עמים .
Our midrashist appears to have kept the homily of Jer. 3:19 when he refers
to the fruit of Israel as "fleet" (like a deer, see Piska 316, "E2".).
Also cf. B.T. Baba Bathra 122a.

S7. Isaiah 27:9.

E3. "El" can refer to "gods". Thus <u>strange</u> "el" would refer to "idols".

E4. The end of the verse reads: "So that the Asherim and the sun images
shall rise no more".

Another interpretation:

"The Lord did set them down alone":

Ultimately I will cause you to dwell[L4] with repose[E5] in the world.

"And there was no el נכר with him":

There will not be amongst you men engaged in any type of business,[E6] as it is said, "There shall be the fistful of the grain in the earth,"[S8] --so that the grains shall produce loaves by the handful; "May his fruit rustle like the Lebanon,"[S9] --so that the grains will rub against each other and let their flour drop to the ground and you will come and take a handful of it and it will come to provide your sustenance.

END OF PISKA

S8. Psalms 72:16.   S9. Psalms 72:16.

L4. The midrashist here combines a root meaning of חנה , "dwell", with a root meaning of נחת , "repose" to interpret ינחנו .

E5. The midrashic comment here is in the form of paraphrase and takes ינחנו as a hiph'il, "cause to repose (root: נוח)", "give him rest".

E6. I.e. it will be as if there will be "no trading". The word may have been taken as a derivation of Heb. מכר or of כרה, "trading", (see Deut. 2:6, Job 6:27, and Job 40:30.) J.H. Schorr, "The Method of the Sages etc." says: עמו אל נכר = ὁμιλεῖν χρεία = engaged in business. However we shall be safe to claim that whatever the midrashic derivation, the homilist found in vs. 13, דבש מסלע, תנובת שדי, a clear indication that food would be provided miraculously. J. Klausner, Messianic Idea etc.,(B 231) pp. 408-413, p. 507, pp. 340-344 places our pericope within those traditions which discuss the Messianic Era rather than the Era of Resurrection. He compares our pericope with the traditions in B.T. Kethubot, 111b, B.T. Sabbath 30b, Kallah Rabbathi ch. 2, Syriac Baruch 29:5-8, Irenaeus (Haer. 5:33). See Klausner,(B 231) p. 342 -344. Also cf. B.T. Berachoth 17a, and Moore, Age etc.,(B 271) vol. 2, p. 365, p. 378.

13

"He made him ride on the high places of the earth":

This refers to the Land of Israel[E1] which is higher than all the other countries. This is according to the matter of which Scripture states, "We should go up at once and possess it."[S1] And it also states, "So they went up and spied out the Land,";[S2] "And they went up into the South, and came unto Hebron."[S2] And it also states, "And they went up[L1] out of Egypt (and they came to the Land of Canaan)."[S3]

"And he did eat of the fruitage of the fields":

This refers to the fruitage[E2] of the Land of Israel for it is easier to eat than the fruits of all other countries.

"And he made him to suck honey out of the crag":

For example, in the vicinity of Sachne. It once happened that Rabbi Yehuda said to his son, "Go and bring me dried figs from the

---

S1. Numbers 13:30.   S2. Numbers 13:21,2.   S3. Genesis 45:25.

L1. Thus, in all these instances the use of עלה shows that the Land of Israel is indeed higher than other countries.

E1. This Piska contains pericopes which are of a single form and identify the references in the verse to specific themes of Jewish interest. This type of "specifying" is often called "pesher" in Qumran literature. Harry Fox in personal correspondence calls passages such as ours by the term "Rabbinic pesher". The first identification uses proof texts to show that Israel must be a higher land than all others because Scripture refers to "going up" to the Land.

E2. The homily based upon Jer. 3:19, "Land of the deer" (see "E2" to Piska 315), may have been used as a reference behind the "fleetness" (קל) of eating Israel's fruit. Compare the similar traditions and expressions in B.T. Kethuboth 112a (cf. Rashi to B.T. Rosh Hashanah 13a).

barrel." He replied, "Father, it is of honey!" He said to him,

"Dip your hand into it and you will lift out dried figs from it."[E3]

"And oil out of the flinty rock":

This refers to the olives of Gush Halab.[E4] It once happened that

Rabbi Yosi said to his son in Sepphoris, "Go up and bring us olives[*] [T1]

from the upper story." He went and found the upper story covered with

oil.[**] [T2]

END OF PISKA

---

[*] Ln: dried figs
[**] Ln: honey

T1. The story in Ln exemplifies the "honey" passage of the previous pericope ("suck honey out of the crag"). It appears to have become assimilated with the previous passage and its reading is likely corrupt.

T2. Ln appears corrupt in this reading as well.

E3. I.e. the honey obviously came from the dried figs and therefore illustrates the verse. Sachne is north of Sepphoris in Upper Galilee (see S. Klein, "Topographical Material of Eretz-Yisrael", [B 233] Hazofeh, vol. 7, p. 120.)

E4. The story teller either means that the olives of Gush Halav were so rich they yielded oil without pressing or that the olives were supposed to be so dried that their abundant yield of oil illustrates the miraculous nature of the produce of the Land. The story in Ln which is not concerned with olives but with honey is either corrupt or else it is a variant of the story in the preceding pericope which is retold here. The reading in F is more plausible as it presents à cogent reference to the oil verse. Gush Halab is Giscala, also in Galilee (see Neubauer's Geographie du Talmud, [B 274] Paris, 1868, p. 230.)

14

"Curd of oxen and milk of sheep":

This occurred in the days of Solomon,[E1] as it is said, "Ten fat

oxen, and twenty oxen out of the pastures and a hundred sheep...."[S1]

"With fat of lamb and rams...":

This occurred in the days of the Ten Tribes, as it is said, "And

eat the lambs out of the flock and the calves out of the midst of the

stall...."[S2]

"With kidney fat of wheat":

This occurred in the days of Solomon, as it is said, "And Solomon's

provision for one day was thirty _kor_ of fine flour."[S3]

"And of the blood of the grape thou drankest foaming wine":

This occurred in the days of the Ten Tribes, as it is said, "That

drank wine in bowls...."[S4]

Another interpretation:[E2]

S1. 1 Kings 5:3.   S2. Amos 6:4.   S3. 1 Kings 5:2.
S4. Amos 6:6.

E1. This Piska continues to exegete Deut. 32:13. While the previous
Piska enumerated the blessings of the Land, this Piska enumerates the
enormous richness of the Land during First Temple times. It is not
clear why the exegesis of this verse was split into two sections.

E2. Here "Another interpretation" actually means "a further interpretation". It does not refer to a variant tradition but to a complementary
facet of interpretation. The midrash presents the basics of Judaism as
the Land, the Temple, the Torah, Exile-and-Redemption. The verse is
exegeted to underscore the importance of these themes as the foci of
Judaism. He presents his material in such form as to argue that just
as some of these themes have become established so will the others
become established, with assurance and certainty,   in the
future. Thus he establishes a base for hope of future redemption.

13

"He made him ride on the high places of the earth":

This refers to the Temple which is higher than the whole world, as it is said, "Then thou shalt arise and get thee up unto the place."[S5] And Scripture also states, "And many peoples shall go and say: 'Come ye, and let us go up[E3] to the mountain of the Lord'."[S6]

"And he did eat of the fruitage of the field":

This refers to the baskets of the first-fruits.[E4]

"And he made him to suck honey out of the crag and oil out of the flinty rock":

This refers to the libations of oil.

14

"Curd of oxen and milk of sheep with fat of lambs":

These refer to the sin-offering, the burnt-offering, peace-offerings, thanks-giving offerings, guilt-offerings and minor sacrifices.

"With kidney fat of wheat":

This refers to the dishes of flour.[E5]

S5. Deuteronomy 17:8.   S6. Isaiah 2:3.

E3. The Temple is the high place of the world. See M. Eliade, The Sacred and the Profane, (B 139) p. 43; p. 63.

E4. The entire section is in "pesher form", i.e. the midrashist identifies the poetic imagery of the verse with traditional institutions and beliefs.

E5. Dishes of flour were used for the mincha offering, see B.T. Krithoth 6a where סלתות,שמנים,יינות,בהמות are mentioned as the main Temple provisions.

"And of the blood of the grape thou drankest foaming wine":

This refers to the libations of wine.

Another interpretation:

"He made him ride on the high places of the earth":

This refers to the Torah, as it is said, "The Lord made me as the beginning of His way."[S7] [E6]

S7. Proverbs 8:22.

E6. ירכבהו --made him ride or made it ride. What is the antecedent of "it"? The midrashist finds it in " קנו " in Deut. 32:11. In P.314,"E1". we saw that קנו referred to the giving of the Torah and also here the midrashist relates to Proverbs 8:22, " קנני ". (There were 155 (קנה) parshiot in Palestinian cycle of Torah readings. See A. Epstein "Some sources etc.",[B143] p. 54 and p. 58). Proverbs 8 discusses the virtues of wisdom which to the Rabbis meant "Torah" (cf. B.T. Kiddushin 49b, Syriac Baruch 51:3ff. and Moore Notes,[B271] vol. 3, p. 82, n. 32 to vol. 1, p. 265. Silberman thinks that רכב (ride) suggests דרך (road) for the homilist who then drew upon Prov. 8:22. The midrashist exegetes the images of the verse to refer to the various components of Rabbinic methods of study in a similar fashion to the way that the preacher read "Temple" concepts into these images. The pesher[B17] approach to interpreting verses in this way occurs also in Gen. R. 66:4, p. 748. The midrash, (having discussed the physical aspect of the Land described in Gen. 27:28),[B17] p. 748, continues:
Another interpretation:
"From the dew of the heaven": This refers to Zion, as it is said "As the dew of Hermon which descends upon the mountains of Zion (Ps. 133:3)."

"And from the fat of the earth": This refers to the sacrifices.

"And much corn": This refers to the first fruits.

"And wine": This refers to the libations, (cf. Canticles R. 1:19).

Another interpretation:
"From the dew of heaven": This refers to Scripture.

"And from the fat (משמני) of the earth": This refers to Mishna (משנה).

"And much corn": This refers to Talmud.

"And he did eat of the fruitage of the field":

This refers to Scripture.[E7]

"And he made him to suck honey out of the crag":

This refers to the Mishna.[E8]

"And wine": This refers to Haggadah.

This passage seems to be related to the same cycle of midrashim of which Piska 309 is a section:

...Three are called possessions of God: "The Torah" is called God's possession", as it is said, "The Lord possessed me as the beginning of His way." "Israel" is called "God's possession" ..."The Temple" is called "God's possession"...

These three "possessions" fix the main foci of the Jewish world-view. Thus it is that these foci come to the fore again here in Piska 317. "The high places" are defined as Temple, Torah, and Israel (the land and the people). The midrashist finds קנו in Deut. 32:11 (=קנין = possession) to be the apparent antecedent of "He made him (ride the high places..."). The midrashist homiletically shows that the "Torah", the reference of Proverbs 8:22, which is termed קנני is related to קנו in Deut. 32:11. And so Piska 314, "El", relates the "eagle's nest (קנו)" to "the giving of the Torah". Thus Piska 314 is also related to the "קנין "cycle. Interestingly, Frag. Targ. to Gen. 1:1 takes ראשית as a reference to Wisdom; the source of this interpretation can be found in Gen. R. 1:5 which relates ראשית of Gen. 1:1 with ראשית of Prov. 8:22 and interprets it in reference to Torah.

E7. Now that the midrashist has identified Deut. 32:14 as a reference to Torah, he continues to identify the imagery of the verse with Rabbinic subjects. The "field produce" is linked to the subject matter of Scripture which is readily cultivated. Perhaps כתובות = תנובות.

E8. "Honey suckled from the crag" is identified with Mishna. The phrase שן סלע (Job 39:28, Jud. 15:13, 1 Sam. 14:4) suggesting, perhaps, the identification. The image presents midrashic teachings as sweeter than those of unadorned Scripture; however, mishnaic teachings are also like rocks which are difficult to grasp and to cultivate (cf. Rashi to B.T. Erubin 54b).

"And oil out of the flinty rock":

This refers to the <u>Talmud</u>.[E9]

"Curd of oxen and milk of sheep with fat of lambs":[E10]

These refer to the arguments <u>a fortiori</u>, the arguments by

analogy, logically proposed interpretations and refutations.[L1]

L1. דין refers to a deduction based upon an argument from
traditional sources. It is not in the same category as הלכה which refers
to teachings which have been received as authoritative, --as in
Mishna Yevamoth 8:3:נקבל הלכה אם . הלכה must be accepted as binding
whereas דין is only as acceptable as the strength of its argument allows
it to be and it is subject to counter argument and refutation -- תשובה .
Thus Mishna Yevamoth 8:3 declares:ואם לדין יש תשובה .

E9. "Oil from flint stone" is associated here with the study of the
Talmud which I take here to refer to the study of midrash(see above
"E6" to Piska 317 and P.T. Shabbath 16:1). The typology of Torah study
is ingeniously developed here by association. Although Midrash
Haggada appears corrupt at the point of "L2":בלשיים שבללן ; this
reading enables us to unravel "E9" as follows:
    שמן is associated with בלול (mixing) and בלול was used by the
Rabbis to refer to "expounding" see Jastrow s.v. ביל, בול, and <u>Aruch Compl.</u>
s.v. בל and B.T. Men. 65a הוה בייל לישנא ודריש. See E.S. Rosenthal
"אבל, יבל ", <u>Lěšōnēnū</u>, (cf. also E.Y. Kutcher, "Marginal Notes to
Mishnaic Lexicon etc." <u>Lěšōnēnū</u>,31 (1966) p. 111, p. 117.),
Also see Sifre Deut. 48: "The words of the Torah are compared with oil
and honey". Also see Cant. R. 1:20 and 1:3 and Deut. R. 7:2. In Tanna
DeVe Eliahu ch. 2 it is said that God passed out Torah as oil and fat
which are poured quietly --i.e. these laws are not immediately sensed
in the literal words of the Torah --the laws are quietly submerged
within the Torah. Cf. Seder Eliahu Rabba,(B 42) p. 12.

E10. The homilist takes "oxen and sheep" to refer to exegetical
arguments which argue from cases of strong import (oxen) to cases of
minor import (sheep). He finds in the parallelism of חלב (milk) with
חלב (fat) an allusion to arguments by analogy. In the phrase of
"rams of the breed of Bashan" he finds reference to the "attack"
of argumentative exegesis. In the words "he-goats" he finds
allusion to the logical analysis of a proposed exegesis which breaks the
force of the attack (cf. Sifre Deut. Piska 58 and Mishna Krithoth 3:9).

"With the kidney fat of wheat":

These refer to those laws which are the essence of the Torah.[E11]

"And of the blood of the grape thou drankest foaming wine":

This refers to the <u>Aggadah</u> which lures man's heart as wine.[E12]

Another interpretation:

"He made him ride on the high places of the earth":

This refers to the world,[*] [E13] as it is said, "The boar out of the woods ⟨ יער ⟩ doth ravage it."[S8]

S8. Psalms.   *Ln: This world.

E11. Kidney fat refers to the "bulk" of the wheat which the midrashist compares to the "halachot", the traditional laws which constitute the <u>bulk</u> of Torah study for the Rabbis. [(B 249)] Cf. Mishna Hagigah 1:8, S. Lieberman, <u>Tosefta Kifshuta</u>, vol. 8, <u>Erubin</u>,p. 139, B.T. Shabbath 32a, Avoth de R. Nathan (ed. Schechter) "A" (ch. 27, 42b) and "B" (ch. 35, 42b), [(B 104)] see also A.I. Baumgarten, "The Akiban Opposition" <u>HUCA</u>, vol. 50 (1979), p. 83.

E12. The point is that the skilfully produced <u>haggadic</u> homily makes the audience compliant (as if from wine) to the Rabbinic views concerning repentance and perfect faith. Perhaps this homilist knew of an interpretation like that in B.T. Sotah 7b where the very term הגדה, perhaps, is derived as if it came from נגד "to pull", so that Job 15:18 אשר חכמים יגידו ולא כחדו אבותיהם is seen as if it were a sermon on the value of repentance: "For the wise tell encouraging stories of ancestors.."

E13. The midrashist finds the antecedent of "him" to refer back to Deut. 32:11 " יעיר ". The midrashist relates this to " יער " in Psalm 80:14. This Psalm describes how the vine of Israel is ravaged by the nations. (See further Tanhuma Buber Shmini para. 14 p. 32: ואת החזיר ." זו מלכות אדום הרשעה שנאמר יכרסמנה חזיר מיער and to the same purpose see Lev. R. 13:5).(Cf. <u>Conclusion</u> no. 7). The midrashist has related Deut. 32:11 and Ps. 80:14 to show that it is the "eagle" which stirs up the nest of the nations to ravage Israel. God is responsible for Israel's subjugation to the nations. Now that the theme of "nations and oppresion" has been alluded to, he finds further detailed allusions along the same lines in Deut. 32:13-14.

"And he did eat of the fruitage of the field":

This refers to the Four Kingdoms.[E14]

"And he made him to suck honey out of the crag and oil out of
the flinty rock":

This refers to the oppressors[L2] who have taken possession of the
Land of Israel and it is more difficult to get a penny from them than
from a flint. On the Future Morrow, Israel will inherit their properties
and it will be as pleasing to them as oil and honey.

"Curd of oxen":

This refers to their councillors[L3] and their consuls.[E15]

L2. The reason that "oil" is interpreted here to refer to מציקים
is simply that מצק means "to pour oil" as it does in B.T. Hor. 12a.
Cf. Targ. Onk. here שמן=קרוין שליטי see A. Oppenheimer, The Am-Ha-aretz,
p. 202, n. 12: "These are the conductores, the large scale tenant-farmers,
who were given the land expropriated by the Romans after the Great Revolt
against them, cf. ibid. p. 73 note b; (metzikim) Roman tax collectors.

L3. הפיטקים is the Greek "hypatikos" and the term הגמון here may
simply be a glossed explanation of "hypatikos".

E14. Those who eat "the produce of the field" are identified as the
"Four Kingdoms". This is probably due to an association of the image
of the consumed produce in Deut. 32:13 with Israel in Dan. 7:23-28
which is consumed by the four beasts. The Four Kingdoms are considered
to be Babylonia, Medes (Persia), Greece, Edom-Rome, (cf. Isaiah 10:5).

E15. חמאת בקר was probably read as (חמ) את פקק (ר) since " ב " is
allowed to interchange with " פ" in midrashic exegesis. "Hegemon" may
be a gloss to explain "hypatikos". See Krauss, Rome and Persia, p. 138.
שמן = מציקים because יצק means to pour oil (cf. Gen. 28:18). For the
meaning of " מציקים ", oppressors see above L2 and S. Freyne,
Galilee: from Alexander the Great to Hadrian 323 BCE to 135 CE,(B, 165)
p. 167 f. and S. Klein, Neue Beitrage zur Geschichte und Geographie
Galilaas, (B 232)Vienna, 1923, p. 13, n. 7., and M. Gil, "Land Ownership
in Palestine under Roman Rule",(B 169) Revue Internationale des
Droits de l'Antiquité, 17 (1970), p. 40-44. Cf. Targ. Onk. here
דשליטון (= בקר), רברביהון), צאן (= כרים (=כרים).
It is possible that סלע here has also contributed to the typological
"authority" as סלע = שילטונוהי in Targ. to Is. 31:9 (cf. G.R. Driver

"With kidney fat":

    This refers to the high commanders.[E16]

"And rams":

    This refers to their centurions.* [E17]

"Of the breed of bashan":

    This refers to the officials** who are appointed from birth.[E18]

---

in the *Journal* of *Semitic* *Studies*, 13 (1968).

* Ln: Vile ones

** Ln: their centurions who are appointed...

E16. כליות (kidney) is midrashically equated with <u>kiliarchoi</u>, i.e. "officers of thousands". Cf. Targ. Onk. here, חיליהון = כליות .

E17. אילים may be taken here in the sense of "leaders" or "chiefs" as in Ex. 15:15 or 2 Kings 24:-5. Cf. Targ. Onk. here תקיפיהון (= אלים).

E18. It is possible that בשן = βασανος (trial, gentile courts cf. Schorr[B 312] p. 10 in reference to Sifre Deut.) and our text is a corrupted reading for the Greek. The point would be to refer to the Roman judges or perhaps, the verse ואילים בני בשן was possibly read as חילי ממני משינים through interchanging ב with פ and א with ח . The reference is to those soldiers who received commissions on account of their birth status (the sense of Targ. Onk. בני בשן = עמא דארעהון?). <u>Beneficarii</u> were specially appointed soldiers for privileged duties. For the expression מכין השינים as referring to the birth canal see B.T. Nida 41b, P.T. Yevamoth 6:1, Mishna Rosh Hashanna 2:8 and see E.Z. Melamed, "Euphemism etc."[B 263] in *Sefer* <u>HaZikaron</u> <u>le</u> <u>Vinyamin</u> <u>de</u> <u>Vries</u> (editor: E.Z. Melamed), Jerusalem, Tel Aviv University, 1968, p. 138. Ln here reads בני פוקרים which seems to be a corruption of <u>beneficarii</u> (possibly read in parallel structure (יחלב) בקרו -- בני (ואילים), so that likewise we may read <u>kiliarchoi</u> as derived from (חלב) כליות -- כרים).

"And he-goats":

This refers to their senators.* E19

"With kidney fat of wheat":

This refers to their matrons.E20

"And the blood of the grape thou drankest foaming wine":E21

On the Future Morrow Israel** will inherit their properties and

it will be as pleasing to them as oil and as honey.

Another interpretation:

"With kidney fat of wheat":

In the Future every single grain will be like two kidneysE22 of

---

* Ln: Saracenyrkin

** Ln: This refers to Israel who on the Future Morrow will inherit...

E19. Is "goat-skin" here a reference to high office? Has the midrashist of F construed עתודים to mean "striped" in reference to the purple border of the senatorial toga? In Ln עתוד is taken as "centurion". Perhaps ע (gutteral) was taken in interchange with קנ and ר was taken as ד (the shapes of the letters being almost identical, see Rashi to B.T. Krithoth 7b מתחלפת ב"ד"ר .) In its own way F may have midrashically read עתור (ב)שן that is, "Senator".

E20. "Matrons" here refers to a position of rank. כליית read as כלה.

E21. Perhaps חמר (wine) has been turned about to refer to מחר , the Future Morrow (World to Come). Cf. Pseudo-Jonathan:
מן ענבא חד מפקין כור אחד
In epic fashion, the midrashist ends where he began, (cf. Targ. Onk. אחסנתהון = עתודים, property) with the statement that Israel will inherit the properties of their oppressors (see Piska 317 "L2"). Cf. Marqah 4:9 - "When you arrive there you will find all great glory. You will make an end of the nations and seize all their possessions."

E22. כליות is plural, therefore taken as "two". See next note.

a large ox - weighing four[*] Sepphorian pounds. And if you should be amazed at this matter, consider the turnip heads. It once happened the weight of a turnip head was thirty Sepphorian pounds. And it once happened that a fox made his nest in a turnip head. It once happened with some plants; there was a mustard stalk which had three twigs on it and one of them separated and they used it to cover a potter's hut. They struck it and they found in it nine <u>kabim</u> of mustard. Said Rabbi Shimon the son of Halafta, "There was a cabbage stalk in the middle of my house and I used to go up and down it as one goes up and down a ladder."

Another interpretation"

" And the blood of the grape thou drankest foaming wine":

That you should not become wearied by treading or harvesting but you will bring it in a wagon and stand it in a corner and it will constantly renew the supply that you may drink from it as you drink from a jug.[E23]

END OF PISKA

---

* Ln: fourteen

E23. See Moore, <u>Ages</u> etc.,[(B 271)] vol 2, p. 365, p. 378. See Klausner, The <u>Messianic</u> etc.(B 231) ¸p. 342ff., p. 507ff. Cf. Kalla Rabathi ch. 2, B.T. Kethuboth 111b, B.T. Shabbath 30b. See the parallels in Klausner, op. cit., p. 410 and p. 367. Parallels mention 30 kegs of wine in each grape. Perhaps the abundance is adduced from the word חמר which besides "wine" also refers to the measurement of 1 kor (10 ephas) cf. Targ. Onk. to Lev. 27:16 and Targ. to Ez. 45:4.

15

"But Jeshurun waxed fat, and kicked":

According to the bounty do they rebel.[*] [E1] And similarly
you will find that the people of the Generation of the Flood rebelled
against the Holy One, Blessed Be He, specifically under circumstances[T1]
of food and drink, and under circumstances of tranquility. And what
does Scripture say about them? "Their houses are tranquil without
fear...."[S1]

 --the rest of the baraita is as related in eleh devarim etc.[E2]

S1. Job 21:9.

[*] Ln: is their outlook   T1. I.e. because of food etc.

E1. This Piska will present Deut. 32:15 so as to show the entire range
of Israel's sacred histroy from pre-Israelite times, i.e. the Flood Era
to the Messianic Era. Also see Tanhuma Buber Genesis vol. 1, p. 26,
n. 308 and A. Büchler, Studies in Sin etc. (B 117) p. 112. The midrash
here is based upon the wording of Neh. 9:25f. See notes to "E3"
below, Piska 318 where the Sam. and Sept. texts have readings which
traditions are preserved in Sifre here. See also Seder Eliahu Rabba
ch. 29 p. 144. (Silberman notes that the Job passage is the basis of
the reference to the Flood generation's rebellion through gluttony.)

E2. The omitted section: (Sifre Deut. Piska 43)
    "Their bull gendereth etc.",(Job 21:10) "They send forth their
little ones like a flock etc.", (Job 21:11), "They spend their days in
prosperity etc.", (Job 21:13), --this instigated them: "And they said
unto God,'Depart from us'", (Job 21:14), "What is the Almighty that we
should serve Him etc., (Job 21:15),(what profit should we have?)". They
said: It amounts to a drop of rain -- we do not need Him -- "And
there went up a mist from the earth (and watered the whole face of the
ground)" (Gen. 2:6).
    The Almighty said to them: "Through this very goodness with which
I have graced you, you lord it over Me -- through it I will punish you:
"And the rain was upon the earth forty days and forty nights." (Gen.
7:12).
    Rabbi Yosi ben Dormasqit says: Just as they cast their eyes, (עין),
the upper and the lower, in order to perform their lusts so also did
the Almighty open upon them the fountains, (מעין), the upper and the
lower, in order to destroy them, as it is said, "On the same day were
all the fountains of the great deep broken up, and the windows of
heaven were opened." (Gen. 7:12). ❀

170

Piska 318

And so we have found that the People of the Tower rebelled against

the Holy One, Blessed Be He, specifically under circumstances of

tranquillity,* as it is said, "And all the earth was of one language."S2 E3

{✲   This passage lends itself to two interpretations. B.T. Sanhedrin
198a, containing a tradition which is related to our pericope, alludes
to Gen. 6:2, "(And the b'nai elohim saw the daughters of man, that they
were pleasing {Targ. Ps. - Jon. refers to how the women painted themselves and exposed themselves seductively},) and they took them women
from all which they chose." It is therefore possible that the allusion
of our pericope refers to the lusting eyes of the heavenly beings
(b'nei elohim) and the eyes of the lower beings (daughters of man).It
is not clear whether Ibn Ezra (B 10) would have agreed with this
identification of the "upper and lower eyes" in our pericope. In his
commentary to Gen. 6:12, he says, "How pleasant is the exposition that
they gave; namely, that because the people destroyed their way with
water so did God punish them with water, just as their waters were
from above and below so were the waters which destroyed them." While
his reference here may be to the mixing of sexual fluids of upper beings
with the sexual fluids of lower beings his reference may simply be,
on the other hand, to promiscuity -- the fluids of the upper male and
the lower female during intercourse. A. Weizer's note (B 10) that
it refers to unnatural mixtures, seems to me to be only conjecture.
Our midrash in Sifre may refer to these "liquids" as the "fount of
the upper ones, the fount of the lower ones".}

* Ln: of food and drink and under circumstances of tranquillity.

S2. Genesis 11:11.

E3.   I.e. unity presupposes a state of tranquillity. Piska 43.
      "And all the earth was of one language and of one speech. And it
came to pass as they journeyed east, that they found a plain in the land
of Shinar; and they sat there." (Gen. 11:1f.) --Now the "sitting"
which is mentioned here specifically means "eating and drinking".
This is according to the matter of which Scripture states, "And the
people sat --to eat and to drink--, and rose up to make merry." (Ex. 32:6)
This instigated them to say, "Come let us build a city etc." (Gen. 11:4)
What does Scripture say about them? -- "So the Lord scattered them
abroad from thence." (Gen. 11:8)#
      {#"Come let us build us a city -- lest we be scattered abroad
         upon the face of the whole earth."
      "So the Lord scattered them abroad from thence."
These passages are used to illustrate that God makes his punishment fit
the crime. In Marqah 2:8 a list of proof texts to this same effect is
given, e.g. "They had said: Let us make war on them. The True One
said: Prepare now to war with Me."

אמרו נעבד עמון קרב
וקשטה אמר אזדמנו כדו לקרבי

If the form and style of Marqah's statements here and elsewhere are
not evidence of the antiquity of these forms which are also found
in our Sifre pericope and throughout Rabbinic literature, surely they
are at least evidence that by the time of Marqah (3rd - 4th C) these
forms had wide circulation and had been well established. Indeed in
regards to our c oncern here he writes, "You waxed fat..."
--with food unfried and drink ungulped. (4:8) And if I understand
him correctly he tells us (4:7) that Moses and Abraham concluded
covenants with God and that these covenants were kept and honored by
God who gave Jacob a land of bounty, so much so that they "kicked"
through the myriads of blessing (cf. Deut. 31:20

אשר נשבעתי...
אכל ושבע...
וניאצוני

also see Neh. 9:25f. and Sam. Pent. Deut. 32:15).

"All these things Moses, the great prophet, condenses into
one utterance in this Song. 'Jacob ate and was satiated',
just as according to the words of the Song (-praise) ' he
waxed fat' so according to the Song 'And he kicked' --
by his very blessings."

I take this translation to be correct and I think it is quite superior
to that offered by MacDonald (B16) (Vol. 1, p. 158, see esp. n. 142)
since I am unable to see why ויבעט must mean here "was prosperous"
as he says. In light of the exegesis offered in Sifre it is quite
possible to mean "kicked" -- which is, after all, the only sense it has
in Scripture. The original Marqah passage runs as follows:

כל אלון מליה צמחנון נביה רבה משה במלה
חדה בהדה שירתה יאכל יעקב וישבע מן מלי
תשבחתה שמן כשירה ויבעט בברכאתה

This passage, then, not only agrees with our Sifre pericope in exegesis
of Deut. 32:15, it provides the very word our midrash in Sifre uses as
its starting point -- "satiated", שובע . Marqah has supplied us with
a Hebrew Samaritan reading of the verse (also found in LXX) i.e.
יאכל יעקב וישבע   which he then relates to the following
וישמן -- ויבעט   to show that Israel was overfed (cf. Marqah 4:8
--"food unfried") and kicked through the blessings provided by the
Song's covenant. Could it be that our Sifre passage is based upon this
very text and (יאכל וישבע   ) "exegesis" cited in Marqah - וישבע   ?
It would explain the weight placed upon לפי שובע מרדים   in Piska 318.
Now Marqah refers to #1) shirta, #2) tushbahta, #3) shira. #1) and #3)
are equivalent terms for Song, the one in Aramaic and the other in
Hebrew. While #2) could be translated "song" we may raise the question
why Marqah did not refer to the Song as shirta which is his usual
designation of the Song (Deut. 32). It is possible that "tushbahta"
here is not meant as Song but as "blessing" and refers to the word 'שבע "
which appears in Samaritan Pent. (cf. Septuagint) Deut. 32:15 in reference

to the blessings promised to Israel (and traced by Marqah to the
terms of the Abrahamic and Mosaic covenants). So much for the
Memar Marqah. A close reading of Sifre Deut. Piska 318 will provide
evidence that the homilists of this midrash were aware that the text
of Nehemiah 9:25f preserved a tradition, linguistically, thematically,
and perhaps even Scripturally (did Neh. 9:25f know of a variant of
Deut. 32:15? Is the variant of LXX and Sam. based upon a gloss
connecting Deut. 32:15 and Deut. 31:20 or Neh. 9:25f?),

Deut. 32:15 reads: (M.T.): וישמן ישורון ויבעט

Sam. Deut. 32:15 reads: יאכל יעקב וישבע ישמן ישרון ויבעט

Neh. 9:25f reads: ויאכלו וישבעו וישמינו...וימרו וימרדו

Sifre Deut. Piska 318 reads: לפי שובע מרדים

It is therefore very likely that the midrashist included a tradition in
his midrash which reflected an unaccepted reading in his received
Scripture but he would have been able to justify his use of this
tradition since he could have been alluding to Neh. 9:25f which was in
his received Scripture. He was, thus, able to derive the very lesson
that Marqah derived -- a lesson likely associated with the verse
prior to the times of Marqah and the midrashist -- i.e. sin is the
result of abundance. I suspect that the midrashist, with his mind's
eye still upon Neh. 9:25f, (cf. Deut. 31:20), interpreted וינאץ
(in Deut. 32:19: cf. Piska 320) again to mean that Israel sinned
through God's bounty:

Deut. 32:19 (M.T.) reads: וירא ה׳ וינאץ

Neh. 9:25 reads: ...בטובך הגדול ויומרו וימרדו...ויעשו נאצות גדולת

Sifre Deut. Piska 320 reads: וירא ה׳ וינאץ -- רבי יהודה אמר ממה
שהנאם משלו מנאצים לפניו

The conclusion that "Israel's sins were the result of her blessings"
was a received tradition by both Marqah and the midrashist, leads us
to speculate upon the nature of variant readings and midrashic
exposition.

Four possibilities present themselves:

    1) The variant reading is responsible for the midrash.
    2) The midrash is responsible for the variant reading.
    3) Traditions float freely and are read into texts by various
       groups who are unaware of the process others use for exegesis
       (e.g. variant readings).
    4) Verses, somewhat similar in form and content, suggest similar
       interpretations to independent exegetes.

While all of these possibilities may at one time or another contain
some truth, I submit that the "1)" is actually the most likely cause
of the common understanding of Deut. 32:15 in Marqah and Sifre. The
term " שבע " was not used by the midrashist haphazardly, his verse
(according to the mss.) used וישמן alone. That he then uses the
terminology of Neh. 9:25 - מרד as opposed to בעט of Deut. 32:15
and continues to relate Deut. 32:19 וינאץ with Neh. 9:25f
נאצות ...... בטובך shows his awareness that Deut. 32 and Neh. 9
(cf. Deut. 31:20) are to be related. The awareness must stem from,
("at the origin of this midrash") a knowledge of the variant reading

And so we have found that the People of Sodom rebelled specifically

under the circumstances of food,[*] as it is said, "As for the earth,

out of it cometh bread..."[S3] --And the Mishna:[**] [E4] -- And likewise

---

for why else would the midrashist use Neh. 9:25f without direct
reference to it. "2)" is possible but assumes that the LXX text
postdates the midrashic tradition, a contention that would have to be
proven since the recording of the LXX text was centuries before the
recording of the midrash. "3)" and "4)" do not explain the common
language between the midrash and the variant reading without straining
the imagination.

[*] Ln: specifically under circumstances of food and specifically
under circumstances of drink and under circumstances of tranquillity.

[**] Ln: related in Eleh Devarim.

S3. Job 28:5.

E4. The omitted section: (Piska 43)
    "As for the earth, out of it cometh bread", (Job 28:5). "The
stones thereof are the place of sapphires", (Job 28:6). "That path
no bird of prey knoweth", (Job 28:7). "The proud beasts have not
trodden it etc," (Job 28:8). --The People of Sodom said, "We have food!
We have silver and gold! Let us arise and cause the 'Law of Hospitality
to Wayfarers' to be eradicated from our land!"
    The Almighty said to them, "Through this very goodness with which
I graced you, you seek to cause the 'Law of Hospitality to Wayfarers'
to be eradicated from amongst yourselves -- I, then, will cause you to
be eradicated from the world".
    What does Scripture say about them? --"He breaketh open a shaft
from where men sojourn."; (Job 28:4)."A contemptible brand etc.";
(Job 12:5)."The tents of robbers prosper, and they that provoke are
secure." (Job 12:6). This instigated them --"against he whom the
Lord brought into their hand." (Job 12:6). And so does Scripture say,
"As I liveth saith the Lord God...Behold this was the iniquity of thy
sister Sodom: (pride, fullness of bread, and careless ease)". (Ez. 16:48).
So much so -- "Neither did she strengthen the hand of the poor
and needy. And they were haughty..." (Ez. 16:50). Similarly you may
cite, "For the drink was finished." (Gen. 13:10). What is it that
Scripture implies, "And they gave their father wine to drink." (Gen.
19:33)? And from whence did they have wine in the cave? But it was
providentially supplied for the occasion. And so does Scripture state,
"And it shall come to pass in that day that the mountains shall drop
down sweet wine." (Joel 4:18).
    If He bestows such to those who provoke Him, how much more
so will He act kindly towards those who perform His will!
    (Here "Mishna" means "Baraita".)

Piska 318

Scripture states, "As I live saith the Lord God, if Sodom (thy

sister and her daughters) hath done...."[S4]

And once Rabbi Gamliel and Rabbi Yehoshua and Rabbi Elazar

ben Azaria and Rabbi Akiba entered Rome -- and the rest of this

is a Baraita in Eleh Devarim --[E5]

S4. Ezekiel 16:48.

E5. The omitted section:(Piska 43).
   And once Rabbi Gamliel and Rabbi Yehoshua and Rabbi Elazar-
ben Azaria and Rabbi Akiba entered Rome. The reverberating noise
of the city could be heard from the Palatium to an extent of one
hundred and twenty mils.[+] They began to cry but Rabbi Akiba rejoiced. They said to him, "Akiba, why is it that we cry but you
rejoice?" He replied, "Why do you cry?" They said to him,
"And should we not lament the fact that the nations which worship
idols, sacrifice to gods and prostrate themselves to graven images
dwell securely, peacefully and tranquilly while the House of the
footstool of our God is a fiery ruin and a den for the beasts of the
field." He replied to them, "For that very reason I rejoice: if He
grants such beneficence to those who provoke Him, how much more so will
He act kindly towards those who perform His will!"

[+] Cf. Lam. R. to Lam. 5:18.
See W. Bacher, "Rome dans le Talmud et le Midrasch,"[(B 97)] REJ, 33,
1896, p. 195f. where Bacher discusses this passage and convincingly
argues that פטיליון refers to the Palatium, the district of Rome,
situated on a height, which housed the palace of the emperor. In
accordance with Bacher's suggested interpretation of the passage I
have translated the third person plurals in the second sentence as
passives, which sense is common in Hebrew and Aramaic third person
plurals.}

And similarly you will find that the People of the Desert
rebelled specifically under circumstances of food and drink, as
it is said, "And the people sat down to eat and to drink, and
rose up to make merry."[S5] What is it the Scripture says about
them? "They have turned aside quickly out of the way...."[S6]

The Holy One, Blessed Be He, said to Moses: Tell Israel:
When you enter the Land, ultimately you will rebel specifically
under circumstances of food and drink and under circumstances
of tranquillity, as it is said, "For when I shall have brought them
into the Land which I swore unto their fathers, flowing with milk
and honey; and they shall have eaten their fill, and waxen fat;
and turned unto other gods...."[S7]

So Moses said to Israel: When you enter the Land ultimately
you will rebel specifically under circumstances of food and drink
and specifically under circumstances of tranquillity, as it is said,
"Lest when you have eaten and are satiated...[S8]and when thy herds and
thy flocks multiply[S9]...then thy heart be lifted up and thou forget
the Lord thy God...."[S10]

And similarly you will find that the sons and daughters of Job
were stricken with punishments specifically under the circumstances

---

S5. Exodus 32:6.   S6. Exodus 32:8.
S7. Deuteronomy 31:20.   S8. Deuteronomy 8:12.
S9. Deuteronomy 8:13.   S10. Deuteronomy 8:14.

of food and drink,* as it is said, "While he was yet speaking there
came yet another, and said: "Thy sons and thy daughters were yet
eating and drinking wine in their eldest brother's house; and
behold, a great wind came..."[S11] And similarly you will find that
the Ten Tribes were exiled specifically under circumstances of food,
drink, and tranquillity, as it is said, "That lie upon beds of
ivory...";[S12] "That drink wine in bowls,";[S13] "Therefore now shall
they go captive at the head of them that go captive."[S14]

And similarly you will find that in the Days[L1] of the Messiah[E6]
ultimately they will rebel specifically under circumstances of food
and drink,** as it is said, "But Jeshurun waxed fat and kicked ...and

* Ln: food and drink and tranquillity

** Ln: and tranquillity

S11. Job 1:18.   S12. Amos 6:4.   S13. Amos 6:6.
S14. Amos 6:7.

L1. The homilist supposes that ישורון signifies the name that
Israel will be called in the Messianic Era. The reference to that era
here is in fact a reference to the three generations which will precede
the era of great peace. It is hardly feasible to think that the
midrashist could think that Israel will rebel in the World to Come.

E6. The "Days of the Messiah" refers to those times of upheaval and
change when the judgment comes, see Klausner, Messianic etc.,[B 231]
339ff. Note that our text preserves the sense of the LXX (Jacob
ate - was satiated and kicked) and Sam. (Jacob ate was satiated and
grew fat...).

Piska 318

he forsook God who made him."

This is like the parable of someone who had a calf. He searched out, cut down and fed vetch to it in order that it would be able to plough with him. When the calf grew older, its master placed a yoke upon it. The calf leaped and broke the yoke and severed the carved ends. And in this regard does Scripture say, "Thou hast broken the bars of wood but thou shalt make in their stead bars of iron."[S15] [E7]

"Thou didst wax fat":

In the days of Jereboam.[E8]

"Thou didst grow thick":

In the days of Ahab.[E9]

"Thou didst become gross":

All this happened in the days of Jehu.[E10]

S15. Jeremiah 28:13.

E7. The Rabbis understood that Israel accepted upon themselves the commitment to be loyal to God and the Torah. They used the metaphorical phrases "accepting the yoke of the Kingship of Heaven" and the "yoke of the commandments". The image in this Piska builds upon this metaphor by claiming that in the Future Era Israel's faith will be unbreakable, i.e. the yoke will be of iron. Israel will not be able to פורק עול   , to rebel.

E8.   The personages mentioned in our Piska are described in the Bible as "they who did that which was evil in the sight of the Lord". For Jereboam see 1 Kings 13:28, 2 Kings 3:3, et passim.

E9. For Ahab see 1 Kings 22:39 et passim.

E10. For Jehu see 2 Kings 10:29 et passim.

Another interpretation:

"Thou didst wax fat":

In the days of Ahaz.[E11]

"Thou didst grow thick":

In the days of Menasseh.[E12]

"Thou didst become gross":

All this happened in the days of Zedekiah.[E13]

Another interpretation:

"Thou didst wax fat, thou didst grow thick, thou didst

become gross":

When someone is fat in the inside, he causes ridges on the out-

side. And in this regard does Scripture say, "Because he hath covered

his inside with his fatness he made collops of fat on his loin

ridges". [S16] [E14]

Another interpretation:

"Thou didst wax fat, thou didst grow thick...."

This refers to the three generations which precede[L2] the Days of

---

S16. Job 15:27.

E11. For Ahaz see 1 Kings 22:51 et passim.

E12. For Menasseh see 2 Kings 23:12 et passim.

E13. For Zedekiah see 2 Kings 24:7 et passim. The first mentioned kings (Jereboam, Ahab, Jehu) were kings of Israel -- the three latter ones (Ahaz, Menasseh, Zedekiah) were kings of Judah.

E14. We seem to have an allegorical interpretation before us: inside imperfection (improper understanding) shows up as outer imperfection (improper behavior).

L2. In some traditions our whole period of three generations preceding

---

the Days of the Messiah is called by the "Days of the Messiah".
Thus sometimes the term refers to those three generations which precede
the Future Morrow of peace. Now the traditions mentioned in this Piska
are largely reported as Tannaitic traditions in B.T. Sanhedrin 108a ff.
Then on 111a we find a tradition in the name of Simaye reporting that
only two of 600,000 entered the promised land and we find that Raba
declared the ratio would be the same in the "days of the Messiah".
Raba may have known a tradition similar to the one we have here. At
any rate we can see that the "Days of the Messiah" refer to a transition
point just as the journey through the desert did. In this regard one
may note the baraita cited in B.T. Sanhed. 99a: The Days of the Messiah
will be 40 years, (in comparison with the journey in the desert) while
another tradition understood them to be 400 years, as was the time
between Abraham and the Exodus, which is also said to have been three
generations see Gen. 15:13ff.). B.T. Sanhedrin 99a distinguishes
between the "Days of the Messiah" and the "World to Come". Israel
can and will sin in "the Days of the Messiah", according to our homilist,
but one would be hard pressed to think of Israel sinning in "the World
to Come" {which I do not think could refer to the after-life of the soul
in this passage.
    L. Finkelstein, (Mabo le-Massektot Abot ve-Abot d'Rabbi Natan:)
Introduction to the Treatises Abot and Abot of Rabbi Nathan, JTS, (B153)
New York, 1950, p. 217ff and p. xxxii ff argues that עולם הבא   refers
to the after-life existence of the World of Souls where one waits to
be resurrected to the Messianic Age. His arguments are not entirely
satisfying and do not close the issue of the identification of עולם הבא .
It may well be that the terms   עתיד לבא, עולם הבא
                          גן עדן, ימות המשיח
were used loosely and interchangeably so that ultimately only context can
now tell us the usage of these terms and where context cannot, the
identification of these terms remains ambiguous. Nevertheless, in
Sifre traditions akin to our passages we may note Sifre Deut. Piska 34
which interprets Proverbs 6:22:
    "When you walk, it (Torah) will lead you" -- In This World.
    "When you lie down, it will watch over you" -- In the time of death.
    "And when you awake" -- In the Days of the Messiah.
    "It will talk with you" -- In the World to Come.
Similarly we note Sifre Deut. Piska 47 which interprets Deut. 6:21:
    "That your days may be multiplied" -- In This World
    "And the days of our children" -- In the Days of the Messiah.
    "As the days of Heaven upon the earth" -- In the World to Come.
The progression is: This World, (death), the Days of the Messiah, the
World to Come. Thus it would seem that "the World to Come" refers to
the Era of Peace, the End of Days, when the Torah will communicate
easily with Israel and the Heavenly Kingdom is upon the earth.}.

the Messiah,[E15] as it is said, "Their land also is full of horses,

neither is there any end of their chariots,";[S17] "Their land also

is full of silver and gold neither is there any end of their

treasuries,";[S17] "Their land is also full of idols; everyone

worshipeth the work of his own hands, that which his own fingers

have made."[S17]

"And he forsook the God who made him":

And in this regard does Scripture say, ("Who hath stretched out

the heavens and hath established the earth."[S18]), "For My people

have committed two evils...."[S18a] [E16] The Holy One, Blessed Be He,

---

S17. Isaiah 2:7,8.   S18. (Ln) Isaiah 51:13.
S18a. Jeremiah 2:13.

E15. The sense of "wax fat" here is applied to fatness or fullness of
the Land which is supposed to precede the blissful Era of resurrection.
However the fullness is not that of blessing but of abomination. Three
texts are seen as pointing to the three generations prior to the Days
of the Messiah (also, as Lichtenstein[B 247] points out the three
expressions "fat", "thick", "gross" point to three generations). These
generations of sin symbolize the breaking point -- the fullness
of the measure of sin before the final judgment. The homilist understands
Is. 2 as referring to those days of final judgment when the terror of
the Lord will approach (Is. 2:10). See further, R. Le Déaut La Nuit
Pascale,[B 242] p. 147ff., who finds in Gen. 15:16 the model for three
generations of tribulation followed by redemption. See also, Y.
Zakovitch, The Pattern of the Numerical Sequence 3-4 in the Bible,[B354]
Ph.D. Dissertation, Jerusalem, Hebrew U., 1977, ch. 2, p. 157ff.

E16. Friedmann [B 47] follows the reading in Ln here and emends:
    This is according to the matter of which Scripture states,
    "And thou hast forgotten the Lord thy Maker, Who hath stretched
    out the heavens and hath established the earth." (Is. 51:13).
He takes "For My people..." as a separate citation. The first
citation works well in that it mirrors Deut. 32:15, "And he forsook
the God Who made him". The second citation (Jer. 2:13) is to equate
the "forsaking" of God mentioned in Deut. 32:15 with God's "forsaking"
Israel and so the point is made that the punishment is "measure for
measure".

said to them: In the measure that you have meted out to Me, have
I meted out to you -- "I have abandoned My house, I have forsaken
My heritage...,";[S19] "And he forsook the tabernacle of Shiloh."[S20]
And Scripture also states, "For thou hast forsaken thy people the
House of Jacob."[S21]

Another interpretation:

"And he forsook God Who made him":

This is according to the matter of which Scripture states,
"And He brought me into the inner court of the Lord's house, and
behold, at the door of the Temple of the Lord, between the porch
and the altar, were about five and twenty men, with their backs toward
the Temple of the Lord...."[S22 E17]

Rabbi Dostaye the son of Yehuda says: Do not read "And he forsook
God Who made him; and he dishonored" but rather "And he forsook God
Who made him, that the Rock should dishonor his salvation."[E18] This is

---

S19. Jeremiah 2:13.   S20. Psalms 78:60.
S21. Isaiah 2:6.   S22. Ezekiel 8:16.

E17. See my article, "Allusions to Christian and Gnostic Practices in
Talmudic Tradition,"(B 103) Journal for the Study of Judaism, vol. 12,
no. 1, pp. 101-109 where I suggest that the "turning of the back" was
understood by the Rabbis as a symbol of adherence to gnostic doctrines
of sacred and demonic space.

E18. The translation of this passage is quite difficult; yet,given the
way in which the proof texts of this pericope are used,it appears to
me that צור is to be understood here as subject of the verse and not
object, cf. A Rozenzweig, Festschrift zu Israel's Lewy's siebezigsten
Geburstag (editors: M. Brann and J. Elbogen) reprinted Makor,
Jerusalem, 5732, p. 317, p. 223 (notes).(B 297) L. Silberman translates;
not -- "he discarded his saving Rock" but "and the Rock discarded His
salvation", (This is measure for measure, נבל = discard).

according to the matter of which Scripture states, "Do not contemn us, for Thy name's sake, do not dishonor the throne of Thy glory."[S23]

16

"They roused Him to jealousy with strange gods":

For they went and made things of foreignness.[E19] And so does Scripture state, "And also Maacah his mother he removed from being queen because she had made an abominable image for an Asherah."[S24]

"With abominations they did provoke Him":

This refers to the act of sodomy.[E20] And so does Scripture state, "Thou shalt not lie with mankind as with womankind; it is an abomination."[S25] And Scripture also states, "And also a male prostitute there was in the land."[S26]

S23. Jeremiah 14:21.   S24. 1 Kings 15:13.
S25. Leviticus 18:22.   S26. 1 Kings 14:24.

E19. This comment is made in reference to the entire verse, "They roused Him to jealousy with strange gods, with abominations did they provoke Him." The midrashist notes the parallelism of the verse, "foreignness"= "abominations" and shows through a proof text that abominable images (idols) were in fact made just as Moses had foretold.

E20. The midrashist wishes to note here that the parallelism of "strange gods" and "abominations" does not give rise to a needless repetition because "abomination" can also refer to the act of sodomy as the proof text from Lev. 18 shows. The midrashist again notes that we have a proof text showing that such acts of sodomy were in fact practised just as Moses had foretold.

17

"They sacrificed unto demons -- no-gods":

Had they worshipped the sun and the moon, the stars and the
constellations -- things which are necessary for the world since
the world derives benefit from them, there would not have been a
double jealousy[E21] but they worshipped things that were of no
benefit to them but were harmful to them.

"Unto demons":

What is the method of a demon? He enters[L3] a person and casts

---

E21. The "double jealousy" stems from the double reference "roused to
jealousy" and "provoked". Had they sacrificed in a humanly understand-
able fashion it would have been insult enough but they sacrificed
irrationally and thereby added insult to injury, i.e. they did not
evaluate their motivations properly, see "E25", Piska 318. It seems
to me that the midrashist understood the words of the verse לא אלה
to mean "without any point, any substance" and thereby confirmed the
idea that שערום = שערו .

L3. Midrash Leqah Tob reads כופה אותו על פניו giving the understanding
that one is being "thrown into a fit upon his face". Hizkuni to
this verse explains the term "shed" here as "because they overpower
(שודים) the mind of man, so are they called "shedim"." In our
Sifre passage, the way the shed possesses one is by entering. Perhaps
the homilist of Sifre Ha'azinu has examined the wording of Deut. 32:17
and found in וזבחו לשדים an allusion to זובח וקטר . B.T. Krithoth
3b and B.T. Sanhedrin 65a show that there were two traditional understandings of מקטר לשד . Abaye explains the terminology to mean that
one has summoned shedim for the purpose of utilizing their powers to
perform supernatural (על מנת לחברו) acts. Rashi understands
the Talmudic passage to mean that Abaye considered the word מקטר to
refer to "sacrificing" to a shed for the purpose of summoning him. One
may suggest an alternative interpretation of מקטר against the view of
Rashi. Abaye may have understood מקטר as the act of "binding"
oneself to a shed, see J.N. Epstein, REJ vol. 73 (1921), p. 33, who
discusses the magical connotations of קושר and see I. Gruenwald,
Apocalyptic etc., p. 66, n. 135 who suspects that קושר in the
Sandelphon traditions (e.g. "Ma'aseh Merkabah," G. Scholem, Jewish
Gnost. etc., Appendix "C", para. 20, p. 111:
            דהוא קטר תגא למריה דתיסק
can be compared with B.T. Hag. 13b:
        דאמר שם אתגא ואזל ויתב
--illustration is my own) may mean to conjure. Thus מקטר may be

him into a fit.[E22]

"Gods that they knew not":

That even the Gentile Nations of the World are not acquainted
with them.

---

taken to mean "conjuring the attachment of a shed by the use of a
magic name". Perhaps Rashi actually understood the use of מקטר in
this way and offered his interpretation to explain the term זובח וקטר .
Thus מקטר can refer to sacrifices or to conjuring. I interpret
B.T. Krith. 3b and B.T. Sanhed. 65a to show that Ravva and Abaye
argued about the meaning of מקטר . Ravva understood it to mean
"sacrificial worship" while Abaye understood it to mean "conjuring".
Now the homilist of Sifre Ha'azinu may have, as Rashi may have,
equated the terms זובח וקטר and קטר . He thereby discovered
that Deut. 32:17 was speaking of "conjuring", and thus discussed
what happens when one conjures shedim. He possibly paraphrased his
understanding of "binding oneself" to a demon (through sacrifice)
by simply stating -- "it enters him". Perhaps our homilist here is
the same one who understands further in this Piska that when Israel's
ancestors summoned shedim, their hair did not stand on end. In this
way he draws a contrast between serious conjuring and mindless
conjuring. He claims that Israel's ancestors were guilty only of the
latter and thereby deflates the seriousness of Israel's unfaithfulness
to God. It is noteworthy that our homilist considers summoning a
shed to be an offense mentioned in the Song of Moses and he thereby
voices his disapproval of practices known to us from Sefer HaRazim
and Merkabah texts.

E22. I suspect we have a folk etymology here which derives שד from
Aram. שדי (B 71) "to cast down" (cf. Targ. to Job 28:6). See also
Aruch Compl. s.v. כף , and perhaps כופה here is taken as the
active form with the meaning "to cast into a fit" as opposed to its
usage as "compelled" as in B.T. Rosh Hashannah 28a (perhaps in this
B.T. source also כופה means "to be thrown into a fit"). Some texts
of midrash actually add "on his face" to make its sense clear
(see Midrash Haggadol as cited in Midrash Tannaim (B 26)). For
the method of exegesis of "discovering" roots in obscure words
cf. Ruth Rabba 1:5. See "E5", Piska 321.

"New gods that came up of late":

Whenever a gentile sees it he says, "This is an idol of the Jews!" And so does Scripture state, "As my hand has reached the kingdom of the idols, whose graven images were from Jerusalem and from Samaria." [S27] This teaches that Jerusalem and Samaria supplied molds[E23] to the whole world.

"Your ancestors did not שערו them":

That the hair ⟨ שער ⟩ of your ancestors did not stand up in their presence.[E24]

S27. Isaiah 10:10.

E23. "Graven images" is understood here to refer to "molds" which are engraven.

E24. See Rashi to Deut. 32:16 and cf. 1Q pesher Hab. 4:9 (Hab. 1:11):
אז חף רוח ויעבר וישם כוחו לאל **זו**
In our passage שערום is taken to mean "to cause the hair to stand on end" which is a sign of reverence. Our text here presents exegetical problems in the understanding of Deut. 32:17. The Massoretic Text reads, "Which your fathers dreaded not (שערום לא)." The homilist tells us the etymology of שערום which he knows means "dread". It derives from שיער , "hair" and hence means "hair-raising". Thus שערום is an expression of fear. Midrash Haggadol [(B 20)] to Deut. 32:17 connects the word שערום of Deut. 32:17 with
תסמר שערת בשרי
of Job 4:16 which refers to "hair-raising" experience. Hoffman, in his text of Midrash Tannaim here, places the reference to Job 4:16 in petite. That at some point in the period of composition of Sifre Ha'azinu, שערום was exegeted in terms of Job 4:16 (cf. M. Dahood, "Hebrew-Ugaritic Lexicography", Biblica 50 (1964), p. 337) can be seen from Avoth de Rabbi Nathan "B" 38. ARN "B" understands Job 4:16 to refer to the fear experienced by Israel as they perceived an indiscernible form at the Theophany of Sinai. The relationship between the homilies of ARN "B" and Sifre Ha'azinu deserves attention. Suffice it to say here that at many points in this work I have drawn upon parallels between the two and noted them, e.g. "L1", Piska 306; "L6", Piska 306; "L1", Piska 310; "E5", Piska 329; "E4", Piska 331.
Another example in Rabbinic literature where hair raising denotes fear can be found in Tanhuma Buber, Balak 24 (cf. Num. R. 20:20) where someone's hair was said to have stood on end when he realized that he

Another interpretation:

"Your ancestors did not שערו them":

For your ancestors did not evaluate them ⟨ שער ⟩ to know whether or not they had any use.[E25]

---

had eaten swine's flesh. It would appear then, that the homilist understood the passage in one of two ways:
1) The spirits and images that the ancestors of the Israelites worshipped had no substance and no reality for the worshippers in that the spirits could not evoke fear, "hair-raising" awe.
2) The ancestors of Israel did not worship ("have hair-raising awe") idols at all.

Usages of the raising of body hair to express "fear" are widespread in religious literatures. For instance, the vision of a spectre of ones's family i.e. the wandering spirit of a dead man, is said to make the hair of the beholder of the spirit to rise: "The spectre which makes the hair (šārtu) of my body to rise...(see F. Thureau-Dangin, "Rituels et Amulettes contre Labartu", [B 332] Revue d'assyriologie et d'archeologie orientale, vol. 18, no. 4, Paris, 1921, p. 187. See his p. 187, n. 2 for two other parallels to our matter in Assyrian sources). Cliff Hospital pointed out to me similar usages of "hair-raising" to denote "fear" in Indian Literature. See The Bhagavad Gita, [B 6] translated by F. Egerton, Harper Torch Books, Harper and Row, New York, 1965:

I desire to see thy form as God (11:3 -- the request is granted and then we read:)...Then filled with amazement, his (body) hair standing upright (Cliff Hospital assures me the reference is to "body-hair"), Dharamjaya bowed with his head to the God and said...(11:14).

(The fear of killing elicits this response which allows us to get a sense of the deep emotion expressed by "hair-raising" images:) My limbs sink down and my mouth becomes parched and there is trembling in my body and my hair stands on end (1:24).

In later Indian Literature we hear that joyous, ecstatic experience can also cause one's hair to stand on end (see Bhāgavata Purāna with Cūrnika Commentary, [B 6] Bombay, 1910).

The point of our midrash (following interpretation #1 above which is the interpretation of Deut. 32:17 given by ARN "B" ch. 38 which believes the reference of the verse to be to those who worshipped idols in the days of Enos) is that the later Israelites invent new gods and, unlike their ancestors, they revere their gods in fear and ecstacy.

E25. שערום is taken here as if from שער "to evaluate" which has the sense of "esteem", cf. Koran sura 6:91: They have not estimated God with the estimation that is due Him. See above "E20".

Another interpretation:

"Your ancestors did not שערום them":

Do not read "שערום (fear them)" but " שעום (regarded

them)."[E26] For even though they sacrificed and made offerings to

them, they did not revere them. This is according to the matter

of which Scripture states: "And to Cain and his offering, He did

not regard ⟨ שעה ⟩."[S28]

END OF PISKA

S28. Genesis 4:5.

E26. The dropping of letters is admissible in midrashic exegesis.
See A. Rosenzweig, op. cit., (B 297) p. 318 and p. 250 for further
examples of this method. Here the midrashist drops " ר"
from שערום to get שעום . In Gen. God did not שעה (have regard)
for Cain's sacrifice although he offered one. So,here also "your
ancestors" had no regard (שעום) for the false gods although they
did offer sacrifices to them.

18

"Of the Rock that begot thee thou wast unmindful":

The Holy One, Blessed Be He, said to them: You have made Me feel as if I were a male who sought[L1] to give birth.[E1] --Were it[E2] a recovering woman, sitting upon the birthstool, would she not experience pain? This is according to the matter of which Scripture states,[T1] "For the children are come to the birth, and there is not strength to bring forth."[S1]

--Were it a sick woman who was having her first child, would she not experience pain! This is according to the matter of which Scripture states,[T1] "For I have heard a voice as of a woman in travail, the anguish as of her that bringeth forth her first child."[S2]

S1. 2 Kings 19:3.   S2. Jeremiah 4:31.

T1. Omitted in Ln possibly due to homoioteleuton. ("Scripture states").

L1. The sense of מבקש ל... is "unsuccessfully attempt". Midrash Tannaim actually spells this out as:
מבקש לילד ואינו יולד
See "E3", Piska 319. Also Piska 322: בקשו לברוח.
In Sifre 319 here it has the force of "hypothetically". (See P. Saydon, "The Conative Imperfect in Hebrew", VT, 12 (1962).

E1. The passage is arranged in order of ascending degrees of pain in order to show that the pain of a male who midrashically aches in childbirth, which is a pain of no fruition, is (hypothetically) the severest pain . Such is the pain that Israel is pictured giving to God through her behavior. The masculine form ילדך is used in Deut. 32:18 as if to imply (so the midrashist believes) that the pain is like that of a male hypothetically giving birth. For the use of בקש ל... meaning to perpetrate a scheme which is ultimately doomed to failure (and therefore is only a hypothetical scheme) see Esther 2:4, Gen. R. 84:1 and B.T. Berachoth 12b. Friedmann[B 47] thinks that the midrashist took צור as an allusion to צער but even if he is mistaken, the picture of pain fits the verse. See further Conclusion no. 7.

E2. Here we have an exclamatory usage of אילו as described in L1, Piska 306.

--Were it that she had two in her womb, would she not experience pain! This is according to the matter of which Scripture states, "And the children struggled together with her."[S3]

--Were it a man, whose nature is not one of giving birth, who sought to give birth, would the experience of pain not be doubly doubled! This is according to the matter of which Scripture states, "Ask ye now and see whether a man doth travail with child."[S4]

Another interpretation:

"Of the Rock that begot thee thou wast unmindful":

Would you have Me forget the merit of your ancestors![E3]

And so does Scripture state, "Look unto the rock whence ye were hewn and to the hole of the pit whence ye were digged,[S5] (Look unto Abraham your father and unto Sarah that bore you)."

_____

S3. Genesis 25:22.   S4. Jeremiah 30:6.
S5. Isaiah 51:1.

E3. Deut. 32:18 reads: צור ילדך תשי   and the midrashist shows that "צור " may be a reference to Abraham (see also Yalkut Shimoni (766) to Balak 23). The verse continues ותשכח אל מחללך   and this is seen as a reference to Sarah. Indeed Isaiah 51:2 refers to Abraham by צור and to Sarah by תחוללכם   . If תשכח is read as a hiph'il we could render the verse as "Would you have God forget (Sarah and Abraham) that bore thee". The lesson is that if Israel continues upon her present course, God may be incited to forget the merit of Israel's forebearers since their behavior was unlike anything Israel now does. It is noteworthy that Ibn Ezra to Deut. 32:18 equates תשי   with תש (forget) as in Proverbs 4:5. Cf. N.A. van Uchelen, "The Targumic Version of Deut. 33:15, Journal of Jewish Studies, (B 340) vol. 31 (1980), no. 2, p. 199ff.

Piska 319

Another interpretation:

"Of the Rock that begot thee thou wast unmindful":

Whenever I desire to favor you, you weaken the Strength of Heaven:[E4] You stood by the Sea and said, This is my God and I will adore Him."[S6] --I desired to favor you. Then you reversed yourselves and said, "Let us make a captain and let us return to Egypt."[S7]

You stood at Mount Sinai and said, "Of all the Lord hath spoken, we will perform and we will hearken." [S8] --I desired to favor you. Then you reversed yourselves and said about the Golden Calf, "This is thy god, O Israel."[S9]

Thus it is that whenever I desire to favor you, you weaken the Strength of Heaven.

S6. Exodus 15:2.   S7. Numbers 14:4.
S8. Exodus 24:7.   S9. Exodus 32:4.

E4. This notion of "the weakening of the Strength of Heaven" has been discussed by I. Abrahams, Studies in Pharisaism, (B 84) 16, p. 180, "God is likened to a sculptor whose art is nullified by the vacillation of the model." Also see D. Patte, Early Jewish Hermeneutic etc., (B 284) p 106. For the midrashist, God's kingship in the world is dependent upon His saving of Israel, as the homilist notes at the end of the Piska 306. Thus it is that if Israel does not allow God to save her she indeed weakens the Power of Heaven (a term which stands for God). The midrashist thinks that Deut. 32:18 שׁי comes from שׁשׁן "to weaken" (cf. Num. R. 9:1 where it is claimed that the "yod" of שׁי in Deut. 32:18 is to be written in a small form as if it were non-existent). This midrash is part of those cycles of midrashim which posit that it was Abraham, who through his constancy, gave God his sovereignty upon the earth, see Piska 313, "E5". Israel may be about to reverse this process by her lack of probity.) Cf. Lam. R. 1:35 where this midrash is attributed to Azariah in the name of Judah in the name of Symon.

Piska 319

"And didst forget God that bore thee ⟨מחוללך⟩":

Rabbi Meir said: God who experienced pangs ⟨החיל⟩ concerning you; God who experienced pain concerning you.[E5] This is according to the matter of which Scripture states, "Pangs ⟨חיל⟩, as of a woman in travail."[S10]

Rabbi Yehuda says: Who made you full of cavities ⟨מחיילים⟩.[E6] Another interpretation:

"And didst forget the God that bore thee ⟨מחוללך⟩"

God who fixed ⟨החיל⟩ His name upon you yet did not fix it upon any other people or kingdom.[E7] And so does Scripture state, "I am the Lord thy God who took you out of the Land of Egypt."[S11]

Rabbi Nehemiah says: God who makes you sicker* than all other peoples when you do not occupy yourselves with Torah. And so does Scripture state, "The voice of the Lord is upon the waters - (until)-

---

* Ln: more profane

S10. Psalms 48:7.   S11. Exodus 20:2.

E5. מחלל seems to be related to חיל "to writhe with pain". God's fathering of the Jewish nation is a painful task. See also Marmorstein, The Old Rabbinic Doctrine II, Essays in Anthropomorphism, (B 260) p. 70 for the idea that God shares Israel's distress. Cf. Midrash Tannaim, p. 195.

E6. See also Num. R. 9:1 where מחילים is understood as "hearts and kidneys". The point is that God knows our thoughts (heart) and inner feelings (kidneys). Also see "E8" and E10 to Piska 309.

E7. The emphasis here is upon "thy God", Ex. 20, cf. Num. R. 9:4. By His deliverance of Israel, God has caused His name to be associated with Israel's salvation history. See P.T. Sukka 3:4 and cf. Dev. R. (ed. Lieberman), p. 28.

...the voice of the Lord makes the "hinds" ⟨אילות⟩[L2] [E8]
weak ⟨יחולל⟩ ".[S12]

Another interpretation:

"And didst forget the God that bore thee ⟨מחוללך⟩":

The God who forgives you ⟨מוחל לך⟩ concerning all your

transgressions.[E9]

END OF PISKA

S12. Psalms 29:3-9.

L2. אילות has probably been read midrashically as אולת.While the
proof text of Ps. 29:9 appears in Midrash Tannaim (p. 195), the passage,
remarking that Israel is turned sick before the gaze of the world
community when they do not "do" the Torah, is missing in that work.
The expression עושה את התורה may well be taken here to mean "to study
Torah", see N. Broznick "עשות ספרים הרבה אין קץ", "Beth Mikra,25 (1980),
p. 213ff. The passage then means that:"God makes Israel sick before the
gaze of others"as a proof text can be interpreted to show that the Voice
of the Lord turns ignoramuses sickly. Perhaps יחולל has been understood to be a form of חלה and see G.R. Driver in Mélanges de l'Univer-
sité Saint-Joseph (Beyrouth), vol. 45 (1969) and the article
"Alexandrian Analogical Word-Analysis and Septuagint Translation
Techniques: a case study of חלל-חיל - חול " in Textus,vol. 8 (1973).

E8. As L2, or read יחול לאילות= "sickens because of TORAH." For
אילת= TORAH. See B.T. Erub. 54b.

E9. The midrashist splits up מחלל into מחל לך "forgives you".
In Ln the text assumes ("and so does Scripture state {?}")
"ותשכח אל מחללך " (Deut. 32:18). Cf. Tanna DeVe Eliahu ch. 26.
אל תקרי מחללו אלא מחל לו
Cf. Seder Eliahu Rabba,B32a p. 134 n. 25 and cf. B.T. Shabboth 118b.

19

"The Lord saw it and spurned":

Rabbi Yehuda says: "From that with which He graced[E1] them from His own, they spurned Him."

Rabbi Meir says: "Because of the provocation of His sons[E2] and daughters." And are not such matters to be argued by a fortiori arguments:

If even when they provoke, they are called "sons",

then how much more so are they to be called "sons"

when they do not provoke!

20

"And He said, 'I will hide My face from them'":

The Holy One, Blessed Be He, said, "Behold I will remove[E3] My Shekina[L1] from amongst them."

L1. The term שכינה not only represents the "divine presence" but also signifies "divine favor and care".

E1. Friedmann sees a midrashic play upon the word " וינאץ ". According to him, the midrashist has broken the word up and extricated the word " נאה " from it. Thus it means "to despise (נאץ)" that which was given to be "of benefit (נאה)". Another possibility is that the midrash plays upon the scriptural word "ירא " which in itself can refer to "needed provision", cf. Gen. 22:8, Deut. 33:21 but the midrashist has underscored his point by dropping the "r" (see "E25", to Piska 318) so as to change ירא into יאה , Friedmann's[B 47] text is significant-ly different from F's[B 48] here. The point in F's version is that the homilist paraphrases the verse to mean "The hand that fed him, he bit." L. Silberman translates here "They spurned him by means of the very things (good) He had given them".

E2. Meir sees in the usage of "sons" here the lesson that even when Israel sins, they are still God's children. But see the Christian usage of Deut. 32:19 in polemic against the Jews, e.g. Justin Martyr, Dialogue with Trypho,[B 261] p. 338, ch. 123, and p. 332, ch. 119.

E3. This midrash, like other ancient versions (e.g. Targumim, Peshitta, LXX) preserves an understanding of אסתירה as if it read אסירה . In

"I will see what their end will be":

For I know what is to be their final[L2] disposition.

Another interpretation:

Behold I will deliver them into the hands of the Four Kingdoms so that they will be enslaved by them.[E4]

"I will see what their end will be":

And I will know what they are at their end.

"For they are a generation of perversenesses":

--"A perverse generation"? "A generation of perversity". --

Specifically "A generation of perversities" is written here:

They are wayward and perfidious.[E5]

---

this way it may be argued that variant readings of הסיר , in other ancient versions where M.T. reads הסתר , (cf. Talmon, "Q.T. Text" in Qumran & the History of the Biblical Text,[B 329] p. 29ff., p. 109ff., and E.R. Rowlands, "The Targum and the Peshitta Version of the Book of Isaiah",[B 298] VT 9, (1959), p. 188) are preserved in midrashic lore so that הסתר may be generally equated with הסיר for the midrashist. Is. 50:6 LXX, indeed rendered M.T. הסתרתי- (לא) -- as apostrepsein to prosopon. The midrash introduced here by the "another interpretation" sees a derivation of אסתירה from מסר "to hand over". The idea is that the way God hides His face is by delivering Israel into the hands of oppressors. God uses agents to punish but redeems by Himself. Cf. Ben Sira 18:24. Cf. Marqah 4:12, אסתלקו טבאתי מנון .

L2. The midrashist has to paraphrase Deut. 32:19 lest we think that אחריתם could refer to Israel's destruction, whereas it refers to their future end (see also Targ. Onk. here). I take the version in Midrash Tannaim (p. 196) to mean that God will remove his Shekina from them to let them know - להודיעם - that which could be their end, or what could transpire at their end.

E4. The homilist equates God's hiding His face with the state of Israel's exile.

E5. The homilist finds the plural הפכנים aptly describes these people as "two-faced", turning about, and then about once again. The homily acts as an introduction to the next verse where the homilist finds the claim that Israel was unsteady in her faith, first worshipping

"Children in whom there is no faithfulness":

You are children in whom there is no constancy.[E6] You stood

at Mount Sinai and said, "Of all that the Lord hath spoke, we will

do and we will hearken".[S1] I responded, "You are heavenly beings".[S2]

When you said about the Golden Calf, "This is thy god, O Israel",[S3]

so I also said to you, "Then like a man you shall die".[S4] I brought

you into the Land (of your ancestors) and built for you the Chosen

Temple. I said that you would never be exiled from it. When you said,

"We have no portion with David,"[S5] so I also said, "And Israel shall

surely be exiled from upon its land."[S6]

---

the Golden Calf and then rejecting the ideals of David. Cf. Tanhuma
Buber, addition to Shelach 7, vol. 2, p. 180. For the sense of
ho poneros, see C. Taylor, Pirqe Aboth, Sayings of the Jewish Fathers;
Ktav, New York, 1969, Excursus 5, p. 128ff. Cf. Marqah 2:3 "...believed
but they were unworthy","...believed but did not remain steadfast "
(quotes Ex. 5:21, and Ex. 14:21). L. Silberman translates: "It is
not written 'a generation that will overturn תהפוך ' but 'a perverse
generation' that is, they are wayward; they are perfidious."

S1. Exodus 24:7.   S2. Psalms 82:6.   S3. Exodus 32:4.
S4. Psalms 82:2.   S5. 2 Samuel 20:1.   S6. Amos 7:17.

E6. Since the homily exists here in a similar way to the presentation
of Justin Martyr, Dialogue with Trypho, p. 352, ch. 132; p. 178,
ch. 20-21; p. 331, ch. 119, I assume that the passage antedates the
Christian polemic. Would Jews use an anti-Jewish polemic unless this
existed before Christians used it against Jews?

Rabbi Dostaye the son of Yehuda says:[E7] Do not read "in whom there is no faithfulness (אמון)" but "in whom there is no amen". For they did not want to respond "amen" after the prophets when they blessed them. And so does Scripture state, "That I perform the oath that I swore unto your fathers, to give them a land flowing with milk and honey, as at this day".[S7] And not one of them opened his mouth to say "amen" until Jeremiah himself came and answered "amen", as it is said, "Then I answered and said, 'Amen Lord'."[S8]

21

"They have roused M.e to jealousy with a no-god; they have provoked Me with their hot airs":

You see the case of the man who worships an image -- something which he sees. Yet they worshipped shadows, yea, not only shadows but the very steam that rises from the pot. This is like the matter of which it is said,[E8] "They have provoked Me with their hot airs."

S7. Jeremiah 11:5.   S8. Jeremiah 11:5.

E7. Rabbi Dostaye's insight ties together verses 20-35 into a unit forecasting the consequences of Israel's refusal to acknowledge the covenant. Dostaye's statement makes God's reaction more immediate than does the introductory statement.

E8. For Talmudic references regarding shadow-worship see LF's notes to this passage. However, his sources should be considered with caution as to their applicability here. For a discussion concerning midrashim such as ours which contain both a lead verse and a proof text, both verses being the same, see E. Katz, "It is This which Scripture says", Hadarom, no. 44 (5737) p. 207ff. Katz argues against the view of Heinemann and maintains that the form such as that of our midrash is "original".

"And I will raise them to jealousy with a no-people
⟨ בלא עם ⟩ ":

Do not read "בלא עם " but rather " בלוי עם "[*][E9] This refers
to those who come from the nations and the kingdoms and remove them
from their houses.

Another interpretation:

This refers to those who come from Barberia and Mauretania
that go naked in the market place. You have no greater example of
a shameful, despicable person than he who goes naked in the market
place.

"I will provoke them with a vile nation":

This refers to the <u>minim</u>. And so does Scripture state, "The
vile[L3][E10] person says in his heart, 'There is no God'."[S9]

---

* Ln: בלוי עם

S9. Psalms 14:1.

L3. According to this passage, מינים are people who do not believe
in God. Cf. Tosefoth B.T. Avodah Zarah 26b " איזהו מין " . The
proof text of Ps. 14:1 continues: "They are corrupt, they do
abominable deeds." The midrashist accounts for the existence of <u>minim</u>
through his interpretation which allows the possibility that they serve
God's purposes. See also F. Dexinger, "Die Sektenproblematik," <u>Kairos</u>,
21 (1979), no. 4, p. 273ff and S. Lachs, "R. Abbahu and the Minim,"
<u>JQR</u>,60 (1970),p. 197ff.

E9. See B.T. Yevamoth 63b which refers to our passage by תניתא
and thereby indicates it to be Tannaitic. The Sifre homilist finds a
midrashic derivation of בלא עם as בלוי עם
    a) "caravan nations" who are bands of outlaws (cf. Piska 317, "E15").
    b) "dregs and rags" (cf. Jeremiah 38:11-12) worn by uncivilized
       peoples who go "naked" in the streets. According to B.T. Yev. 63b
       such people are <u>despised</u> by God.

E10. נבל properly "the fool". B.T. Yev. 63b attributes our midrash
to Rabbi Eliezer. See also B.T. Berachoth 12b. Ben Sira (50:25) takes

22

"For a fire is kindled in my nostril":

When retribution comes from me, it will come only in "nostril".

Where is "nostril"?[E11] In Hell, as it says, "And burneth unto the

depths of the nether-world."

"And it shall devour the land with its produce":

This refers to the Land of Israel.[E12]

---

the word נבל to refer to the Samaritans of Shechem –

וגוי נבל הדר בשכם

parallel to

ושלישי איננו עם (=בלא עם)

While Midrash Tannaim p. 196, likewise identifies the term בלא עם
with the Samaritans (= צרי). R. Herford, Christianity in Talmud and
Midrash, 1903, p. 235, p. 378 ff. identifies the minim with
Christians while M. Friedlander, Der vorchristliche jüdische Gnosticismus, 1898, sees them as gnostics. Geza Vermes, "The Decalogue and the
Minim", (B 342) In Memoriam Paul Kahle, Berlin, 1968 (p. 232ff.),
thinks the term "minim" first referred to "gnostics" and in later usage
came to mean "Christians", (see also F. Dexinger, "Die Sektenproblematik
in Judenthum ", Kairos, 21 (1979). However, Paul in Romans 10:19
refers to our verse and takes בלא עם as signifying the gentiles
who had "now" to come into Christianity so as to absorb the divine
promises given to the prophets. Thus, Christianity was seen as a
reference point of this verse from early times, even if the term minim
only later came to signify them. For מינים see also Sifre Deut. Piska
331 and B.T. Pesachim 140 a.

E11. Here we have an instance of "the nostril" as the symbol of "angry
vengeance". In Deut. 32:22, the homilist finds an equation between
"the burning nostril" (a common phrase in the Bible) and the burning
in the nether world. The conclusion is drawn that Hell is the source
of punishing vengeance.

E12. The explanations here differ according to a schema (see further
Piska 322) attributed to Nehemiah and Judah. Deut. 32:22 gives rise to
two interpretations, one expounding that it refers to the Land of Israel
and the other expounding that it refers to the Nations of the World
who possess the entire world (and the fulness thereof as in Psalms
24:1). Marqah also knows the expression "Earth and the fulness thereof" –see Marqah 4:8 –in connection with Deut. 32:22 he states 410:
"For a fire is kindled in my anger...the Land will be destroyed and
all its inhabitants. In their evil doing the foundations of the
mountains will be swept away."

"And setteth ablaze the foundations of the mountains":

This refers to Jerusalem. This is according to the matter of which Scripture states, "Jerusalem -- the mountains are about her (and the Lord is about His people)."[S10]

Another interpretation:

"And it[L4] shall devour the land with its produce":

This refers to the world "and the fulness thereof."

"And setteth ablaze the foundations of the mountains":

This refers to the Four Kingdoms.[E13] And so does Scripture state, "...and behold[*] there came four chariots:...:"[T1] [S11]

END OF PISKA

----

*Ln: I lifted up mine eyes and saw and behold Four Kingdoms came out from between the two mountains and the mountains were mountains of brass."

S10. Psalms 125:2.   S11. Zechariah 6:1.

T1. Ln's "Four Kingdoms" in lieu of M.T. "four chariots" is likely an error by association.

L4. The midrashist understands by this that the Gentile Nations of the Earth and their wealth will be consumed.

E13. The Piska ends with an apocalyptic view of God's anger wreaking destruction upon the nations. Zechariah 6:1 is used to allude to the destruction of the Four Kingdoms (=four chariots of the mountains) since Deut. 32:23 speaks of the burning of the foundations of the mountains. Ln has actually written "Four Kingdoms" for M.T. "four chariots" - most likely in error by association with the midrash.

23

"I will gather evils upon them":

Behold I will gather together all retributions and bring all
of them upon them at one time.

Another interpretation:

Behold, I will gather them all together into the net[E1] and
bring upon them all their retributions -- all at once.

Another interpretation:

"I will gather ⟨ אסוף ⟩ evils upon them" is not written here,
but rather[E2] "I will bring to an end ⟨ אספה ⟩". For all the

---

E1. Friedmann[(B 47)] follows the first printed edition and omits this
section. Ln reads חרים here and thereby indicates that עלימו of
Deut. 32:23 is midrashically read here as חרים (net). Ln seems to
preserve the crux of the interpretation while F: לתוך מצודה is
fully consonant with the artistic literary mode of Sifre Ha'azinu --
the subtle hiding of the word plays by the substitution of synonyms
for Scriptural words. Ln חרים should, in my estimation be taken as
"net" (cf. Koheleth 7:26 מצודים וחרמים) and the word is used as an
interpretation of עלימו by interchanging ע with ח and ל with ר
(חירם = חרים). Alternatively, one may think that עלימו itself
has been translated as חרים (a net or a trap) because the midrashist
may have taken as root עלם , "that which has been concealed". According to the midrashist, it is the nations who are to be judged at once.
The alternative traditions, concerning this verse, fit the "Israel
vs. the nations" format of interpretations ascribed at times to
Yehuda and Nehemiah. See "E4", Piska 325. Of the two interpretations
here, Silberman writes: the first interpretation makes evils = רעות
the object of the verb; the second makes עלימו the object.

E2. While אסף means "to gather" and סוף means "to destroy", the
homilist clarifies here that the sense of אספה in Deut. 32:23 must
be "to destroy". This interpretation understands the topic of the
verse to concern Israel. See Piska 321, "E1" and Piska 325, "E4".
L. Silberman translates "My arrows, I will destroy them (בם)": It
is not written, "I will use up my arrows on them" but "my arrows,
I will destroy."

retributions will be brought to an end but the people will not

be brought to an end. And so does Scripture state, "I will bring

to an end my arrows upon them" --"My arrows will bring them to an

end," is not written here, but rather "I will bring to an end my

arrows upon them". My arrows shall be brought to an end but the

people shall not be brought to an end.

Another interpretation:

"I will use up my arrows upon them":

This refers to the arrows of famine. And so does Scripture

state, "When I shall send upon them the evil arrows of famine."[S1]

24

"The wasting of hunger and the devouring of the fiery bolt":

For they shall be plagued by the famine and cast out into the

streets.[E3] And so does Scripture state, "And people to whom they

prophesy shall be cast out in the streets of Jerusalem...."[S2]

"And Keteb Meriri...":

According to your method[E4] you must learn that all who are

possessed by a demon do froth.[*E5]

---

* Ln: are bitter

S1. Ezekiel 5:16.   S2. Jeremiah 14:16.

E3. מזי is taken here as akin to the Syriac zwa, "to project outwards"
and is considered here as "cast out". It is not likely that Vs. 26:רעב
has been taken as רחב (street) by virtue of a ע with ח interchange.
The uncited portion of the proof text is intended to be read here,
"...because of the famine". It is most likely that רעב in Deut. 32:23
does refer to "famine" and so is associated with the proof text of
Jer. 14:16 that mentions being cast into the streets because of famine.
L. Silberman writes me: Verse 24 specifies 'my arrows', in Verse 23
the words are obscure. The midrashist is required to explain them;
hence, מזי = מוצאים and לחומי = מושלכים .

"And the teeth of cattle...":

Do not read " וְשֵׁן בְּהֵמוֹת אֲשַׁלַּח בָּם " but rather

" וְשֵׁן בָּהֲמוֹת אֲשַׁלַּח בָּם ":* that they should become repeatedly frenzied** on account of each of their sins.[E6]

E4. Cf. Lam. R. to Lam. 1:3, and Num. R. 12:3 (keteb yashud of Ps. 91:6, where "yashud" is to be taken as "shed" -- a demon. (Cf. Midrash Tehillim 91:3, p. 199) See "E21", Piska 318.

E5. The method being that names are to be broken up for homiletical purposes. For the understanding (F) of מרירי as "froth","spittle" cf. Deve Eliahu ch. 27 "רירו יורד".(cf. Seder Eliahu Rabba p. 136) and cf. L. Finkelstein, "Prolegomena etc" PAAJR,vol. 4 (1933), p. 43. This fits in with the word-derivation of the earlier comment ("E22", Piska 318): the manner of the shed is to "cast one into a fit". In Num. R. 12:3, it is clear that נכפה means "to fall into a frenzy" and so כופה would subsequently mean "to throw into a fit", i.e. to drive one mad. For the method of interpreting names homiletically see Gen. R. 42:8 and B.T. Yoma 83b. Ln's מורר can mean "bitter" - "afflicted". F's reading appears to be better.

* Ln: וְשֵׁן בָּהֶם אֲשֶׁר בָּם

** F: possibly "searching out sins" (מחזיר) or = Ln: "heating up and recovering (i.e. cooling off) " (מתחזיר)

E6. The midrashist understands that the image of the tooth refers to rabid madness. He undoubtedly wants his midrashic interpretation considered seriously as reflecting the intended meaning of the verse, even if he is aware that some of his play is not textually supportable. Nevertheless, the net effect is a dramatic portrayal of the actual sense of the verse's threat. Now שן can be taken to mean "repetition (שנה)", while בהמה has been taken to mean "frenzy (המה)". In Ln שן also has sense of "changing (fluctuate·)" i.e. לשנות; and אשלח is converted into אשר by an interchange of ל with ר . This המה produces "inner" turmoil (בם). The play is further enhanced by taking בהמה not only as המה or המם (also המה = frothing wine) in reference to "frenzy" ("frothing") but also as חום , heat;or חמה ,anger. See further Conclusion no. 7.Perles (Beth Talmud, editor: I.H. Weiss, Vienna 5641, p. 114f.) understands here, "Do not read behemot but rather beḥamut (בחמות)", i.e. not "cattle"but rather "heat" or,if from חמה , "anger". He suggests that the expositor actually intended us to understand that God will stir up the people to commit grievous sins. He goes on to say that the next passage to this one continues the theme by showing that someone was "heated up" to stretch his foreskin (an act of renouncing covenant and so Jewish identification as well) and eventually died from sores caused by the operation. I do not agree with

Perles. First of all, the theology of such a passage, would run
counter to the sense of Scripture in this case; Deut. 32:21 claims that
God will send punishments upon the people <u>because</u> of their sins. The
punishments (and not the sins) are enumerated in the verses of which
Deut. 32:24 is a unit. Would the midrashist even think that God would
increase their sins! Secondly, if Perles is correct then the reading
דבר אחר should be omitted from the text and "both" traditions (one being
the conclusion of the other) presented as one single tradition.
Rosenzweig, (B 297) (<u>Tifereth Israel</u>, p. 228)interprets the pericope
to refer to God's making murderous teeth (he thinks the midrashist takes
שׁן בְּהֵמֹת as בְּהֵמֹת שֵׁן). Another understanding of the text which
suits the scriptural sense and Rabbinic views of Ha'azinu acknowledges
the text to read בְּהֵמֹת = בְּהֵמֹת -- the people will be stirred up into
a frenzy (מהמם) on account of their sins. Scripture is understood
to be referring to "rabid teeth" as an image of the mechanism which
drives people into a frenzy. The "another interpretation" pericope
deserves some comment. This pericope sees the nature of the punishments
to be completely different than in the first tradition. בהמות is still
understood to mean " מהמם " in this second tradition which speaks of the
natural consequences of "heated frenzy" (plays upon בהמות as מהמם and
as מחמם) whereby someone actually would inflict a wound upon himself
during a fit. This is unlike the first passage which took the frenzy
in itself to be the punishment. The final tradition, also introduced
as "another interpretation", took the verse literally (animals will
bite people) and backs up the interpretation by reference to such an
event having actually occurred. While the forms of the pericopes here
seem so similar it may appear that each succeeding tradition is based
upon a "novel reading" of the tradition which precedes it. By changing
a few letters we can see how each tradition is built upon the one that
preceded it but we must not assume that they therefore are telling us
the same information. These switches are made to show us different
facets. Whether the redactor here played with a single tradition,
whether various preachers preached a single tradition in a slightly
different form so as to give a well known midrash a new meaning, or
whether traditions just circulated in different forms cannot now be
determined. It may even be that the original teaching contained all
these traditions in the order we have them and were passed down as an
intriguing unit of lore in which he interpreted in three different
ways and presented all the possibilities. The speculations upon these
"another interpretation" forms are many but that each interpretation
presents some new insight is obvious from our investigation. The
midrashist had much to work with in בהמות : מות, המה, חֵמָה, חם.

Another interpretation:

That one of them would become inflamed and pull himself and raise an ulcer so that he gradually die of it.[E7]

Another interpretation:

"And the teeth of cattle will I send upon them":

That his own cow will bite him and raise an ulcer so that he gradually die of it.[E8]

They said that it once happened that ewes were biting and killing.[E9]

"With the venom of crawling things of the dust":

That they, themselves, would be forced to crawl in the dust.

Rabbi says: This refers to the snakes, whose kingdom is specifically that of the dust.

25

"Without shall the sword bereave":

From here they said,[E10] "In a time of war stay your travel and in

---

E7. Here שן בהמות is read either as שנומי מות(ב interchanged with ו) or שנומי בהמה (ulcer in rage). For further plays involving נומי see Gen. R. 46:8: ונמלתם taken as נומימלתם .

E8. This interpretation combines the sense of a biting, domesticated animal (בהמות) and a raised ulcer leading to death (נומי מות).

E9. Cf. P.T. Ta'anith 3:6 חמור נושך וממית and B.T. Ta'anith 22a where such plagues are referred to as משולחת .

E10. מכאן אמרו in midrash halacha generally signifies a scriptural source for a Mishnaic, Baraitaic , or Toseftaic ruling. There is an analogous term מכאןסמכו which is used to signify scriptural "hinges" for Rabbinic enactments, see P.T. Shevi'ith 10:2 and commentaries. Our statement in Sifre is actually cited as a baraita in B.T. Baba Kamma 60b where the need of various scriptural supports for the idea is discussed. Deut. 32:24 is taken to mean that in time of war ("the sword") there is bereavement if one travels ("without").

a time of famine increase your travel." And so does Scripture state,
"If I go forth into the field, then behold the slain with the sword!
And if I enter the city then behold them that are sick with famine."[S3]
And Scripture also states, "He that is in the field shall die by the
sword and he that is in the city, famine and pestilence shall devour
him."[S4]

"And in the chambers terror":

One would consider the sword as it came to the marketplace.[E11]
If he were able to flee and escape from it, then the chambers of his
heart would produce an ulcer through their beating upon him so that
he would gradually die.

Another interpretation:

"Without shall the sword bereave...":

On account of that which they did in the streets[E12] of Jerusalem.
And thus does Scripture state, "For according to the number of thy
cities are thy gods, O Judah; and according to the number of the
streets of Jerusalem have ye set up altars to the shameful thing...."[S5]

"And in the chambers terror":

On account of what they did in the innermost chamber.[L1] And so
does Scripture state, "Son of man, hast thou seen, what the Elders of
the House of Israel do in the dark, every man in his chambers of
imagery? For they say: The Lord seeth us not, the Lord hath
forsaken the land."[S6]

S3. Jeremiah 14:18.   S4. Ezekiel 7:15.
S5. Jeremiah 11:13.   S6. Ezekiel 8:12.

"...both young man and virgin":

This is more dire than all other horrors except for "the suckling with the man of gray hairs."[E13] And so does Scripture state, "The man with the woman shall be taken, the aged with him that is full of days."[S7]

Another interpretation:

"Both young man":

You have caused Me to harm My chosen ones. And so does Scripture

---

L1. חדרי חדרים must be understood here to refer to a completely private place.

E11. Deut. 32:24 is paraphrased midrashically : As the sword came to the broad place (חוצה) there was reflection (שכל) but in the chambers (of the heart) there was an ulcer (נומא = אימה).

E12. The play here is occasioned by Deut. 32:25 מחוץ = חוצה (street) as in Jer. 11:13.

S7. Jeremiah 6:11.

E13. The midrashist may be using as his base an understanding of the structure of Scripture which posits that the worst tragedy is always placed at the end of a verse (see B.T. Baba Bathra 8b concerning Jer. 15:12). The homilist may have understood the word מלא in the proof text to mean מלא , "without days", or perhaps "full of days" may have been understood to refer to a child whose age can only be measured in "days" as opposed to "years". In either case the reference would be to a child. Cf. Matthew 24:18. Here גם---גם refers to a progression of tragedies (one worse than the others) while עם states equivalence of tragedy. Thus the literal sense of the proof text illustrates that the word עם is meant to signify equivalence: "full of days" = "aged".

state, "And Joshua the son of Nun, the servant of Moses of His

chosen ones,[E14] answered."[S8]

"And virgin":

This teaches us that they were as clean of sin as a virgin who

had never tasted sin in her life.

"Suckling":

This teaches us that they would suckle[E15] the words of the Torah

as a suckling suckles milk from the breasts of his mother.

"With the man of gray hairs 〈 שיבה 〉:

Do not read "the man of שיבה (gray hairs)" but rather

" ישיבה (great academy)".[E16] This teaches us that all of them were

worthy to sit[E17] in the great academy. And so does Scripture state,

---

S8. Numbers 11:28.

E14. As Moses was over 80 years of age when Joshua served him the
sense of בחור could not be "young man" but "chosen one". The homilist
may have had in mind that when a student is exiled, his teacher is to
be exiled with him, see B.T. Makkoth 10a. So it is that when God is
forced to punish His nation, His elect are also punished for not having
taught the people to behave in better ways.

E15. Cf. B.T. Erubin 54b.

E16. See B.T. Hagiga 14a: זקן - זה שראוי לישיבה

E17. "To sit" i.e. "to be elected to".

"All the mighty, doers of war."[S9] Now what "might" can people display who are going into exile?[L2] And what "war" can people "do" when they are bound in fetters and put into chains? Rather:

"(All the) mighty"[E18]--This refers to the mighty ones of the Torah.[*] This is like the matter of which Scripture states, "Bless the Lord, ye angels of His, <u>mighty</u> in strength, the <u>doers of His word</u>."[S10]

"doers of war"[E19]--That they discuss and argue in the war of the Torah, as it is said, "Wherefore it is said in the <u>Book</u>[E20] of the Wars of the Lord."[S11]

And Scripture also states, "And all the men of might, and the חרש and the מסגר , a thousand":[S12]

---

* Ln: of the war of the Torah

S9. 2 Kings 24:16.   S10. Psalms 103:20.
S11. Numbers 21:14.   S12. 2 Kings 24:16.

L2. The midrashist indicates by these remarks that his "pesher" allegory is justified since the literal sense of the verse cannot be interpreted without major difficulties.

E18. See B.T. Hagiga 14a: גבור זה בעל שמועות

E19. Ibid: ואיש מלחמה זה שיודע לישא
                   וליתן במלחמתה של תורה
      See also printed Tanhuma Noah 3.

E20. בספר מלחמות ה׳   is to be understood: "Through the Torah Scroll are the Wars of the Lord."

" חרש" --one speaks and all are quiet.[E21]

" מסגר" --all sit before him and learn from him.[E22]

One פותח [L3] and another סוגר [E23] to fulfill that of which it is

said, "And he shall פתח but not סוגר and he shall סגר but

not פותח ."[S13]

END OF PISKA

S13. Isaiah 22:22.

L3. Friedmann reads: "after opening none can close". The
phrase seems to be attached to the praises of the "מסגר "
(closer = סוגר) as if it were a midrashic play on the term, " סוגר".
However, this reading does not adequately account for the notation
that "all sit before the מסגר to learn from him". F is likely
correct in taking פותח אחד as the better reading and finding here
a reference to both the חרש and the מסגר , חרש= פותח =engrave,
סוגר = מסגר . The reading of Friedmann represents an emendation
of a clever scribe, who changed אחד into אחר , because he did not
realize that מסגר was to be read midrashically here as סחר "to sit
around". One may wonder exactly how the copyist understood מסגר
to mean "none may close" since סגר actually refers to "closing".
We might also speculate here that סוגר = practical instruction
(as opposed to פותח = scriptural exegesis). Josephus, Antiquities I,
p. 226-230, (ed. Loeb. Vol IV, p. 113 para. 3) alludes to Gen. 22:9
(i.e. 1) Abraham built an altar,
    2) arranged the wood,
    3) ויעקד את יצחק בנו   )
by noting that Abraham prepared an altar, laid wood on it and then
gave him instruction. Since עקד means to bind (feet to head) it
has a similar sense to סוגר . It is interesting to note that LXX
translates עקד in Gen. 22:9 by συμποδίζειν (bind the feet) the
very word which translates תרגל (to teach to walk in Hos. 11:3: the
meaning of עקד as "instruct" could well have been taken by Josephus
just as LXX used σμμποδίζειν in Hos. 11:3: "Yet it was I who
taught Ephraim to walk. I took them by their arms.... I led them with
cords...with bands of love." Thus Hos. 11:3 itself equates good
instruction with being led by "fetters". Perhaps סוגר also has the
sense of "discipline" -not only in its harsh sense but also in its
academic sense. The midrashist's play on סוגר (=surround=sitting
around) is only etymological fun and not a serious derivation.

S13. Isaiah 22:22.

E21. Read as חרש , "a deaf mute". See B.T. Sanhedrin 38a:

כיון שפותחין הכל נעשין כחרשים .‏ (Note also חרש = חכם in Jer.
10:8-9 and Is. 60:20).

E22. I suspect that מסגר is read here midrashically as אסחרו
which in Targum to the Psalms 1:1 means " sit ". Kohut in
Aruch (s.v. סחר) notes that סחר means to "sit for purposes [B77]
of eating or of studying as is noted in the Meturgamman".

E23. The passage means either:
1) legal decisions (see "L3" on previous page) are not made until
   theoretical discussions are concluded, and then, once decisions
   are made, further discussions cannot be reopened,
   or
2) If the subject of the debate is declared "fit", the ruling
   stands, and if declared "unfit", the ruling likewise stands.
Cf. Koran sura 35:2, "That which Allah openeth, none can withhold it,
and that which He withholdeth none can release thereafter -- He is
the mighty, the wise." I understand this passage as follows:
   It seems to me that the best way to view this passage is to suppose
that חרש here is equated with פתח . Both words can mean "engrave",
Targumim translate both by גלף . (See my article "A Distinctive Usage
of Pth etc."[B 101] H.S. 20-21, p. 60f. and M.H. Gottstein "Theory
and Practice of Textual Criticism" Textus, vol. 3 (1963) Jerusalem,
Heb. U. ed. C. Rabin,p. 153, notes LXX Is. 45:8 is influenced by
Is. 28:24 חרש = פתח). Noting the equation of חרש and פתח , we
are faced with two possible interpretations of our pericope:
1) B.T. Hagigah 14a equates "poteah" with "divre Torah" in a
   tradition related to our pericope. The B.T. tradition can be
   interpreted to mean that the פותח refers to the teacher who deals
   with scriptural theory and literary structure (cf. Tanhuma
   V'Ethanen 5 פתחו של יהושוע- and cf. Tanna Deve Eliahu ch. 14
   refers Isaiah 42:18,חרשם,to scholars and also says
   פתח בדבר תורה). For the method of deriving halacha from
   Scripture see E.E. Urbach
   "הדרשה כיסוד הלכה ובעית הסופרים"
   in G. Scholem Jubilee Volume, 1968.
   B.T. Sanhedrin 38a, in a tradition related to our pericope, also
   takes the סוגר to refer to the decider of the halacha:
   כיון שסוגרין בהלכה שוב אין פותחין.
   The point of the Babylonian traditions may well be that
   decisive laws are not to be proclaimed until the conclusion
   of all theoretical argumentation; but, once this has occurred
   and the decision has been promulgated no further arguments may
   be entertained. This view of the פותח and the סוגר may perhaps
   be traced to Palestinian traditions. Both P.T. Nedarim 6:8
   and P.T. Sanhedrin 1:2 use 2 Kings 2:24 (the same verse under
   discussion in our pericope) to find reference to 2 types of
   scholars -- the מסגר and the חרש . A tradition related to
   our pericope in Tanhuma Noah 3 supports our interpretation

here by saying:

עד שמעמידין דבר על בריו -- והלכה לאמתה .

See also Ch. J. Kossowski, Thesarus Talmudus, (B72)
s.v. מסגר but also see B.T. Gittin 88a which does not contain
mention of "divrei Torah" or "halacha" in its reading --.٠
Are B.T. Hag. 14a and B.T. Sanhed. 38a later expansions of
the tradition in B.T. Gittin 88a? -- could B.T. Hag. 14a and
B.T. Sanhed. 38a contain early glosses? If we accept that our
interpretation of the passage will hold, we may further wish to
explain B.T. Moed Katan 28b in which Akiba describes himself
by the term "last" as a reference to the authority Akiba
enjoyed -- he was the promulgator of laws which should be
taken as final decisions.

2) According to the interpretation of the pericope offered above
in #1 we find that אחד פותח ואחד סוגר would mean that
"one person interprets while another decides". But the phrase
could also mean "Both the poteah and the soger have a common
feature". Tanhuma Noah 3 also supports such an interpretation
of our pericope (here corrected by the reading in Otzar
HaGeonim (B32)):

Tanhuma Noah 3	:	Otzar HaGeonim Le-Masekhet Sanhedrin
	:	(Teshuvot Uferushim), Mossad HaRav
	:	Kook, Jerusalem 1966, p. 329.
חרש - שבשעה שאחד מהן מדבר	:	חרש - שבשעה שאחד מהן מתיר
נעשה הכל כחרשין	:	
מסגר-כיון שאחד מהן סוגר דברי	:	
טמאה וטהרה או איסור והתר אין	:	
בעולם שיכול לפתוח לטהר ולהתיר	:	...מי שיכול לפתוח ולטהר
לקים מה שנאמר ...	:	לקיים...

According to this interpretation: heresh=poteah=declare permiss-
ible, masger=declare forbidden.
We now find that the proposed midrashic etymology in our
pericope works as follows: The פותח is called a חרש because
no one will challenge him (חרש =mute, they are silent). The
מסגר is so called because people sit attentively (ג and ח
interchange, סחר = sit in study). Also the פותח is the one
who "opens" or "loosens" (cf. Job 12:4). The סוגר is the one
who "binds up", that is, he forbids (cf. Matt. 18:18) because
סוגר can mean "to bind" (cf. Job 11:10). The Tanhuma passage
introduces these etymologies in its exposition which appears
to be a later reworking of traditions related to that found
in our Sifre text. It may well be that B.T. Gittin 88a was
expanded and expounded in two versions. One like the tradition
of B.T. Hagigah 14a which equates פותח with דברי תורה ,
and another like the Otzar Ha-Geonim text which equates פותח
with מתיר . A complete investigation of the Tanhuma passage
of Noah 3 will show that both the B.T. tradition and the
Otzar HaGeonim tradition have been synthesized and woven skilfully into a single literary unit.

26

"I thought I would make an end of them $\langle$ אפאיהם $\rangle$":

    I thought in <u>my</u> <u>anger</u> -- <u>where</u> <u>are</u> <u>they</u> $\langle$ באפי איה הם $\rangle$.[E1]

"I should make their memory cease from among men":

    I thought -- they should not be in the world. But what could I do to them -- "(If it had not been the Lord who was for us. Say now Israel:) If it had not been the Lord who was for us when men rose up against us."[S1] [E2](If it had not been: "And he said to destroy them...if it had not been for Moses, His chosen...."[S1a])

Another interpretation:

    I thought in my anger -- where are they!

"I should make their memory cease from among men":

    That they should not be in the world. But what could I do --"<u>Except</u> the Lord of Hosts had left unto us a very small remnant...."[S2]

S1. Psalms 124:1,2.   S1a. (Ln) Psalms 106:23.
S2. Isaiah 1:9.

E1. The <u>hapax</u> <u>legomenon</u>, אפאיהם , is analyzed by considering it as three words: אפ(י) אי(ה) הם

E2. The midrashist searches Scripture to find those decisive factors which prevented God from destroying Israel and considers Deut. 22:37 as a prediction of those events described as actually happening by Scripture. The point is that God must preserve Israel since He is identified with them and their defeat would appear as God's defeat.

Another interpretation:

I would make an end of them -- were it not...as it is said,
"And He thought to destroy them were it not that Moses His
chosen stood before Him in the breach."[S3]

27

"Were it not for the accumulated ⟨אגור⟩ anger of his
enemy":

Who caused them[E3] to take retribution against these? The
anger of the Gentile Nations that had accumulated within their
inwards.

"אגור" -- אגור specifically means "accumulated",[E4] as it
is said, "The words of Agur the son of Jakeh."[S4] And Scripture also
states, "May He incite death against them, let them go down alive into
the nether-world; for evil in their accumulation (מגורם)[E5] is
within them".[S5]

S3. Psalms 120:23.   S4. Proverbs 30:1.   S5. Psalms 55:16.

E3. "Them" is a euphemism for "Me" and "Gentile Nations" is a
circumlocution for "Israel".

E4. The midrashist does not want us to translate "אגור " as "I was
in dread". He therefore builds upon the Rabbinic notion that "Agur
the son of Jakeh" is to be identified with Solomon who collected
(agur) proverbs. See Canticles Rabba 1:10 which appears to preserve
an explanation of Avoth de R. Nathan "A", ch. 39 (missing in ARN "B",
ch. 43, end) but it is noteworthy that Cant. R. uses the terminology
and methodology of ARN "A" ch.39 to exegete names that we find in ARN
"B", ch. 43. L. Silberman thinks that our midrash may mean that God
caused the nations to take retribution against Israel (אגור   changed
midrashically to גרם).

E5. The proof text reads מגורם   which must mean "their accumulation"
in this context.

"Lest they alienate them in their distresses":

In the time of Israel's distress the Gentile Nations of the
World treat them as strangers and pretend that they never knew them.
And so we find that when they sought to flee northwards they did not
care for them but they delivered them up. This is like the matter
of which it is said, "Thus says the Lord: For three transgressions
of Tyre, and for four, I will not turn away the punishment; because
they delivered up a whole people to Edom."[S6] They sought to flee to the
south and they delivered them up, as it is said, "Thus says the Lord:
For three transgressions of Gaza, and for four, I will not turn away
the punishment; because they carried into exile a whole people to
deliver them up to Edom."[S7] They sought to flee to the east and they
delivered them up, as it is said, "Thus says the Lord: For three
transgressions of Damascus...."[S8] They sought to flee to the west
and they delivered them up, as it is said, "The oracle concerning
Arabia, in the thickets in Arabia you will lodge, O caravans of
Dedanites...."[S9]

In the time of Israel's fortune, the Gentile Nations of the World
deceive them and pretend to be their brothers. And so did Esau say to
Jacob, "I have enough, my brother, keep what you have for yourself."[S10]
And so did Hiram say to Solomon, "What kind of cities are these which
you have given me, my brother."[S11] [E6]

S6. Amos 2:6.   S7. Amos 1:6.   S8. Amos 1:3.   S9. Isaiah 21:13.
S10. Genesis 33:9.   S11. 1 Kings 9:13.

E6. The mention of Esau here may be accounted for perhaps by the equation
of Esau with Edom (=Rome) as is commonly known but the mention of Hiram

"Lest they should say, 'Our hand is triumphant, the Lord
has not wrought all this'":

Just as those fools said, "Have we not by our own strength
taken horns for ourselves."[S12]

28

"For they are a nation devoid of counsel":

Rabbi Yehuda interpreted it to refer to Israel. Rabbi Nehemiah
interpreted it to refer to the Gentile Nations of the World.

Rabbi Yehuda interpreted it to refer to Israel:

Israel destroyed the good counsel that was given to them.

"Counsel" specifically refers to "Torah", as it is said, "I have
counsel and Toshia."[S13] [E7]

"And there is no understanding in them...":

---

of Tyre (who aided Solomon in the building of the Temple) is somewhat
difficult to account for. The midrashim based upon Ez. 28:2 (see
Yalkut Shimoni Ez. 28-367) understands Hiram to have been wicked.
Perhaps this passage is based upon an early tradition known to ben Sira
50:25 which mentions Seir and Philistia as enemies of Israel. As
Philistia may have been identified with Phoenicia (both being sea
faring peoples) and as Tyre was the leading port of Phoenicia ben
Sira may have referred to Tyre as Philistia. (Otherwise it is not
clear what he meant. Josephus, <u>Against Apion</u> [B 13] 1:70, also notes
the hostility of Tyre. Thus the midrashist may have an acute reason for
telling his audience to be wary of the sweet talk of the nations like
Tyre. L. Silberman suggests the reference may be to the Seleucid empire.

S12. Amos 6:13.   S13. Proverbs 8:14.

E7. "Toshia" refers to "Torah" in Rabbinic literature, e.g.
Tanhuma [B 25] Jethro 9: יצפון לישרים תושיה
and also see B.T. Gittin 70a.

There is not one of them who will reflect and say:
Yesterday one person of us could pursue one thousand of the
Gentile Nations and two could put ten thousand to flight. Yet
now one person of the Gentile Nations could pursue one thousand
of us and two could put ten thousand to flight ..."unless
their Rock had given them."

Rabbi Nehemiah interpreted it to refer to the Gentile Nations:
The Gentile Nations destroyed[*] the Seven Commandments[E8] that I
gave to them.

"And there is no understanding in them...":

There is not one of them who will reflect and say: Now one of
us could chase one thousand of Israel and two could put ten
thousand to flight. As for the Messianic Era, could one of
Israel pursue one thousand and could two put ten thousand to
flight..."unless their Rock had given them!"

---

* Ln: have not the

E8. For the concept of the Seven Commandments given to the nations
see A. Lichtenstein, The Seven Laws of Noah, (B 246) New York, the Rabbi
Jacob Joseph School Press, 1981. As for the end of this pericope, F
punctuates the passage to mean that now none will think that they will
be defeated by Israel in the Messianic Era but it will happen. So F
places the words "unless their Rock..." as the caption of the next
passage rather than the conclusion of this one. Nevertheless, I feel
that it belongs at the end of this passage to indicate that in the
Messianic Era God will help Israel. "Give them" means "give the
Gentiles to Israel". Nowadays it is natural for the Gentiles to win
but in the Future they will lose and not understand the reason.

Piska 322

It once happened in the Judean War that a commander of a ten-division of cavalry, on horseback, chased an Israelite man with the intention of killing him but he could not catch him. Before he finally caught up to the man, a snake had come out and bit* the man upon his heel. He said to him: (Please say one thing to whomever.) Do not think that because we are mighty they have been delivered into our hands..."unless their Rock had given them."^{E9}

END OF PISKA

---

* Ln: wrapped itself around his heel

E9. I have underlined what may be circumlocutions here if we assume (as in Ln) that the Jew is speaking. Hebrew reads "we are mighty" but perhaps sense is "you are mighty" as is the reading in Midrash Tannaim. Hebrew reads "They have been delivered" but perhaps sense is "We have been delivered". Hebrew reads "our hands" but perhaps the sense is "your hands" (see variants in F). The point, would be, according to only Yehuda (not Nehemiah) that the Gentile Nations could not have persecuted the Jews so successfully in the past had God not allowed it to happen by delivering them into the hands of the nations. However, if the Roman is the speaker, Silberman is correct in taking the words literally. This too suggests the view of Yehuda. The passage is either an added gloss to Yehuda's words or else the view of Nehemiah is an interpolation for the sake of consistency in presenting Yehuda - Nehemiah arguments.

29

"If they were wise they would understand <u>this</u>":

If Israel would reflect upon the words of the Torah that I gave to them, no nation or kingdom could rule[L1] over them.[T1] And <u>this</u> specifically refers to the Torah, as it is said, "And <u>this</u> is the Torah which Moses set...."[S1]

Another interpretation:

"If they were wise they would understand this":

If Israel would reflect upon that which was told them by Jacob, their father, no nation or kingdom could rule over them.[T1] And what did He say to them? "Accept upon yourselves the kingship of Heaven, subdue each other with the fear of Heaven, act charitably towards each other."[E1]

S1. Deuteronomy 4:44.

T1. Omitted in Ln possibly due to homoioteleuton,("kingdom could rule over them").

L1. Schorr, p. 13f comments that the homilist took
אחריתם (v. 32:29)= ἀχεῖρωσις (or ἀχεῖρωτος) = unconquered and perhaps אחריתם corrresponds to "another nation" so the combined sense is," You would be unconquered by another nation."

E1. We seem to have here a midrashic interpretation or at least an allusion to an interpretation of a specific verse which is not cited. Perhaps the allusion is Gen. 49:1-2 where "hear" may have been taken as a reference to the recitation of "Hear, O Israel,..." which is referred to by the Rabbis as "acceptance of the yoke of the Kingship of Heaven", while "gather yourselves" may refer to pacifying each other, and "assemble in a group" may refer to "mutual charity" (cf. Targ. Ps.-Jon. to Gen. 49:1f, B.T. Pesachim 56a, and comments of Pardo to this Piska). Hoffman, in his notes to <u>Midrash Tannaim</u> (B 26) on Deut. 32:29 suggests that reference is made here to the word "and <u>this</u>" of Gen. 49:28 (="understand <u>this</u>" of Deut. 32). The midrash may interpret, I believe, Gen. 49:28, "and this" as a reference to the qualifications of the remainder of the verse:
    1) they have a <u>Father</u> (להם אביהם)

30

"How should one chase a thousand...":

Since you have not fulfilled the Torah, how can I fulfill the promise you sought,[E2] that one of you should chase one thousand of the Gentile Nations and two would put to flight ten thousand and now one of the Gentile Nations can chase one thousand of you and two of them put to flight ten thousand.

"Except their Rock had given them over and the Lord had delivered them up":

I do not deliver you up through My own agency but through the agency of others.[E3] And there was already an incident in Judah in which the flies delivered them up.

Rabbi Hanina, a citizen of Tibi'in says: This is comparable to one

---

2) making one <u>bend</u> according to his <u>bent</u>
(ויברך אותם איש אשר כברכתו)
3) <u>giving</u> <u>blessing</u> (ברך אותם).
These qualifications roughly correspond to the advice stated in our pericope. The order of the verse, when exegeted this way, corresponds on a one to one basis with the order in the pericope. Pardo's (B 283) solution does not allow for the order of items exegeted from Gen. 49:1-2 to correspond exactly to the ordering of items in the pericope. Cf. S. Schechter, "Some Aspects of Rabbinic Theology", JQR vol. 7 (1895), p. 203.

E2. Cf. Lev. 26:8.

E3. The hiph'il form הסגירם suggests that God causes others to deliver Israel up to the enemy.

who says to another, "I will sell you a slave and deliver him later." -- But I am not so, for I sell and immediately deliver.[E4]

Another tradition:[E5]

"And the Lord had delivered them":

I deliver you who are like the case of defiled people, shut up by the hands of the pure; or perhaps what is meant is that they are like pure people shut up by the hands of the defiled![E6] Yet this cannot be for they shut up only those who are defiled, as it is said, "And the priest shall shut up the plague for seven days...."[S2]

S2. Leviticus 13:4.

E4. LE favors the note of Hoffman to Midrash Tannaim to this verse. My translation is based upon their idea of taking "kiri" as "kairos" --"time delayed" sale. Since the verse says that God will sell -- and deliver, the midrashist points out that the two are not synonymous. The point is that God delivers immediately upon sale!

E5. Asterisks (**) represent L.F.'s additions to this text.

E6. Lou Silberman renders this: "I deliver you as impure ones into the hands of pure ones -- or *this may not be so* but rather as the pure into the hands of the impure. No -- only the impure are shut up, as it says...." The word " הסגיר " here is taken in the sense of "shutting up a leprous person". The midrashist wants to interpret the verse to Israel's credit but explains that he cannot find a way. L.F, "Studies in Tannaitic Midrashim, (B159) p. 213, considers the clause " ביד טהורים ..." as a gloss on the verse which was carried over into our text by "overquotation". Since our text is to be considered "written", this conjecture is quite speculative.

31

"For their צור is not as our צור ":

Not according to the[T2] dominion[E7] that you give to us do you give to them. For when you give dominion to us we act toward them with the quality of mercy but when you give them[T2] dominion they act toward us with the quality of cruelness -- They behead[E8] us, they burn us, they crucify us.[E9]

"Even our enemies, themselves, being judges":

You have written in the Torah that an enemy cannot judge nor testify:[E10] "...and he who is not an enemy,"[S3]-- i.e. he may

testify against him.

"...neither sought to harm him,"[S4]-- i.e. he may

judge him.

And you have appointed over us enemies as witnesses and judges!

S3. Numbers 35:23.   S4. Numbers 35:23.

T2. Has the repeated phrase "give dominion" here caused the scribe to omit a passage in Ln by homoioteleuton?

E7. " צור " here is taken as, "dominion", "power", "rock".

E8. Since the tortures in this pericope describe specific methods of execution, "killing" here may refer to "beheading" as it sometimes does (e.g. Mishna Sanhedrin 7:1). Compare here Josephus, Apion 2:30.

E9. See Aruch Compl. s.v. צלב (=aufhangen).

E10. Here we have a full protest against God's injustices to Israel. The redactor is not concerned that he has included a pericope that challenges the ideas presented in Piska 307. By claiming that "You have written" and then proceeding with a midrashic commentary to the verse (cited as baraita in B.T. Sanhedrin 29a, also see Mishna Sanhedrin 3:5; cf. E.Z. Melamed, The Relationship between The Halakhic Midrashim and The Mishna and Tosefta, 265 Jerusalem, 5727, p. 144)the midrashist does not distinguish between the written word and Rabbinic interpretation. Rabbinic interpretation to him is indeed the meaning of the written word. See Targumim to Deut. 32:31.

32

"For their vine is the vine of Sodom...":

Rabbi Yehuda interpreted it in reference to Israel.

Rabbi Nehemiah interpreted it in reference to the Gentile Nations
of the World.

Rabbi Yehuda says:

Are you indeed from the vine of Sodom or from the planting
of Gommorah? But surely you are distinctly from the Holy
Planting, as it is said, "Yet I planted thee a noble vine,
wholly a right seed."[S5]

"Their grapes are grapes of gall":

You are the children of the first[E11] Adam whom[*] I punished with
the edict of death, placed upon him and his succeeding generations
until the end of all generations.

"Their clusters are bitter":

The bitterness of the great ones among you is spread out
amongst them as a cluster. And "cluster" specifically refers to

---

The exegesis of Numbers 35:23 which is presented here is an outgrowth
of apparently repetitious phrases which require clarification to show
that they are indeed not repetitious.

*Ln: Adam who punished you with the edict of death with all succeeding
generations until....

S5. Jeremiah 2:21.

E11. " רוש " (gall) here is seen as "ראש ", i.e. "the first one --
Adam". Israel has shown itself to be a "true" son of sinful Adam
and therefore will suffer the consequences. Schorr, p. 13f. claims
ענבימו = ἀναφῦμα   such that ענב = ἀναφῦω   = sprout,
(=children).

"great one", as it is said, "There is no cluster to eat nor

first ripe fig which my soul desireth...."[S6] [E12]

33

"Their wine is the venom of serpents":

Those angers of the pious ones[E13] and reverers of Heaven[*]

amongst you are as serpents.

"And the head of asps which is cruel":

For the chief[E14] ones amongst you are like the asp which is

cruel.

---

[*] Ln: upright

S6. Micah 7:1.

E12. The verses of the proof text Mich 7:1,2:"...no cluster...The
חסיד is perished out of the earth and the ישר ...." For the term
"cluster" in reference to "great ones" see B.T. Hulin 92a and the end
of Mishna Sotah. Cf. S. Krauss, Griechische und lateinische Lehnworter,
(B 7.4) s.v. אסכולי , s.v. אשכולות . While Silberman plausibly sees
here a condemnation of even the pious, it may mean that the harsh words
of the pious are taken by the homilist to be necessary. Israel has
become so sinful that her leaders have now to take extreme measures.

E13. The parallelism in Micah 7:1,2, of cluster with חסיד and ישר,
explains why cluster = חסיד and ישר (Targum trans. אשכול = חסידיא).
Perhaps יינם is construed here as יראים or perhaps the actual
understanding of the midrash is that חמת תנינים is taken as
המתונים which renders חסידים as its synonym. See "E15", Piska
323. Schorr, p. 13f. takes יינם as ὲννόημα = thoughtful
(מתונים) or as ὲυνόημα = good willed(חסידים).Also see G. Porton,
"The Grape Cluster etc", JJS,vol. 27 (1976), p. 159ff. Perhaps the
tradition here is related to B.T. Yoma 23a which claims that the
sign of a scholar is that he takes vengeance and bears a grudge like
a snake. See Rabin (B291) akhzar ("cruel") = "zealous").

E14. "Head" is understood as "chief ones".

Another interpretation:

"Their wine (יינם) is the anger of serpents":

The anger of the humble (המתונים   ) and reverers of

Heaven[*] E15 amongst you, is as that of serpents.

"And the head of asps which is cruel":

The chief ones among you are like the asp which is cruel.^{**}

---

* Ln: fearers of sin.
** Ln: omits "which is cruel".

E15. Either " חמת תנינים " is taken as " המתונים   " or
" פתנים   " is taken as " מתונים " using a פ with מ interchange.
Now מתונים is used in Avoth de Rabbi Nathan "B" ch. 1 with a meaning
of "a patient, respectful teacher." But D. Winston Thomas, "The Root
צנע in Hebrew and the meaning of קדרנית in Malachi 3:14, (B 331)"
Journal of Jewish Studies, vol. 1, (48 - 49), p. 187, finds "matan"
in Ethiopic = measure = honor = שער = צנע   which suggests to me
that מתונים in ARN "B" ch. 1, refers to those who measure and
calculate their responses in due measure to the needs of the situation.
But Winston argues convincingly that Heb. צנע and Ethiopic "matan"
actually means "to show honor". Such a meaning may lie behind the
story, I believe, of B.T. Berachoth 20a:
                מתון מתון ל‎ מאה זוזי שויא .
Thus מתון would refer to one who honors God without regard for his
own welfare. The point of the story in B.T. Ber. 20a being that
"to be a matan is certainly worth the expense of 400 zuz." The usual
interpretation, to the effect that, had he waited and not acted upon
impulse, he could have saved 400 zuz, misses the point of the story;
namely, that earlier generations were happy to honor God through self-
sacrifice. Thus the term מתון may mean here,(and perhaps in Mishna
Avot ch. 1), "one who fears" and so the Sifre parallels, חסידים and
ירא שמים and מתונים, may all be synonyms in this passage. One
suspects that our Deut. 32 verse " ראש פתנים " has been
midrashically played upon to yield ירא שמים in Sifre. L. Silberman writes that this pericope is negative. It condemns even the best
people of those days.

Rabbi Nehemiah interpreted it in reference to the Gentile
Nations of the World:

> And it is certain that you are of the vine of Sodom
> and of the planting of Gommorah. You are the disciples of
> the primordial serpent[L2] who corrupted[E16] Adam and Eve.

32

> "Their clusters are bitter":
> For the bitterness of the great ones among you is spread
> out among them as a serpent.[E17]
> "Their clusters are bitter":
> And "cluster" specifically refers to a "great one", as it is
> said, "There is no cluster to eat (nor first ripe fig which
> my soul desireth.)."[S7]

END OF PISKA

S7. Micah 7:1.

L2. Compare Targum Onkelos to Deut. 32:32 -- ריש חוין   .

E16. Here the word פתנים   has been understood as פתה   (seduce).
Thus ראש פתנים   = primordial seducer.

E17. Lou Silberman notes here, "a serpent's poison spreads through
the entire body of the person who was bitten."

34

"Is this not laid up in store with Me":
  Rabbi Eliezer the son of Yosi Hagelili says:
  Concerning the cup which has been laid up and forestalled

I might have thought that it would have become totally diluted, so
Scripture says, "foaming wine".[S1] [E1] I might have thought that it
would be only half full, so Scripture says, "full of mixture".[S1] [E2]
I might have thought that it wouldn't lack even a single drop,[E3] so
Scripture says, "And He poureth out of the same,":[S1]

From that very drop there drank the Generation of the Flood,
and the Generation of the Dispersion, and the People of Sodom[*]
and Pharaoh and all of his troops, Sisera and all his hordes,
Sennacherib and all his devotees, Nebuchadnezzar and all his
troops -- and from that very drop, all those who have come

---

* Ln: and Gomorrah

S1. Psalms 85:9.

E1. "Foaming wine" is discussed by D.T. Tsumura, "Two-fold Image of
Wine in Psalm 46:45", (B 334) JQR, vol. 71, no. 3, (Jan. 1981), p. 168.
The point of the midrash is that the wine of punishment, though set
aside, remains potent and full.

E2. The midrashist equates כמוס of Deut. 32:34 with כוס of
Psalm 75:9. This text of Psalms is then given a fully treated
exegesis, cf. Tsumura op. cit. p. 169. Is wine here taken as a
symbol of blood, as a symbol of punishment?

E3. It may well be that the custom of removing ten drops of wine
from a cup during the Passover recitation of the ten plagues is based
upon the notion that the plagues foreshadow 10 punishings of the nations
from the cup of wrath -- the 7 mentioned in our pericope plus those of
Persia, Greece and Rome.

into the world will drink in the future, until the end of
all generations. And so does Scripture state, "And in this
mountain will the Lord of Hosts make unto all peoples a feast
of fat things, a feast of wines on the lees [S2] (fats full of
marrow, lees well refined and death shall be swallowed forever
and the Lord God shall wipe away the tears from every face and
the shame of His people He shall remove from off the face of the
whole earth, for the mouth of the Lord hath spoken":[S2])

I might have thought that "fat" refers to things that are
of benefit and that "lees" refers to things that are
of no benefit at all, so Scripture states "fats full of
marrow",[S2] "lees well refined."[S2] It refers to fats which contain
nothing but froth. And so does Scripture state, "Babylon hath
been a golden cup in the Lord's hand, that made all the earth
drunken."[S3] (And Scripture also states, "The cup of your
sister you shall drink--deep and wide; she shall be for a
mockery and a derision--much for it to contain".[S3a]):
Just as it is normal that once golden things are broken they
can be restored; so too, once the retributions cease from the
Gentile Nations, in the Future the retributions will be
reestablished upon them. Concerning the time when the
retributions arrive upon Israel--what is stated in
Scripture? "Thou shall drink it and drain it, and thou shalt

S2.   Isaiah 25:6.   S3.   Jeremiah 51:7.
S3a. (Ln) Ez. 23:32.

craunch the sherd thereof":[S4]

Just as it is normal that once sherds are broken they
cannot be restored; so too, once the retributions cease
from Israel,[*][T1] in the Future the retributions will not be
reestablished upon them.

"Sealed up in my treasuries":

Just as a treasury is sealed and does not permit interest to
accrue; so too, the deeds of the wicked[**][E4] do not permit interest
to accrue.

Unless it be as you have said they would have destroyed
the world.

And so does Scripture state, "Woe to the wicked, it shall be ill
with him; only the work of his hands shall be done him."[S5] But
the deeds of the righteous permit interest to accrue and interest
on interest. And so does Scripture state, "Say ye of the
righteous, that it shall be well with him; for they eat the
interest of their doings."[S6]

Another interpretation:

Just as a treasury is sealed and is not depleted of anything; so
too, the righteous do not receive their due in This World. And
from whence do we know that the righteous do not receive in This

---

* Ln: Those nations   ** Ln: Israel

S4. Ezekiel 23:34.   S5. Isaiah 3:10.   S6. Isaiah 3:10.

T1. Omitted in Ln possibly due to homoioteleuton, ("Scripture states").

E4. The point here is that the wicked are not paid back more than they

World what is due them?[*] --As Scripture states,[T2] "How great

is Thy goodness which you have stored away for those who

fear You."[S7] And from whence do we know that the wicked do

not receive in This World what is due them? --As Scripture

states,[T2] "Is this not laid up in store with Me?" When do

these and those receive their due? In the future when

redemption comes to Israel, as is said, "Vengeance is Mine

and recompense."[E5]

END OF PISKA

---

deserve. Had this not been so they would have caused the world to be
destroyed. But the righteous are paid back more than they deserve for
their goodness accumulates interest. Ln reads "Israel" here where F
reads "the wicked". It is not clear what the intent of Ln is, if it
is not simply a mistake; perhaps the sense is that "what is laid up in
store" is due the nations while "what is sealed up in the treasuries"
is due Israel -- for good or for bad.

* Ln is corrupt here.

S7. Psalms 31:20.

T2. As Scripture states, "How great is Thy goodness which You have
stored away for those who fear You."--omitted in Ln.Possible homoioteleuton.

E5. The midrashist understands the scriptural term "vengeance" to refer
to the punishment of the wicked while the term "recompense" refers to
the reward of the righteous. Thus the two expressions -- vengeance
and recompense -- are seen not to be repetitive or redundant but of
serious import.

35

"Vengeance is Mine and recompense":

I will punish them Myself, not through an angel and not

through a sent one,[E1] according to the matter of which Scripture

states, "Come now and I will send thee to Pharaoh."[S1] And

Scripture also states, "And the angel of the Lord went forth and

smote in the camp of the Assyrians...."[S2]

Another interpretation:

"Vengeance is Mine and I will recompense it" is not written

here but distinctly "Vengeance is Mine and recompense" -- I

recompensed in This World the reward of the deeds that your fathers

did before Me.[E2] And so does Scripture state, "I will not keep silent

---

S1. Exodus 3:10.   S2. 2 Kings 19:35.

E1. The word "לי" found in Deut. 32:35 is the subject of this passage.
In Mechilta to Ex. 12:12, the use of the first person in Ex. 12:12
is taken by the midrashist to refer to God's acting (without angels)
"by Myself". The use of messengers or angels to punish the enemies
of God and the Jewish people is not unknown in Biblical literature
as witnessed by the proof texts here (cf. Ex. 33:15 ff.). In a version
of the Septuagint to Isaiah 63:9 we find M.T. " צר " read as ציר
(cf. Prov. 25:13): "a messenger (Gk. Is. 63:9: presbeis)" so that the
sense of Is. 63:9 is rendered "not by means of a messenger".
(Cf. M. Dahood, "Sir 'emissary' in Ps. 78:44", Biblica, 59 (1978), p. 264.)
In the Qumran literature Isaiah Scroll 21:2 we find the reading
"צירי " (B 313) See further, I.L. Seeligman, The Septuagint Version of
Isaiah, p. 62; J. Goldin, "Not by means of an angel and not by
means of a messenger", (B 173) Studies in the History of Religion,
p. 412ff., and E.E. Urbach, Sages, (B 339   ) p. 136 - 137 and p. 741,
n. 5.

E2. Deut. 32:35 does not use what we would call the "future tense" here,
i.e. it does not say "I will recompense". The point is that Israel's
ancestors were punished in this world for their sins, a sign that their
sins were not very grave (see above Piska 307), and thereby they are
allowed to enjoy perfect salvation in the Era of Resurrection. The
reason the word "fathers" is mentioned by the midrashists is because
the final proof text concludes with the words "on account of their
(i.e. "fathers") profaning of the Land".

except I have recompensed."[S3] And Scripture also states, "And first

I recompensed their iniquity and their sin double."[S4]

"Against the time when their foot shall slip":

 This is according to the matter of which Scripture states,

"The foot shall tread it down, even the feet of the poor and the steps

of the needy."[S5] [E3]

"For the day of their calamity is at hand":

 Rabbi Yosi said: If retribution is still coming slowly towards[E4]

S3. Isaiah 65:6.   S4. Jeremiah 16:18.   S5. Isaiah 26:6.

E3. The proof text ends with the words "even the feet of the poor and
the steps of the needy" so that it may be clearly seen that Israel will
be reduced to poverty as punishment for their sins. The midrashists
thereby indicate that the impoverished state of the Jews is in fact
a merciful punishment since the nation will continue to exist and will
not be destroyed by severer, sudden punishment.

E4. The argument may proceed as follows: Since retribution is meted
out slowly to Israel who was to be punished immediately, Israel should
not be dismayed that retribution has not yet touched the nations whose
punishment was supposed to be delayed to the distant future. The time
elements are relative and work in Israel's favor for their punishment
("at once") is slow in coming, how much slower will be that of the
nations ("to be in the future"). The midrashist thus prepares the way
for an explanation of why the wicked nations who torment Israel enjoy
happy lives -- their time has not yet come for punishment. The midrashist is thus able to present a comparison between Israel's
"merciful" punishments and those "cruel" punishments which will in the
future afflict the nations. In the next pericope he explains that when
punishment finally does arrive upon the nations it will be of such
immediate intensity as to destroy them completely. In Piska 321 he
mentioned a similar fate where the first interpretation of אספה
was taken as referring to the sudden punishing of the nations while the
second interpretation was construed as referring to the cessation of
punishments upon Israel. However, Silberman raises the possibility
that ממשמש   here could be seen as implying an imminent punishment
for Israel and all the more so for Israel's enemies.

those of whom Scripture says,[E5]"For the day of their calamity is at

hand", then how much more slowly   shall it come towards those of

whom Scripture states, "And after many days shall they be punished."[S6]

"And the things that are to come upon them will make haste":

When the Holy One, Blessed Be He, brings retribution upon the

Gentile Nations, He causes the world to quake upon them. And so does

Scripture state, "They fly as a vulture that hasteneth to devour."[S7]

And Scripture also states, "That say: 'Let Him make speed, let Him

hasten His work, that we may see it; and let the counsel of the Holy

One of Israel draw nigh and come."[S8] Yet when the Holy One, Blessed

Be He, brings punishments upon Israel He does not do so abruptly but He

prolongs it.[*] How does He do this? -- He hands them over to the Four

Kingdoms that they should be subjugated by them. And so does Scripture

state, "Fear not for I am with thee, saith the Lord, to deliver you.

(and to save you)."[S9]

END OF PISKA

---

* Ln: He does not prolong it for them.

S6. Isaiah 24:22.   S7. Habakuk 1:8.
S8. Isaiah 5:19.   S9. Jeremiah 1:8.

E5. Israel will always continue to exist because God preserves it by
protracting the punishemnt due the Jews over the years of exile rather
than concentrating their punishment into a single, abrupt action which
would destroy them.

36

"For the Lord will judge His people":

When the Holy One, Blessed Be He, judges the Gentile Nations
He is joyful, as it is said, "When the Lord will judge His people
(and repent Himself for His servants)." But when the Holy One, Blessed
Be He, judges Israel, He -- as if it were possible -- feels regret,
as it is said, "And repent Himself for His servants". Now "repentance"
specifically means "regret", as it is said, "For it repenteth Me
that I have made them."[S1] And Scripture also states, "It repenteth
Me that I have set up Saul to be King."[S2]

"When He sees that their stay is gone":

When He[E1] sees their destruction by means of the captivity where
all had departed.[*]

Another interpretation:

When they abandon hope of redemption.

Another interpretation:

"When He sees their stay is gone, and there is none remaining to shut up or left at large":[**]

When He sees that the penny has perished from the wallet,[E2] as it

---

[*] Ln: He sees all going before Him when the captivity has brought
perdition.
[**] Ln omits "Another interpretation....or left at large."

S1. Genesis 6:7.   S2. 1 Samuel 15:11.

E1. The question here is whether "He" in Deut. 32:36 refers to God or
to Israel. Thus the homilist offers two interpretations of the verse.
Schorr, p. 13f., sees יך = δόδs (=departure= גלות).

E2. Deut. 32:26 is compared with 2 Kings 14:26 (see "E4") where the
word " עני " occurs. Thus the reference to "stay" in Deut. 32:26 must
be to a "wallet", which being emptied ("is gone"), renders the nation

is said, "And when they have made an end of emptying the stay of the holy people, all these things shall be finished."[S3]

Another interpretation:

"When He sees that their stay is gone":

When He sees they no longer have men like Moses who pray[E3] for them, as it is said, "And He thought to destroy them were it not for Moses, His chosen one."[S4]

Another interpretation:

"When He sees...":

When He sees that they no longer have men like Aaron to pray for them, as it is said, "And he stood between the dead and the living and the plague ceased."[S5]

---

in a state of poverty (עני). And so a proof text is brought showing that "stay" can refer to "wealth":

כי יראה כי אזלת יד = כי ראה ה׳ את עני

S3. Daniel 12:7.   S4. Psalms 106:23.   S5. Numbers 17:13.

E3. Either: The word " יד ", "stay" literally means "hand". The hand is a symbol of prayer, cf. B.T. Sotah 38a, Mishna Tamid 7:2. Cf. Marqah's reference to "like Aaron","like Eliezar", "like Phineas", (5:2). Cf. G. C. Greenstein, "'To grasp the hem' in Ugaritic literature", [B 178] VT vol. 32 (1982) no. 2, p. 217f. ("To raise the hand" = "to pray"). See Schorr, p. 13-14, who equates יד = ειδω = those who know;

Or: יד = ידיד (His beloved) see M. Delcor, "Two Special Meanings of the Word יד in Biblical Hebrew", Journal of Semitic Studies, Vol. 12-13 (1967-68), p. 230ff.

Another interpretation:

"When He sees...":

When He sees that they no longer have men like Phineas to pray for them, as it is said, "And Phineas stood and prayed."[S6]

Another interpretation:

"When He sees that their stay is gone, and there is none remaining, shut up or left at large":

"There is none shut up and there is none left at large -- and there is no deliverer of Israel."[E4]

END OF PISKA

S6. Psalms 106:30.

E4. The point here is that God will redeem Israel (ועל עבדיו יתנחם) when it looks bleakest for them. So it was in 2 Kings 14:26 and so it will be again. The midrashist has offered seven explanations of "stay" to emphasize the desperation of their plight -- all possibilities of redemption have been exhausted. Thus the community listening to these homilies, having experienced the Destruction of the Temple, the failure of Bar Kochba's revolt and the persecution of the Roman Empire, finds a message of hope in their time of despair. These verses had been used before to this effect, before the Fall of the Temple; see 2 Maccabees 7:6. The word " עזוב " here means "aid". Cf. B.T. Sanhed. 97a (=סומך סומך) and Rashi to Deut. 32:36, also Anonymous, "עצור ועזוב " עוד לענין Lĕšōnenū 33 (1968) no. 1, p. 70ff. and especially A. Ahuvya, "עצור ועזוב " עוד לענין, Lĕšōnenū,31 (1967), no. 3, p. 160. Cf. " עצור ועזוב בישראל", ibid,30 (1966),no. 3, p. 175.

37

"And he will say: 'Where are their <u>princes</u>...'":

Rabbi Yehuda interpreted it in reference to Israel while Rabbi Nehemiah interpreted it in reference to the Gentile Nations of the World.

Rabbi Yehuda says: In the future it will be that Israel will say to the Gentile Nations of the World, "Where are your councillors and your consuls."[E1]

END OF PISKA

E1. "Elohim" in Deut. 32:37 is understood by the midrashist here in its profane sense of "princes".

38

"Who did eat the fat of their sacrifices...":

For we would give them soldiers' store, and present them
with the soldiers' gift and bestow upon them "salt money".[E1]

"Let them rise up and help you":

It is not written here "Let them rise up and they will help
you (ויעזרו אתכם)" but specifically "Let them rise up and He[E2]
will help you (ויעזרכם)".*

---

*Ln: ויעזרוכם

E1. "Fat" is interpreted as "store". "Sacrifices" is taken as
"gifts". "Drink offerings" is understood as an allusion to "salt-
money". See notes in F here.

E2. <u>Either</u>: a)"Yehuda" emphasizes the consonantal reading (כם) יעזר
("He will save...") as opposed to the vocalized reading (כם) יַעְזְרֻ
("They will save...") to emphasize that He, God, will rescue Israel,

   <u>Or</u>:   b) More likely we have an instance, already noted in E25
to Piska 306, whereby the editor introduces a refutation,based upon a
grammatical point, of a position which he is about to bring."Nehemiah"
understands the words יקומו ויעזרכם to mean "Rise up and help Yourself" (see note here in Sifre Bamidbar-Devarim, with notes of Wilna
Gaon, 5626: ויעזר את עצמם). The plural forms of ויעזרכם יקומו are
not of consequence, God as אלוהים being defined by the Royal
plural (cf. Joshua 24:19 אלהים קדשים) and a switch in persons from
3rd to 2nd also being possible when addressing God (e.g. Ps. 68:36
נורא אלהים ממקדשיך). Hence יעזרכם =Let Him help Himself
(Yourself). But the refutation of this position is that this possibility
of a grammatical switch in persons (from 3rd to 2nd) is allowable
only if two separate words (i.e. יעזרו אתכם) are used but not if
only one word (יעזרכם) is used. Thus the interpretation falls
apart because Deut. 32 uses only one word and not two. There is no
difference between F (יעזרכם) and Ln (יעזרוכם) except that F
follows the Massoretic spelling (defective) while Ln presents the
Massoretic reading (full) but not the spelling.
   "Nehemiah's" midrash may be dated to first century traditions
evidenced in the Synoptic Gospels. I raise now the possibility of
legends concerning Judaism's Temple and Christianity's Passion being
built upon the same midrashic typology developed from Deut. 32:37-39.
If Mt. 27:40 and Mk. 15:29 tell us that Jesus=Temple then I posit that
the Passion of the Synoptics follows a tradition similar to Piska 328,
Piska 329 <u>mutatis mutandis</u>: The slashing of the Temple curtain (=Lk
23:45, Mt. 27:51, Mk 15:38, cf. H.L. Chronis, "The Torn Veil: Cultus
and Christianity in Mark 15:37-39", <u>JBL</u>, vol. 101 (1982), p. 97ff),

Rabbi Nehemiah says:

This refers to evil Titus, the son of Vespasian's wife, who

entered the Holy of Holies and slashed two curtains with a sword

and said, "If He be God let Him come[E3] and oppose this!"

"Who did eat of the fat of their sacrifices..."

He said: Moses led these ones astray by telling them, "Build

an altar, and offer burnt sacrifices upon it, and pour libations

---

"If He be God let him come and oppose this"(=Lk 23:35-39, Mt. 27:40-43,
Mk. 15:30), allusions to resurrection of the dead (=Mt. 27:52 esp.
"after two days he will revive us" = Lk 24:7, Mt. 27:63, Mk. 16:9).
Cassuto (Bibl. and Or. Studies,p. 98) has pointed out that Hosea 5:14
rephrases Deut. 32:39. Since the conclusion of this section ends
in Hosea 6:2

יחיינו מימים ביום השלישי יקומנו ונחיה לפניו

and Hosea 6:2 is cited in Piska 329 we might suppose that the synoptic
saying to the effect that the Temple would be rebuilt in 3 days
(Mt. 27:40 and Mk. 15:29) was intended to refer to Jesus' resurrection
based upon Hos. 6:2 and midrashim upon Deut. 32, to which Hos. passages
are related. We might even suggest that Deut. 32:40 ("I live forever")
has influenced Mt. 28:7 and Mk. 16:19. (Since John's passion is centred
about "paschal lamb" typology the above motifs are absent.) We may thus
argue for an early date (late 1st century) for the ancestry of the
"Nehemiah" legend (based upon a dating of the passion sections to this
time) unless the parent of the Jewish and Christian legends goes back
to a legend concerning desecrations of the Temple prior to the
destruction of 70.Cf.D. Senior, "Death of Jesus and Resurrection of
Holy Ones", CBQ 38 (1976), p. 312. Also compare Wisdom of Solomon
2:17ff, to Mt. 27:40-43. Cf. M. Gertner, "Midrashim in the New
Testament", Journal of Semitic Studies, Vol. 7 (1962), no. 1, p. 262ff.

E3. Here "elohim" is taken in its sacred sense as a reference to
Israel's God. Also see S. Lieberman, Greek etc.,(B248) p. 164f, for
the claim that the expression "son of Vespasian's wife" here is to
cast aspersion upon Titus' legitimacy, a remark aimed at Roman morals,
although in actuality the Rabbis did accept that Vespasian was the
legitimate father of Titus. According to the midrashic Titus, how was
Moses supposed to have led Israel astray? He ordained rites which had
no redemptive effect or protective power against Rome, whereas the
Roman pagan rites were effective (see Tosafot to B.T. Av. Zarah 29b:
"ישתו ").

over it," according to the matter of which it is said,

"The one lamb thou shalt offer in the morning and the other

lamb thou shalt offer at dusk...and the drink offering

thereof". [S1]

"Let Him rise up and help you, let Him be your protection":

The Holy One, Blessed Be He, is forgiving towards everything.

He exacts immediate[E4] punishment for the desecration of His name.

END OF PISKA

S1. Numbers 28:4.

E4. The use of "See now" in Deut. 32:39 is used by the preacher to substantiate that teaching which says that God will punish desecration of His name immediately. The foregoing story of evil Titus and the calumnies intimated by verse 37 and 38 are offered as examples of profaning God's name. That verse 39 begins by words "See--now", the midrashist takes as evidence that God reacts to profanation of His name with immediate punishment --now. The probable refutation of this position found above, "E2" implies that Israel will say to the nations in the Messianic Era, "Where are your councillors? Let them rise up and help you!" That is the position of Yehuda.

39

"See now that I, I am He":

This refutes those who say there is no heavenly rulership.[E1]

E1. The aggadist compares verses 37 and 39: "Where is (are) their ruler (rulers)?" ("elohim" can be singular or plural). --"I, I am that!" The antecedent of That is taken to be ruler(s). Thus the ruler(s) speak(s) out and identifies Himself (themselves) so that His (their) existence is demonstrated. Thus it is that those who denied that there were heavenly powers are now refuted by the Power(s) making contrary claims by the presentation of actual evidence. So the midrashist is convinced that God himself will answer those who deny His existence. But still, there may be others who asked the question, "Where are their rulers?" and heard the answer "I, I am That!" who would think that the antecedent of "That" refers to "rulers" such that a plurality of rulers has been indicated by the response. Thus the midrashist shows that the verse indicates God will tell them "and there is no god with Me!". The midrashist adds a further proof text to explain a similar use of a double "I" in Scripture which also had to be qualified to show that there is only one God: "I am the first and I am the last and besides Me there is no God." That this proof text is placed in our texts after a discussion of God's omnipotence rather than after the discussion of how many gods exist indicates that the discussion of omnipotence is an interpolation into the midrash. Cf. Philo, Post., (B 34) ch. 58 (167-169) and see Koran sura 112:3.

This pericope has received attention from A.F. Segal in his study Two Powers in Heaven[1]. Segal identifies three traditions (there are actually four - see E3, Piska 329) and attempts to analyze them[2].

To begin, we should note that Segal's rendition of ולא כבר כתוב as "Has it not elsewhere been said" is more properly translated as "Has it not yet been written?" Although the word כבר is used in many ways in Rabbinic literature, its use in this phrase is meant to suggest that we have an opposing statement. It is important to see this element of opposition in כבר because it introduces the plan of the pericope. The midrashist finds in Scripture mention of people who make heretical claims and also the opposition to these claims. If anyone should claim that there are two deities we may take assurance in the fact that God will respond in opposition to them: And he (the heretic) will say, "Where are their gods? (Deut. 32:37)". Then God will answer, "See now that I, I am 'that' (Deut. 32:39)." The homilist proceeds to explain that we might think אלוהימו is a plural and refers to "gods" so that the response -- "I, I am 'that' (in reference to the word אלוהימו) apparently confirms that there are two deities. Thus the midrashist points out that God must correct this impression by stating outright, "And there is no god with Me (Deut. 32:39)." The homilist states that God's answer will be

definitive and refute the heretics to their faces. Now Segal
misses the intent of the proof text, Isaiah 44:6, which is brought
to show that double usages of "I" in Scripture (e.g. "I am the
first and I am the last.") when referring to God are of necessity
always defined by Scripture as referring to a single God ("And but
for Me, there is no god.") Segal has not analyzed the form of the
midrash well and believes that this proof text is meant to show
some kind of refutation against those who deny God's ability
to kill or to bring to life. Segal has missed the point that there
is an interpolation in the text here and the proof text of Is. 44:6
does not refer to the interpolation but to that which preceded the
interpolation, the question of how many deities exist. The homilist
himself indicates that we have an interpolation into the text --
"or according to the theme...." Herford correctly saw this
(Christianity in Talmud and Midrash, p. 299) passage as an interpolation, omitted it from his translation so that Deut. 32:39 ("And
there is no god with Me") and Isaiah 44:6 ("And but for Me there is no
god.") are juxtaposed. Now this interpolation is designed to show
another understanding of the heretical denial and divine response.
The nations, according to this alternate view, ask איה אלוקימו :
"Where is the power of their God?" And God replies, "I kill and I
make alive, I wound and I heal." God has ultimate power. After the
interpolation -- או כעניו which is indicative of a parenthetical
remark, the homilist returns to his original theme of showing that
God is first, last, and alone, for the midrashist is no longer concerned
with showing that God has powers over life and death, having already
finished that topic.

A more serious error is Segal's mistaken translation of the passage that begins "Another interpretation: 'I kill and I make alive'."
He states here that the question of interpretation concerns whether
only one power kills while another makes alive or whether one power
by Himself can kill people and give life to people. In spite of the
fact that the midrashist has already disposed of the claim that
there even exists another power besides God, Segal sums up his
mistranslation (Just as wounding and healing is by one (power), so
is death and life by one (power) alone.)[3] by saying, "One god might
be thought to be in charge of killing while another is in charge of
revivication."[4] Segal understands that the Rabbis countered this
alleged claim by pointing out that wounding and healing are done by
one God and so must one God also kill and give life. Segal does not
explain why the heretics would have agreed that wounding and healing
are done by one God from the verse, any more than they would accept
that killing and giving life are done by one God. Nevertheless, he
finds in this passage (really concerned with showing that a person
can be resurrected) an alleged reference to "two-power" heresy which
is the topic of his inquiry. His finding is wrong. The midrashist
is concerned with finding some type of Scriptural support for the
notion that there will be a resurrection of the dead. The homilist
at the outset found an answer to show that there is only one God

and now queries whether the verse: "I kill and I make alive" means
1) God kills one person and gives another life; or 2) He resurrects
him . The homilist solves the problem by investigating the next part
of the verse which states, "I wound and I heal". Now since healing
is not able to be done to one who has not first been wounded it is
clear that the verse means that God heals the one He has wounded. We
are concerned with the plight of one victim. Therefore, the parallel
structure of the verse dictates that "I kill and I make" alive refer
to one victim as well. The order of the words thus shows that God
kills someone and then makes the same person alive. Now the
midrashist states that we have here a remez, a hint, not a clear proof
of resurrection because we arrive at our conclusion by assuming a
parallel structure of meaning within the verse. Segal's translation
of רמז as "sure allusion" is incorrect. The homilist merely stated
that there are divine promises(הבטחות) which contain allusions(רמז)
to the resurrection of the dead.

Segal then examines a final passage in this midrash based upon מציל
and concludes that the midrashist is referring to the "standard motif
that families will be split up on the day of judgement". There is no
basis for his comment. The homilist believes God is responding in
vs. 39 ואין מידי מציל to challenges posed in vs. 37 -- fathers save--
צור חסיו בו (צור refers to "fathers", see N.A. van Uchelen, "The Targumic Version of Deut. 33:15, JJS, vol. 31 (1980), no. 2, p. 199ff)
while חסיו refers to "safeguarding") and vs. 38 --
סתרה יקומו ויעזרכם יהי עליכם סתרה (סתרה can refer to shelter. For
the idea of the soul being sheltered and safeguarded until the time
of the resurrection see F.C. Porter, "The Pre-existence of the Soul
in the Book of Wisdom and in Rabbinical Writings",[B287] Old Testament
and Semitic Studies in Memory of William Rainey Harper, (editors,
R.F. Harper, F. Brown, G.F. Moore), Univ. of Chicago Press, 1908,
pp. 205-270). Now verse 39:"And none can save out of My hand" when
taken in response to the claim that "fathers can save their children"
is seen to be an explicit denial of such saving. That brothers cannot
save one another is shown by reference to Psalm 49:8 -- "A brother
shall not redeem-redeem a man." The midrashist explains the apparently
redundant פודה -- פודה to refer to two certain brothers, Ishmael
(brother of Isaac), Esau or Edom, (brother of Jacob). So the
midrashist says -- Since I know that Ishmael and Esau are not saved by
merit of their fathers how do I know that they will not be saved by the
merit of their brothers? -- Ps. 49:8 is exegeted to show that indeed
they cannot be so saved.

Notes:
1. See A.F. Segal, Two Powers in Heaven: Early Rabbinic Reports about
   Christianity and Gnosticism, Leiden, E.J. Brill, 1977.

2. Segal, p. 84ff. The title erroneously reads "Sifre Deut. 379 (and
   reads so in his Index to Rabbinic sources as well)". It should
   read "Sifre Deut. 329".

3. Segal, p. 85.

As for he who says there are[T1] two[*] heavenly rulerships,[E2] we refute him by citing, "And yet has it not been written, 'And there is no God with Me.'"

Or concerning the declarations that He has not the power to kill nor the power to give life, not the power to cause injury nor the power to give benefit, Scripture states, "See now that I, I, am He, I will kill and I will make alive...."[E3] And Scripture also states, "Thus saith the Lord, the King of Israel, and his Redeemer, the Lord of Hosts, I am the first and I am the last and besides Me there is no other God."[S1]

Another interpretation:[**]

"I will kill and I will make alive":

This is one of the four assurances which contain an allusion to the Resurrection of the Dead: "I will kill and I will make alive,"; "My soul will die the death of the righteous";[S2] "Reuben will live and will not die";[S3] "After two days He will revive us."[S4]

---

4. Segal, p. 87. Why does Segal mention Hosea 6:2 here when the reference is obviously to Deut. 32:39?

*Ln: There is no heavenly rulership.
** Ln: omits "Another interpretation".

S1. Isaiah 44:6. S2. Numbers 23:10. S3. Deuteronomy 33:6.
S4. Hosea 6:2.

T1. Since the proof text in Ln supports a reading like that of F but is irrelevant to the present reading in Ln, I assume Ln to be corrupt in its reading here.

E2. See R.T. Herford, Christianity in Talmud and Midrash,[(B194)] London, Williams Norgate 1903, p. 262 and 265, n. 1. Herford omits the apparent interpolation in his translation of the passage, p. 299.

I might understand that the reference to "death" applies
to one person while the reference to "life" applies to another, so
Scripture states, "I wound and I heal": Just as it is only
feasible that the references to "wounding" and "healing" apply to
the same person; so too, do the references to "death" and "life"
refer to the same person.[E4]

"And there is none that can deliver מידי ":
Fathers do not[T2] deliver their sons:[E5] Abraham does not deliver

---

E3. Here ends the apparent interpolation. The passage as it now
stands refutes four groups: Those who deny God exists, those who
believe in more than one god, those who deny God is omnipotent,
and those who believe an ancestor can save a son. See below E5 .

T2. Ln's scribe wrote " את " but whole context shows this was a mistake
of " אין ".

E4. The midrashist examines the order of terms in Deut. 32:39:
1a) kill.........1b) make alive
2a) wound........2b) heal
and concludes that since 2b) is of necessity performed upon the subject
of 2a) (well people need not be healed), then 1b) is to be understood
as applying to the subject of 1a). Thus the verse implies that God
makes alive the one whom He has killed. This interpretation seems to
have been known to the author of 4 Maccabees 18:18 who quotes Deut.
32:39 to show that there is an afterlife for those who die as martyrs
for their laws which "are the length of your days". Cf. Philo, Som.2,
ch. 44 (297).[B 34]

E5. We have now to see what the scoffers said in Deut. 32:37f.:
1) צור חסיו בו   (cf. Is. 51:2 Abraham)
2) יקומו ויעזרכם....
3) יהי עליכם סתרה
(That סתר refers to שאול or the after life, see M. Dahood,
"Hebrew-Ugaritic Lexicography", Biblica 50 (1969), p. 344.).
But God answers in Deut. 32:39:
ואין מידי מציל
The homilist takes צור to refer to Abraham - the Father, the Patriarch,
and may also take ידי as ידיד (=Abraham; cf. Is. 41:8). See M. Delcor,
"Two Special Meanings of the Word יד in Biblical Hebrew", Journal of
Semitic Studies ,12-13 (1967-8), p. 230ff. See also B. T. Shab. 55a.
For the use of נצל as "safekeeping" for the afterlife see the usage

Ishmael and Isaac does not deliver Esau. I only know from here
that fathers do not deliver their sons. From whence do I know that
brothers do not deliver brothers? I know it from the Scripture which
states, "Truly no man can redeem his brother."[S5] --Isaac does not
deliver Ishmael and Jacob does not deliver Esau. And even should
a person give Him all the money in the world, he is not permitted
to be ransomed, as it is said, "Truly no man can redeem his
brother (or give to God his ransom);[S5]for the redemption of their
soul is priceless."[S6] The soul is so priceless that when a person
sins against it there is no price which may restore it.

END OF PISKA

---

of מוצל in ARN "B" ch. 25,(B 1   ) cf. "El", Piska 341. Also
note how our tradition is used by ARN "B" ch. 27 (beginning). That
Deut. 32:39 here is an answer to verse 38 see Hizkuni(B 9   ) to
Deut. 32:39. Also see Urbach, Sages,(B 339)p. 500 for similar ideas
in Fourth Ezra and Pseudo-Philo. Cf. A. Marmorstein, Doctrine of Merits,
p. 38, (B 260) . See further Conclusion no. 7.

S5. Psalms 49:8.   S6. Psalms 49:8.

40

"For I lifted up My hand to heaven (and I said, 'as

I live forever')":

When the Holy One, Blessed Be He, created the world He

purposely created it^{E1} by means of command and by means of an oath.^{*E2}

---

* Ln: by means of command and _not_ by means of an oath.

E1. Ln reads better than F here. Cf. A. Marmorstein, <u>Doctrine of</u>
<u>Merits</u>, p. 176. The sense runs well -- the world was not created
by means of an oath -- and so the midrashist must explain "then why
did He later make one". The oath is that none shall escape punishment
in this world or the next.
    In his work, <u>Divine Name and Presence</u>: the Memra, $^{(B\ 190\ )}$p. 51ff.
Robert Hayward examines Frag. Targ. (Ginsburger) (cf. B 56, p. 8):
    And the world was created by mercy, and by mercy it is sustained.
Then he looks at Mechilta (to Ex. 22:26) <u>Kaspa</u> 1:58f, (cf. B. 15 p. 317):
    For by mercy I created My world.
And also Mechilta <u>Nezikin</u> 10:158 (cf. B. 15 p. 286):
    Come and see the mercies of Him who said, and the world was there.
Finally he adduces Sifre Deut. Piska 330:
    When the Holy One, Blessed Be He, created, He did not create
    except by a <u>ma'amar</u>, nor did He create except by an oath.
On the basis of these sources Hayward announces that "we deduce that
the <u>Memra</u> represents YHWH in His good mercies...and the <u>ma'amar</u> which
He utters on this occasion is broadly similar to the <u>Memra</u>." (Hayward,
p. 53.)
    Now the question arises as to how exactly Hayward
understands the term "oath" in the Sifre passage. The possibilities are:
  1) <u>oath</u> is used as an opposite of <u>ma'amar</u> and so should be taken as
    a reference to the opposite of "mercy", i.e. it refers to
    "justice". The continuation of the Sifre passage which speaks
    of the punishment of the wicked through this oath could substan-
    tiate such an interpretation.
  2) <u>oath</u> is used as a synonym of <u>ma'amar</u> and the sentence means that
    God used only <u>ma'amar</u>, which is namely, only <u>oath</u>. Consider
    the continuation of the Sifre passage;such an interpretation I say
    would refute his claim that <u>ma'amar</u> refers to mercy. Perhaps
    Hayward thinks this statement in Sifre is independent of the
    explanation which follows which mentions the punishment of the
    wicked. The later explanation has midrashically turned around
    the word "oath" in order to serve its own needs. Thus he might
    argue that the statement he has quoted is substantial to prove
    his point.
  3) <u>oath</u> here is taken as a technical term from the vocabulary of
    "magic" texts and it means to summon into existence by the proper
    enunciation of divine names. In this case also we would have to say

that the continuity of the midrash is broken by a later
stratum that understands oath purely as a vehicle of
punishment and that this stratum has changed the original
intent of the first passage that speaks of God creating by
means of an oath.
Hayward answers this question with recourse to possibility #2, "the
notion has already been mentioned in the Sifre Deuteronomy 330,
where the very same oath which created the universe is equivalent
to the m'mr , the Hebrew version of Memra." He compares this
notion with Jubilees 12:4 (and has created everything by His word),
Jubilee 36:7 (a great oath...by the Name...which created the heavens
and the earth...), 1 Enoch 69:16ff. (this oath...the heaven was
suspended...the earth was founded...) and concludes:
     First, the oath is responsible for the creation and the
     ensuing stability of the created order, as in Jubilees 36:7
     and the Sifre Deuteronomy 330(Hayward, p. 12f).
Hayward assumes a single tradition of Memra-theology(where the world
was created by an oath)is present in all of these passages. In order to
do this he will have to explain the history of the tradition in Sifre
Deut. Piska 330 which "understands" the oath as מאמר , a tool of
punishment which God was forced to take reluctantly against those of
little faith. Now the examples adduced by Hayward from Jubilees and
Enoch understand the oath as a powerfully divine name which can work
wonders, it can cause mighty wonders to occur -- create a world or
destroy a land. If the reading in Sifre Deut. 330 is as given by F
and followed by Hayward then oath can have no other meaning than that
of Enoch, and it stems from the "magic" vocabulary of Apocalyptic.
It is not certain that it must parallel ma'amar, and it is not
certain that it reflects an aspect of God's mercy. Perhaps Hayward
would have been better off to argue either #1 or #3 above. However,
I accept the reading of Ln: "and not by means of an oath". The
midrash rejects the notion of the tradition found in Enoch and
Jubilees. God did create by ma'amar, not by oath. It was only later
that He resorted to oath, once those "of little faith" vexed Him.
According to the proof text the oath was first taken after the Exodus,
not during creation. Thus the midrash plays down the idea of the
magic use of the divine name and understands "oath" to mean "promise"
not a "magical rite". The world was created only by mercy. The notion
of the gnostics -- that the creation was evil and that matter was
base is rejected. Another midrash follows the same pattern of thought;
namely, the world was created by blessing and should so continue, it
is man's rebelliousness which leads to curse, not God's creation.
  See Gen. R. 1:10,(B.17) p. 9 .

E2. In Deut. 32:40, the midrashist understands "lifting up the
hands" as a sign of an oath as in Gen. 14:22. Cf. Marqah 4:12,(B16   )
"As live forever" -- is a strong oath.

And who caused Him to take oath? It was those who lacked faith who
caused Him to take oath, as it is said, "And He lifted up His hand
concerning them, to cast them down in the desert[E3](and to cast their
seed down amongst the nations)";[S1] "I have lifted up my hand,[E4]
concerning the nations."[*] [S2]

"And I said, 'As I live forever'":

For the response of the Holy One, Blessed Be He, is not as
the response of one who is made of flesh and blood. The response of
one who is made of flesh and blood is as follows: The councillor enters
into his administrative area. If he is able[**] to exact punishment from
those he sentenced, he exacts it, and if not, then he is unable
to exact punishment. But He Who Spoke and The World
Existed is not so. If He does not exact punishment from the living, He
exacts it from the dead. If He does not exact it in This World, He
exacts it in the World to Come.

END OF PISKA

---

*Ln: omits "S2".
**Ln: If he immediately is able.

S1. Psalms 106:26.   S2. Ezekiel 36:7.

E3. Some texts read here in accordance with Massoretic text Ez.20:5:
"And I lifted up My hand to the seed of the house of Jacob."

E4. The Massoretic reading of Ez.36:7 is as follows:
   "I have lifted up My hand, I swear the nations which are about you
   shall bear their shame." Yet, the sense of the pericope remains
that the sinners of Israel shall not escape punishment. Ln's
reading incorporates Psalm 106:26 "and to cast their seed down amongst
the nations". Perhaps F adds Ez. 36:7 to show that while there is an
oath to condemn the sinners of Israel there is also an oath to punish
the nations and to redeem Israel.

41

"When I whet My lightning sword":

When retribution goes out from before Me, it is as fleeting
as lightning.. Nevertheless -- "And My hand shall take hold on
judgement; /[E1]I will render vengeance to My adversaries," --behold
one-- "and will recompense them that hate Me," --behold two.[E2]

Another interpretation/

"I will render vengeance to צרי ":

This refers to the Samaritans, as it is said, "When the צרי
of Judah and Benjamin[E3] (heard of the exiles building the temple)."[S1]

S1. Ezra 4:1.

E1. What is contained in slashes here /..../ is thought by L.F. to
be a gloss.

E2. " שנון " taken as "whet" in the translation of the verse can also
be taken midrashically as "repetition" i.e. "a double sword" -- a
double punishment which is to be related to the doubled expression
"vengeance and recompense" of this verse (41).

E3. The play here is made upon צרי which again appears in Ezra 4:1
in reference to the Samaritans who were the adversaries (צרי) of
Judah and Benjamin, the returning exiles from Babylonia. Cf. the
note to Ben Sira 50:25 in E10 , Piska 320.

"And will recompense them that hate Me":

This refers to the minim.[E4] And likewise does Scripture state, "Do not I hate them, O Lord, that hate Thee? And I do strive against those that rise up against Thee; (the end of their hatred is that they become my enemies)."[S2]

END OF PISKA

S2. Psalms 129:31.

E4. "Those who hate God" are said to be minim by definition. See also B.T. Shabbath 116a and Avoth deRabbi Nathan "A",ch. 16. Also see Herford, Christianity in Talmud and Midrash, p. 156ff.

42

"I will make Mine arrows drunk with blood":

Now is it possible for arrows to be drunk with blood! Rather,
it means[E1] "Behold I will make other creatures drunk from that which
my arrows accomplish."

"And My sword shall devour flesh":

Now is it possible for a sword to devour flesh! Rather it means,
"Behold I will feed other creatures from that which My sword
accomplishes". And so does Scripture state, "And thou son of man,
speak unto the birds of every sort (and to all the birds of the Heavens:
'Gather and come to My sacrifice which I offer')."[S1] And Scripture
states, "That ye may eat fat* abundantly and drink blood (to
drunkenness.)"[S1] And it states, "The flesh of the mighty shall ye eat
...(and the blood of the princes of the earth you will drink)."[S2]
And Scripture continues, "And ye shall be filled at My table with horses
and horsemen...".[S3] And Scripture says, "The sword of the Lord is
filled with blood, it is made with fatness,"[S4] [E2] -- on what account?--
"for the Lord hath a sacrifice in Bozrah, and a great slaughter in
the Land of Edom."[S4]

---

* Ln: bread
** Ln: with fat and blood

S1. Ezekiel 39:17. S2. Ezekiel 39:18. S3. Ezekiel 39:20
S4. Isaiah 34:6.

E1. The midrash paraphrases verse 42 in such a way as to show that the
punishments to come to Israel's oppressors are punishments for the murder
of Israel, God's people and nation.

E2. The readings of Massoretic text are noted by Friedmann[(B47)]
here to vary from citations in the manuscripts.

"With the blood of the slain and the captives":[T1]

On account of that which they did to the slain of My people.
And so does Scripture state, "O that My head were waters, and Mine eyes
a fountain of tears, that I might weep day and night for the slain
of the daughter of My people."[S5]

"And the captives":[T1]

On account of that which they did to the captivity of My
people. And so does Scripture state, "And they shall take them captive,
whose captives they were; and they shall rule over their oppressors."[S6]

"From the head is the פרעות of the enemy":

When the Holy One, Blessed Be He, brings retribution (פורענות)
upon the Gentile Nations,[E3] He does not bring it upon them for their
own crimes alone but for these as well as those of their

S5. Jeremiah 8:23.   S6. Isaiah 14:2.

T1. Omitted in Ln possibly due to homoioteleuton ("with the blood of
the slain and the captives").

E3. פרעות is taken here as "punishment" (פרענות) while ראש is
taken as "the ancestors" (first ones). Hence the point of the midrash
is to show that reward and punishment are fully given   on Judgement
Day, retroactively to the beginning of history . This midrashic statement serves as a theodic statement. L. Silberman raises an interesting
insight here. We are   dealing with accumulative punishment and
reward -- "Not only the punishment due them but also the punishment due
their ancestors...not only the good things due them...."

ancestors[T2] from Nimrod on. When He brings blessings upon Israel
He brings upon them both those which they themselves have
earned and also those of their ancestors[T2] from Abraham on.
Another interpretation:

"From the head of פרעות , the enemy":

What was seen, to hang upon the head of Pharaoh all the
retributions? It was on account of the fact that he was the first
to enslave Israel.[E4]

END OF PISKA

T2. Omitted in Ln possibly due to homoioteleuton ("and their
ancestors").

E4. The homilist finds a message in Deut. 32:42. Since פרע may
have two meanings: 1) a head of (hair)
                    2) punishments
the question arises as to why the oppressive King of Egypt was called
Pharaoh. The answer is found in the verse מראש פרעות אויב,
i.e. he is the archetype (ראש) of the enemy who oppresses Israel but
eventually will be mortally punished (פרעות). Pharaoh, indeed, the
midrashist notes, experienced both. The term "Pharaoh" incorporates
the idea of an "archetype" (a head) and of ensuing punishment upon
him. The plural פרעות is thus explained to refer to the oppressors
throughout Jewish history as "pharaohs" since they will undergo the
same sure retribution as did Pharaoh of Egypt. L. Silberman finds an
intriguing alternative and suggests we might consider the translation
here: "What was seen hanging over the head of Pharaoh? All the
retributions because he was the first to enslave Israel." This is an
example of how an ancestor will suffer for the evils perpetrated by
his "descendants in evil".

43

" הרנינו ‎, O ye nations, because of His people":

In the Future when the Holy One, Blessed Be He, brings
redemption to Israel, the Gentile Nations of the World will be
angered before Him.[E1] And this would not be their first time for they
already were enraged at an earlier occasion. This is according to the
matter of which Scripture states, "The nations heard, they were
angered."[S1]

Another interpretation:

" הרנינו ‎, O ye nations because of His people":

In the Future, the Gentile Nations of the World will rejoice[E2]
on account of Israel, as it is said, "Rejoice, O ye nations, because
of His people". And also the heavens[E3] and the earth! As it is
said, "Sing, O ye heavens, for the Lord hath done it; Shout, ye

---

S1. Exodus 15:14.

E1. The "nations" here are taken as the "nations of the world" and
the term הרנינו ‎ of this verse (43) is taken in the sense of
"complain" rather than "rejoice". Cf. Hizkuni[B9] to Deut. 32:43
who equates it with לשון יללה ‎ (woes). Silberman finds other
references - J. Ber. IV, 7d and J. Ber. IX, 14b.

E2. In this passage the midrashist takes הרנינו ‎ in the sense of
"rejoice". Thus we have two possibilities in interpreting this verse:
either the nations will praise Israel or they will be jealous of them
and complain (see above E1). Schorr, p. 13f. sees
הרנינו ‎ = ορνΰεῖν = roused (מתרגש).

E3. The midrashist understands that all of nature will applaud
Israel's redemption. Those elements which the midrashist cited .
in Piska 306 which Israel corrupted are now seen to rejoice with
Israel. No longer need they witness Israel's wrong doing. Can it
be that the midrashist believed that nature suffers a kind of exile
due to Israel's state of exile? Is redemption seen here as a cosmic
event rather than a national one?

lowest parts of the earth."[S2] From whence do we know that this
is so of the mountains and the hills? As it is said, "The
mountains and the hills shall break forth before you into singing."[S3]
From whence do we know that this is so of the trees? As it is
said, "And all the trees of the field shall clap their hand."[S4]
From whence do we know that this is so of the Patriarchs and
the Matriarchs? As it is said, "The _Sela_ dwellers[E4] will exult,
at the head, the mountains will shout."[S5]

"For He doth avenge the blood of His servants, and doth
   render vengeance to His adversaries":

   Two vengeances:[E5] He takes vengeance on murder and he takes
vengeance on theft.[L1] And from whence do we know that all thefts which
the Gentile Nations of the World committed against Israel are accounted
unto them as if they had spilled innocent blood? As it is said, "I
will gather all the nations and will bring them down into the valley

---

S2. Isaiah 44:23.   S3. Isaiah 55:12.
S4. Isaiah 55:12.   S5. Isaiah 42:11.

L1. חמס, "violence", was usually understood by the Rabbis to refer
to theft see _Aruch_ _Compl._ s.v. חמס .

E4. The "_sela_ _dwellers_" verse may be seen to refer to the Patriarchs
(mountains) and Matriarchs (sela) as they seem to be midrashically
implicit in the proof text ending -- "at the head, the mountains will
shout". _Rocks_ and _mountains_ symbolize Sarah and Abraham, cf. Is. 51:1f,
see Piska 319, see also B.T. Rosh Hashannah 11a, see further Num. R.
20:16 and Ex. R. 28:1, for הורים = הרים see Yalkut Psalms 878. Also
see N.A. van Uchelen, "The Targumic Version of Deut. 33:15, _JJS_, vol. 31,
n. 2, p. 199ff.(B 340)

E5. The word _avenge_ is mentioned twice in vs. 43: יקום ונקם . The
midrashist explains the two punishments to be in return for two major
crimes, "murder" and "violence" (= חמ , according to the Rabbis the
term חמס could refer to "theft" e.g. B.T. Gittin 49b).

of Jehoshaphat, and I will enter into judgement[E6] with them there for My people Israel,"[S6]; "Egypt shall be a desolation, and Edom shall be a desolate wilderness, for the <u>theft</u> against the children of Judah, because they have shed innocent <u>blood</u> in their land."[S7]-- At the very moment: "But Judah shall be inhabited forever, and Jerusalem from generation to generation,"[S8]; "And I will hold as innocent their blood that I have not held as innocent; and the Lord dwelleth in Zion."[S9]

"And doth make expiation for the land of His people":

From whence do we know that the slaughter[E7] of Israel at the hands of the Gentile Nations of the World effects expiation for them in the World to Come?[L2] We know it from that which is said, "A Psalm of Asaph. O God, the heathen are come into Thine inheritance,"[S10]; "They have given the dead bodies of Thy servants..."[S11] "They have shed their blood like water."[S12]

S6. Joel 4:2.   S7. Joel 4:19.   S8. Joel 4:20.
S9. Joel 4:21.   S10. Psalms 79:1.   S11. Psalms 79:2.
S12. Psalms 79:3.

L2. Has נקם been taken as "save" as suggested by G.R. Driver, "Archaeological Discovery and the Scriptures", <u>Christianity</u> <u>Today</u> 12 (1968), p. 3ff?   The מדרש may not be playing upon the words "and doth make expiation for the land of His people" as much as it is rendering the verse as "by the spilled blood of His servants...doth make expiation".

E6. The reading of this verse in Massoretic version is: "For My people and for My heritage Israel."

E7. The midrashist takes אדמתו (land) as דמו (blood). However, see L2 above.

Another interpretation:

"And אדמתו doth make expiation for His people":

From whence do you say that the descent of the wicked[E8] into Gehinnom[L3] effects expiation for them?* It is said from that which is stated, "I have granted thy expiation; Egypt, Ethiopia and Seba are beneath you,"[S13]; "Since thou are precious in My sight and honorable, and I have loved thee (and I have put[T1] אדם in thy nether places)."[S14]

Rabbi Meir used to say:" The Land of Israel[L4] expiates for whoever dwells upon it, as it is said, "As for the nation that dwells in her, its sin is נשוא ."[S15]

.

---

* Ln: for Israel in the World to Come.

S13. Isaiah 43:3.   S14. (Ln) Isaiah 43:4.
S15. Isaiah 33:24.

T1. Ln's extended reading of the verse to include אדם   here is superior to the reading of F since it relates to אדמתו   in Deut. 32:43 - the reading אדם as in M.T. is to the point as stated in Targum to Is. 43:4:

ואנא רחימתך ומסרית עממיא תחותך - (אדם=עממיא)

L3. Perhaps אדמה is seen as ארץ   thus equivalent to underworld and after world. See,"Ereş: Underworld: Two more suggestions", W.L. Holladay, V.T. 19 (1969),p. 123f. and M. Dahood, "Hebrew-Ugaritic Lexicography", Biblica 50 (1969), p. 337.

L4. For the idea that ארמהcan refer to the Land of Israel in Scripture see P. Winter, (Mitteilungen)"Nochmals zu Deuteronomium 32:8", Zeitschrift fur die Alttestamentliche Wissenschaft,vol.75 (1963),p. 222, n. 13.

E8. The midrashist takes אדמתו (land) as אדם   ("nations" - see Targ. Is. 43:4 but as Edom by B.T. Berachoth 62b). This part of the proof text is omitted in F but is retained in Ln: The final proof text here shows that God will save Israel because He loves them. The word תחתיך has been explained here in two senses:
    1) your nether places (=beneath you)
    2) your replacements (i.e. your "scapegoats").
See further no. 7, Conclusions.

--Still, the exegesis hangs upon that which itself is unsupported,[E9] ("For the land is filled --the Holy One of Israel."[T2] But still the exegesis hangs upon that which is unsupported,) for we do not know if the sense is that their sins will be <u>razed</u> upon the land or whether their sins will be <u>raised</u> upon it! Since Scripture states, "And His land <u>expiates</u> for His people," we see that their sins are <u>razed</u> upon it and not <u>raised</u> upon it.

And similarly was Rabbi Meir wont to say: Whoever dwells in the Land of Israel, and reads the profession of the <u>shma</u> -- mornings and evenings, and speaks in the holy tongue, will be a citizen in the World to Come.

T2. Ln is probably quoting Jer. 51:5,"For their land is full of guilt against the Holy One of Israel," and indeed this is the actual reading in the first printed edition (Venice 1545). This also is ambiguous as we do not know whose land is referred to in the verse.

E9. The point is that the exegesis of the proof text is uncertain because נשוא (B 8) can mean either "forgiven" or "borne" (cf. Gen. 4:13 where Onkelos renders "forgiven" while Ps.-Jon (B 55) renders "borne". Since the point in the proof is unsupported,no conclusions concerning its sense may be drawn. Generally, ambiguity in statements may be due to homonyms (the sense of the passage not specifying the intended meaning of the term) or else due to unclear positioning of punctuation,e.g. we have קדוש ישראל : either "the holy one, Israel"; or "the Holy One of Israel". I suspect that there was an original passage in our midrash based upon the tradition which appears in Ln that stated that Jeremiah 51:5 קדוש ישראל itself was ambiguous "because we do not know if the verse means that 'Israel is Holy because they fill the Land' or if the verse refers to 'God' and not to Israel at all. The final solution of these problems is then brought from Deut. 32:43: "And the Land expiates for His people". The problem of the meaning נשוא in Is. 33:24 prevented clarification, as did the problem of the meaning of קדוש ישראל in Jer. 51:5. Deut. 32:43 is considered to be a clear statement showing that the Land effects atonement for those who dwell upon it. It may be that אדמתן was taken to mean דם (m) or אדם (m) because it is taken to be the subject of a masculine verb. אדמה is not easily taken as a masculine noun. However, in spite of this, the English translations agree upon treating it as one here which conforms

You have attested: How notable is This Song![E10] For we find in

it "that which is in the present" and we find in it "that which

was in the past" and we find in it "that which will be in the

Future to Come" and we find in it "that which is in This World" and

we find in it "that which will be in the World to Come"!

(END OF THE SONG)

END OF PISKA

---

to the view of Meir. L. Silberman finds my attempt to render the
Hebrew פרק = נשא   (sins removed because of the land) vs נשא (sins
carried) by raze and raise somewhat misleading. --"The question is:
does the Land expiate for the sins or are the sins placed upon it?"

E10. Indeed, the redactor of the midrash Sifre to Ha'azinu often
presents all of these themes as a combined interpretation of a single
verse. The same sentiment is expressed by Jewish apologists throughout
the ages:
    Commentary of Ramban[B 35]to Deut. 32:40:
        It would have earned belief therein because all its words have
        been fulfilled by now...certainly we shall continue to believe
        and look forward with all our heart for the word of God by
        the mouth of His prophet...
    Josephus, Antiquities 4:44:[B 11]
        Then he recited to them a poem in hexameter verse...containing
        a prediction of future events, in accordance with which all has
        come and is coming to pass, the seer having in no whit strayed
        from the truth.
    Philo, Moses 2:288: [B 34]
        Some of these have already taken place, others are still looked
        for, since confidence in the future is assured by fulfilment in
        the past.
    Philo, Virtues 72-75:[B 34]
        ...past sins...present admonitions...exhortations for future
        ...happy fulfilment...life immortal.
Interestingly the same sentiment is said by M.P. Horgan (Pesharim:
Qumran Interpretations of Biblical Books,[B 204] CBQ, Biblical Assoc.
of America, monograph series 8, Washington, 1979, p. 255) to characterize
raz-pesher in Daniel:
        To illuminate the meaning of the past and present events, to
        predict the future and to press toward the eschatological
        cataclysm and deliverance.

44

"And Moses came":

Here it states, "And Moses came" while elsewhere it is stated,

"And Moses went,"[S1] It is impossible to state,"And Moses came" while

it yet states, "And Moses went." And it is impossible to state,"And Moses

went ," while it yet states,"And Moses came." You must conclude from

this: there came his transfer:[E1] that authority was being placed in the

hand of another.

S1. Deuteronomy 31:1.

E1. This passage is quite difficult to interpret. Rashi to Deut. 32:44
interprets it to mean that Moses came with his "explainer" (meturgaman)
which he surrendered to Joshua,cf. Sifre Deut. Piska 305. It appears
that Levy accepted this interpretation and read accordingly,
"steward" (see Fürst,[B66] s.v. דייתיכוס),cf. Piska 305 for the
bestowing of the "explainer" who would explain the master's words to the
public. Jastrow [B68] (s.v. דייתיכוס) maintains the reading of the
mss. and explains it to mean that Moses' time of successorship had
arrived. I also maintain that the reading of the mss.should be maintained but understand the sense to be that an actual transfer of authority
occurred in a "split second". {Cf. D. Daube, "A Reform in Acts and its
Models", in Jews, Greeks and Christians: Religious Cultures in Late
Antiquity (Essays in Honor of William David Davies), ed. R. Hammerton-
Kelly and R. Scroggs, Leiden, Brill, 1976, p. 157, n. 51.} I believe
the midrashist wishes to tell us that the prophecy of Ha'azinu represents
the prophecy of Moses at the exact point of the transfer (between "And
Moses went"and "And Moses came"). Zayit Ra'anan (on Yalk. Shimoni to
Deut. 32:44) suggests that we have here a sense of דיתקי "a testament of
successorship", "a will". Thus "Moses came" and "Moses went" is taken
as a reference to the point of death that Moses had reached. Moses'
contract, as it were, had been fulfilled and was now given to Joshua.
Indeed, Friedmann[B47] thinks that the term דייתיכוס is a euphemistic term for "dying" (he made his will). See Piska 341 (E1) and
particularly see Gen. R. 58:2 (p. 620):

בא השמש -- קודם שלא השקיע הקבה שימשו
של משה הזריח הקבה שימשו של יהושע

The word בא actually was taken to refer to the death of Moses and the
successorship of Joshua just before Moses died. Perhaps we have the
source of a mystical explanation of the successorship of Joshua in
Midrash Tannaim's [B26] (citing Midrash Haggadol) version of
"דייתיכוס ": "כוס ובידו ", which perhaps gave rise to the statement
in Ma'aseh Merkabah,(ed. Scholem, Jewish Gnosticism etc.,[B305]
Appendix "C", para. 13, p. 109):שלש אותות כתב משה ליהושע בכוס

"And he spoke all the words of this song into the ears
of the nation":

This teaches that he submerged[E2] them into their ears.

"He and Hosea the son of Nun":

Why do I require these words, for has it not yet been stated,
"And Moses called to Hosea the son of Nun, 'Joshua,'"?[S2] What is
the import of the Scripture which states, "He and Hosea the son of
Nun"? --It is to inform one of the righteous behavior of Joshua. I
might have thought that when he was granted authority his opinion of
himself became inflated! Scripture therefore states, "He and Hosea the
son of Nun" --he, Hosea remained the righteous one. Even though he
was granted the position of being the overseer of Israel,[*] he was still
Hosea in respect to his righteous behavior.

A similar case to this you may cite:

"And Joseph   was in Egypt":[S3]

And do we not know that Joseph was in Egypt! It is to inform one
of the righteousness of Joseph who used to shepherd his father's sheep.

Thus Joshua received the ability to perform miracles. We should also
note here, in passing, that Josephus does not use the Septuagint
"diatheke" to refer to the covenant, nor should we attempt to do so here.

* Ln: congregation

S2. Numbers 13:16.   S3. Exodus 1:5.

E2. The homilist realizes that the phrase "into the ears" is an
obvious consequence of speaking and need not have been mentioned by
Scripture unless the apparently extra word באזניהם was meant to supply
us with new information. The homilist tells us the significance of the
phrase -- Moses spoke in such a way that his words sank deeply into the
ears of the people; they have been preserved throughout the ages and
many generations have taken them to heart.

Now even though he was granted the position of a king in Egypt, he
was still <u>Joseph</u> in respect to his righteous behavior.

A similar case to this you may cite:

"And David was the youngest":[S4]

And do we not know that David was the youngest! It is to inform
you of the righteousness of David who used to shepherd his father's
sheep. Now even though he was granted the position of King over Israel,
he was still <u>David</u> in respect to his "youngest"[E3] types of behavior.

END OF PISKA

S4. I Samuel 13:14.

E3. The homilist wishes to point out the significance of the Scriptural
appellation of monarchs by their names given in youth. Hosea was given
the royal appellative "Joshua", Joseph became "Zaphnath Paneach". The
point is that these men, in their monarchical roles, kept the righteousness
of their youth. The form of the "David" pericope has been stylized to
fit the form of the other passages with which it is connected. Its sense
is: Why speak of David as "youngest" when he was a king? --Because he
maintained his "youngest behavior" in respect to his righteousness.
Apparently, Hebrew should have read הקטן בצדקו but under influence
of other passages here reads, דוד בקטנו .

46

"And he said unto them: 'Set your heart unto all the words wherewith I testify against you this day'":

It is incumbent that a person should have his heart, his eyes, his ears concentrated upon the words of the Torah. And so does Scripture state, "Son of man,[E1] behold with thine eyes and hear with your ears (and set your heart to) that which I declare unto thee,";[S1] "And set your heart unto the entering in of the House...(into the exiting out of the Temple...)"[S1] --The argument is a fortiori:

Now if a person must have his heart, his eyes, and his ears concentrated upon the Temple which was visible to the eyes and was measured by the hand, how much more so is such concentration necessary in respect to the words of the Torah which are as mountains suspended by a hair![E2]

"That ye may charge your children therewith to observe":

He said to them: Just as I hold it to your credit that you will sustain the Torah after I am gone. So, you also must hold it to your children's credit that they will sustain the Torah after you have gone.

S1. Ezekiel 44:5.

E1. "Set your heart" immediately follows "Son of Man" in the Massoretic version.

E2. The point here is that there are many laws derived from words in the Torah such that without deep concentration of thought it is impossible to gain a concrete notion of the source of these laws. Cf. Mishna Hagigah 1:8.

There is a story: Our master[E3] had come from Laodicea when Rabbi Yosi the son of Rabbi Yehuda and Rabbi Elazar the son of Yehuda entered and sat down before him. He said to them, "Come closer,[*] I must hold it to your credit that you will sustain the Torah after I am gone. So, you also must hold it to your children's credit that they will sustain the Torah after you have gone".

Is it not that Moses was unsurpassed! Yet were it not for those others who accepted the Torah from Moses, it would not have had such value for him. {As for we who are limited,}[E4] how much more would the Torah be without value unless others accept it from us![**] [T1]

For this reason is it stated, "That ye may charge your children therewith."

END OF PISKA

---

* Ln: come closer, come closer

** Ln: If Moses was not great or if there was another, we would have accepted his Torah even if his Torah would not have been equivalent. So all the more so should we accept Moses' Torah!

T1. Neither F nor Ln here contains a decidedly superior reading.

E3. Is the reference here to Rabbi Yehuda HaNasi, the compiler of the Mishna who is often referred to as "Rabbenu " or is it to Rabbi Yehuda, the father of Yosi and Elazar?

E4. I have used {....} to indicate F's emendation of the text which has not the support of any manuscript. According to his view, the midrashist intends to say that the Torah of Moses would have had no value had Moses been unable to transmit it. Friedmann accepts the reading as found in Ln and it appears to me that we have a tradition with a similar form in Sifre Deut. Piska 342 (Finkelstein p. 393, line 5) which deals with Moses' blessings. However, there are possible understandings of F's text which require no emendation:
    We may suppose that Moses would not have been great were it not for those others who received the Torah from him; thus, all the more so

His <u>Torah</u> would not have been comparable (to what we received,
were it not for those who received it from Moses first. --
Lichtenstein suspects it means "were it not for those who keep
its laws").
The sense of Torah here need not be limited to the sense of <u>written</u>
<u>Torah</u>. If we accept my proposal in L1 , Piska 306 that אילו- אין) לא)
is meant to signify a rhetorical exclamation at times, we may render
the passage before us as:

> If Moses had not been unsurpassed and if others had not accepted
> the Torah from him, would it have had no value! Now that this
> is so, how much more value does it have!

For the reading "now that this is so" see Yalkut Shimoni to Deut. 32:46
(947)⁽ᴮ 60 ⁾. This form also can be used to interpret the statement
in Sifre Deut. Piska 342.

47

"For it is no vain thing from you":

There is nothing so empty in the Torah that if you interpret it you would not receive the benefit of some reward in This World while the principal is maintained for you in the World to Come. Know that this is so, for they said: Why is it written, "And the sister of Lotan is Timna,";[S1] "And Timna was a concubine"?[S2]

--This was written because she said, "I am not sufficiently worthy to be his wife so I will be his[E1] concubine!" And why should we care so much? But it is to inform you of the belovedness* of Abraham. There were some who did not desire to be of kingship and of royalty but ran to be attached to him. And are not these matters to be argued, a fortiori:

Since kings[E2] and royalty ran to be attached to Esau who had only one fulfilled commandment in his possession; namely, that he had honored his father, how much more so were they running to become attached to Jacob, the righteous one, who kept the entire Torah,[E3] as it is said, "And Jacob was a perfect man dwelling in tents."[S3]

---

* Ln: Praiseworthiness

S1. Genesis 36:22.   S2. Genesis 36:12.   S3. Genesis 25:27.

E1. Timna was the concubine of Eliphaz, the son of Esau. Cf. N. Leibowitz, Studies in Devarim, (B 244) p. 355.

E2. Lotan was a king.

E3. Jacob was thought to have dwelled in the tents "of Torah" see Targum Onkelos to Gen. 25:27.

Piska 336

"And through this thing ye shall prolong your days
(upon the earth)":

This is one of the things that he who does them eats of their
fruits in This World while there is "length of days" for him in the
World to Come. And it is stated explicitly here in reference to
Torah study.

From whence do we know that this is also the case in reference
to the honoring of one's father and mother? We know it since
Scripture states, "Honor your father and your mother in order that
your days may be prolonged...."[S4] --For the sending away of the
mother bird? It is written, "You shall surely send away the mother,
and the children you may take for yourself in order that it may be
good for you and that you may prolong your days,"[S5] --For the making
of peace? It is written "And all thy children shall be taught of the
Lord;[* E4] and great shall be the peace of your children." [S6 T1]

END OF PISKA

---

* Ln: ends citation here.

S4. Exodus 20:12.   S5. Deuteronomy 22:7.   S6. Isaiah 54:13.

T1. F continues the proof text and reads "peace of your children", so
that the Biblical context of the verse in Isaiah (verses are sometimes
to be read in conjunction with their surrounding verses for proof text
purposes) which is referring to the great era of redemption proves to the
satisfaction of the homilist that he who brings peace is assured of a
place in the World to Come.

E4. Cf. Mishna Peah 1:1 and cf. B.T. Kiddushin 40a (gives another
exegesis of "for the making of peace"). The method of exegesis in our
Sifre passage is obscure. Did רב (great) suggest to the homilist that
"prolonged days (רבים)" was to be the reward for "making peace"?
Perhaps the sense of "And all thy children shall be taught of the Lord"

---

itself implied that such children would enjoy the World to Come
(the context of Is. 54:13) for in only this Era of the Future would
they be taught directly by God. Thus "learning from the Lord"
could have been taken as equivalent to "the Next World". See "E6"
Piska 310 for the source of the idea that in the Next World, God will
teach people directly. It is certainly possible that the word
שלום has been played upon here and is construed both in the sense of
"peacemaking" as well as "the Next World". For the notion that שלום
refers to the Next World see B.T. Ketuboth 104a (בא שלום).

48

"And the Lord spoke unto Moses at the very height
of this day (saying).":[E1]

In three places it is stated "at the very height of this day":

It is stated "at the very height of this day"[S1] in reference to

Noah. This teaches us that the generation of Noah said: "We

swear -- may such befall from such, if, when we sense his

movement, we let him be![E2] And furthermore we shall take axes

and hatchets and chop up the ark in front of him." So the

Holy One, Blessed Be He, said, "Behold I will bring him in at

noon and whoever is able to oppose, let him come forward and

oppose!"

And what did He see to say in reference to Egypt "At the very

height of this day all the hosts of the Lord departed"?[S2]

This was because the Egyptians said: "We swear, may such befall

from such, if, when we sense their movement, we let them be!

S1. Genesis 7:13.   S2. Exodus 12:17.

E1. "The very height of this day" is taken in the sense of "broad
daylight", " high noon".

E2. I take אם -איו as an oath formula here together with כך וכך or
כך מכך cf. Lieberman, Greek etc., (B 248) p. 123. Also see the
rendition of L. Ginzberg, Legends of the Jews, (B 171) Phila, JPS,
1968, vol. 3, p. 445:
    God said, "If Noah enters the ark at night his generation will
    declare: He could do so because we were not aware of it, or
    we should not have permitted him to enter the ark alone, but we
    should have taken our hammers and axes and crushed the ark!
    Therefore", said God "do I wish him to enter the ark at the
    noon hour. Let him who wishes to prevent it try to do so."
    (Cf. Gen. R. 32:12).

And furthermore we shall take swords and sabers
and kill them with these." So the Holy One,
Blessed Be He, said, "Behold I will take them
out at noon and whoever is able to oppose, let
him come forward and oppose!"
And what did He see to say here (in reference to Moses)
"At the very height of this day"?

This was because Israel said: We swear, may
such befall from such, if when we sense his
movement, we let him be! We will not abandon the
man who took us out of Egypt and split the sea
for us, and (brought down the Torah for us and)
brought down the manna for us, and brought across
the quail for us and performed miracles and
wonders for us." So the Holy One, Blessed Be
He, said: "Behold, I will bring him into the cave
at noon and whoever is able to oppose, let him
come forward and oppose!"
--For this reason it is stated, "And the Lord
spoke unto Moses at the very height of this
day, saying...."

END OF PISKA

49

"Ascend unto this mountain of Abarim":

It is an "ascent   " for you and not a "descent   ".[L1]

"(Unto) This mountain of Abarim":

For it was called by four titles:[E1] "Mountain of Abarim"; "Mountain

of Nebo"; "   Hor   HaHar"; "Rosh HaPisgah". Why was it called the

"Mountain of Nebo"?[E2] It was called such since there were buried

within it these three prophets* whose deaths were not caused by sin.

And these are they: Moses, Aaron and Miriam.

"Which (אשר) is in the Land of Moab":

This teaches us that He showed him the succession[E3] (שלשלת   )

---

* Ln: dead people

L1. Here "ascent   " means "promotion", "improvement in condition
and status" while "descent   " means "decline in condition and status".
For example of such usage see B.T. Kethuboth 61a
"עולה עמו ואינה יורדת עמו"   "
and Kohut, Aruch Completum s.v. על (Hinaufsteigen).

E1. I do not believe we should see Abarim here as if it were construed
as ארבע (four) but rather I believe we should see this name as an
introduction to the explanation of נבו . Abarim then is understood
as עברים , sins. (It   is unlikely   that the words "without sin"
in our pericope may in fact be a circumlocution, a euphemism, with the
actual meaning here of "with sin", cf. Piska 340. See also ARN (B1)
"B" ch. 25: אין בידך עון   and see also next note.)

E2. Nebo is taken here as if it were related to "nevi'im", prophets.
See Marqah 2:12 - "Mount Nebo" - for The Prophethood.(B16)
The reading of Ln is also very acceptable: These three dead people
--Moses, Aaron and Miriam. I suspect that according to Ln the sense is
that "passed - ons" (עברים   )are in it -- (= נבו omitting the
letters איתן which appear to be dropped for midrashic purposes when
appropriate to do so. Alternatively, we may have a midrashic reading of
נבו as אין בו(F)i.e. No sinners are in it.)

E3. אשר   may here be taken to refer to a chain "of succession"
-Aram. אשר   =chain (= שרשרת   or שלשלת) as it may also have been
taken in Piska 357 where " אשר " again leads to a comment concerning a
chain of succession.

of kings which were in the future to arise from Ruth the Moabite.[E4]

"Which (אשר) is over against Jericho":

This teaches us that He showed him by succession (שלשלת)
of prophets which were in the future to arise from Rahab the
prostitute.

"And see all the Land of Canaan":

Rabbi Eliezer says: The finger of the Holy One, Blessed Be He,
became a metatron[*] for Moses which showed him all the settlements of
the Land of Israel.[E5] "Until here is the boundary of Ephraim; until
here is the boundary of Menasseh."

Rabbi Yehoshua says: Moses himself saw it. How was this
accomplished? He put such power into the eyes of Moses that he saw
from one end of the world unto the other.

END OF PISKA

---

* Ln: with the finger of Moses there was a metatron i.e. a surveying
guide for Moses....

E4. These comments are based upon the identification of Ruth with
Moab and Rahab with Jericho.

E5. In accordance with the teaching of Rabbi Yehoshua we find that also
Marqah records traditions to the effect that Moses was provided with
remarkable powers of vision:
   With his eyes (בעיניו) he saw the angels of heaven in their ranks,
   as it says, "And he saw the form of the angels (a targumic rendition,
   M.T. Num. 12:8 has "the form of the Lord")".
   After that he saw all the land (ארעה) from the river Pishon as
   far as the river Euphrates and even to the distant sea. (2:12).

   ...When the great prophet Moses stood on the top of Mount Nebo...
   His Lord exalted him and He unveiled the light of his eyes and showed
   him the four quarters (ארבעת רבעת עלמה   ) of the world. (5:3).

   "His eye was not dim" -- for he was prepared for the recording
   of the Law and to see (צפו) the four quarters of the world. (5:4).

Since Rabbi Yehoshua argues that Moses actually saw the Land with
his eyes, we understand that Rabbi Eliezer must have argued that he
did not see it with his eyes. The expression "to show by means of
the finger" means to show through the medium of prophecy. It would
be more accurate to translate מראה as "(give) vision" rather than
"to show". The "given vision" is considered, however, to be effected
by means of the instrument of vision. Since מראה signifies
"showing something" (in our case taken as "vision"), the metaphor
is maintained by referring to the medium of prophecy (i.e.רוח הקודש   )
as "the finger" (since fingers are used to show things). New
Testament illustrates a similar point:
Luke 11:20 (RSV): If it is by the finger of God that I cast out...
Matthew 12:28: But if it is by the spirit of God that I cast out...
The origin of the expression may lie in the fact that ירה means "to
stretch out the finger" (see Gesenius s.v. הורה). Cf. Prov. 6:13.
The Church Fathers use "the finger" to refer to the instrument through
which prophecy is effected. See St. Irenaeus, Ancient Christian Writers,
"Proof of the Apostolic Teaching", (translated by J.P. Smith), London,
Longman, Green and Co., 1952, ch. 26 and notes to ch. 26. Cf. Anaf
Yosef to Lev. R. 11:9. Also see Tanhuma Buber, Shmini 11, vol. 2,
p. 28, n. 67, Targ. to Ez. 3:22. The various textual readings of
this Sifre pericope show that the copyists had difficulty understanding
the term "metatron". Friedmann suggests that מראה here is a gloss to
explain "metatron", a reasonable suggestion if other uses of מראה באצבע
are put aside. Ln reads באצבעו של משה היה מטטרון מראה   which I
have attempted to explain as a glossed interpretation as if "metatron"
in Ln was also taken in the sense of a metator or guide. The phrase
באצבעו של משה   in Ln may again mean that Moses was shown the Land
through his spirit of prophecy. Cf. Gen. R. 5:3 and Marmorstein,
Studies in Jewish Theology, p. 6, n. 3. However, it cannot be denied
that the reference in Ln may be to the angel Metatron:
היה מטטרון מראה למשה   which can mean: "It was Metatron who showed
Moses". Since the name Metatron is not clearly attested in Tannaitic
literature, either the dating of our passage in Sifre or our notions of
the history of the term "metatron' will be greatly affected by understanding here the reference to be an angel. So we should either accept Ln
as a corrupt reading here or render it as I have indicated in my
translation of Ln (guide = מראה), Piska 338. See however, Urbach,
Sages, (B 339) p. 743f., n. 15. As for the claim that Moses was able to
see "from one end of the world to the other" see Piska 306 ("E14") and
Piska 35,(E2") where I consider עולם to mean a unit of space. It may
either mean that Moses was able to see from one border of the Land of
Israel to the other, or that his eyesight was so keen that he could see
from the earth to the heavenly realms. (See Sifre Deut. Piska 88
where " מסוף העולם עד סופ   etc." refers to the route of the sun
and the moon.) For other traditions concerning what Moses saw
spacewise and timewise see Mechilta Beshalach (B 15) p. 184 to Ex. 17:14.

50

"And die in the mount whither thou goest up":

He said to Him:[E1] Master of the Universe, why should I die? Is it not better that they should say "Blessed is Moses" from sight than that they should say "Blessed is Moses" from report? Is it not better that they should say "This is Moses who took us out of Egypt, and split the sea for us, (brought down the Torah for us and) and brought down the manna for us, and performed miracles and wonders for us" than that they should say, "Such and such was Moses, such and such did Moses"?

He replied to him: "Cease, Moses, it is My decree which is apportioned equally to all people, as it is said, "This is the law of a man: that he dies -- in a tent...."[S1] And Scripture also states, "And this is the law of the man of the Lord God."[S2] [E2]

The Ministering Angels said to the Holy One, Blessed Be He: "Master of the Universe, why did the first Adam die?"

S1. Numbers 19:14.   S2. 2 Samuel 7:19.

E1. The method of aggadic narrative here is accomplished by inter-weaving "proof texts" into a coherent story.

E2. "Law of the man of the Lord" is a possible translation of the words תורת האדם אדוני ה׳   2 Samuel 7:19, which allows the preacher to see, by comparison with Num. 19:14 which speaks of the law of a man -- to die, that Moses had to die. I.e. even the man of the Lord (=Moses, see Deut. 33:1) is subject to the law of man -- mortality. Now the homilist weaves his story by dwelling upon this above exegesis. The word used for "man" in Num. 19:14 which tells us that "man" must die is "adam". Thus it was that the angels could have argued that Num. 19:14 may imply that only those men (adam) who are sinners like Adam must die (cf. E.E. Urbach, Sages, p. 246, and p. 875, n. 15f.). God could have answered the angels by saying that the term "adam" in Num. 19:14 is used to refer to all Mankind (who descend from Adam) and all must die. According to Avoth de Rabbi Nathan "B" ch. 25, Moses died without sin due to the decree put upon Adam and hence upon Mankind. See also Marqah 5:1 "Adam tasted

He replied to them, "Because he did not perform my commandments."

They said to Him: "And behold Moses has performed your commandments!"

He replied to them: "It is my decree apportioned equally to all
people," as it is said, "This is the law of the man: that he dies
-- in a tent...." ("and this is the law of the man of the Lord.")
"And be gathered unto thy people":

Near Abraham, Isaac and Jacob; (your fathers); near Amram and
Kehath; (your fathers); near Miriam and Aaron your brother.[E3]

" As Aaron thy brother died":

This is the type of death that you desired.[E4]

And from whence did Moses desire the type of death that Aaron had
had? When the Holy One, Blessed Be He, said, "Take Aaron and Eleazar
his son...";[S3] "And strip Aaron of his garments".[S4]--This refers to the

---

death prepared, Moses fasted for life prepared." Also see Marqah 5:1,
"The powers called to their Lord that death should not come near him."

S3. Numbers 20:25.   S4. Numbers 20:26.

E3. This comment may be an attempt to explain עמיך   as a plural
form.

E4. The midrashist ponders the point here of telling Moses that he
will die like Aaron. Schorr p. 14 claims the play is on
את = εὐχή =want (= חמדת   ).

priestly garments.[*] "And he put them on Eleazar."[S5] And so the second

and so the third.[E5] He said to him: "Enter the cave!" And he entered.

"Go up on the bier!" And he went up. "Stretch out your hands!" And

he stretched. "Stretch out your feet!" And he stretched out.[E6]

"Close your mouth!" And he closed. "Shut your eyes!" And he shut.

At that time Moses declared, "Happy is he who dies by this type of

death!" For this reason is it stated, "As Aaron thy brother died."

-- It is the type of death that you desired.

END OF PISKA

---

* Ln: He stripped off the priestly garments.

S5. Numbers 20:28.

E5. The midrashist may have been reluctant to name the actual garments
alluded to here out of a feeling of propriety that undergarments
should not be named. See E.Z. Melamed's article "Euphemism etc.".

E6. For the notion that "stretching out the feet",as a term of dying,
is a Palestinian term see P. Robinson, "To stretch out the feet:
a formula for death in the Testaments of the Twelve Patriarchs,"
JBL 97 (1973) and M. de Jonge, "Again to stretch out the feet in the
Testament of the Twelve Patriarchs," JBL, vol. 99 (March 1980). Is the
usage of פשט רגל as a sign of one's preparing for death, related to
the expression of later Hebrew פשט רגל which means "to go
bankrupt"?

51

"Because ye trespassed against Me":

It was you who caused them[E1] to trespass against Me.

"Because ye sanctified Me not":

It was you who caused them not to sanctify Me.

"Because ye rebelled against My commandment":[S1 E2]

It was you who caused them to rebel against my commandment.

The Holy One, Blessed Be He, said to Moses: Did I not say the following to you: "What is that in your hand?";[S2] "Cast it upon the ground!"[S3] -- and you cast it (from your hand). Now you did not complain concerning these miracles which were due to that which had been in your hand, so why should you have complained concerning this simple matter!"[E3]

S1. Numbers 27:14.   S2. Exodus 4:2.   S3. Exodus 4:3.

E1. עַל אֲשֶׁר is understood both here and in the following passage to mean: "on account of those others" (whom you made transgress against Me).

E2. "Because ye rebelled against My commandment" is not found in Deut. 32:51 but in Num. 27:14 and has come into our Sifre text here because the Rabbis likewise (see above "E1") exegeted it by using the principle that עַל אֲשֶׁר is to be taken as a reference to "others" whom Moses caused to sin. These verses then are read to mean: "Because you sinned -- by making others sin." Num. 27:14 may be taken as the reference point in Deut. 32:51 which alludes to Meribat-Kadesh, the place where Moses caused others to trespass.

E3. The homilist here pictures God's argument as follows:
Since your staff had long belonged to you and had been in your control, you should have been reluctant to believe that it could behave in a supernatural fashion and do extremely bizarre things, yet you did believe in its powers without protest;so, why did you protest concerning the small matter of taking water from a rock which had never been under your control (Your rod had to change to perform miracles but perhaps this rock had always had the ability to produce water). Thus you, Moses, acted inconsistently according

And from whence do we know that Moses did not depart from
the world until the Holy One, Blessed Be He, wrapped him in His
wings?[E4] We know it from that which is said, "Therefore ye shall
not bring this assembly...."[S4]

END OF PISKA

---

to your own logic.

S4. Numbers 20:12.

E4. See E1, Piska 341.

52

"For from afar thou shalt see the land, but thither thou shalt not come":[E1]

E1. "E4" Piska 340 is best considered to be part of Piska 341 as it describes (Moses') death before the Israelites entered into the Land. Friedmann (B 47) points out that the verse which is exegeted to imply Moses' ascension in the "wings of the Shekina" is Deut. 32:52, "For from נגד thou shalt see the Land". See also Marqah 5:3 - כבודה קרב לה ואגפפה . Midrash Leqah Tob supplies Deut. 35:52 as a proof text to the midrash. It is noteworthy (in F) that the term the midrash uses here is צרר (wrap by pulling closed) which is a synonym for Scripture's נגד which can have the sense of "enclosing". This is shown by Leqah Tob's (or his source's) view that Judges 9:17 נגד ויצל shows נצל in the context of נגד (sheltering). See also E5 , Piska 329, and ARN "B" ch. 25. If כנפים here refers to the hems, then perhaps the idea is that Moses is protected by God's grace -- see E.C. Greenstein "'To grasp the hem' in Ugaritic literature," VT, 32 (1982), p. 218. (B 178) Now the proof text we have in our Sifre text comes from Num. 20:12 and, as it is in all the mss., I take it to be an original reading and not a corruption. This verse explains that Moses will not live to bring the people into the Land and thus introduces the passage nicely. It seems to me that Num. 20:12 does not belong as the proof text of Piska 340 (which rightly plays off of Deut. 35:52) but acts as an introduction to the dialogue between God and Moses concerning the entrance of Moses into the Land. Perhaps our entire Piska once belonged to a lost midrash on Num. 19-20. At any rate it is difficult to see how this verse, Num. 20:12, relates to Piska 340 mentioning God's enwrapment of Moses. In order to understand the exegesis here we must take stock of several terms:

      (pass) עבר can mean "retired" see Mishna Horayoth 3:1. (B 41)
      "come"= בא can mean "died" see Cant. R. 58:2 (see also E1 Piska 334).

Also see printed Tanhuma: V'Ethanan 5.
I understand the midrash as follows:
    God: You cannot bring the people into the Land   לא תביאו
    Moses: Fine, I will retire.
    God: There you will not be, even if retired.   ושמה לא תעבור
    Moses: I will die to get there and be buried there.
    God: There you will not be, even if dead.   ושמה לא תבוא
            You will not enter -- neither as king nor as commoner (עבר),
            neither alive nor dead (בא).
For another form of the midrash see Sifre Deut. to Deut. 34:4, Piska 357. For a related version see Mechilta Beshalach (B 15) to Exodus 17:14 (p. 183) where it seems that the verses are taken as:
    (God:) "You cannot bring the people..."
    (Moses:) I will be a commoner
    (God:) A king cannot be a commoner
    (Moses:) I will enter by the underground tunnel of Caesarea.

It is stated here, "but thither thou shalt not come."[*] And it

is stated further on, "But thither thou shalt not pass."[**] [S1] It is

impossible to state, "But thither thou shalt not pass"[**] for it has

yet stated "But thither thou shalt not come."[*] And it is impossible

to state "But thither thou shalt not come"[*] for it yet states, "But

thither thou shalt not pass"![**] (And why does Scripture state, "But

thither thou shalt not come", "But thither thou shalt not pass"?)--Moses

said to the Holy One, Blessed Be He: "(Master of the Universe) If I

cannot enter it as a king so I will enter it as a commoner. If I

cannot enter it alive so I will enter it dead." --The Holy One,

Blessed Be He, replied: "But thither thou shalt not come...but thither

thou shalt not pass. Neither as king nor as commoner, neither alive

nor dead."

END OF PISKA

END OF SIDRA

(God:) "Thither thou shalt not cross!"
(Moses:) My bones shall cross over the Jordan.
(God:) You shall not cross over this Jordan. (cf. Rashi to Deut.
4:22)
See also S.E. Loewenstamm, "The Death of Moses", G. Scholem Jubilee Vol.,
Jerusalem, Magnes, 1938, p. 16ff.

* F: come -- Ln: pass
** F: pass -- Ln: come

S1. Deuteronomy 34:4.

281

CONCLUSION

Richard S. Sarason recently wrote:

> "What has not been attempted, and to my mind should be, is a
> kind of phenomenological analysis of the texts which asks what
> we may learn about the world view and thought processes of the
> documents' compilers, not only from what they say, but also
> from how they say it[1]."

After some elaboration he continues:

> "Given the nature of our evidence, then, including its peculiar
> literary characteristics, I can only suggest that the most
> fruitful course for future scholarship on these materials must
> be to get back onto the page[2]."

He then poses a number of questions to be studied[3]:

> What do the literary and formulaic traits of the texts reveal
> about their formulation and redaction?
>
> How are we to evaluate the attributions and attributed materials
> they contain?
>
> What sort of world view is expressed, or presupposed, by the
> conceptions put forth in the texts, and through their instinctive
> modes of formulation?
>
> What does the text tell us about its intended audience?
> What sorts of conceptual traits and prior ideas and concerns
> does it take for granted on the part of that audience?
> Who would understand these texts?
>
> What can we learn about the conception and valorization of
> Scripture on the part of the framers of these texts from the
> detailed operations performed therein on scriptural passages?

How are the earlier aggadic midrashim related to the Talmuds?

Is there any conceptual and literary coherence between the two?
I should like to deal with these questions as they relate to Sifre
Deut. to Ha'azinu.

1. Formulation and redaction.

Internal evidence shows us that our midrash has been carefully constructed
as a whole. The traditions are ordered in a sequence which deals with
past, present, future[4]; while individual traditions are ordered in a
sequence that best emphasizes the point being made. For example, in
the first passage of our midrash the point is that Israel has shown
herself unworthy of being the bearer of the covenant[5]. The point is made
by listing the many witnesses against Israel beginning with Israel herself
and ending with the insignificant ant. The ordering of the series shows
careful construction and editing. It is my feeling that these texts were
constructed from oral traditions which were set down in writing[6]. The
amount of time required to "work out" the midrashim is more than could be
done in the space of an immediate hearing. The parallels found in the
Talmudim and the later collections of midrashim have already an immediate
sense which is seen to be the sense of our midrashim but which is phrased
without the subtlety of our Sifre text. It may well be that the Talmudim
and later midrashim are heir to the oral forms behind the traditions of
our Sifre text which was recorded at the close of the Tannaitic period.
While Finkelstein also thinks our Sifre Ha'azinu is a written document he
does not seem to think it was really composed before the close of the
P.T.[7] and his proofs that it existed in writing are questionable[8].

2. Attributions

Where the manuscripts agree upon the name of the tradent I see no reason

to dispute the attribution and would urge that the burden of proof is
upon him who would dispute any given attribution.

3. Relationship between <u>what</u> is said and <u>how</u> it is said.

The relationship is complete. As I have indicated in my Introduction, the
forms of the tradition are entirely consistent with the content of the
tradition[9]. Parables are used to show the close relationship between
Israel and God. The parable form is an entertaining form and distracts
from the force of verses which may appear to be harsh upon Israel[10].
Aggadic narratives are used to subtly serve as exemplary behavior, e.g.
martyrdom and the justice of dying for religious causes[11]. The very
assimilation of an "alien word" into the midrashic context mirrors the assimilation of "alien Israel" into God's ultimate plan. Midrash uses
totally Rabbinic form and informs the audience without any delay that the
midrashist is uttering "truth". The forms of the traditions are the
forms of speaking "truth"[12].

4. <u>The</u> <u>intended</u> <u>audience</u>.

The audience of Sifre must be seen as extremely literate in Rabbinic
literature. The subtle nuances, turns of traditional phrase to indicate
"novel" meaning, allusions to <u>halacha</u>[13] and <u>talmud</u>[14], point in this
direction.

5. <u>Concerns</u>

The midrash addresses the plight of Israel, i.e. her sufferings, and
promises future reward for the righteous[15]. It castigates sin[16] but
maintains that Israel is the beloved of God[17]. Interestingly it contrasts
how Israel behaves as a conqueror and how Rome acts[18]. It may be that
these midrashim reflect a view that Bar Kochba was tolerant of non-Jews or
else is imagining how things must have been in Hasmonean times. The point
of the midrash is to maintain Israel's loyalty to her traditions

and to encourage an optimistic view amongst Jews.

6. <u>Who</u> <u>would</u> <u>understand</u> <u>these</u> <u>texts</u>?

Anyone familiar with the entire corpus of Rabbinic literature who knew Scripture by heart and had a vivid imagination could understand these texts after a period of study. The numbers of Greek and foreign terms show us that these midrashim were current while this language was spoken in Palestine. Interestingly, I have noticed some midrashic plays which presuppose a knowledge of Aramaic idiom and conclude from this that if the midrashic traditions behind our text were not partially in Aramaic, at least the audience would be expected to know these allusions to the Aramaic[19]. Since the majority of the traditions in our midrash can also be found in the Targumim which are of Palestinian origin, i.e. Ps.-Jon. and Frag. Targ., we may assume that these traditions were very popular and contained the traditional exposition of <u>Ha'azinu</u>. Thus, while the traditions would be known widely, the fascination with our Sifre midrashim would be in unravelling the allusions which would yield traditions known to the audience since childhood. Sifre Deut. to <u>Ha'azinu</u> is a sophisticated work.

7. <u>The</u> <u>Conception</u> <u>of</u> <u>Scripture</u>

For the Rabbis, Scripture represented the perfect description of reality which if probed deeply enough could yield information concerning Israel's past, present and future as an eternal construct. Scripture is the shadow of "midrashic reality". By our isolating the words of Scripture and observing their behavior in the context of words with similar acoustical traits, the Scriptures 'act' as a living organism and allow unsuspected levels of meaning to be exposed in the words examined[20]. This process of determining the precise function of Scriptural words is usually referred to as Talmud[21].

A further note is necessary here to suggest that it may well be the case, and the Rabbis may well have been aware of it, that Scripture consciously interprets Scripture. In an enlightening article entitled "The Prophet Hosea and the Books of the Pentateuch", [B 119] p. 79ff, U. Cassuto demonstrates how the author of Hosea utilized Deut. 32 and, in some sense, interpreted it. It can now be demonstrated that Sifre Ha'azinu utilized insights gleaned from Hosea and transferred them back to an understanding of Deut. 32. Occasionally we find a Hosea text quoted in Sifre as a proof text but more often we find the tradition mentioned in the Hosea text without any citation from Hosea. For instance, compare Piska 319 (Deut. 32:18):

צור ילדך תשי (ותשכח אל מחללך)

...אילו חיה יושבת על המשבר לא הייתה מצטערת...

אילו היה זכר שאין דרכו לילד ומבקש לילד לא היה צער כפול ומכופל.

and Hosea 13:13:   ...חבלי יולדה יבאו לו

כי עת לא יעמד במשבר בנים

The similarity is heightened by the Targum to Hosea 13:13:

עקא וזיע כחבליו על ילדה ייתון ... ארי כען איתי עלוהי עקא כאתתא

דיתבה על מתברא וחיל לית לה למילד.

That Hosea is not cited in Sifre in instances like this suggests that the tradition in the Sifre midrash may have at one time served as a midrash directly upon the verse in Hosea (the transference of midrashim from one verse to another has been discussed by Ch. Albeck[P 87]) or that Hosea traditions on Deut. 32 have their own history and were received independently of Hosea quotations. Passages such as Hosea 2:16 and 9:10 which are actually cited in Piska 313 may show that there was at least some recognition that parts of Hosea's message could act as a commentary to Deut. 32 for, indeed, these proof texts are not utilized by Sifre to show merely the usage of a word or a concept but to tie together Deut. 32 and Hosea 2 and 9 as if Hosea 2 and 9 intended to define the Song of Moses.

It is possible that the complex of midrashim in Piska 311 has been determined by the wording of Hosea 2:1 such that the numbers of Israel are as the sands of the sea because the other nations would not accept the Torah (does אשר לא ימד ולא יספר explain Hab. 3:6 (וימדד) in Piska 311?) so that only the children of Israel are the children of the living God (which explains the parable of Piska 312).

While Piska 329 (Deut. 32:39) can be explained on its own terms, we may well wonder if Hosea 5:13 as elaborated in Hosea 6:1-3 has influenced Sifre Ha'azinu. We may compare particularly here ואין מידי מציל with Hosea 13:14-15 מיד שאול אפדם ... כי הוא בין אחים יפריא on which Targum Hosea remarks:

בית ישראל מיד קטול פרקתנון ארי אינון מתקרן בנין

so that בין is read as בן while אחים is taken as "evil" (see Rashi ad. loc.) and compare this with Piska 329:

אין אבות מצילים את הבנים.

Similarly Hosea 8:14 ושלחתי אש may explain the need to push ושן בהמות אשלח as מתחמם in Piska 321. Also Hosea 13:6 שבעו וירם לבם על כן שכחוני may well lie behind the explanation of Deut. 32:15 וישמע ישורון ויבעט in Piska 318: לפי שובע מרדים . It is possible that Hosea 2:16

ושמתים ליער ואכלתם חית השדה lies behind the comment of Piska 317: זה העולם שנא׳ יכרסמנה חזיר מיער . ויאכל תנובות שדי אלו ארבע מלכיות (see Ibn Ezra to Hos. 2:20)

The message of Hosea 14:10   כי ישרים דרכי ה׳

וצדיקים ילכו בם ופשעים יכשלו בם

as understood by the Targum:

וצדיקיא דהליכו בה יחון בהון בחיי עלמא

ורשיעיא יתמסרון לגיהנם על דלא הליכן בהון.

acts as a fitting comment to sum up the theology of Song midrash and
such is the message of the conclusion of Piska 333 (end of the Song) as
well.

We may well posit that there existed a very early tradition of
commentary upon the Song of Moses, as early as the time of Hosea (if
Cassuto's argument is as correct as it appears) and that some sections of
this "Hosea" tradition (probably dependently but perhaps not altogether
so) were preserved, interpreted and reinterpreted over the years (as
evidenced in Targum to Hosea) until they were artfully recorded in Sifre
Ha'azinu. Thus the contention of L. Finkelstein in New Light etc.,that
Sifre traditions can be traced back to the time of the Prophets, may,
with qualification be correct in spite of the situation that Finkelstein
does not present the strongest arguments for his case. A good case
can be made in regards to the Sifre midrash on the Song of Moses.

8. Relationship of our midrash of Sifre Ha'azinu to the Talmudim.

A number of traditions found in our midrash can be found in the Talmudim
and in the later midrashim in forms slightly different from those
that occur in our Sifre text[22]. I suspect that the influence of the
Talmudim upon the later compilations of midrash is both direct and
indirect. Direct in that the compilers of the later midrashim knew
the Talmudic traditions and incorporated these versions into the later
compilations (and perhaps later copyists have also done this to the Sifre

texts at points[23]) and indirect in that the versions of the midrashim
known to the later compilers appear to have included forms of the
oral versions which were known to the Talmudic sages and continued in
oral form after the close of the Talmuds. Indeed, a comparison of
such forms with our Sifre Ha'azinu text often shows us that the Sifre
texts are more difficult to comprehend as they contain
subtle allusions which are spelled out clearly in the Talmudic texts and
the later compilations of midrashim. This I think is because oral forms
must be more direct than written forms which can be consulted for long
periods of time (whereas oral materials depend upon their immediate impact
for effect). Thus it is, I believe, that one may consider Sifre Deut.
to Ha'azinu to represent an early written text (such written aggadic
texts are mentioned in Talmudic literature in reference to the times of
Rabbi Hiyya and Rabbi Yochanan, the close of the Tannaitic period[24])
based upon traditions which circulated orally in forms close to those
which are preserved in the Talmudim.

9. Conceptual and literary coherence between the two corpora.

If the Talmudic references as found in Finkelstein be looked at carefully,
one will note a very close conceptual and literary coherence. I have
outlined such coherence at several points in my work[25]. As for the
Targumim, midrashim, and Talmudic passages that bear upon the verses
of the Song of Moses one will find such close correspondence of
traditions that one will be forced to admit that, although the formulation
in each case is particular to the needs of the context in which the
traditions are found, these Rabbinic works preserve the authentic Tannaitic
teachings of the Song of Moses. If one then proceeds to consider Samaritan,

Philonic, and Christian exegesis, one will gain an appreciation for
the wide circulation of these traditions and in some cases may consider
the traditions to have come into the hands of the Tannaim from very
ancient sources. Nevertheless, from a literary point of view, Sifre
Deut. to Ha'azinu presents a unified, coherent, running interpretation
while the Talmudim use these traditions to serve their own purposes
which are not concerned with the exegesis of the Song of Moses. We
are therefore in a most fortunate state that we have Sifre Deuteronomy
to Ha'azinu as a section of the grand corpus of the Rabbinic library.
I have tried in this work to make this literary gem more accessible by
presenting a detailed analysis of it. If I have succeeded at any point
I will have fulfilled the task my teacher, Lou H. Silberman, set for
himself and his students: "...to hearken to R(edactor)'s text and thus
to seek to understand his hearkening to the traditional material he
had at hand and behind that to understand the hearkening to Scripture
of those whose interpretations are woven together by R. into his own
statement of the faith of Israel"[26].

1.   See R.S. Sarason, "Toward a New Agendum for the Study of Rabbinic Midrashic Literature", in Jacob J. Petuchowski and Ezra Fleischer (ed.), Studies in Aggadah, Targum and Jewish Liturgy in Memory of Joseph Heinemann, Hebrew University, Jerusalem, 1981, p. 57f.

2.   Ibid. p. 67f.

3.   Ibid. p. 68f.

4.   E.g. in Piska 313 we are given an exegesis of a verse which is seen to reflect past and future (but in doing so addresses the present: see "S12".). It seems to me that the point of stressing Israel's unique relationship to God reflects a Rabbinic message to encourage Jews to believe that although they are treated as the most despised of all nations in actual fact they are the most glorified of all. It is a message, not so much chauvinistic as practical, which kept Jews loyal to their faith through the most difficult persecutions. There is a "chronological" sequence to the presentation; nevertheless, any of the pericopes here may be read as an independent unit and appreciated as such.

5.   So is the impression gained from the beginning of Piska 306.

6.   See Piska 306 "E47". My assumption is that oral traditions are passed on in a form that is quite transparent so that the materials could be readily understood while written materials (at least of the early Amoraic period) were phrased with great subtlety and are not able to be deciphered at first glance. Perhaps in this way the prohibition of writing midrashim was somewhat mitigated. For the interdiction of writing midrashim and for sources indicating that midrashim were in fact written during the close of the Tannaitic period, see Julius Kaplan, The Redaction of the Babylonian Talmud,$^{(B 215)}$ Jerusalem, Makor, 5723, ch. 19. Also see Jonah Fraenkel, "Remarkable Phenomena in the Text-History of the Aggadic Stories", Proceedings of the Seventh World Congress of Jewish Studies in the Talmud, Halacha and Midrash,$^{(B 163)}$ World Union of Jewish Studies, 1981, p. 45ff. In "Studies in the Tannaitic Midrashim", p. 211 (PAAJR, vol. 5, 1933-44), L. Finkelstein compares Piska 306 and Piska 311 (see also p. 204f) with Midrash Haggadol on the same verses treated by Sifre and concludes on the basis of similar readings that Midrash Haggadol (which he sees as Mechilta on Deut. of school of Yishmael) and Sifre Deut. share a common written source. While Midrash Haggadol may indeed reflect the School of Yishmael it seems to me that we must say in regards to the treatment of Ha'azinu in these works that both Midrash Haggadol and Sifre share the very same text here because Midrash Haggadol has borrowed the Sifre text (with corruptions in places) which itself is a text of the School of Yishmael in its final form (See Epstein, Introd. etc.$^{(B 147)}$ p. 628ff) and so no proof can be brought from his citations to show that both Sifre and Midrash Haggadol used a common written source. However, I believe that it is quite plausible to accept that our Sifre texts were transmitted in writing because they preserve excellent traditions which became corrupted in the course of later oral transmissions. A case in point can be found in the "English summary" of Y. Sussman, "The 'Boundaries of Eretz-Israel'", Tarbiz,$^{(B 327)}$ vol. 45 (1976), no. 3-4, p.ii ff: "The text of this baraita was formerly known in four versions... the Rehovot inscription now supplies a fifth. Its version agrees with

that found in Sifre..."

7.   See Introduction, n. 12.

8.   See above n. 6.

9.   See Introduction, n. 6.

10. E.g. Piska 306 "E13".

11. See Piska 307.

12. That is to say, they are those verse forms used to "derive" accepted
halacha from Scripture. The word "midrash" itself often interchanges
with "Talmud", 'Talmud' being the word to describe the traditional process
(applying traditional forms) to Scripture. The sources for this phenomenon
are discussed by M. Güdemann, "Haggada und Midrasche-Haggada: Eine Beitrag
zur Sagengeschichte", (B 182) Jubelschrift zum Neunzigsten Geburstage
des Dr. L. Zunz, Berlin (5644) reprinted Makor, Jerusalem, 5729, p. 111ff.
Ch. Grunhut – ספרא ושאר ספרי דבי רב (B 181) Festschrift zum
Siebzigsten Geburstage David Hoffman's, L. Lamm, Berlin, 1914, p. 4ff.
L. Finkelstein, "Midrash, Halakhot and Aggadot", (B 155) Yitzhak F. Baer
Jubilee Volume, on the occasion of his seventieth birthday, (ed. S. Baron
et al) Historical Society of Jerusalem, Jerusalem, 1960, p. 28ff.
It should be noted that Finkelstein's claim that Talmud can also refer to
Scripture (ibid. p. 36) is by no means certain but that "Torah" can refer
to midrash (=Talmud) is certain (cf. B.T. Kiddushin 49b and P.T. Moed
Katan 3:7). It is true that Jastrow (B 68) and the other lexicographers
understand Talmud to mean Scripture in the phrase "Talmud Lomar". B.
Wacholder, privately, suggested the formula allows us to suppose a dialogue
between Moses and God before the Torah was finalized. Moses pointed to
ambiguities in a proposed version (יכול) and God corrected (תלמוד לומר),
"the Torah is now to read". He cites Sifra to Lev. 1 as evidence. Another
plausible explanation of the term can be given. Let us look at the familiar
usage of this term as found in the Passover Haggadah (cf. Mechilta to
Ex. 13:14):

> (Ex. 13:8: And you shall interpret (והגדת) to your son on
> that day -- "Because of this God made for me my Exiting from
> Egypt.")
> If so, "on that day" -- It is possible ...while it is still day!
> Talmud Lomar, "Because of this". "Because of this" I distinctly
> explain "at the time when mazza and maror are set before you".

In the passage it is clear that the Biblical "והגדת " has been
understood as פתח (i.e. "to interpret" and so Passover "Haggadah" =
"the interpretation"). It is also clear from the context that " אמרתי "
must be taken as "explain" just as Obadiah of Bertinoro explains the
word in Mishna Pes. 10:5. Now what does the word "Talmud Lomar" mean
here? Clearly it means that we have reason to interpret the verse of
Ex. 13:8 in such a way to show that "this" is to be taken as a demonstrative
pronoun which expresses immediacy; one could point to the "this". "This"
is an important part of the verse and contains a definite teaching although
it does look insignificant and trivial. But the point is that there is a
reason for the inclusion of "this" -- namely to teach you that the
"explanation" must be carried on at the time when one eats mazza and maror
which is definitely at night (see Ex. 12:18). The phrase Talmud Lomar
does make sense. In B.T. Krithoth 13b (B.T. Zev. 18b, B.T. Beza 4a) there

arises a question whether תלמוד should be permitted to a drunk teacher. The passage assumes that we are talking about discussing legal matters from the wording of Scripture (i.e. מדרש) but not stating rules of practice (הוראה). The passage equates תלמוד with אמורא -- interpreting. Rav, when intoxicated, refused to do Talmud lest he come by dint of habit to express the rules of practice which is forbidden to an intoxicated teacher. Thus _Talmud_ means "to interpret legal possibilities from the words of Scripture". And so in B.T. Baba Kamma 104b the word _Talmud_ is explained to mean, that when used in midrash halacha (Sifra to Lev. 5:23 is under discussion there), it refers to interpreting redundant or apparently trivial Scriptural words to throw light upon vagaries in Scripture's commandments. According to E. Weisberg, "Towards a clarification of the expressions 'Talmud' and 'Talmud Lomar'", (B 347) Lĕšŏnenū, vol. 39 (1974-5), nos. 1-2, p. 147ff). לומר is to be taken as a sign of quotation. He projects that the original usages of Talmud contained _Lomar_ only when followed by a Biblical verse which it cited. Thus, if we can trust his assumptions based upon manuscript examination, we should take "Talmud Lomar" to mean: "There is a clarification to be interpreted,quote:..." We also find in the mss, " מה תלמוד " (Weisberg claims later scribes confused this into "מה תלמוד לומר ") "what is the decisive explanation of a law which requires these Scriptural words?" Either _Lomar_ indicates a citation (I have seen no evidence of this in Rabbinic works) or means "to interpret" (the "Talmud is to interpret"). And so I believe that _Talmud_ refers to the form of midrash halacha which is meant to show how Scripture yields halacha (while הוראה refers to the form of teaching practical cases of Law - as established usage, cf. P.T. Shab. 16:1 and B.T. Baba Mezia 43b).

13.   See the rather complicated allusions in Piska 317, "E7" - "E12" which indicate a sophisticated audience.

14.   The midrash not only alludes to the technical forms of Scriptural analysis it makes use of the forms as well, e.g. Piska 306 "E56".

15.   Cf. Piska 307, Piska 324.

16.   See Piska 308 "E5".

17.   See Piska 322 "E2".

18.   See Piska 323 "E7".

19.   E.g. Piska 321 "E22".

20.   And this midrashic ploy, I believe, is quite early as evidenced in the Antitheses of Matthew 5:21ff:
   A.   You have heard that it was said (=the pronunciation given by
        the teachers...)"_____ ".
   B.   But I say unto you (I pronounce it with an acoustical shift...)
        "_____ ".
We can now fill in the blanks (by retroversion into Hebrew):

5:21	A.	לא תרצח	do not murder.
5:22	B.	לא תרגז	do not be angry.
5:27	A.	לא תנאף	do not commit adultery
5:28	B.	לא תאב	do not lust.
5:33	A.	לא תשא..לשוא	do not swear vainly.
5:33	B.	לא תשא:לשוא	do not swear -- it is vanity

5:38 A. עין תחת עין   eye revenge for eye
5:39 B.   תחת   replace -- to be struck again

5:43 A. ואהבת לרעיך   love only thy neighbor.
5:44 B. ואהבת לרעיך   love your enemies (רעים לך   ).

See further M. Kister, "Sayings of Jesus and the Midrash", (B230)
Jerusalem Studies in Jewish Thought 2 (1982), Hebrew University, p. 7ff for
existing midrashic materials which help explain the expansion of the
Antitheses in Matt. 5:17ff.

21. Talmud is also able to be seen more critically as the "disciplining"
of Scripture to conform to Rabbinic "oral" tradition.

22. See. E.Z. Melamed, Halachic Midrashim of the Tannaim in the Talmud
Babli, (B264) Jerusalem, 1943, p. 458ff. and see above Piska 306
"E47". See Bibliography for detailed studies concerning midrash and Talmud
(not our particular midrash only) of Albeck, Zunz, Friedmann, Hoffman, J.N.
Epstein, Lauterbach, Finkelstein, Wacholder, etc.

23. See the variants in Finkelstein which periodically agree with B.T.

24. See the sources mentioned in J. Kaplan, The Redaction of the Babylonian
Talmud, Jerusalem, Makor, 5723, ch. 19.

25. E.g. Piska 306; Finkelstein (B48) p. 338 (B.T. Ta'an 7:1), Finkelstein
(B48) p. 340 (B.T. Bab. Bat. 25a, B.T. Yoma 21a, B.T. Bab. Bat. 147a),
and see above n. 22.

26. See L.H. Silberman, "A Theological Treatise on Forgiveness: Chapter
Twenty-Three of Pesiqta deRab Kahana" (B317) in Studies in Aggadah, Targum
etc. p. 96.

LOOKING AHEAD

The focus of this study of Sifre Ha'azinu centered upon three concerns;

textual, linguistic and exegetical. One may suppose that in the near

future a new edition of Sifre Deuteronomy will appear that will correct

the errors noted by Finkelstein in the Introduction to his edition and

that will utilize materials which were unavailable to him. Also, as our

knowledge of Rabbinic usages expands, better interpretations of Sifre

should emerge. For instance, contrary to the usual Rabbinic usage, I

translated לקיים (usually: "to certify") by the sense of "to contradict"

in Piska 306. The context called for such, the author of Midrash

Haggadol explained לקיים in this way (unless his text actually read

"contradict"), the Rabbinic usage of לענות (Deut. 31:21) in the proof

text of the passage calls for the understanding of "to contradict". In

Sifre Deut. Piska 189 the Rabbis explained לענות in Deut. 19:16 as

להכחיש and Malbim uses this verse to explain Job 16:8: לענות ב' =

לקום ב' =contradict (my denial, כחשי). The transitive use of the

piel in Piska 306 requires more detailed investigation for the full

appreciation of the " לקיים " midrash. Finally we note the pressing

question concerning which traditions are cited in "home" settings and

which at "visiting" settings. Many of the traditions in Sifre Ha'azinu

can be found in Sifre Ekeb. Only detailed studies designed to locate

the actual "home" of traditions can enlighten us in regard to the primary

exegetical techniques of the Rabbis. While my work has touched upon these

matters in regard to the Song midrash of Ha'azinu, it remains for those

adept at producing critical editions, Rabbinic lexicons, and literary

studies to help us better incline our ears at the proper angle to hear

more clearly, the words of the Sages.

BIBLIOGRAPHY

1. Aboth de R. Nathan, ed. S. Schechter, New York, Feldheim, 1945.

2. Amram Gaon, Seder Rav Amram HaShalem, ed. D. Goldschmidt, Jerusalem,Mossad HaRav Kook, 1971.

3. The Apocrypha and Pseudepigrapha of the Old Testament in English with Introductions and Critical and Explanatory Notes to the Several Books, R.H. Charles et al., London, Oxford University Press, 1968.

4. Apocalypse de Baruch (Introduction, tradition du Syriaque et Commentaire), ed. P. Bogaert, Paris, 1969.

5. Bhāgavad Gītā, ed. F. Egerton, New York, Harper Torch Books, 1965.

6. Bhāgavata Purāna with Cūrnika Commentary,Bombay, 1910.

7. Biblia Hebraica, ed. R. Kittel et al, Stuttgart, 1962.

8. The Bible in Aramaic, ed. A. Sperber, 1959-1962.

9. Ḥizkuni (of Hezekiah bar Manoah to the Torah), ed. Ch. D. Chavel, Jerusalem, Mossad HaRav Kook, 1981.

10. Ibn Ezra's Perushei HaTorah, ed. A. Weizer, Jerusalem, Mossad HaRav Kook, 1977.

11. Josephus with an English Translation, ed. and tr. H. St. Thackery, Cambridge, 1961.

12. Koran, English and Arabic: The Meaning of the Glorious Koran, tr. M. Pickthall, Karachi, n.d.

13. The Works of Flavius Josephus, tr. W. Whiston, New York, Leavitt and Allen, 1853, (edition referred to unless otherwise noted).

14. Mechilta de-Rabbi Shimon bar Yochai, ed. J.N. Epstein and E.Z. Melamed, Jerusalem, Academy for Jewish Research, 1955.

15. Mechilta de-Rabbi Yishmael, ed. Ch. Horowitz and Y. Rabin, Jerusalem, Bamberger and Wahrmann, 1960.

16. Memar Marqah, ed. J. Macdonald, Berlin, Alfred Töpelmann, 1963.

17. Midrash Bereshith Rabba, critical edition with notes and commentary, ed. J. Theodor and Ch. Albeck, Jerusalem, Wahrmann, 1965.

18. Midrash Rabba im Kol Hamefarshim, Wilna, reprint Jerusalem, 5721.

19. Midrash Devarim Rabba, ed. S. Lieberman, Jerusalem, Wahrmann, 1964-65.

20. Midrash Haggadol (to Sefer Devarim) on the Pentateuch, ed. S. Fisch, Jerusalem, Mossad HaRav Kook, 1972.

21. Midrash Leqaḥ Tob (styled P'sikta Zutarta), ed. S. Buber and
    M. Katznelenbogen, 1884.

22. Midrash Pesiqta Rabbathi, ed. M. Friedmann, Tel Aviv, 5723.

23. Midrash Rabba (with Etz Yosef and Anaf Yosef commentaries), Warsaw,
    5627.

24. Midrash Tanḥuma, ed. S. Buber, Jerusalem, 1963-64.

25. Midrash Tanḥuma (with Etz Yosef and Anaf Yosef commentaries),
    Jerusalem, 5735.

26. Midrash Tannaim zum Deuteronomium, ed. D. Hoffman, Berlin,
    M. Poppelaver, 1908-9.

27. Midrash Tehillim (Schachar Tob),ed. S. Buber, Wilna, 5651 and
    Jerusalem 5737.

28. Midrash Vayikra Rabba (Leviticus Rabba), ed. M. Margulies,
    Jerusalem, Ministry of Education and Culture, 1953-1960.

29. Mikraot Gedolot, Jerusalem, Schocken, 1958-59.

30. The New Testament in Modern Speech, tr. R.F. Weymouth, London,
    James Clarke and Co., 1937.

31. The Old Testament in Greek According to the Septuagint,
    ed. H.B. Swete, Cambridge University Press, Cambridge, 1887.

32. Otsar Ha-Geonim le Masekhet Sanhedrin, ed. Ch. Z. Taubes,
    Jerusalem, Mossad HaRav Kook, 1966.

33. The Essential Philo, ed. N.H. Glatzer, Schocken, New York, 1971.

34. Philo in Ten Vols. and two supplementary Vols., tr. F.H. Colson
    et al., London, Heinemann, 1929-1961.

35. Perush HaRamban al HaTorah, ed. Ch. D. Chavel, Jerusalem, Mossad
    HaRav Kook, 5720-27.

36. Rabbenu Bahya on the Torah, ed. Ch. D. Chavel, Vol. 3: Numbers --
    Deuteronomy, Jerusalem, Mossad HaRav Kook, 1968.

37. Rashi al haTorah, ed. A. Berliner, (new edition with an
    appendix of variants in the readings of Rashi as found in
    the Commentary of Ramban to the Torah and with textual
    clarifications by Ch. D. Chavel,) 1969-1970.

38. Saadiah Gaon, Kitab al Amanat wa'l-I'tiqadat, ed. S. Landover,
    (Paris, 1880), tr. S. Rosenblatt, The Book of Beliefs and
    Opinions, 1948.

39. Igeret Rav Sherira Gaon, ed. B. Lewin, Jerusalem, 5732.

40. Samaritan Chronicle No. 2, ed. J. Macdonald, Berlin, Walter
    de Gruyter and Co., 1969.

41. The Six Orders of the Mishna, ed. H. Albeck and H. Yalon,
    Jerusalem, Dvir, 1952-1956.

42. Seder Eliahu Rabbah Veseder Eliahu Zuta, ed. M. Friedmann,
    Jerusalem, Wahrmann, 5720.

43. Seder Olam Rabba, ed. d. Ratner, New York, 5726.

44. Sefer Ben Sira HaShalem, ed. M.H. Segal, Jerusalem, Mossad
    Bialik, 5732.

45. Sefer HaRazim, ed. M. Margalioth, Tel Aviv, 1966.

46. Sifra, ed. I.H. Weiss, Vienna, 5622.

47. Sifre de-be Rab, ed. M. Friedmann, Vienna, 1864.

48. Sifre on Deuteronomy, ed. L. Finkelstein, JTS, 1969.

49. Sifrei al Sefer Bamidbar Ve-Sifrei Zuta, ed. H.S. Horowitz,
    Leipzig 1917, reprint Jerusalem, Wahrmann, 1966.

50. Talmud Bavli, Vilna, Romm, 1886.

51. Talmud Yerushalmi, Vilna, Romm, 1922.

52. Tanna Deve Eliahu with Ziquqin de nura uviurin de'esha
    commentary (2 versions), Lublin, 5657.

53. Targum Neophyti, Palestinian Targum m.s. Bibliotheca Vaticana,
    1968.

54. Targum to the Five Megillot, ed. B. Gross, New York, Hermon
    Press, 1971.

55. Pseudo-Jonathon (Thargum Jonathon ben Usiël zum Pentateuch),
    ed. M. Ginsburger, Berlin, S. Calvary and Co., 1903.

56. Das Fragmententhargum (Thargum jeruschalmi zum Pentateuch),
    ed. M. Ginsburger, Berlin, S. Calvary, 1889.

57. Tosefta, ed. M.S. Zuckermandel with supplement to the Tosefta by
    S. Lieberman, Jerusalem, Bamberger and Wahrmann, 1937.

58. Yalkut Ha-Makhiri of Yishiahu, ed. Y. Shapiro, reprint Jerusalem,
    5724.

59. Yalkut Shimoni, ed. I. Shiloni, Jerusalem, Mossad HaRav Kook, 1973.

60. Yalkut Shimoni, with Zayit Ra'anan and Introduction by B. Landau,
    Jerusalem, 5720.

2. Dictionaries and Concordances

61. Bacher, W. Erche Midrasch, (Vol. 1), Tannaim, (Vol. 2) Amoraim ,
    Jerusalem, Carmiel, 1970.

62. Bauer, W.A., A Greek Lexicon of the New Testament and other
    Early Christian Literature, Revised and Translated by
    W. Arndt and F.W. Ginrisch, Chicago, Univ. Press, 1957.

63. Ben Yehuda, E., A Complete Dictionary of Ancient and Modern
    Hebrew, Jerusalem, 1952.

64. Brown, F., Driver, S.R., Briggs, C.A., A Hebrew and English
    Lexicon of the Old Testament, Oxford, Clarendon Press, 1959.

65. Even-Shoshan, A., HaMilon HeHahadash, Jerusalem, Kiryath Sepher,
    1969.

66. Fürst, J., Glossarium Graeco-Hebreum oder Der Griechische
    Wörterschatz der jüdischen Midraschwerke, ein Beitrag zur

Kultur - und Altertumskunde, Strassburg, Karl J.
Trubner, 1890-91.

67. Gesenius, F.H.W., Hebrew and Chaldee Lexicon to the Old
Testament, Scriptures, Tr. and rev. by S.P. Tregelles,
reprinted Grand Rapids, Eerdmans, 1957.

68. Jastrow, M., A Dictionary of the Targumim, the Talmud Babli
and Yerushalmi, and the Midrashic Literature, New York,
Pardes, 1950.

69. Hebrew-English Lexicon of the Bible, New York, Schocken, 1978.

70. Interpreter's Dictionary of the Bible, ed. G. Buttrick et al.,
New York, Abingdon, 1962.

71. Kohut, A., Aruch Completum of Nathan Ben Yechiel, Vienna, 1926.

72. Kossowsky, B., Thesarus Sifre, Jerusalem, Ministry of Education
and Culture, Government of Israel, 1971-74.

73. Kossowsky, Ch. Y. and Kossowsky, B., Thesarus Talmudus, Jerusalem,
Ministry of Education and Culture and JTS, 1954--.

74. Krauss, S., Griechische und lateinische Lehnwörter in Talmud,
Midrasch und Targum, Berlin, Calvary, 1898-99.

75. Krauss, S., et al, Supplement Volume to Kohut, Aruch Completum,
New York, 1955.

76. Kutcher, E. (ed.), Archive of the New Dictionary of Rabbinical
Literature, Ramat Gan, 1972.

77. Levita, E., Meturgeman, Isny, 1541, reprint Israel, 1967.

78. Levy, J., Chaldäisches Wörterbuch über die Targumim und einen
grossen Theil des rabbinischen Schriftthmus, Cologne,
J. Meltzer, 1859.

79. Levy, J. Neuhebraisches und chaldäisches Wörterbuch über die
Talmudim und Midraschim, Leipzig, 1876-1879.

80. Liddel, H.G., and Scott, R., A Greek-English Lexicon, Revised
by H.S. Jones, Oxford, 1968.

81. Mandelkern, S., Concordanctiae Veteris Testamenti Hebraicae
Atque Chaldaicae, Tel Aviv, 1964.

82. Smith, J. Payne, A Compendious Syriac Dictionary, Oxford,
Clarendon Press, 1903.

3. Secondary Sources

83. Abelson, I., The Immanence of God in Rabbinical Literature, London,
1912.

84. Abrahams, I., Studies in Pharisaism and the Gospels, New York,
Ktav, 1967.

85. Adrath, A., "The aggadot of the Sages as developed literature",
Alei Siah, 2, (5736), Heb.

86. Ahuvya, A., "Again ozer ve'azov", Lěšonenu, 31 (1967), Heb.

87. Albeck, Ch., "The Method of the Sages' Exegesis", The Oral Law:
    Lectures at the second national congress for the Oral Law,
    ed. Y.L. Hacohen Maimon, Jerusalem, Mossad HaRav Kook,
    5729, Heb.

88. Albeck, Ch., Untersuchungen über die halachischen Midraschim,
    Berlin, 1927.

89. Albright W., "Some Remarks on the Song of Moses in Deuteronomy
    32", VT, vol. 9 (1959).

90. Alon, G., Jews, Judaism and the Classical World: Studies in
    Jewish History in the times of the Second Temple and Talmud,
    tr. I. Abrahams, Jerusalem, Hebrew University, 1977.

91. Aphraates, Demonstrations of Aphrahat, the Persian Sage, ed.
    J. Gwynn, Grand Rapids, Eerdmans, 1955.

92. Ashkenazi, M.D., Toledot Adom, Jerusalem, Mossad HaRav Kook, 1974.

93. Bacher, W., Die Proömien der alten Jüdischen Homilie, Leipzig,
    Hinrich, 1913.

94. Bacher, W., The Legends of the Amoraim of Eretz Israel, Tel Aviv,
    5685, Heb.

95. Bacher, W., The Legends of the Tannaim, Tel Aviv, 5682, Heb.

96. Bacher, W., "The Origin of the Word 'Haggadah'", JQR,4 (1982).

97. Bacher, W., "Rome dans le Talmud et le Midrasch", REJ,vol. 33 (1896).

98. Bacher, W., Tradition und Tradenten in den Schulen Palästinas
    und Babylonians, Leipzig, Gustav Frock, 1914.

99. Bamberger, B.J. "Philo and the Aggadah", HUCA 48.

100. Baron, S., A Social and Religious History of the Jews (10 vols.),
     Philadelphia, JPS, 1952.

101. Basser, H., "Distinctive Usage of pth in Rabbinic Literature",
     Hebrew Studies, vols. 20-21 (1979-80).

102. Basser, H., "The Rabbinic Attempt to Democratize Salvation and
     Revelation", Studies in Religion, 12 (1983).

103. Basser, H.W., "Allusions to Christian and Gnostic Practices in
     Talmudic Tradition", JSJ, vol. 12 (1976), no. 1.

104. Baumgarten, A.I., "The Akiban Opposition", HUCA,vol. 50 (1979).

105. Ben David, Y., "Machat Poranotan shel resha'im", Lěšonenū, vol. 41
     (1977), Heb.

106. Blau, L., Das altjudische Zauberwesen Jahresbericht der
     Landes-Rabbiner Schule in Budapest, Budapest, 1898.

107. Bloch, R., "Methodological Note for the Study of Rabbinic Literature",
     Approaches to Ancient Judaism, Theory and Practice, ed. W.S. Green,
     Missoula, Scholars Press, 1978.

108. Bohrer, Y.L., "A Historical and Methodological Explanation of
     Aggadic Sources", Samuel K. Mirsky Memorial Volume: Studies in Law,

Philosophy and Literature, ed. G. Appel, New York, Yeshiva
University-Sura Institute for Research, 1970, Heb.

109. Bokser, B., "Justyn Martyr and the Jews", JQR, vol. 54 (1974), no. 3.

110. Bonsirven, J., Palestinian Judaism in the time of Jesus Christ,
New York, Holt, Reinhardt and Winston, n.d.

111. Bonsirven, L., Textes Rabbiniques Des Deux Premiers Siècles
Chrétiens, Pontificio Institute Biblico, Rome, 1955.

112. Bowker, J., The Targums and Rabbinic Literature: An Introduction
to Jewish Interpretations of Scripture, Cambridge, Cambridge
University Press, 1969.

113. Braver, A., "The Debate between a Sadducee and Pharisee in the
Mouths of Cain and Abel", Beth Mikra, vol. 44 (1971), Heb.

114. Bright, J., A History of Israel, London, SCM, 1972.

115. Broznick, N., "Asot sefarim harbeh ayn ketz, Koheleth 12:12",
Beth Mikra, vol. 25 (1980), Heb.

116. Buchanan, G., "Midrashim pre-tannaïtes: à propos de Prov. I-IX,
Revue Biblique vol 72 (1965).

117. Büchler A., Studies in Sin and Atonement in the Rabbinic Literature
of the First Century, Ktav, New York, 1967.

118. Büchler, A., "The Minim of Sepphoris and Tiberius in the Second and
Third Centuries", Studies in Jewish History, London, Oxford
University Press, 1956.

119. Cassuto, U., Biblical and Oriental Studies, vol. I: Bible
(tr. I. Abrahams), Jerusalem, Magnes, 1973.

120. Ceresko, A., "The Law Book of the Josianic Reform", CBQ 38 (1976)

121. Chronis, H., "The Torn Veil: Cultus and Christology in Mark 15:37-39,
JBL, vol. 101 (1982).

122. Craigie, P., The Book of Deuteronomy, (The New International
Commentary on the Old Testament), Grand Rapids, Eerdmans, 1976.

123. Dahood, M., "Hebrew-Ugaritic Lexicography", Biblica 50 (1964).

124. Daube, D., The New Testament and Rabbinic Judaism, London,
University of London, 1956.

125. Daube, D., "Rabbinic Methods of Interpretation and Hellenistic
Rhetoric", HUCA, vol. 22 (1949).

126. Daube, D., "A Reform in Acts and its Models", on Jews Greeks and
Christians: Religious Cultures in Late Antiquity (Essays
in Honor of William David Davies); ed. R. Hammertone-Kelly
and R. Scroggs, Leiden, Brill, 1976.

127. Davies, W.D., Torah in the Messianic Age and/or the Age to Come,
Philadelphia, Society of Biblical Literature, 1952.

128. De Jonge, M., "Again 'to stretch out the feet' in the Testament
of the Five Patriarch", JBL, vol. 49 (1980), no. 1.

129. De Lange, M.R.M., <u>Origen and the Jews</u>: <u>Studies in Jewish-Christian Relations in Third Century Palestine</u>, Cambridge, Harvard University, 1976.

130. Delcor, M., "Two Special Meanings of the Word 'yad' in Biblical Hebrew", <u>Journal of Semitic Studies</u>, 12-13 (1967-8).

131. Derrett, J.D.M., "Allegory and the wicked vine dressers and Sifre Deuteronomy Piska 312", <u>Journal of Theological Studies</u>, 25 (1974).

132. De Vries, B., "Concerning the Form of the Halachot in the Tannaitic Era", <u>Studies in Talmudic Literature</u>, Jerusalem, Mossad HaRav Kook, 1968, Heb.

133. De Vries, B., "The Literary Categories of the Aggadah", <u>Studies in Talmudic Literature</u>, Jerusalem, Mossad HaRav Kook, 1968, Heb.

134. De Vries, B., "The Literary Nature of Aggadah", <u>Studies in Talmudic Literature</u>, Jerusalem, Mossad HaRav Kook, 1968, Heb.

135. Dexinger, F., "Die Sektenproblematik im Judenthum", <u>Kairos</u> 21 (1979).

136. Driver, G.R., "Hebrew Notes on the Wisdom of Jesus Ben Sirach", <u>JBL</u> 53 (1939).

137. Driver, S.R., <u>A Critical and Exegetical Commentary on Deuteronomy</u>, International Critical Commentary, Edinburgh, T. and T. Clark, 1960.

138. Eissfeldt, O., <u>The Old Testament, An Introduction</u>, tr. P. Ackroyd, New York, Harper and Row, 1965.

139. Eliade, M., <u>The Sacred and the Profane: The Nature of Religion</u>, tr. W. Trask, New York, Harcourt, Brace and World Inc., 1959.

140. <u>Encyclopedia Judaica</u>, 16 volumes, Jerusalem, Keter, 1971.

141. <u>Ephraem, Syrus, Opera omnia quae extant graecae, syriacae, latinae...</u>, ed. J.M.H. Salvioni, Vatican, 1732-46.

142. Eppenheim, Ch.,"Observations on the Relationship between the Haggadot of the Sages and various Targumim," <u>Beth Talmud</u>, vol. 2 (5642). Reprint: Jerusalem, 5729.

143. Epstein, A., "Some Sources of Midrashim", <u>Of Jewish Antiquities, Studies and Notices</u>, vol. 2, ed. A.M. Haberman, Jerusalem, Mossad HaRav Kook, 5717, Heb.

144. Epstein, A., "Sifra and the Bablyonian Talmud, Sifre and the Palestinian Talmud", <u>Of Jewish Antiquities, Studies and Notices</u>, vol. 2, ed. A.M. Haberman, Jerusalem, Mossad HaRav Kook, 5717, Heb.

145. Epstein, B., <u>Torah Temima</u>, Tel Aviv, 5716, Heb.

146. Epstein, J.N., "Gloses Babylo-Araméenes", <u>REJ</u>, vol. 73 (1921).

147. Epstein, J.N., <u>Introduction to Tannaitic Literature: Mishna, Tosephta and Halachic Midrashim</u>, edited by E.Z. Melamed, Jerusalem, Magnes, 1957, Heb.

304

148. Epstein, J.N., "Siphre zu Deuteronomium unter Benutzung des Nachlasses von Dr. H.S. Horovitz sel. A. mit kritischem Apparat und Noten herausgegeben von Dr. Louis Finkelstein, Lieferung 1-4, Bogen 1-16, Breslau, 1935-1937", *Tarbiz*, vol. 8 (1936-37), Heb.

149. Farbridge, M.H., *Studies in Biblical and Semitic Symbolism*, New York, Ktav, 1970.

150. Finkelstein, L., "An old baraita on Deuteronomy", *Eretz-Israel*, vol. 10 (1971), Heb.

151. Finkelstein, L., "Fragment of an Unkown Midrash on Deuteronomy", *HUCA*, vols. 12-13, (1937-1938).

152. Finkelstein, L., "Improved Readings in the *Sifre*", *PAAJR*, vol. 4 (1932-33).

153. Finkelstein, L., *Introduction to the Treatises Abot and Abot of Rabbi Nathan*, New York, 1950.

154. Finkelstein, L., "La Kedousha et les benedictions du Schema," *REJ*, vol. 93 (1932).

155. Finkelstein, L., "Midrash, Halachot and Aggadot", *Yitzhak F. Baer Jubilee Volume (on the occasion of his 70th birthday)*, ed. S. Baron *et al.*, Jerusalem, Historical Society of Jerusalem, 1960.

156. Finkelstein, L., *New Light from the Prophets*, London, Vallentine, Mitchell, 1969.

157. Finkelstein, L., "Prolegomena to an Edition of the Sifre on Deuteronomy", *PAAJR*, vol. 3 (1932).

158. Finkelstein, L., "Source of Tannaitic Midrashim", *JQR*, vol. 31 (1941).

159. Finkelstein, L., "Studies in Tannaitic Midrashim", *PAAJR*, vol. 6 (1935).

160. Finkelstein, L., "The Mekilta and Its Text", *PAAJR*, vol. 5 (1934).

161. Finkelstein, L., "The Transmission of Early Rabbinic Tradition", *Exploring the Talmud*, ed. H.Z. Dimotrovsky, New York, Ktav, 1926.

162. Fox, H., "'As if with a finger' --The Text History of an Expression Avoiding Anthropomorphism", *Tarbiz*, vol. 49 (1980), nos. 3-4, Heb.

163. Fraenkel, J.,"Remarkable Phenomena in the Text History of the Aggadic Stories", *Proceedings of the Seventh World Congress of Jewish Studies in the Talmud, Halacha and Midrash*, Jerusalem, World Union of Jewish Studies, 1981, Heb.

164. Fraenkel, J., "Time and Its Shaping in Aggadic Narrative", *Studies in Aggadah, Targum and Jewish Liturgy in Memory of Joseph Heinemann*, Jerusalem, Hebrew University, 1981, Heb.

165. Freyne, S., Galilee from Alexander the Great to Hadrian 323 B.C.E. to 135 C.E.: A Study of Second Temple Judaism, Michael Glazier and University of Notre Dame Press, Notre Dame, 1980.

166. Friedländer, M., Vorchristliche judische Gnosticismus, Gottingen, Vandenhoek and Ruprecht, 1898.

167. Gager, J., "The Dialogue of Paganism with Judaism, Bar Cochba to Julian", HUCA, vol. 44 (1973).

168. Gerhardssohn, B., Memory and Manuscript, Oral Tradition and Written Transmission in Rabbinic Judaism and Early Christianity, Lund, 1961.

169. Gil, M., "Land Ownership in Palestine under Roman Rule", Revue Internationale des Droits de l'Antiquité, vol. 17, (1970).

170. Ginzberg, L., On Jewish Law and Lore, New York, Atheneum, 1977.

171. Ginzberg, L., The Legends of the Jews, tr. H. Szold, Philadelphia, JPS, 1968.

172. Goldin, J., "The Home of a Pharisee", AJS Review, vol. 5 (1980).

173. Goldin, J., "Not By Means of an Angel and Not By Means of a Messenger", Studies in the History of Religions, ed. J. Neusner, Leiden, Brill, 1968.

174. Goldin, J., "Of Change and Adaptation", History of Religions, vol. 4-5 (1964-66).

175. Goldin, J., The Song at the Sea: Being a Commentary on a Commentary in Two Parts, New Haven, Yale University, 1971.

176. Goshen-Gottstein, M.H., "Theory and Practice of Textual Criticism", Textus, vol. 3, ed. C. Rabin, Jerusalem, Hebrew University, 1963.

177. Grayson, K., "Hilaskesthai and related words in LXX", NTS, vol. 27 (1981), no. 5.

178. Greenstein, E.C. "'To grasp the hem' in Ugaritic Literature", VT, vol. 32 (1982), no. 2.

179. Gruenwald, I., Apocalyptic and Merkabah Mysticism: A Study of the Jewish Esoteric Literature in the Time of the Mishna and Talmudim, Hebrew University (dissertation), Jerusalem, 1968-69, Heb.

180. Gruenwald, I., Apocalyptic and Merkavah Mysticism, Leiden, Brill, 1980.

181. Grünhut, Ch., "Sifra ve-shaar Sifre deVe Rav", Festschrift zum siebzigsten Geburstage David Hoffman's, ed. L. Lamm, Berlin, 1914, Heb.

182. Güdemann, M., "Haggada und Midrasch-Haggada: eine Beitrag zur Sagengeschichte",Jubelschrift zum neunzigsten Geburstage des L. Zunz, Berlin, 5644.

183. Gutman, Y.M., "The Sense of Scripture and Midrashic Methodology", Hazofeh, vol. 5, Reprint Jerusalem, Makor, 1972, Heb.

184. Haas, L., "Bibliography on Midrash", In The Study of Ancient Judaism, vol. I, ed. J. Neusner, New York, Ktav, 1981.

185. Halevy, A.A., The Gates of the Aggadah: Concerning the Essence of the Aggadah, Its Types, Methods, Aims and Influence upon the Culture of Its Times, Tel Aviv, 1963, Heb.

186. Halperin, Y., Seder HaDorot, Jerusalem, 5716.

187. Hardy, W.D., "The Horse in Zecharaiah", In Memoriam Paul Kahle, ed. M. Black and G. Fohrer, Berlin, Alfred Töpelman, 1968.

188. Haupert, R., "The Transcription-Theory of the Septuagint", JBL, 53 (1939).

189. Hayman, A.P., "Disputation Against Sergius", Corpus Scriptorum Orientalium, Tome 153, Scriptores Syri, vol. 339.

190. Hayward, R., Divine Name and Presence: The Memra, Oxford, Publications of the Oxford Centre for Postgraduate Hebrew Study, 1981.

191. Heinemann, I., The Methodology of the Aggadah, Jerusalem, 1950, Heb.

192. Heinemann, J., Aggadah and Its Development, Jerusalem, Keter, 1974, Heb.

193. Heinemann, J., "The Proem in the Aggadic Midrashim", Scripta Hierosolymitana (Studies in Aggadah and Folklore), vol. 22 (1971).

194. Herford, R.T., Christianity in Talmud and Midrash, London, Williams Norgate, 1903.

195. Herr, M.D., "The Conception of History Among the Sages", Proceedings of the Sixth World Congress of Jewish Studies, Vol. 13, Jerusalem, World Union of Jewish Studies, 1977, Heb.

196. Herr, M.D., "Persecutions and Martyrdom in Hadrian's Days", Scripta Hierosolymitana, vol. 23 (1972).

197. Heschel, A.J., Theology of Ancient Judaism, London and New York, Soncino, 1962-1965, Heb.

198. Hidal, S., "Reflections on Deuteronomy 32", Annual of the Swedish Theological Institute, vol. 11 (1978).

199. Hirschensohn, Ch., Berure Ha-Middoth, Jerusalem, 5689.

200. Hoffer, A.I. "In Explanation of Ani Vehu Hoshia Na", Ha-Tsofeh le-Hokhmat Yisrael, vol. 1 (5671), n. 1 (Reprint Jerusalem, Makor, 5732), Heb.

201. Hoffman, D., "Concerning the Study of Tannaitic Midrashim", tr. into Hebrew by A.Z. Rabinowitz, M'silot l'Torat HaTannaim, Tel Aviv, 5688.

202. Hoffman, D., Zur Einleitung in die halachischen Midraschim, Beilage zum Jahresbericht des Rabbiner Seminars, Berlin, 1888.

203. Holladay, W.L., "Ereş-Underworld; Two More Suggestions", VT, 19 (1969).

204. Horgan, M.P. _Pesharim: Qumran Interpretations of Biblical Books_,
     Washington, CBQ, Biblical Association of America, Monograph
     Series 8, 1979.

205. Howe, F.R. and G.R., "Moses and the Eagle (Deut. 32:11)", _Journal
     of the Scientific Affiliation_, vol. 20 (1968), no. 1.

206. Humbert, P. "'Qânâ' en Hebreu Biblique", _Festschrifft Alfred
     Bertholet zum 80 Geburstag_, ed. W. Baumgertner, O. Eissfeldt
     et al., Tubingen, 1950.

207. Irenaeus, _Proof of the Apostolic Preaching_, volume 16 of _Ancient
     Christian Writers_, tr. and annotated by J.P. Smith, London,
     Longmans, Green and Co., 1952.

208. _The Jewish Encyclopedia_, (12 Volumes): _The History, Religion,
     Literature and Customs of the Jewish People from the Earliest
     Times to the Present Day_, ed. I. Singer, New York, Funk and
     Wagnalls, 1912.

209. Johnston, R.M., "The Study of Rabbinic Parable: Some Preliminary
     Observations", _SBL seminar papers_, 1976, Scholars Press,
     Missoula, 1976.

210. Kadushin, M., _A Conceptual Approach to the Mekilta_, New York,
     JTS, 1969.

211. Kadushin ., M., "Aspects of the Rabbinic Concept of Israel",
     HUCA, vol. 19, (1945-46).

212. Kadushin ., M., "The Election of Israel in Words of the Sages",
     Proceedings of the Rabbinic Assembly of America, vol. 8
     (1941-44).

213. Kadushin , M., _The Rabbinic Mind_, New York, 1952.

214. Kahana, M., _Prolegomena to a New Edition of the Sifre on
     Numbers_, unpublished, diss. Hebrew University, April 1982.

215. Kaplan, J., _The Redaction of the Babylonian Talmud_, Jerusalem,
     Makor, 5723.

216. Kasher, R., Again, "Azur Ve'azov", _Lesonenu_, 31 (1967), no. 3, Heb.

217. Katz, E., "It is this which Scripture says", _HaDarom_, vol. 44
     (5737), Heb.

218. Katz, J., _Exclusiveness and Tolerance_, New York, Schocken, 1962.

219. Kimmelman, R., "Rabbi Yochanan and Origen on the Song of Songs:
     A Third Century Jewish-Christian Disputation," _HTR_, vol. 73
     (1980), nos. 3-4.

230. Kister, I., "Sayings of Jesus and the Midrash", _Studies in Jewish
     Thought_, 2 (1982).

231. Klausner, Joseph, _The Messianic Idea in Israel_, New York, Macmillan,
     1955.

232. Klein, S., _Neue Beitrage zur Geschichte und Geographie Galilaas_,
     Vienna, 1923.

233. Klein, S., "Topographical Material of Eretz-Israel", Hazofeh, vol. 7 (1923), Heb. (Reprint Jerusalem, Makor, 1972).

234. Kohler, K., Jewish Theology Systematically and Historically Considered, New York, 1928.

235. Krauss, S., Persia and Rome in Talmud and Midrashim, Jerusalem, Mossad HaRav Kook, 1947-8, Heb.

236. Krauss, S., Talmudische Archäologie, 3 vols., Hildesheim, Olms, 1966.

237. Kutscher, E.Y., "Marginal Notes to the Mishnaic Lexicon and a Grammatical Note (p. 107-111)", Lĕšōnenū,31 (1966), Heb.

238. Lachs, S., "Rabbi Abbahu and the Minim", JQR,60 (1970).

239. Lauterbach, J.Z., "Midrash and Mishna", JQR, vol. 5-6 (1916).

240. Lauterbach, J.Z., Rabbinical Essays, Ktav, 1973.

241. Le Déaut, R., "À propos d'une definition du Midrash", Biblica,50 (1969).

242. Le Déaut, R., La Nuit Pascale; Essai sur la Signification de la Pâque Juive à partir du Targum d'Exode 12:42, Rome, Institut Biblique Pontifical, 1963.

243. Lehrer, M., "In the Heavens and upon the Earth and in the Four Corners of the World", Benjamin De Vries Memorial Volume, ed. E.Z. Melamed, Jerusalem, Tel Aviv University, 1968, Heb.

244. Leibowitz, N., Studies in Devarim, Jerusalem, World Zionist Organizations, 1980.

245. Leibowitz, N., Studies in Shmot, Jerusalem, World Zionist Organizations, 1980.

246. Lichtenstein, A., The Seven Laws of Noah, New York, Rabbi Jacob School Press, 1981.

247. Lichtenstein, A.Y., Zera Avraham (to Zeh Sefer Sifre) vol. I, Dyhrenfurt, 5571; vol. 2, Radwil, 5580.

248. Lieberman, S., Greek in Jewish Palestine in the 2-4 Centuries C.E., New York, Feldheim, 1965.

249. Lieberman, S., Tosefta Kifshuta, New York, JTS, 5715-5733.

250. Lieberman, S., Hellenism in Jewish Palestine: Studies in the Literary Transmission, Beliefs and Manners of Palestine in the 1st Century B.C.E. -- 4th Century C.E., New York, JTS, 1962.

251. Lieberman, S., "Siphre zu Deuteronomium etc.", Kiryath Sepher, vol. 14 (5693).

252. Lieberman, S., Siphre Zutta, New York, JTS, 1968, Heb.

253. Loewenstamm, S.E., "The Death of Moses", Gershom G Scholem Jubilee Volume on the occasion of his sixtieth birthday, Jerusalem, Magnes, 1958, Heb.

254. Malbim, M.L., Otzar ha-Perushim, Jerusalem, Pardes, 1956.

255. Mann, J., and Sonne, I., The Bible as Read and Preached in the Old Synagogue, Cincinnati, HUC-JTR, 1966.

256. Margolioth, A., "The Concept "D'RSH" in the Talmud and the Midrashim", Lěšonenū, vol. 20, (1957), Heb.

257. Margolioth, R., "Citations of Verses in the Talmud and Midrash", Sinai: Jubilee Volume ed. Y.L. HaCohen Maimon, Jerusalem, Mossad HaRav Kook, 5718 (p. 226ff), Heb.

258. Marmorstein, A., "Essay on the Historical Value of the Aggadah", Studies in Jewish Theology, ed. J. Rabbinowitz and M.S. Lew, London, Oxford University, 1950, Heb.

259. Marmorstein, A., Studies in Jewish Theology, ed. J. Rabbinowitz and M.S. Lew, Oxford, Oxford University Press, 1950.

260. Marmorstein, A., The Doctrine of Merits in Old Rabbinic Literature and the Old Rabbinic Doctrine of God (parts 1 and 2), New York, Ktav, 1968.

261. Martyr, J., Dialogue with Trypho (in writings of Saint Justin Martyr, vol. 6 of Fathers of the Church), tr. T. Falls, New York, Christian Heritage, 1948.

262. Meeks, W., "Moses as God and King", Religions in Antiquity: Festschrift for E.R. Goodenough, ed. J. Neusner, Leiden, Brill, 1968.

263. Melamed, E.Z., "Euphemism and Scribal Circumlocutions in Talmudic Literature", Benjamin De Vries Memorial Volume, ed. E.Z. Melamed, Jerusalem, Tel Aviv University, 1968, Heb.

264. Melamed, E.Z., Halachic Midrashim of the Tannaim in the Talmud Babli, Jerusalem, 1943, Heb.

265. Melamed, E.Z., The Relationship between the Halachic Midrashim and the Mishna and Tosefta, Jerusalem, 5727, Heb.

266. Metal, Z., The Samaritan Version of the Pentateuch in Jewish Sources, Tel Aviv, 1974.

267. Mihaly, E., "A Rabbinic Defense of the Election of Israel", HUCA, vol. 35 (1964), Ktav, 1968.

268. Milik, J.T., The Books of Enoch: Aramaic Fragments of Qumran Cave 4, ed. J.T. Milik, Oxford, Clarendon Press, 1976.

269. Moeshet, M., and Klein, Y., "Concerning the root KNN in the language of the Sages by comparison with Akkadian", Lěšonenū, vol. 40 ('76).

270. Moore, G.F., "Intermediaries in Jewish Theology -- Memra, Shekinah, Metatron", HTR, vol. 15 (1922).

271. Moore, G.F. Judaism in the First Centuries of the Christian Era, the Age of the Tannaim, 3 vols, Cambridge, Harvard University Press, 1927-1928.

272. Muilenberg, J. "The Form and Structure of the Covenantal Formulations", VT, vol. 9 (1959).

273. Neaves, Lord, The Greek Anthology, Philadelphia, J.B. Lippincott
     and Co., (Ancient Classics for English Readers, ed. W. Collins),
     1874.

274. Neubauer, A., Géographie du Talmud, Paris, 1868.

275. Neusner, J., Aphra'at and Judaism, the Jewish-Christian
     Argument in Fourth Century Iran, Leiden, Brill, 1971.

276. Neusner, J., "From Exegesis to Fable in Rabbinic Traditions
     About the Pharisees", JJS, 25 (1974).

277. Niehaus, J., "Raz-pešar in Isaiah XXIV", VT, vol. 3 (1981), no. 3.

278. Noy, D., Introduction to Aggadic Literature, (mimeographed),
     Jerusalem, 5726, Heb.

279. Noy (Neuman), D., Motif-Index of Talmudic-Midrashic Literature,
     Bloomington, 1954 (Diss.).

280. Nyiro, L., Literature and Its Interpretations, tr. S. Simon,
     The Hague, Mouton and Akademiai Kiado, Budapest, 1979.

281. Oppenheimer, A., The Am Ha-aretz: A Study in the Social History
     of the Jewish People in the Hellenistic Roman Period, Leiden,
     Brill, 1977.

282. Origen, The Song of Songs: Commentary and Homiles, vol. 26 of
     Ancient Christian Writers, tr. and annotated by R.P. Lawson,
     London, Longmans, Green and Co., 1957.

283. Pardo, D., Siphre de-be-Rab, Heb. (comm.), Jerusalem, 5730.

284. Patte, D., Early Jewish Hermeneutic in Palestine, Missoula, Society
     of Biblical Literature and Scholars Press (Dissertation Series,
     no. 22), 1975.

285. Perles, A.Z., "The Sense of Two Pericopes in Siphre", Beth Ha-Talmud,
     ed. I.H. Weiss, Vienna, vol. I (5641), Heb.

286. Pool, D. de Sola, The Kaddish, New York, The Union of Sephardic
     Congregations, 1964.

287. Porter, F.C., "The Pre-existence of the Soul in the Book of Wisdom
     and in Rabbinical Writings", in Old Testament and Semitic Studies
     in Memory of William Rainey Harper, ed. R.F. Harper, F. Brown,
     G.F. Moore, Chicago, University of Chicago, 1908.

288. Porton, G.C., "Defining Midrash", in The Study of Ancient Judaism,
     vol. 1, J. Neusner, New York, Ktav 1981.

289. Porton, G.C., "The Grape-Cluster in Jewish Literature and
     Art of Late Antiquity", JJS, vol. 27 (1976), no. I.

290. Rabin, Ch., "Observations concerning the root QNN/KNN", Lěšônenū,
     vol. 40, 1976, nos. 3-4, Heb.

291. Rabin, Ch., "Three Hebrew Terms from the Realm of Social
     Psychology, (akhzar, bataḥ, ba'at)", Hebräische Wortforschung
     in honor of W. Baumgartner, ed. J. Barr, et al., Leiden, Brill,
     1967.

292. Rabinowitz, Z.M., "The Oldest Form of Rabbinic Midrashim According

to the Genizah Material", Proceedings of the Fifth World Congress of Jewish Studies, Jerusalem, Academic Press, vol. 3, 1969.

293. Rafal, D., "The Song of 'Ha'azinu'", Beth Mikra ,31 (1966),3; 32(1967),1; 33(1968),2.

294. Randall, G.H., Barnabas, Writer of 'the Epistle of Barnabas', London, Macmillan, 1877.

295. Robinson, P., "To stretch out the feet: a formula for death in the Testament of the Twelve Patriarchs", JBL ,vol. 97 (1973).

296. Rosenthal, E.S., "YBL, 'OBL", Lešonenū ,vol. 32 (1968).

297. Rosenzweig, A., "Die Al-tikri-Deutungen: ein Beitrag zur Talmudischen Schniftdeutung", Tiffereth Israel, Festschrift zu Israel's Lewy's siebigsten Geburstage, ed. M. Brann and J. Elbogen, Jerusalem, Makor, 5732.

298. Rowlands, E.R., "The Targum and the Peshitta Version of the Book of Isaiah", VT, vol. 9 (1959).

299. Ruether, R., Faith and Fratricide: The Theological Roots of Anti-Semitism, New York, Seabury Press, 1974.

300. Safrai S. and Stern, M., (editors), Compendia Rerum Judaicorum ad Novum Testamentum, The Jewish People in the First Century, Historical Geography, Political History, Social, Cultural and Religious Life and Institutions, vol. 1, 1974, Assen, Van Gorcum, vol. 2, Philadelphia, Fortress Press, 1976.

301. Sanders, E.P., "Rabbi Akiba's View of Suffering", JQR, vol. 53 (1973), no. 4.

302. Sanders, E.P., Paul and Palestinian Judaism, Philadelphia, Fortress Press, 1977.

303. Sarason, R.S., "Toward a New Agendum for the Study of Rabbinic Midrashic Literature", Studies in Aggadah, Targum and Jewish Liturgy in Memory of Joseph Heinemann, Jerusalem, Hebrew University, 1981.

304. Sawyer, J., "Spaciousness (an important feature of language about salvation in the O.T.)", Annual of the Theological Institute (in Jerusalem), vol. 6 (1967).

305. Saydon, P., "The Conative Imperfect in Hebrew", VT,12 (1962).

306. Schechter, S., "The Mechilta to Deuteronomy", JQR,16 (1904).

307. Schechter, S., Some Aspects of Rabbinic Theology, London, Adam and Charles Black, 1909.

308. Schechter, S., Studies in Judaism (first series), Philadelphia, JPS, 1919.

309. Scholem, G., Jewish Gnosticism, Merkabah Mysticism and Talmudic Tradition, New York, JTS, 1965.

310. Scholem, G., Major Trends in Jewish Mysticism, New York, Schocken, 1961.

312

311. Scholem, G., *The Messianic Idea in Judaism and Other Essays in Jewish Spirituality*, New York, Schocken, 1972.

312. Schorr, J.H., "The Method of the Sages to Interpret Hebrew Words According to Their Sense in Foreign Languages", *HeHalutz*, Vol. 12 (5647), Heb.

313. Seeligman, I.L., *The Septuagint Version of Isaiah*, Leiden, 1948.

314. Seeligman, I.L., "The Beginnings of Midrash in the Book of Chronicles", *Tarbiz*, vol. 49 (1980), nos. 1-2, Heb.

315. Segal, A.F., *Two Powers in Heaven: Early Rabbinic Reports about Christianity and Gnosticism*, Leiden, Brill, 1977.

316. Senior, D., "Death of Jesus and Resurrection of Holy Ones", *CBQ*, 38 (1976).

317. Silberman, L.H., "Between Chaos and Creation: A Survival Myth", *Central Conference of American Rabbis Journal*, Summer 1977.

318. Silberman, L.H., "Unriddling the Riddle: A Study in the Structure and Language of the Habakuk Pesher", *Revue de Qumran*, vol.3 (1961).

319. Silberman, L.H., "A Theological Treatise on Forgiveness: Chapter twenty-three of Pesiqta de Rab Kahana", *Studies in Aggadah, Targum and Jewish Liturgy in Memory of Joseph Heinemann*, Jerusalem, Hebrew University, 1981.

320. Simon, M., *Verus Israel: Etude sur les relations entre Chrétiens et Juifs dans l'empire romain*, Paris, Editions E. de Boccard, 1964.

321. Slomovic, E., "Towards an understanding of Exegesis in the Dead Sea Scrolls", *Bar Ilan*, vol. 7-8 (1970).

322. Smith, J.Z., "Sacred Persistence: Towards Redescription of Canon", *Approaches to Ancient Judaism*, ed. W.S. Green, Missoula, Scholars Press, 1978.

323. Sonne, I, "Use of Rabbinic Literature as Historical Sources", *JQR*, vol. 36 (1924).

324. Stein, E., "Die Homiletische Peroratio in Midrasch", *HUCA* vol 8-9 (1931-32).

325. Stern, D., "The Case of Mashal", *Prooftexts*, vol. 1 (1981), no. 3.

326. Strack, H., *Introduction to the Talmud and Midrash*, New York, Atheneum, 1969.

327. Sussman, Y., "The 'Boundaries of Eretz-Israel'", *Tarbiz*, vol. 45, (1976), no. 3-4, Heb.

328. Tam, J., *Sepher HaYashar*, Berlin, 1898.

329. Talmon, S., "Aspects of the Textual Translation of the Bible in the Light of the Qumran Manuscripts", *Qumran and the History of the Biblical Text*, ed. F.M. Cross and S. Talmon, Cambridge, Harvard University Press, 1975.

330. Taylor, C., Pirqe Aboth: Sayings of the Jewish Fathers, New
York, 1969.

331. Thomas, D.W., "The Root ZN' in Hebrew and the Meaning of
QDRNYT, Malachi 3:14", JJS, vol. 11 (1948-49).

332. Thureau-Dangin, F., "Rituels et Amulettes contra Lebartu",
Revue d'assyrologie et d'archeologie orientale, vol. 18
(1921), no. 4.

333. Tiede, D.L., The Charismatic Figure as Miracle Worker, Missoula,
SBL, 1972.

334. Tsumura, D.T., "Two-fold Image of Wine in Psalm 46:45", JQR,
vol. 71 (1981), no. 3.

335. Ugolino, B., Thesaurus Antiquatum Sacrarum Comlectens, Venice,
J.G. Herthz and S. Colitti, vol. 15, 1753.

336. Urbach, E.E., "Ascesis and Suffering in Talmudic and Midrashic
Sources", Yitzhak E. Baer Jubilee Volume, ed. S. Baron et al
Jerusalem, Historical Society of Jerusalem, 1960.

337. Urbach, E.E., "The Derasha as the base of Halacha and the problem
of the Sofrim", G. Scholem Jubilee Volume on the occasion
of his sixtieth birthday, Jerusalem, Magnes, 1958, Heb.

338. Urbach, E.E., "The Homiletical Interpretations of the Sages and
the Expositions of Origen on Canticles, and the Jewish-
Christian Disputation", Studies in Aggadah and Folk Literature,
Jerusalem, Magnes, 1971.

339. Urbach, E.E., The Sages: Their concepts and beliefs, tr. I. Abrahams,
Jerusalem, Hebrew University, 1975.

340. Van Uchelen, N.A., "The Targumic Version of Deuteronomy 33:15",
JJS, vol. 31 (1980).

341. Verecundi Iuncensis, "Commentarii Super Contra Ecclescastice",
Corpus Christianorum series Latina, vol. XCIII.

342. Vermes, G., "The Decalogue and the Minim", In Memoriam Paul Kahle,
ed. M. Black and G. Fohrer, Berlin, 1968.

343. Vermes, G., Scripture and Tradition in Judaism, Leiden, Brill, 1973.

344. Wacholder, B., "The Date of the Mekilta De-Rabbi Ishmael", HUCA,
vol. 39 (1968).

345. Wacholder, B., "A History of the Sabbatical Readings of Scripture
for the Triennial Cycle", Prolegomenon to the Bible as Read
and Preached in the Old Synagogue, vol. 1(J. Mann), 1971.

346. Wacholder, B., Essays on Jewish Chronology and Chronography, New
York, 1976.

347. Weisberg, E., "Towards a Clarification of the Expressions 'Talmud'
and 'Talmud Lomar'", Lĕšōnenu, vol. 39, (1974-5), nos. 1-2.

348. Weiss, I.H., Dor Dor veDorshav, New York, 1924.

349. Wolfson, H.A., Philo: Foundations of the Religious Philosophy in
Judaism, Christianity, and Islam , 2 vols., Cambridge, Harvard
University Press, 1948.

350. Wright, A.G., The Literary Genre Midrash, New York, Alba House, 1967.

351. Wright, G.E., "The Lawsuit of God", Israel's Prophetic Heritage: Essays in Honour of James Muilenberg, ed. B.W. Anderston et al, New York, Harper and Bros., 1962.

352. Y'aqwb, "Mamra dlwqbl yhwdya dmry y'akwb", Patrologia Orientalis, 38(1976), no. 174.

353. Zahari, H., Aggadic and Halachic Midrashim in the Commentary of Rashi to the Torah (by comparing material), Jerusalem, Aqadmon, 1978, Heb.

354. Zakovitch, Y., The Pattern of the Numerical Sequence 3-4 in the Bible, Hebrew University diss., Jerusalem, Hebrew University, n.d.

355. Zeitlin, S., "Midrash: A Historical Study", JQR, vol. 44 (1953).

356. Zunz, L., Die gottesdienstichen Vortrage der Juden, Frankfurt, A.M. 1892.